# NTC's Beginner's German and English Dictionary

NTC's

# Beginner's German and English Dictionary

Editor
Erick P. Byrd

General Editor
Frank R. Abate

*Printed on recyclable paper*

*NTC Publishing Group*
Lincolnwood, Illinois USA

Manufactured in the United States.

5 6 7 8 9 BC 9 8 7 6 5 4 3 2 1

# Contents

## Introduction

This German-English bilingual dictionary is especially designed to help the English-speaking student learn basic German, and may also be used to help the German-speaking student learn basic English. Approximately 3,500 main vocabulary entries have been compiled in this useful reference. The dictionary also contains hundreds of subentries to highlight idiomatic expressions and shades of meaning.

To enable beginning language students to have a clear understanding of the correct usage of entry words, this dictionary also presents each main entry and subentry in its most common context. At least one example sentence, followed by a translation, illustrates the correct use of each main entry word in context. Verbs are listed by their infinitive forms. Common German verbs are conjugated in the present tense within the entry. Since the conjugated forms of irregular verbs can differ greatly in spelling from their infinitives, these variants are displayed in example sentences where needed.

The typography of this dictionary, designed with beginning learners in mind, allows students to distinguish the various parts of the entries. Entry words are in boldface type, while parts of speech and translated sentences are in italics.

Between the German-English and English-German sections of the dictionary, an 18-page section contains drawings illustrating 174 common words in twenty-one categories that include sports, birds, insects, food, transportation, and animals. Each drawing is labeled both in German and English. The appendices at the back of the book provide tables of names and useful groups of words such as the months of the year, days of the week, parts of the body, and more.

## How to Use This Dictionary

This dictionary provides more information than just the simple translation of a word. The learner will find within each entry a phonetic pronunciation of the word, the part(s) of speech, and an example sentence. When a word has more than one possible translation, the most common meanings are given. Useful expressions or compounds based on this main entry are listed as subentries.

## The Entries

In both sections of the dictionary, entries follow this basic format:

1. *Entry word.* The entry word is in boldface type. Following each German noun is the appropriate article, which also indicates the gender of the noun entry. If the feminine form of a noun is spelled differently, this spelling follows in parenthesis.
2. *Pronunciation.* A simple pronunciation follows each entry. The "Pronunciation" section below outlines the use of the pronunciation guide.
3. *Parts of Speech.* This label, given in italics, indicates whether the entry is a noun, verb, adjective, etc. Abbreviations used for parts of speech are *n.*, noun; *pron.*, pronoun; *v.*, verb; *adj.*, adjective; *adv.*, adverb; *prep.*, preposition; *conj.*, conjunction; *art.*, article; and *interj.*, interjection. Other abbreviations used include *s.*, singular; *pl.*, plural; *m.*, masculine; *f.*, feminine; and *n.*, neuter.
4. *Definition.* The definition gives the basic meaning(s) of the entry word.
5. *Subentries.* Subentries often appear in boldface type to explain the meaning of words or expressions derived from the entry word. As with the main entries, these have a label identifying the part of speech (as applicable) and a translation.
6. *Verb conjugation.* Entries for common German verbs are conjugated in the present tense (first, second, and third person forms for singular and plural).
7. *Illustrative sentence(s).* A sample sentence shows the correct use of the entry or subentry word. Many entries have more than one sentence to illustrate different meanings or uses of the entry word.
8. *Translation.* Every illustrative sentence is translated into English or German as appropriate.

The following are examples of entries in the German-English section:

**Mannschaft, die** [MAHNshahft] *n.* • team
Unsere Korbballmannschaft hat zwölf Spieler.
*Our basketball team has twelve players.*

**singen** [ZINGən] *v.* • to sing
**Sänger, der (-in, f.)** *n.* • singer

| | |
|---|---|
| singe | singen |
| singst | singt |
| singt | singen |

Die Klasse sang ein Lied, um die Show zu beenden.
*The class sang a song to end the show.*

The English-German section follows the same format, except that verbs are not conjugated in the entries. Here is an example of an English-German entry:

**swim, to** [SWIM] *v.* • schwimmen
**swimming pool** *n.* • Schwimmbecken, das; Swimmingpool, der
**swimsuit** *n.* • Badeanzug, der
I learned to swim at summer camp.
*Ich habe im Sommerlager schwimmen gelernt.*

## Pronunciation

Each main entry is followed by a pronunciation. The pronunciation provided for each German word in the German-English section is geared toward a student who is a native speaker of English, and uses sounds familiar to English speakers. Similarly, the pronunciation provided for each English word in the English-German section is geared toward a student who speaks German, and uses sounds familiar to German speakers.

## Pronunciation Guide: German-English

Following is a description of the symbols used to represent German sounds in the pronunciation guides, along with examples and explanation, as needed.

In actual pronunciations, a syllable receiving primary stress is indicated by capital letters.

In some cases, hyphens were inserted at syllable breaks for clarity.

**NOTE:** Symbols in *italic type* represent sounds that are not found in native English words.

## Vowels

| *Symbol:* | *Word:* | **Pronunciation** *Example:* | *As in English:* |
|---|---|---|---|
| ə | bekommen | bəKAWMən | cup, above |
| ə*r* | Ritter | RITə*r* | butter |
| ah/AH | Hand | HAHNT | father |
| ai/AI | jemals, ähnlich | YAImahls, AINli*sh* | plain |
| au/AU | Auto | AUtoh | house |
| aw/AW | Frosch | FRAWSH | ball |
| e/E | decken | DEKən | bed |
| ee/EE | dienen | DEEnən | feel |
| ei/EI | Geist | GEIST | kite |
| *er*/*ER* | schön | SH*ER*N | No English equivalent. Shape your lips as if to make the sound of *oo* as in *boot*, but say *ai* as in *bait*. |
| i/I | Original | awrigiNAHL | it |
| oh/OH | Problem | prohBLAIM | phone |
| oi/OI | neun | NOIN | boy |
| oo/OO | gut | GOOT | tool |
| u/U | dumm | DUM | put, look |
| *ue*/*UE* | grün | GR*UE*N | No English equivalent. Shape your lips as if to make the sound of *oo* as in *boot*, but say *ee* as in *feel*. |

## Consonants

| Symbol: | Word: | Pronunciation Example: | As in English: |
|---|---|---|---|
| b/B | Bibliothek | bibleeohTAIK | baby |
| d/D | denken | DENGkən | delighted |
| f/F | Flußpferd | FLUSpfert | fifteen |
| g/G | gegen | GAIgən | go |
| h/H | Hund | HUNT | happy |
| k/K | Gebdäck | geBAIK | come |
| *kh/KH* | Mittwoch | MITvaw*kh* | No English equivalent. This sound is made by softly "clearing your throat." |
| l/L | Lehnstuhl | LAINshtool | little |
| m/M | Moment | mawMENT | mama |
| n/N | nein | NEIN | noon |
| ng/NG | lang | LAHNG | sing |
| p/P | Papier | pahPEER | puppy |
| r/R | Ritter | RITə*r* | The *r*-sound in German may also be rolled or uvular. |
| s/S | heiß | HEIS | sauce |
| sh/SH | Schiff | SHIF | shoe |
| *sh/SH* | Richter | RI*SH*tə*r* | Similar to the *sh* in *shoe*, but with the teeth less close together. |
| t/T | Tomate | tohMAHtə | test |
| v/V | Welt | Velt | very |
| y/Y | jung | YUNG | year |
| z/Z | sagen | ZAHgən | zero |
| zh/ZH | Orange | awRAWNzhə | measure |

## Pronunciation Guide: English-German

Following is a description of the symbols used to represent English sounds in the pronunciations, along with examples and explanation, as needed.

**NOTE:** Symbols in *italic type* represent sounds or letter combinations that are not found in native German words. For them, no German word is given.

## Vowels

| Symbol: | Word: | Pronunciation Example: | As in German: |
|---|---|---|---|
| ə/Ə | above | əBƏ*V* | bekommen |
| ər/Ə*R* | bird | BƏ*R*D | Ritter |
| *a*/*A* | ask | *A*SK | Väter |
| ah/AH | father | FAH*dhər* | Hand |
| ei/EI | bite | BEIT | Geist |
| au/AU | loud | LAUD | Auto |
| *aw*/*AW* | law | L*AW* | Morgen |
| e/E | wet | *W*ET | decken |
| *ej*/*EJ* | late | L*EJ*T | lesen |
| eu/EU | boy | BEU | Heuer |
| i/I | sit | SIT | Original |
| ie/IE | eat | IET | Fabrik |
| oh/OH | nose | NOH*Z* | Boden |
| *oo*/*OO* | boot | B*OO*T | gut |
| u/U | put | PUT | dumm |

## Consonants

| Symbol: | Word: | Pronunciation Example: | As in German: |
|---|---|---|---|
| b/B | book | BUK | besser |
| d/D | dear | DIER | dort |
| *dh*/*DH* | the | *DH*Ə | (no equivalent) |
| *dzh*/*DZH* | judge | *DZH*Ə*DZH* | joggen |
| f/F | fifty | FIFtie | fast |
| g/G | get | GET | gegen |
| h/H | hand | HAND | halten |
| j/J | yes | JES | Jahr |
| k/K | king | KING | Karte |
| l/L | little | LITl | Lied |
| m/M | meal | MIEL | Milch |
| n/N | nine | NEIN | nach |

| | | | |
|---|---|---|---|
| ng/NG | bring | BRING | langsam |
| p/P | pepper | PEPər | Papier |
| r/R | road, butter (without roll or trill) | ROHD, Bədər | Ring |
| s/S | sense | SENS | dreißig |
| sh/SH | shadow | SHADoh | Fisch |
| t/T | tent | TENT | Tier |
| *th/TH* | thin | *TH*IN | (no equivalent) |
| *tsh/TSH* | church | *TSHƏRTSH* | (no equivalent) |
| ts/TS | oats | OHTS | Station, tanzen |
| *v/V* | village | *V*ILi*dzh* | warm |
| *w/W* | water | *WA*WTər | (no equivalent) |
| *z/Z* | zebra (pronounced as the German word-initial *s* followed by a vowel) | ZIEBrə | sehen |
| *zh/ZH* | measure | ME*zh*ər | Orange |

## Stressed Syllables

In German, as in English, the syllable receiving stress varies from word to word. The stressed syllable in each of the entry words of this dictionary is noted in the pronunciation by capital letters.

## Capitalization

One of the first things English speakers notice about written German is that German nouns are always capitalized. The formal address pronoun *Sie*, its possessive adjective forms, and declined forms are capitalized as well. The personal pronoun *I (ich)* is *not* capitalized in German, nor are the adjectives denoting nationality. Starting with *eine Million* (one million), the cardinal numbers are treated as nouns and are, therefore, capitalized.

## NUMBERS

Students of German will also notice that words representing numbers greater than twenty are written as one word and may sometimes appear extraordinarily long. For example, eight thousand nine hundred fifty-seven is written in German:

*achttausendneunhundertsiebenundfünfzig*

## BASICS OF GERMAN GRAMMAR

### Gender

All German nouns (words for people, places, things, or ideas) have gender. That is, each German noun is considered either masculine, feminine, or neuter. Most of the time, the gender of a German noun must be memorized. This can be easily accomplished if the student simply learns the definite article that goes with each noun at the time the noun is learned. For example, one should know that *man* is not just *Mann* in German, but rather *der Mann*. The article will indicate the gender of the noun—*der* indicates a masculine noun, just as *die*, as in *die Frau* (woman, wife), indicates a feminine noun, and *das*, as in *das Kind* (child), indicates a neuter noun. Each noun entry in this dictionary is accompanied by its definite article. In addition to gender, the article also indicates the number (singular or plural) of the noun. The definite article preceding a nominative plural noun is always *die*. Care should be taken not to confuse the nominative plural with the singular feminine article. Generally, the definite article can be translated by the word "the" in English.

### Case

All German nouns have a grammatical case determined by how they are used in a sentence or statement. German is an *inflected language*, which means that some words (including nouns, adjectives, and pronouns) are spelled differently (usually with different endings) depending on usage in a sentence. There are four cases in German:

1. **Nominative Case**
   The subject of a sentence, the predicate nominative, a direct address, and nouns in apposition to another nominative use the nominative case.
2. **Dative Case**
   The dative case is used for the indirect object, the object of some prepositions, the object of certain verbs, and for the dative of interest.
3. **Accusative Case**
   The accusative is the case of the direct object, the object of some prepositions, definite time expressions without a preposition, expressions of specific measurement or extent, and appositives of words in the accusative.
4. **Genitive Case**
   The genitive case indicates possession or relationship and is also used with certain prepositions.

As mentioned above in the description of gender, the definite article is used to reflect gender and number. In sentences and statements, the definite article also denotes the case of the noun it precedes. The following chart summarizes the various noun attributes as reflected in the definite article:

| | | **Singular** | | **Plural** |
|---|---|---|---|---|
| | *Masc.* | *Fem.* | *Neut.* | *All Genders* |
| Nominative | der | die | das | die |
| Dative | dem | der | dem | den |
| Accusative | den | die | das | die |
| Genitive | des | der | des | der |

The indefinite article (*a* or *an* in English) functions in the same way as the definite article, and also reflects gender and case of the noun it precedes. There is, of course, no plural form of the indefinite article. The following chart shows the use of the indefinite article in German:

| | *Masc.* | *Fem.* | *Neut.* |
|---|---|---|---|
| Nominative | ein | eine | ein |
| Dative | einem | einer | einem |
| Accusative | einen | eine | ein |
| Genitive | eines | einer | eines |

Other words that are declined similarly to the above are possessive adjectives, demonstrative adjectives, and the German negative *kein* (*no* or *none*).

## Verbs

Discussion of German verbs is limited here to only the most essential elements. In this dictionary, all verbs are listed by their infinitives, the most basic form of the verb. As in English, there are both *regular* and *irregular* verbs in German. Typically, regular verbs are those which, when conjugated, follow a strict pattern of inflected endings, according to the person governing the action of the verb.

For example, here is the present tense conjugation of the German regular verb *hören* (to hear):

| | | | |
|---|---|---|---|
| *ich hör<u>e</u>* | I hear | *wir hör<u>en</u>* | we hear |
| *du hör<u>st</u>* | you [sing.] hear | *ihr hör<u>t</u>* | you [pl.] hear |
| *er, sie, es hör<u>t</u>* | he, she, it hears | *sie, Sie hör<u>en</u>* | they, you [formal] hear |

The endings *-e*, *-st*, *-t*, and *-en* are added to the stem of the verb *hör-* and this pattern is followed with all regular German verbs. Irregular verbs are those whose spelling changes in the stem when conjugated. These verbs must, therefore, be learned individually.

Common regular and irregular German verbs are conjugated in the present tense in their entries in this dictionary. Because the pronouns *(ich, du, er, sie, es, wir, ihr, sie, Sie)* do not change, they have been omitted from the conjugations within the dictionary.

## Prepositions

Words that follow prepositions may be in the dative, accusative, or genitive case. The dative case follows these prepositions:

| | | | |
|---|---|---|---|
| *aus* | out of; from | *nach* | to; after |
| *außer* | besides; except | *seit* | since; for |
| *bei* | at; with; near | *von* | from |
| *mit* | with | *zu* | to; at |

For example:

*Willi kommt aus dem Haus.*
Willi comes from (out of) the house.

*Er geht mit seinem Freund.*
He goes with his friend.

*Der Brief ist von meiner Mutter.*
The letter is from my mother.

The accusative case follows these prepositions:

| | | | |
|---|---|---|---|
| *durch* | through | *ohne* | without |
| *für* | for | *um* | at; around |
| *gegen* | against | *wider* | against |

For example:

*Ich habe heute keine Zeit für dich.*
I have no time for you today.

*Er sieht durch das Fenster.*
He looks through the window.

*Sie kam ohne ihren Mantel.*
She came without her coat.

The genitive case follows these prepositions:

| | | | |
|---|---|---|---|
| *anstatt* | instead (of) | *statt* | instead of |
| *außerhalb* | outside (of) | *trotz* | in spite of |
| *diesseits* | on this side (of) | *um . . . willen* | for sake of |
| *innerhalb* | inside (of); within | *unterhalb* | under; underneath |
| *jenseits* | on that side (of) | *während* | during |
| *oberhalb* | above | *wegen* | because of |

For example:

*Mein Haus liegt jenseits der Straße.*
My house is on that side of the street.

*Während des Sommers blühen die Rosen.*
During the summer the roses bloom.

*Innerhalb der Stadt gibt es viel zu tun.*
In (within) the city there is a lot to do.

Note that there are some prepositions that can be followed by either the dative or the accusative case:

| | | | |
|---|---|---|---|
| *an* | on; at; to | *über* | above; over |
| *auf* | on | *unter* | under; below |
| *hinter* | behind | *vor* | before; in front of |
| *in* | in; into | *zwischen* | between |
| *neben* | next to; beside | | |

If the context of the sentence indicates motion or direction toward a goal, the accusative case is used. If a fixed location or motion with a confined space is indicated, the dative case is used.

For example:

*Der Hund läuft hinter das Haus.*
The dog runs behind the house.

*Der Hund steht hinter dem Haus.*
The dog stands behind the house.

## Adjectives

Adjectives in German can be found preceding nouns or following predicate verbs, but still describing the noun. Adjectives must agree with the number and gender of the nouns they modify. Adjectives following definite articles have the following endings:

| | *Masc.* | *Fem.* | *Neut.* | *Plural* |
|---|---|---|---|---|
| Nominative | -e | -e | -e | -en |
| Accusative | -en | -e | -e | -en |
| Dative | -en | -en | -en | -en |
| Genitive | -en | -en | -en | -en |

Adjectives following indefinite articles (*ein, kein*) and all possessive adjectives have the following endings:

| | *Masc.* | *Fem.* | *Neut.* | *Plural* |
|---|---|---|---|---|
| Nominative | -er | -e | -es | -en |
| Accusative | -en | -e | -es | -en |
| Dative | -en | -en | -en | -en |
| Genitive | -en | -en | -en | -en |

Note that predicate adjectives and adverbs are uninflected.

## Adverbs

Adverbs describe adjectives and verbs. For example:

*Der Zug fährt sehr schnell.* The train goes very fast.

In this sentence, *sehr* (very) is an adverb and *schnell* (fast) is a predicate adjective. Note that they take no endings, but, in the comparative and superlative forms, endings are added much as they are in English:

*Das Schiff fährt schnell.* The ship goes fast.
*Der Zug fährt schneller.* The train goes faster.
*Der Wagen fährt am schnellsten.* The car goes fastest.

The comparative is formed by adding *-er* to the ending of the stem. The superlative is formed by adding the contracted preposition *am* in front of the adverb and *-st* to the end of the adjective stem, followed by *-en*.

NTC's

# Beginner's German and English Dictionary

## German to English/*Deutsch zu Englisch*

# A

**Abend, der** [AHbənt] *n.* • evening; p.m.
**Abendessen, das** *n.* • dinner
**am Abend** • in the evening
**am vorigen Abend** • the night before (eve)
**gestern abend** • last evening
**Guten Abend!** • Good evening
**Weihnachtsabend, der** • Christmas Eve
Ich mache meine Hausaufgaben am Abend.
*I do my homework in the evening.*

Es ist 6 Uhr abends und Zeit zum Abendessen.
*It's 6:00 p.m. and time for dinner.*

**Abenteuer, das** [AHbəntoiə*r*] *n.* • adventure
Unsere Reise nach Europa war ein großes Abenteuer!
*Our trip to Europe was a great adventure!*

**aber** [AHbə*r*] *conj.* • but
Ich möchte gern etwas Kuchen, aber ich halte eine Diät.
*I would like some cake, but I am on a diet.*

**Abfall, der** [AHPfahl] *n.* • garbage
Tu den Abfall in den Mülleimer.
*Put the garbage into the can.*

**ablegen** [AHPlaigən] *v.* • to take
**eine Prüfung ablegen** • to take a test
Ich muß eine Prüfung ablegen.
*I have to take a test.*

**Absatz, der** [AHPzahts] *n.* • paragraph
Schreiben Sie für Morgen zwei Absätze aus dem Buch ab.
*Write two paragraphs from the book for tomorrow.*

**abschließen** [AHPshleesən] *v.* • to lock
Schließen Sie Ihr Haus ab, wenn Sie es verlassen?
*Do you lock your house when you leave?*

**abschreiben** [AHPshreibən] *v.* • to copy
Wir schreiben die Fragen von der Tafel ab.
*We are copying the questions that are on the blackboard.*

**absetzen** [AHPzetsən] *v.* • to take off
Ich habe meinen Hut abgesetzt.
*I took off my hat.*

**abwesend** [AHPvaizənt] *adj.* • absent
Die Hälfte der Klasse ist heute abwesend.
*Half the class is absent today.*

**Abwesenheit, die** [AHPvaizənheit] *n.* • absence
Seine Abwesenheit von der Klasse wurde selten bemerkt.
*His absence from class was seldom noticed.*

**acht** [AH*KH*T] *adj.* • eight
Es sind acht Personen im Bus.
*There are eight people on the bus.*

**achtgeben** [AH*KH*Tgaibən] *v.* • to pay attention (to)
Die Studenten geben auf den Lehrer acht.
*The students pay attention to the teacher.*

**achtzehn** [AH*KH*tsain] *adj.* • eighteen
Wir sind achtzehn in dieser Klasse.
*There are eighteen of us in this class.*

**achtzig** [AH*KH*Tsi*sh*] *adj.* • eighty
Viele Leute werden jetzt achtzig Jahre alt.
*Many people now live to be eighty.*

**Adler, der** [AHdlər] *n.* • eagle
Der Adler ist ein Raubvogel.
*The eagle is a bird of prey.*

**adoptieren** [ahdawpTEErən] *v.* • to adopt
Das junge Paar adoptiert ein kleines Kind.
*The young couple is adopting a baby.*

**Adresse, die** [ahDRESə] *n.* • address
Wie ist deine Adresse zu Hause?
*What is your home address?*

**Affe, der** [AHfə] *n.* • monkey
Ich beobachte gern die Affen im Zoo.
*I like to watch the monkeys at the zoo.*

**ähnlich** [AINli*sh*] *adj.* • alike; similar
Diese Kleider sind zu ähnlich.
*These dresses are too much alike.*

Die Brüder sehen sich ähnlich.
*The brothers are similar in appearance.*

**Aktentasche, die** [AHKtəntahshə] *n.* • briefcase
Sie hat ihre Aktentasche im Büro gelassen.
*She left her briefcase at the office.*

**akzeptieren** [ahktsepTEErən] *v.* • to accept
Die Bank akzeptiert diesen Scheck nicht.
*The bank won't accept this check.*

**alle** [AHLə] *adj.* • all
**überall** • all over; everywhere
**vor allem** • above all
Alle Menschen müssen essen, um zu leben.
*All people must eat in order to live.*

**Allee, die** [ahLAI] *n.* • avenue
Die Allee ist in der Nähe des Stadtzentrums sehr breit.
*The avenue is very wide near the city center.*

**allein** [ahLEIN] *adj.* • alone
Ich fühlte mich allein in der fremden Stadt.
*I felt alone in the strange city.*

**alles** [AHLəs] *pron.; adj.* • all; everything
**alles klar! (gut!; schön!)** • all right (OK)
Frau Müller hat alles gesehen.
*Mrs. Miller saw everything.*

**allgemein** [ahlgəMEIN] *adj.* • general
Ich habe allgemeine Anweisungen, aber geben Sie mir bitte Einzelheiten.
*I have general directions, but please give me details.*

**Alphabet, das** [ahlfahBAIT] *n.* • alphabet
Kinder fangen im Kindergarten an, das Alphabet zu lernen.
*Children begin to learn the alphabet in kindergarten.*

**alt** [AHLT] *adj.* • old
**alte Kamerad, der** *n.* • old pal
Wie alt bist du?
*How old are you?*

Ich liebe alte Filme aus den dreißiger Jahren.
*I like old movies from the 1930s.*

**Alter, das** [AHLtər] *n.* • age
Er ist schon sehr klug für sein Alter.
*He is already very smart for his age.*

**Ameise, die** [AHmeizə] *n.* • ant
Ameisen sind fleißige Insekten.
*Ants are hard-working insects.*

**Amerika** [ahMAIrikah] *n.* • America
**Amerikaner, der (-in, f.)** ] *n.* • American
**amerikanisch** *adj.* • American
**Nordamerika** *n.* • North America
**Mittelamerika** *n.* • Central America
**Südamerika** *n.* • South America
Viele Menschen in Amerika habe Vorfahren aus Europa.
*Many people in America have ancestors from Europe.*

Amerikanische Musik ist in der ganzen Welt populär.
*American music is popular around the world.*

**amüsieren** [ahm*ue*ZEErən] *v.* • to amuse
**amüsant** *adj.* • amusing, fun
Die Kinder amüsieren sich am Strand.
*The children are amusing themselves at the beach.*

**an** [AHN] *prep.* • at; on
Das Bild hängt an der Wand.
*The picture hangs on the wall.*

**Ananas, die** [AHnahnahs] *n.* • pineapple
Auf Hawaii pflanzt man Ananas an.
*They grow pineapples in Hawaii.*

**anbieten** [AHNbeetən] *v.* • to offer
Herr Peters bietet uns ein Geschenk an.
*Mr. Peters is offering us a present.*

**andere, -r, -s** [AHNdərə] *pron.; adj.* • other
Dieses Buch gehört mir; das andere gehört dir.
*This book is mine; the other is yours.*

**ändern** [ENdern] *v.* • to change
Er ändert immer seine Meinung.
*He always changes his opinion.*

**anfangen** [AHNfahngən] *v.* • to begin
**Anfang, der** *n.* • beginning

| | |
|---|---|
| fange an | fangen an |
| fängst an | fangt an |
| fängt an | fangen an |

Um wieviel Uhr fängt der Film an?
*What time does the movie begin?*

**anfassen** [AHNfahsən] *v.* • to touch
Faß den Hund nicht an! Er beißt!
*Don't touch the dog! He bites!*

**angeboren** [AHNgəbohrən] *adj.* • natural
Er hat ein angeborenes Talent für Musik.
*He has a natural gift for music.*

**Angelegenheit, das** [AHNgəlaigənheit] *n.* • business; matter
**sich um seine eigenen Angelegenheiten kümmern** • to mind one's own business
Dies ist eine private Angelegenheit.
*This is a private matter.*

**angeln** [AHNGəln] *v.* • to fish
**angeln gehen** • to go fishing
Wir angeln gern im Sommer.
*We like to fish in the summer.*

**angenehm** [AHNgənaim] *adj.* • pleasant
Wir machten einen sehr angenehmen Spaziergang auf dem Lande.
*We had a very pleasant walk in the country.*

**Angestellte, der** [AHNgəshteltə] *n.* • employee
Die Gesellschaft hat zehn Angestellte.
*The company has ten employees.*

**Angst, die** [AHNGST] *n.* • fear
**Angst haben** • to (have) fear
**vor etwas Angst haben** • to be afraid of
Ich habe Angst um mein Leben, wenn er fährt.
*I fear for my life when he is driving.*

Mein kleiner Bruder hat vor Spinnen Angst.
*My little brother is frightened of spiders.*

**anhalten** [AHNhahltən] *v.* • to stop
Laßt uns an der Tankstelle anhalten.
*Let's stop at the gas station.*

**Anhalter reisen, per** [AHNhahltər reizən, per] *v.* • to hitchhike
In einem Sommer reiste mein Vater per Anhalter durch Frankreich.
*One summer my father hitchhiked through France.*

**ankommen** [AHNkawmən] *v.* • to arrive; to come

| | |
|---|---|
| komme an | kommen an |
| kommst an | kommt an |
| kommt an | kommen an |

Komm nicht zu spät an!
*Don't arrive too late!*

Der Zug kommt um 11 Uhr an.
*The train comes at eleven o'clock.*

**ankündigen** [AHNk*ue*ndigən] *v.* • to announce
Sollten wir deinen Eltern unsere Pläne ankündigen?
*Should we announce our plans to your parents?*

**Ankunft, die** [AHNkunft] *n.* • arrival
Wir erwarten die Ankunft des Flugzeugs.
*We are waiting for the plane's arrival.*

**Anrichte, die** [AHNri*sh*tə] *n.* • dresser; sideboard
Diese Anrichte hat vier Schubladen.
*This dresser has four drawers.*

**ansehen** [AHNzaiyən] *v.* • to look; to watch
Sie sehen sich die Bilder an.
*They're looking at the pictures.*

Wir sehen uns eine neue Show im Fernsehen an.
*We are watching a new show on T.V.*

**anstatt** [ahnSHTAHT] *adv.* • instead of
Anstatt den Zug zu nehmen, fliegen wir.
*Instead of taking the train, we'll fly.*

**antworten** [AHNTvawrtən] *v.* • to reply
**die Antwort** *n.* • answer

| | |
|---|---|
| antworte | antworten |
| antwortest | antwortet |
| antwortet | antworten |

Ich antworte immer auf seine Briefe.
*I always reply to his letters.*

**Anzeige, die** [AHNtseigə] *n.* • advertisement
In dieser Zeitschrift gibt es viele Anzeigen.
*There are a lot of advertisements in this magazine.*

**anzeigen** [AHNtseigən] *v.* • to announce
**die Anzeige** *n.* • announcement
Wir zeigen unsene Verlobung an.
*We're announcing our engagement.*

**anziehen** [AHNtseeyən] *v.* • to attract
**sich anziehen** • to get dressed
**etwas anziehen** • to put something on (clothes)
Zucker zieht Fliegen an.
*Sugar attracts flies.*

**Anzug, der** [AHNtsook] *n.* • suit
Vater trägt heute seinen blauen Anzug.
*Father is wearing his blue suit today.*

**Apfel, der** [AHPfel] *n.* • apple
Claude macht einen Apfelkuchen.
*Claude is making an apple pie.*

**Apotheke, die** [ahpohTAIkə] *n.* • drugstore; pharmacy
**Apotheker, der (-in, f.)** *n.* • pharmacist
Meine Großmutter kauft ihre Medizin bei dieser Apotheke.
*My grandmother buys her medicine at this pharmacy.*

**Appartement, das** [ahpahrtMAWNT] *n.* • apartment
**Appartementgebäude, das** *n.* • apartment building
Meine Schwester hat ein neues Appartement.
*My sister has a new apartment.*

**Appetit, der** [ahpeTIT] *n.* • appetite
Nachdem ich Sport getrieben habe, habe ich großen Appetit.
*After I exercise I have a big appetite.*

**Aprikose, die** [ahpriKOHzə] *n.* • apricot
Aprikosen sind Pfirsichen ähnlich, nur kleiner.
*Apricots are like peaches but smaller.*

**April, der** [ahPRIL] *n.* • April
**Aprilnarr, der** *n.* • April Fool
Ich habe im April Geburtstag.
*My birthday is in April.*

**Aquarium, das** [ahKVAHreeyum] *n.* • aquarium
Im Aquarium befindet sich eine große Vielfalt von Fischen.
*The aquarium has a large variety of fish.*

**Arbeit, die** [AHRbeit] *n.* • work
Die Wissenschaftler leisten wichtige Arbeit.
*The scientists do important work.*

**arbeiten** [AHRbeitən] *v.* • to work
**bearbeiten** *v.* • to work (something); to process; to treat

| | |
|---|---|
| arbeite | arbeiten |
| arbeitest | arbeitetet |
| arbeitet | arbeiten |

Ich muß am Samstag arbeiten.
*I have to work on Saturday.*

**Arbeiter, der (-in, f.)** [AHRbeitər] *n.* • laborer
Die Arbeiter arbeiten in der Fabrik.
*The laborers work in the factory.*

**Ärger, der** [AIRgər] *n.* • trouble
Er hat Ärger mit seinem Auto.
*He is having trouble with his car.*

**ärgerlich** [AIRgərlish] *adj.* • annoying
Es ist ärgerlich, daß wir so lange warten müssen.
*It's annoying that we have to wait so long.*

**Arithmetik, die** [ahritMAItik] *n.* • arithmetic
Die Kinder lernen Arithmetik.
*The children are studying arithmetic.*

**arm** [AHRM] *adj.* • poor
Diese armen Leute haben nicht genug Geld.
*These poor people don't have enough money.*

**Arm, der** [AHRM] *n.* • arm
**Arm in Arm** • arm in arm
Sie trägt fünf Armbänder an ihrem rechten Arm.
*She is wearing five bracelets on her right arm.*

**Armband, das** [AHRMbahnt] *n.* • bracelet
Sie trägt mehrere Armbänder an ihrem linken Arm.
*She is wearing several bracelets on her left arm.*

**Ärmel, der** [AIRməl] *n.* • sleeve
Die Ärmel sind zu kurz!
*The sleeves are too short!*

**arrangieren** [ahrahnZHEErən] *v.* • to arrange
Arrangieren Sie gern Blumen?
*Do you like to arrange flowers?*

**Art, die** [AHRT] *n.* • kind (sort)
Welche Art von Baum ist das?
*What kind of tree is that?*

**Arzt, der; Ärtzin, die** [AHRTST] *n.* • doctor
Suchen Sie einen Arzt auf, wenn Sie sich nicht wohl fühlen.
*See a doctor if you are not feeling well.*

**Asien** [AHzee-yən] *n.* • Asia
Mein Onkel reist oft nach Asien.
*My uncle often travels to Asia.*

**Assistent, der (-in, f.)** [ahsisTENT] *n.* • assistant
Peter ist Assistent in einem Labor. (Laborassistent)
*Peter is an assistant in a laboratory.*

**Ast, der** [AHST] *n.* • branch
Die Äste der Bäume sind im Winter kahl.
*The tree branches are bare in winter.*

**Astronaut, der (-in, f.)** [ahstrohNAUT] *n.* • astronaut
Astronauten werden ausgebildet, um Weltraumfahrten zu bewältigen.
*Astronauts are trained to endure space travel.*

**Athlet, der** [ahtLAIT] *n.* • athlete
**athletisch** *adj.* • athletic
Man muß ein guter Athlet sein, um Fußball spielen zu können.
*You must be a good athlete to play soccer.*

**Atlantik, der** [ahtLAHNtik] *n.* • Atlantic
Ich wohne in der Nähe des Atlantiks.
*I live near the Atlantic Ocean.*

**auch** [AU*KH*] *adv.* • also; too
Ich möchte auch die neuen Studenten kennenlernen.
*I also want to meet the new students.*

Monika möchte auch kommen.
*Monica wants to come, too.*

**auf** [AUF] *prep.* • on; up
**Auf Wiedersehen!** *interj.* • Good-bye!
Er stellte seine Bücher auf den Schreibtisch.
*He put his books on the desk.*

**Aufgabe, die** [AUFgahbə] *n.* • assignment
Die Aufgabe für morgen ist schwer.
*The assignment for tomorrow is difficult.*

**aufhören** [AUFh*err*ən] *v.* • to stop (oneself)
Du sollst aufhören, zu rauchen.
*You should stop smoking.*

**aufnehmen** [AUFnaimən] *v.* • to record
Der Lehrer nimmt unsere Gespräche in der Klasse auf.
*The teacher records our conversations in class.*

**aufstehen** [AUFshtaiən] *v.* • to get up
Ich stehe morgens um sieben Uhr auf.
*I get up at 7 o'clock in the morning.*

**aufwachen** [AUFvah*kh*ən] *v.* • to wake (up)
Patrick wacht um 7 Uhr auf.
*Patrick wakes up at 7:00 a.m.*

**Aufzug, der** [AUFtsook] *n.* • elevator
Sie nimmt den Aufzug in den dritten Stock.
*She takes the elevator to the fourth floor.*

**Auge, das** [AUgə] *n.* • eye
**Augenbrauen, die** *n.* • eyebrows
**Augenlid, das** *n.* • eyelid
**Augenwimpern, die** *n.* • eyelashes
Meine Eltern haben beide braune Augen.
*Both my parents have brown eyes.*

**Augenblick, der** [AUgənblik] *n.* • instant
Das Licht leuchtete nur einen Augenblick auf.
*The light flashed for only an instant.*

**August, der** [auGUST] *n.* • August
Mein Bruder ist im August geboren.
*My brother was born in August.*

**aus** [AUS] *prep.* • from; (made) of
**aussteigen** *v.* • to get out of
**ausgehen** *v.* • to go out
Sie kommen aus Chicago.
*They are coming from Chicago.*

Dieser Pullover ist aus Wolle.
*This sweater is made of wool.*

**Ausflug, der** [AUSflook] *n.* • tour
**Ausflugsbus, der** *n.* • tour bus
Wir machen einen Ausflug durch Paris.
*We are taking a tour of Paris.*

**Ausgang, der** [AUSgahng] *n.* • exit
**Notausgang, der** *n.* • emergency exit
Die Ausgänge im Theater sind klar gekennzeichnet.
*The exits in the theater are clearly marked.*

**ausgeben** [AUSgaibən] *v.* • to spend (money)
Sie hat all ihr Geld ausgegeben.
*She spent all her money.*

**ausgezeichnet** [ausgəTSEI*SH*nət] *adj.* • excellent
Sie wurde für ihre ausgezeichnete Arbeit belohnt.
*She was rewarded for her excellent work.*

**Auskunft, die** [AUSkunft] *n.* • information
Wenn Sie nicht Bescheid wissen, bitten Sie um Auskunft.
*If you don't know, ask for information.*

**Ausländer, der (-in, f.)** [AUSlendər] *n.* • foreigner
Diese Ausländer besuchen die Vereinigten Staaten.
*These foreigners are visiting the United States.*

**ausradieren** [AUSrahdeerən] *v.* • to erase
Ich radiere meine Fehler mit einem Radiergummi aus.
*I erase my mistakes with an eraser.*

**ausrauben** [AUSraubən] *v.* • to rob
Die Polizei fing den Mann, der den Laden ausgeraubt hatte.
*The police caught the man who had robbed the store.*

**ausruhen** [AUSrooən] *v.* • to rest
Der Doktor verordnete mir, den ganzen Tag auszuruhen.
*The doctor told me to rest all day.*

**ausrutschen** [AUSrutshən] *v.* • to slip
Sei vorsichtig! Rutsch nicht auf dem Eis aus!
*Be careful! Don't slip on the ice!*

**ausschimpfen** [AUSshimfən] *v.* • to scold
Vater schimpft uns aus, wenn wir unartig sind.
*Father scolds us when we are naughty.*

**aussehen** [AUSzaiən] *v.* • to look
**aussehen wie** • to look like
Sie sieht wie ihre Schwester aus.
*She looks like her sister.*

**aussprechen** [AUSshpre*sh*ən] *v.* • to pronounce
Wie spricht man dieses Wort aus?
*How do you pronounce this word?*

**Auster, die** [AUStər] *n.* • oyster
Essen Sie rohe Austern?
*Do you eat raw oysters?*

**Australien** [ausTRAHleeyən] *n.* • Australia
**der Australier, -in** *n.* • Australian (person)
**australisch** *adj.* • Australian
Viele außergewöhnliche Tiere leben in Australien.
*Many unusual animals live in Australia.*

**Außenseite, die** [AUsəntseitə] *n.* • outside
Die Außenseite des Hauses ist weiß gestrichen.
*The outside of the house is painted white.*

**außer** [AUsər] *prep.* • except
Außer mir, können alle andere gehen!
*Everyone else can leave except me!*

**außerordentlich** [AUsərawrdentlish] *adj.* • extraordinary
Marie spielt mit außerordentlicher Begabung Klavier.
*Marie plays the piano with extraordinary skill.*

**Auto, das** [AUtoh] *n.* • auto(mobile); car
**Autowaschanlage, die** *n.* • car wash
Das Auto ist das Hauptfortbewegungsmittel in Amerika.
*The automobile is the standard mode of travel in America.*

**Autor, der** [auTOHR] *n.* • author
Mein Lieblingsautor ist ein Romanschriftsteller.
*My favorite author is a novelist.*

# B

**Baby, das** [BAIbee] *n.* • baby
**Babysitter, der** *n.* • baby sitter
Wie heißt dein neugeborenes Baby?
*What is your newborn baby's name?*

**Bach, der** [BAH*KH*] *n.* • brook; stream
Der Junge fischt in diesem kleinen Bach.
*The boy fishes in this little brook.*

Kleine Bäche werden große Flüsse.
*Little streams become great rivers.*

**Backe, die** [BAHkə] *n.* • cheek
Martine hat immer rote Backen!
*Martine always has rosy cheeks!*

**backen** [BAHkən] *v.* • to bake
**Bäcker, der** *n.* • baker
**Bäckerei, die** *n.* • bakery

| | |
|---|---|
| backe | backen |
| bäckst | backt |
| bäckt | backen |

Der Bäcker backt Brot in seinem Backofen.
*The baker bakes bread in his oven.*

**Backofen, der** [BAHKohfən] *n.* • oven
Das Brot ist im Backofen.
*The bread is in the oven.*

**Bad, das** [BAHT] *n.* • bath
**Badeanzug, der** *n.* • bathing suit
**baden** *v.* • to bathe; to take a bath
**Badewanne, die** *n.* • bathtub
**Badezimmer, das** *n.* • bathroom
**Sonnenbad, das** *n.* • sunbath
**Waschbecken, das** *n.* • bathroom sink
Nach der Arbeit nahm sie ein langes Bad, um sich zu entspannen.
*She took a long bath to relax after work.*

**Bahn, die** [BAHN] *n.* • railway
**Bahnhof, der** *n.* • railroad station
Man kann mit der Bahn durch ganz Europa reisen.
*One can travel throughout Europe by railway.*

**bald** [BAHLT] *adv.* • soon
**Bis bald!** • See you soon!
**sobald wie** • as soon as
Das Flugzeug wird bald ankommen.
*The plane will arrive soon.*

**Ball, der** [BAHL] *n.* • ball
Das Kind wirft den Ball.
*The child throws the ball.*

**Ballon, der** [bahLAWN] *n.* • balloon
Der Ballon fliegt an die Zimmerdecke.
*The balloon is floating to the ceiling.*

**Banane, die** [bahNAHnə] *n.* • banana
Der Affe ißt eine Banane.
*The monkey is eating a banana.*

**Band, das** [BAHNT] *n.* • ribbon
Das kleine Mädchen trägt Bänder im Haar.
*This little girl has ribbons in her hair.*

**Bank, die** [BAHNGK] *n.* • bank
**Bankier, der (-in, f.)** *n.* • banker
Zahlen Sie ihr Geld auf die Bank an der Ecke ein.
*Deposit your money at the bank on the corner.*

**Bank, die** [BAHNGK] *n.* • bench
Sie setzen sich auf eine Bank im Park.
*They sit down on a bench in the park.*

**Bär, der** [BAIR] *n.* • bear
Das Feuer wird die Bären von unserem Lager fern halten.
*The fire will keep the bears away from our camp.*

**Bart, der** [BAHRT] *n.* • beard
Mein Vater trägt einen Bart.
*My father has a beard.*

**Baseballspiel, das** [BAISbahlshpeel] *n.* • baseball
Haben wir genügend Spieler, um Baseball zu spielen?
*Do we have enough players to play baseball?*

**bauen** [BAUən] *v.* • to build; to construct

| | |
|---|---|
| baue | bauen |
| baust | baut |
| baut | bauen |

Wir bauen außerhalb der Stadt ein neues Haus.
*We are building a new house outside of town.*

Die Zimmerleute bauen ein neues Haus.
*The carpenters are constructing a new house.*

**Bauernhof, der** [BAUərnhohf] *n.* • farm
Dieser Bauernhof baut Mais und Weizen an.
*This farm produces corn and wheat.*

**Baum, der** [BAUM] *n.* • tree
Laßt uns in den Schatten dieses Baumes gehen.
*Let's go under the shade of this tree.*

**Baumwolle, die** [BAUMvawlə] *n.* • cotton
**aus Baumwolle (gemacht)** • made of cotton
Das Hemd war aus Baumwolle.
*The shirt was made of cotton.*

**beantworten** [beAHNTvawrtən] *v.* • to answer; to respond
**Antwort, die** *n.* • response
Beantworten Sie die Fragen 1-10 in ihrem Buch.
*Answer questions 1-10 in your book.*

Kann jemand die Frage beantworten?
*Can someone respond to the question?*

**bedeuten** [bəDOItən] *v.* • to mean
**das bedeutet** • that is to say

bedeute bedeuten
bedeutest bedeutet
bedeutet bedeuten

Was bedeutet das?
*What does that mean?*

**bedeutend** [bəDOItənt] *adj.* • great
Abraham Lincoln war einer der bedeutendsten Präsidenten der U.S.A.
*Abraham Lincoln was one of the greatest U.S. presidents.*

**bedienen** [bəDEEnən] *v.* • to run; to serve
Ich weiß nicht, wie man die Maschine bedient.
*I don't know how to run the machine.*

Zuerst bedienen wir unsere Gäste.
*First, we serve our guests.*

**beeilen, sich** [bəEIlən, ZI*SH*] *v.* • to hurry
**Beeile dich!** • Hurry up!
beeile mich beeilen uns
beeilst dich beeilt euch
beeilt sich beeilen sich

Wir beeilen uns, um den Zug zu erreichen.
*We are hurrying to catch the train.*

**beenden** [bəENdən] *v.* • to finish
Ich beendete meine Hausaufgabe um 10 Uhr abends.
*I finished my homework at 10:00 p.m.*

**Befehl, der** [bəFAIL] *n.* • command
Der Offizier gibt den Soldaten Befehle.
*The officer gives commands to the soldiers.*

**Begeisterung, die** [bəGEIStərung] *n.* • enthusiasm
**begeistert** *adj.* • enthusiastic
Du zeigst große Begeisterung für neue Fächer.
*You show a lot of enthusiasm for new subjects.*

**beginnen** [bəGINən] *v.* • to start

beginne beginnen
beginnst beginnt
beginnt beginnen

Der Film beginnt um 19.30 Uhr.
*The movie starts at 7:30 p.m.*

**behalten** [bəHAHLtən] *v.* • to keep
**Andenken, das** *n.* • keepsake (memento)

behalte behalten
behältst behaltet
behält behalten

Ich werde dein Bild in meiner Brieftasche behalten.
*I will keep your picture in my wallet.*

**bei** [BEI] *prep.* • by
**einer nach dem andern** • one by one
**bei Tage** • by day

Seine Eltern wohnen bei einem See.
*His parents live by a lake.*

**beide** [BEIdə] *pron.* • both

Maurice und Alan gehen beide ins Kino.
*Maurice and Alan are both going to the movies.*

**Bein, das** [BEIN] *n.* • leg

Diese Tänzerin hat schöne Beine.
*This dancer has beautiful legs.*

**Beispiel, das** [BEIshpeel] *n.* • example
**zum Beispiel** • for example

Dein Benehmen gibt den anderen ein Beispiel.
*Your behavior sets an example for the others.*

**beißen** [BEIsən] *v.* • to bite

beiße beißen
beißt beißt
beißt beißen

Ich habe Angst vor Tieren, die beißen.
*I am afraid of animals that bite.*

**beklagen, sich** [bəKLAHgən] *v.* • to complain
Er beklagt sich immer über das Wetter.
*He is always complaining about the weather.*

**bekommen** [bəKAWMən] *v.* • to get; to receive

| | |
|---|---|
| bekomme | bekommen |
| bekommst | bekommt |
| bekommt | bekommen |

Wenn du tüchtig arbeitest, bekommst du eine gute Note.
*If you study hard, you will get a good grade.*

Sie bekommt viele Komplimente wegen ihres guten Benehmens.
*She receives a lot of compliments for her good manners.*

**Belgien** [BELGyən] *n.* • Belgium
**Belgier, der (-in, f.)** *n.* • Belgian (person)
**belgisch** *adj.* • Belgian
Man spricht Französisch und Flämisch in Belgien.
*They speak French and Flemish in Belgium.*

**bemerken** [bəMERkən] *v.* • to notice
Sie bemerkt jedes Detail.
*She notices every detail.*

**benehmen, sich** [bəNAImən ZI*SH*] *v.* • to behave
**Benehmen, das** *n.* • behavior
**Benimm dich!** • Behave!
**sich gut benehmen** • to behave well
**sich schlecht benehmen** • to behave badly
Diese Kinder wissen, wie man sich in einem Restaurant benimmt.
*These children know how to behave in a restaurant.*

Diese Kinder benehmen sich alle gut.
*All these children are well behaved.*

**benutzen** [bəNUtsən] *v.* • to use
**nutzlos** *adj.* • useless
**nützlich** *adj.* • useful
Ich benutzte das Lexikon, um Wörter nachzuschlagen.
*I used the dictionary to look up words.*

**Benzin, das** [benTSEEN] *n.* • gasoline
**Benzinpumpe, die** *n.* • gas pump
Unser Auto braucht Benzin.
*Our car needs gasoline.*

**bequem** [bəKVAIM] *adj.* • comfortable
Dieser Lehnstuhl ist sehr bequem.
*This easy chair is very comfortable.*

**bereit** [bəREIT] *adv.* • ready
Wir sind bereit zu gehen.
*We are ready to go.*

Sie war bereit, uns alles zu erzählen.
*She was ready to tell us everything.*

**Berg, der** [BERG] *n.* • mountain
**Bergsteigen gehen** • to go mountain climbing
**Berg-und-Tal-Bahn, die** • roller coaster
In den Bergen ist es immer kühl.
*It's always cool in the mountains.*

**Beruf, der** [bəROOF] *n.* • profession; occupation
Ärzte müssen lange studieren, bevor sie ihren Beruf ausüben können.
*Doctors must study a long time before they can practice their profession.*

Welchen Beruf wirst du ergreifen?
*What occupation are you going to choose?*

**berühmt** [bəR*UE*MT] *adj.* • famous
Dieses Restaurant ist für Meeresfrüchte berühmt.
*This restaurant is famous for its seafood.*

**beschäftigt** [bəSHAIFti*sh*t] *adj.* • busy
Die Sekretärin ist sehr beschäftigt.
*The secretary is very busy.*

**beschmutzen** [bəSHMUtsən] *v.* • to soil
Beschmutze nicht den Teppich mit deinen schmutzigen Schuhen!
*Don't soil the rug with your dirty shoes!*

**beschützen** [bəSH*UE*tsən] *v.* • to protect
Die Katze beschützt ihre Jungen.
*The cat protects her kittens.*

**Besen, der** [BAIzən] *n.* • broom
Er benutzte einen Besen, um den Boden zu kehren.
*He used a broom to sweep the floor.*

**besichtigen** [bəZI*SH*tigən] *v.* • to visit
Wir besichtigen ein Schloß am Rhein.
*We are visiting a castle on the Rhine.*

**besitzen** [bəZItsən] *v.* • to own

| | |
|---|---|
| besitze | besitzen |
| besitzt | besitzt |
| besitzt | besitzen |

Unsere wohlhabenden Freunde besitzen mehrere Häuser.
*Our wealthy friends own several houses.*

**besonders** [bəZAWNderz] *adv.; adj.* • especially; special
Ich schwimme gern, besonders wenn es warm ist.
*I like to swim, especially when it is warm.*

Heute abend kommt eine besondere Show im Fernsehen.
*There is a special show on T.V. tonight.*

**besorgt** [bəZAWRKT] *adj.* • worried
Paul ist um seine Noten besorgt.
*Paul is worried about his grades.*

**Besorgung, die** [bəZAWRgung] *n.* • errand
**Besorgungen machen** • to run errands
Wir haben Besorgungen in der Stadt zu machen.
*We have errands to run in town.*

**besser** [BESə*r*] *adj.* • better
Dieser Kuchen schmeckt besser als jener.
*This cake tastes better than that one.*

**bestehen auf** [bəSHTAIən auf] *v.* • to insist
Er besteht darauf, daß er recht hat.
*He insists that he is right.*

**bestellen** [bəSHTELən] *v.* • to order

| | |
|---|---|
| bestelle | bestellen |
| bestellst | bestellt |
| bestellt | bestellen |

Ich habe eben unser Essen bestellt.
*I have just ordered our meal.*

**bester; beste; bestes** [BESt*ər*; BEStə; BEStəs] *adj.* • best
**der, die, das Beste** • the best
Er ist mein bester Freund.
*He is my best friend.*

**bestrafen** [bəSHTRAHfən] *v.* • to punish
Man wird den Verbrecher bestrafen.
*They are going to punish the criminal.*

**besuchen** [bəZOO*KH*ən] *v.* • to attend; to visit (a person)
**Besucher, der** *n.* • visitor
**Besuch, der (-erin, f.)** *n.* • visit

| | |
|---|---|
| besuche | besuchen |
| besuchst | besucht |
| besucht | besuchen |

Sie besuchen heute abend das Konzert.
*They are attending the concert tonight.*

**Betonung, die** [bəTOHnung] *n.* • accent
Die Betonung ist auf der ersten Silbe.
*The accent is on the first syllable.*

**betreten** [bəTRAItən] *v.* • to enter
Der Lehrer betritt das Klassenzimmer.
*The teacher enters the classroom.*

**Bett, das** [BET] *n.* • bed
**Bettdecke, die** *n.* • bedspread
**das Bett machen** • to make the bed
**zu Bett gehen** • to go to bed
Mein Bett hat eine bequeme Matratze.
*My bed has a comfortable mattress.*

**Bettuch, das** [BETtoo*kh*] *n.* • sheet
Das Zimmermädchen wechselte die Bettücher.
*The maid put clean sheets on the bed.*

**bezahlen** [bəTSAHlən] *v.* • to pay (for)
Mein Vater bezahlt die Karten.
*My father is paying for the tickets.*

**Biber, der** [BEEbə*r*] *n.* • beaver
Die Biber bauen Deiche über den Fluß.
*Beavers build dams across the river.*

**Bibliothek, die** [bibleeohTAIK] *n.* • library
**Bibliothekar, der (-in, f.)** *n.* • librarian
Ich werde diese Bücher zur Bibliothek zurückbringen.
*I am going to take these books back to the library.*

**biegen** [BEEgən] *v.* • to bend
**Biegung, die** *n.* • turn

| | |
|---|---|
| biege | biegen |
| biegst | biegt |
| biegt | biegen |

Er war stark genug, den Ast zu biegen.
*He was strong enough to bend the branch.*

**Biene, die** [BEEnə] *n.* • bee
Bienen machen Honig.
*Bees make honey.*

**Bild, das** [BILT] *n.* • picture
Ich habe ein Bild von meiner Familie auf dem Schreibtisch.
*I have a picture of my family on my desk.*

**Bildhauer, der** [BILThauə*r*] *n.* • sculptor
Der Bildhauer schnitzte eine Figur aus Holz.
*The sculptor was carving a statue from wood.*

**billig** [BIli*sh*] *adj.; adv.* • inexpensive; cheap; cheaply
**billig sein** • to be inexpensive
Ich habe einen billigen Wagen gekauft.
*I bought an inexpensive car.*

**bin** see *sein*

**Biologie, die** [beeohlohGEE] *n.* • biology
Meine Schwester studiert Biologie an der Universität.
*My sister studies biology at the university.*

**Birne, die** [BIRnə] *n.* • pear
Die Fruchtschale ist voller Birnen und Äpfel.
*The fruit bowl is full of pears and apples.*

**bis** [BIS] *prep.* • until
Ich lerne bis vier Uhr.
*I study until four o'clock.*

**bist** see *sein*

**bißchen, ein** [BEES*sh*ən] *adj.; adv.* • a little; a (little) bit
Ich möchte gern ein bißchen mehr Kaffee, bitte.
*I would like a little more coffee, please.*

**bitte** [BITə] *adv.* • please
Kann ich bitte das Salz haben?
*May I have the salt, please?*

**bitten** [BITən] *v.* • to ask (for); to request

| | |
|---|---|
| bitte | bitten |
| bittest | bittet |
| bittet | bitten |

Bitten Sie die Kellnerin um etwas mehr Kaffee.
*Ask the waitress for some more coffee.*

**blasen** [BLAHzən] *v.* • to blow

| | |
|---|---|
| blase | blasen |
| bläst | blast |
| bläst | blasen |

Blas die Kerze aus!
*Blow out the candle!*

**Blatt, das** [BLAHT] *n.* • leaf
**Blatt Papier, das** • sheet of paper
Die Blätter sind schön im Herbst.
*The leaves are beautiful in the fall.*

**blau** [BLAU] *adj.* • blue
Mein Father trägt heute einen blauen Anzug.
*My father is wearing his blue suit today.*

**bleiben** [BLEIbən] *v.* • to stay; to remain

| | |
|---|---|
| bleibe | bleiben |
| bleibst | bleibt |
| bleibt | bleiben |

Ich bleibe heute abend bei meinem Freund.
*I am staying at my friend's house tonight.*

Bleiben Sie sitzen, bis das Flugzeug zu einem völligen Stillstand gekommen ist.
*Remain in your seats until the plane comes to a full stop.*

**Bleistift, der** [BLEIshtift] *n.* • pencil
Ich schreibe lieber mit einem Bleistift, damit ich meine Fehler ausradieren kann.
*I prefer to write with a pencil so I can erase my mistakes.*

**Blick, der** [BLIK] *n.* • view
Man hat einen guten Blick vom Berggipfel.
*There is a fine view from the mountain top.*

**blind** [BLINT] *adj.* • blind
Meine Großmutter ist fast blind.
*My grandmother is almost blind.*

**Blitz, der** [BLITS] *n.* • lightning
Der Turm wurde im Sturm vom Blitz getroffen.
*Lightning struck the tower in the storm.*

**blond** [BLAWND] *adj.* • blond
Die zwei kleinen Jungen sind blond.
*The two little boys are blond.*

**Blume, die** [BLOOmə] *n.* • flower
Diese Blumen wachsen im Wald.
*These flowers grow in the woods.*

**Blumenkohl, der** [BLOOmənkohl] *n.* • cauliflower
Blumenkohl ist mein Lieblingsgemüse.
*Cauliflower is my favorite vegetable.*

**Bluse, die** [BLOOzə] *n.* • blouse
Paßt diese Bluse zu diesem Rock?
*Does this blouse go with this skirt?*

**Blut, das** [BLOOT] *n.* • blood
Er spendet Blut im Krankenhaus.
*He gives blood at the hospital.*

**Boden, der** [BOHdən] *n.* • bottom
Stell die schwereren Sachen auf den Boden der Tasche.
*Put the heavier things in the bottom of the bag.*

**Bohnen, die** [BOHnən] *n.* • beans
**grüne Bohnen** • green beans

Es gibt grüne Bohnen zum Essen.
*We are having green beans with dinner.*

**Boot, das** [BOHT] *n.* • boat
**Segelboot, das** *n.* • sailboat
Wir nehmen ein Boot, um fischen zu gehen.
*We take a boat to go fishing.*

**borgen** [BAWRgən] *v.* • to borrow (from)
Er will immer meinen Wagen borgen.
*He always wants to borrow my car.*

**Botschaft, die** [BOHTshahft] *n.* • embassy
**Botschafter, der (-in, f.)** *n.* • ambassador
Wenn Sie ihren Reisepaß verlieren, rufen Sie die Botschaft an.
*Call the embassy if you lose your passport.*

Der Botschafter arbeitet bei der Botschaft.
*The ambassador works at the embassy.*

**Boulevard, der** [BUləvahrd] *n.* • boulevard
Kennst du den Boulevard St-Michel in Paris?
*Are you familiar with the Boulevard St-Michel in Paris?*

**Boutique, die** [buTEEK] *n.* • boutique
Meine Cousine ist Verkäuferin in dieser Boutique.
*My cousin is a clerk in this boutique.*

**Bowlingspiel, das** [BOHlingshpeel] *n.* • bowling
Meine Eltern lieben das Bowlingspiel.
*My parents like bowling.*

**Brand, der** [BRAHNT] *n.* • fire
**in Brand geraten** • to catch fire
Die Feuerwehr hat den Brand gelöscht.
*The firemen extinguished the fire.*

**braten** [BRAHtən] *v.* • to roast
**Rinderbraten, der** *n.* • roast beef

| | |
|---|---|
| brate | braten |
| brätst | bratet |
| brät | braten |

Wir braten einen Truthahn zum Abendessen.
*We are roasting a turkey for dinner.*

**brauchen** [BRAU*kh*ən] *v.* • to need

| | |
|---|---|
| brauche | brauchen |
| brauchst | braucht |
| braucht | brauchen |

Der kleine Junge braucht Hilfe, um sich anzuziehen.
*The little boy needs help getting dressed.*

**braun** [BRAUN] *adj.* • brown
Der braune Mantel steht ihr gut.
*The brown coat looks good on her.*

**brechen** [BRE*sh*ən] *v.* • to break
**abbrechen** *v.* • to break off

| | |
|---|---|
| breche | brechen |
| brichst | brecht |
| bricht | brechen |

Das Glas kann leicht brechen.
*The glass can easily break.*

**breit** [BREIT] *adj.* • broad; wide
Die Alleen in New York sind sehr breit.
*The avenues of New York are very broad.*

Der Grand Canyon ist sehr breit.
*The Grand Canyon is very wide.*

**Brief, der** [BREEF] *n.* • letter
**Briefkasten, der** *n.* • mailbox
Ich warf den Brief in den Briefkasten.
*I put the letter in the mailbox.*

**Briefmarke, die** [BREEFmahrkə] *n.* • stamp (postage)

Meine Schwester sammelt Briefmarken.
*My sister collects stamps.*

**Brieftasche, die** [BREEFtahshə] *n.* • billfold
Ich bewahre mein Geld in meiner Brieftasche auf.
*I keep my money in my billfold.*

**Briefumschlag, der** [BREEFumshlahg] *n.* • envelope
Falten Sie den Brief und tun Sie ihn bitte in einen Briefumschlag.
*Fold the letter and put it in an envelope, please.*

**Brille, die** [BRILə] *n.* • glasses
**Sonnenbrille, die** *n.* • sun glasses
Ich brauche meine Brille, um dies zu lesen.
*I need my glasses to read this.*

**bringen** [BRINGən] *v.* • to bring

| | |
|---|---|
| bringe | bringen |
| bringst | bringt |
| bringt | bringen |

Der Kellner bringt uns den Kaffee.
*The waiter brings us the coffee.*

**Brot, das** [BROHT] *n.* • bread
**Brot und Marmelade** • bread and jam
Das meiste Weißbrot wird aus Weizenmehl gemacht.
*Most white bread is made from wheat flour.*

**Brötchen, das** [BR*ER*ts*h*ən] *n.* • roll
Ich habe Butter auf das Brötchen gestrichen.
*I put butter on the roll.*

**Brücke, die** [BR*UE*kə] *n.* • bridge
Die "Golden Gate" Brücke ist in San Francisco.
*The Golden Gate Bridge is in San Francisco.*

**Bruder, der** [BROOdər] *n.* • brother
Ich habe einen älteren Bruder, der die Universität besucht.
*I have an older brother who is in college.*

**brünett** [br*ue*NET] *adj.* • brunette
Meine Mutter ist brünett.
*My mother is brunette.*

**Brust, die** [BROOST] *n.* • breast; chest
Mein Hund liebt es, wenn ich ihm die Brust kratze.
*My dog likes for me to scratch his chest.*

**Buch, das** [BOO*KH*] *n.* • book
**Bücherregal, das** *n.* • bookshelf
**Bücherschrank, der** *n.* • bookcase
**Buchhändler, der** *n.* • bookseller
**Buchhandlung, die; Buchladen, der** *n.* • bookstore
**Taschenbuch, das** *n.* • paperback
Ich las zwei neue Bücher während meiner Ferien.
*I read two new books during my vacation.*

**bügeln** [B*UE*gəln] *v.* • to press; to iron
**Bügeleisen, das** *n.* • iron (appliance)
Kannst du bitte meine Hose bügeln?
*Can you press my pants, please?*

**Bürger, der** [B*UE*Rgə*r*] *n.* • citizen
Ich bin Bürger der Vereinigten Staaten.
*I am a citizen of the United States.*

**Bürgermeister, der** [B*UE*Rgə*r*meistə*r*] *n.* • mayor
Das Büro des Bürgermeisters ist im Rathaus.
*The office of the mayor is in city hall.*

**Bürgersteig, der** [B*UE*Rgə*r*shteig] *n.* • sidewalk
Der Hund läuft auf dem Bürgersteig.
*The dog walks on the sidewalk.*

**Büro, das** [B*UE*roh] *n.* • office
Das Büro meines Vaters ist in diesem Gebäude.
*My father's office is in this building.*

**Bürste, die** [B*UE*RStə] *n.* • brush
**Zahnbürste, die** *n.* • toothbrush
Ich nehme eine Bürste für mein Haar.
*I use a brush on my hair.*

**bürsten** [B*UE*RStən] *v.* • to brush

| | |
|---|---|
| bürste | bürsten |
| bürstest | bürstet |
| bürstet | bürsten |

Ich bürste mein Haar jeden Morgen.
*I brush my hair every morning.*

**Bus, der** [BOOS] *n.* • bus
**Ausflugsbus, der** *n.* • excursion bus
Die Kinder warten auf den Bus.
*The children are waiting for the bus.*

**Butter, die** [BOOTə*r*] *n* • butter
**Butterbrot, das** *n.* • sandwich
Peter streicht Butter auf sein Brot.
*Peter puts butter on his bread.*

# C

**Café, das** [kahFAI] *n.* • café
**Straßencafé, das** *n.* • sidewalk café
Wir treffen uns oft im Café.
*We often meet in the café.*

**Chef, der** [SHEF] *n.* • boss
Mein Chef hat für heute morgen eine Versammlung einberufen.
*My boss called a meeting for this morning.*

**Chemie, die** [*sh*eMEE] *n.* • chemistry
Ich unterrichte Chemie und Physik am Gymnasium.
*I teach chemistry and physics at the high school.*

**China** [*SH*EEnah] *n.* • China
**chinesisch** *adj.* • Chinese
**Chinese, der (-in, f.)** *n.* • Chinese (person)
Ich hoffe, eines Tages China besuchen zu können.
*I hope to visit China someday.*

**Chirurg, der (-in, f.)** [*sh*irOORG] *n.* • surgeon
**chirurgische Eingriff, der** • surgery; operation
Der Chirurg arbeitet im Krankenhaus.
*The surgeon works at the hospital.*

**Chor, der** [KOHR] *n.* • choir
Dieser Chor singt sehr gut.
*This choir sings very well.*

**Clown, der** [KLAUN] *n.* • clown
Ich liebe die Clowns im Zirkus.
*I like the clowns at the circus.*

**Compact Disk, die** [KOHMpahkt DISK] *n.* • compact disc
Die Compact Disk ist eine neue Erfindung.
*The compact disc is a new invention.*

**Computer, der** [kawmPOOt*ər*] *n.* • computer
Am Computer kann man sich mit Spielen unterhalten.
*You can entertain yourself with games on the computer.*

# D

**da** [DAH] *adv.* • there
**da drüben** • over there
**da oben** • up there
**da unten** • down there

Hallo, ist dein Vater da?
*Hello, is your father there?*

**da** [DAH] *conj.* • since
Da du schon hier bist, bleib doch zum Mittagessen!
*Since you are here, stay for lunch!*

**Dach, das** [DA*KH*] *n.* • roof
Auf dem Dach liegt Schnee.
*There is snow on the roof.*

**Dachgeschoß, das** [DA*KH*gəshaws] *n.* • attic
Das Haus meiner Großmutter hat ein großes Dachgeschoß.
*My grandmother's house has a big attic.*

**Dame, die** [DAHmə] *n.* • lady
**junge Dame, die** • young lady
**Meine Damen und Herren!** • Ladies and gentlemen!
Sie hat das Benehmen einer Dame.
*She has the manners of a lady.*

**Damespiel, das** [DAHməshpeel] *n.* • checkers
Ich spiele gern Dame mit meiner kleinen Schwester.
*I like to play checkers with my little sister.*

**damit** [dahMIT] *adj.* • in order that; in order to; so that
Ich trage eine Brille, damit ich besser sehen kann.
*I wear glasses in order to see better.*

**Dampfer, der** [DAHMpfə*r*] *n.* • steamship
Der Dampfer kam in New York an.
*The steamship arrived in New York.*

**danach** [daNAH*KH*] *adv.* • afterwards
Wir aßen zu Abend, und danach gingen wir spazieren.
*We ate dinner, then afterwards we went for a walk.*

**Dänemark** [DAInəmahrk] *n.* • Denmark
**dänisch** *adj.* • Danish
**Däne, der; Danin, die** *n.* • Dane
Dänemark ist ein Land in Nordeuropa.
*Denmark is a country in northern Europe.*

**danken** [DANGKən] *v.* • to thank
**Vielen Dank!** • thank you

| | |
|---|---|
| danke | danken |
| dankst | dankt |
| dankt | danken |

Sie danken der Gastgeberin, bevor sie gehen.
*They thank the hostess before leaving.*

**dann** [DAHN] *adv.* • then
Wir fahren nach Hause; dann machen wir Abendbrot.
*We'll get home, then we'll make dinner.*

**darin** [dahRIN] *adv.* • inside
Hier ist ein alter Reisekoffer. Was ist darin?
*Here is an old trunk. What is inside?*

**das** [DAHS] *article* • that; the (neuter); these; those
**das ist** • that is
**das sind** • those are
**das ist schade!** • that's too bad!
**das ist alles** • that's all
Das Kind ist zwei Jahre alt.
*The child is two years old.*

**dasselbe** [dahsZELbə] *pron.* • same
Für mich ist es alles dasselbe.
*It's all the same to me.*

**Datum, das** [DAHtum] *n.* • date
An welchem Datum ist dein Termin?
*What date is your appointment?*

**Dauerwelle, die** [DAUərvelə] *n.* • perm(anent)
Sie geht zum Friseur, um sich eine Dauerwelle machen zu lassen.
*She goes to the hairdresser's to get a perm.*

**Daumen, der** [DAUmən] *n.* • thumb
Das Kind lutscht am Daumen.
*The child is sucking its thumb.*

**Decke, die** [DEKə] *n.* • ceiling
An der Decke ist eine Fliege.
*There is a fly on the ceiling.*

**Decke, die** [DEKə] *n.* • blanket
**bedeckt** *adj.* • covered
**bedecken** *v.* • to cover
Diese Decke ist warm.
*This blanket is warm.*

**Deckel, der** [DEKəl] *n.* • cover (lid)
Dieser Topf hat einen Deckel.
*This pot has a cover (lid).*

**decken** [DEKən] *v.* • to set; to cover
**den Tisch decken** • to set the table

| | |
|---|---|
| decke | decken |
| deckst | deckt |
| deckt | decken |

Der Tisch ist für vier Personen gedeckt.
*The table is set for four people.*

**dein** [DEIN] *adj.* • your
Wo ist dein Heft?
*Where is your notebook?* see also *ihr*

**den, die, das** [DAIN, DEE, DAHS] *pron.* • whom
Der Mann, den wir am Bahnhof sahen, unterrichtet an meiner Schule.
*The man whom we saw at the station teaches in my school.*

**denken** [DENGkən] *v.* • to think
**denken an** • to think of
**nachdenken über** • to think about

| | |
|---|---|
| denke | denken |
| denkst | denkt |
| denkt | denken |

Ich denke, wir kommen zu spät!
*I think we are late!*

**der, die, das; die (pl.)** [DAIR, DEE, DAHS; DEE]
def. art. • the
Die Bücher sind auf dem Tisch.
*The books are on the table.*

**derselbe, dieselbe, dasselbe** [DERzelbə, DEEzelbə, DAHSzelbə] *adj.* • same
Du hast dieselbe Jacke wie dein Bruder.
*You have the same jacket as your brother.*

**Detektiv, der** [detekTEEF] *n.* • detective
Mein Vati liebt Detektivgeschichten.
*My dad loves detective stories.*

**Deutschland** [DOITSHlahnt] *n.* • Germany
**Deutsche (der, die)** *n.* • German (person)
**Deutsch, das** *n.* • German (language)
**deutsch** *adj.* • German
**deutsche Schäferhund, der** • German shepherd (dog)
Die Vorfahren meines Vaters kommen aus Deutschland.
*My father's ancestors come from Germany.*

**Dezember, der** [daiTSEMbər] *n.* • December
Dezember ist der letzte Monat des Jahres.
*December is the last month of the year.*

**Diät, die** [deeAIT] *n.* • diet
**eine Diät halten** • to be on a diet
Hast du bei deiner Diät abgenommen?
*Did you lose weight on your diet?*

**dich** [DI*SH*] *pron.* • you
Dieses Geschenk ist für dich (Sie, euch).
*This present is for you.*

**dick** [DIK] *adj.* • thick
Dies ist eine dicke Decke.
*This is a thick blanket.*

**die** see *den; der*

**Dieb, der** [DEEP] *n.* • thief
Der Dieb entkam durch das Fenster.
*The thief escaped through the window.*

**dienen** [DEEnən] *v.* • to serve
**dienen als** • to serve as
**zu Ihren Diensten** • at your service

| | |
|---|---|
| diene | dienen |
| dienst | dient |
| dient | dienen |

Ich bin bereit, Ihnen zu dienen.
*I am ready to serve you.*

**Dienstag, der** [DEENStahk] *n.* • Tuesday
Die Karten sind am Dienstag für den halben Preis zu haben.
*Tickets are half price on Tuesday.*

**Dienstmädchen, das** [DEENSTmaitshən] *n.* • maid
Das Dienstmädchen macht die Hausarbeit.
*The maid does the housework.*

**diese** [DEEzə] *adj.* • these
Ich erkenne diese Kinder.
*I recognize these children.*

**dieser** [DEEzər] *adj.* • this
**dieses ist** • this is
Dieser Mann ist mein Vater.
*This man is my father.*

**Ding, das** [DING] *n.* • thing
**etwas** *pron.* • something
**Wie geht's?** • How are things?
Ich muß zu viele Dinge erledigen.
*I have too many things to do.*

**Direktor, der (-in, f.)** [diREKtohr] *n.* • principal
Die Schule hat in diesem Jahr einen neuen Direktor.
*The school has a new principal this year.*

**Dollar, der** [DAWLahr] *n.* • dollar
Die Zeitung kostet einen Dollar.
*The newspaper costs one dollar.*

**Dolmetscher, der (-in, f.)** [DAWLmetshə*r*] *n.* • interpreter
Sie arbeitet als Dolmetscherin bei der U.N.O.
*She works as an interpreter at the United Nations.*

**Dominospiel, das** [DAWminohshpeel] *n.* • dominoes
Weißt du, wie man Domino spielt?
*Do you know how to play dominoes?*

**Donner, der** [DAWnə*r*] *n.* • thunder
Meine kleine Schwester hat Angst vor Donner.
*My little sister is afraid of thunder.*

**Donnerstag, der** [DAWnə*r*stahk] *n.* • Thursday
Die Klasse trifft sich am Dienstag und am Donnerstag.
*The class meets on Tuesday and Thursday.*

**Dorf, das** [DAWRF] *n.* • village
Die Kirche ist in der Dorfmitte.
*The church is in the center of the village.*

**dort** [DAWRT] *adv.* • there; from there; around there
**es gibt** • there is; there are

Meine Mutter hat uns dort getroffen.
*My mother met us there.*

**Drache, der** [DRAH*kh*ə] *n.* • dragon
Der Ritter kämpft mit einem Drachen.
*The knight is fighting a dragon.*

**drehen** [DRAIən] *v.* • to turn
**andrehen** *v.* • to turn on
**abdrehen** *v.* • to turn off
Drehe das Fleisch um und brate es auf der anderen Seite.
*Turn the meat over and cook the other side.*

**drei** [DREI] *adj.* • three
Das kleine Kind ist drei Jahre alt.
*The young child is three years old.*

**Dreieck, das** [DREIək] *n.* • triangle
Das Schild ist ein Dreieck.
*The sign is a triangle.*

**dreißig** [DREIsi*sh*] *adj.* • thirty
Der September hat dreißig Tage.
*There are thirty days in September.*

**dreizehn** [DREItsain] *adj.* • thirteen
Auf dem Kuchen sind dreizehn Kerzen.
*There are thirteen candles on the cake.*

**dringend** [DRINGənt] *adj.* • pressing; strong; urgent
Ich habe heute eine dringende Verabredung.
*I have a pressing engagement today.*

**Drogerie, die** [drawgeREE] *n.* • drugstore
Meine Großmutter kauft ihre Medizin in der Drogerie.
*My grandmother buys her medicine at the drugstore.*

**drucken** [DRUkən] *v.* • to print

drucke drucken
druckst druckt
druckt drucken

Hier wird die Zeitung gedruckt.
*This is where they print the newspaper.*

**dumm** [DUM] *adj.* • foolish; dumb; silly; stupid

Es ist dumm, so schnell zu fahren.
*It is foolish to drive so fast.*

Wir lachten über seine dummen Bemerkungen.
*We all laughed at his dumb remarks.*

Das ist ein dummer Witz.
*That's a silly joke.*

Er hat einen dummen Fehler gemacht.
*He made a stupid mistake.*

**dunkel** [DUNGkəl] *adj.* • dark
**eine dunkele Farbe** • a deep color

Es ist dunkel draußen.
*It's dark out.*

Der Himmel wird nach Sonnenuntergang dunkel.
*The sky grows dark after the sun sets.*

**dünn** [D*UE*N] *adj.* • thin; skinny

Die Giraffe hat dünne Beine.
*The giraffe has thin legs.*

**Durcheinander, das** [DUR*SH*einahndə*r*] *n.* • mess

Räum bitte das Durcheinander in deinem Zimmer auf.
*Please clean up the mess in your room.*

**dürfen** [D*UE*Rfən] *v.* • may; to be allowed

darf dürfen
darfst dürft
darf dürfen

Darf ich Ihnen helfen?
*May I help you?*

**Durst, der** [DOORST] *n.* • thirst
**Durst haben** • to be thirsty
**durstig (sein)** *adv.* • thirsty
Darf ich ein Glas Wasser haben? Ich habe noch Durst.
*May I have a glass of water? I am still thirsty.*

**Dusche, die** [DUshə] *n.* • shower
Ziehen Sie eine Dusche oder ein Bad vor?
*Do you prefer a shower or a bath?*

**Düsenflugzeug, das** [D*UE*zənflooktsoig] *n.* • jet
Düsenflugzeuge sind schneller als Propellerflugzeuge.
*Jets are faster than propeller planes.*

**düster** [D*UE*Stə*r*] *adj.* • dim
Das Licht in diesem Zimmer ist zu düster.
*The light in this room is too dim.*

**Dutzend, das** [DUtsent] *n.* • dozen
Mein Bruder wird ein Dutzend Eier kaufen.
*My brother is going to buy a dozen eggs.*

# E

**eben** [AIbən] *adj.* • flat
Man braucht eine ebene Oberfläche, um dieses Spiel zu spielen.
*You need a flat surface to play this game.*

**Ecke, die** [EKə] *n.* • corner
**an der Ecke** • on the corner

Dieser Tisch hat eine scharfe Ecke.
*This table has a sharp corner.*

**Edelstein, der** [AIdəlshtein] *n.* • jewel
Die Krone der Königin ist mit Edelsteinen belegt.
*The queen's crown is covered with jewels.*

**Ehefrau, die; Frau, die** [AIəfrau] *n.* • wife
Seine Ehefrau heißt Madeleine.
*His wife's name is Madeleine.*

**Ehemann, der; Mann, der** [AIəmahn] *n.* • husband
Wie heißt Ihr Ehemann?
*What is your husband's name?*

**ehrlich** [AIRli*sh*] *adj.* • honest
Der Junge gab eine ehrliche Antwort.
*The boy gave an honest answer.*

**Ei, das** [EI] *n.* • egg
**gekochte Ei, das** • boiled egg
**hart gekochte Ei, das** • hard-boiled egg
**Rührei, das** *n.* • scrambled egg
Carole möchte zwei Spiegeleier zum Frühstück.
*Carole would like two fried eggs for breakfast.*

**Eiche, die** [EI*sh*ə] *n.* • oak
Der Tisch ist ganz aus Eiche gemacht.
*The table is made of solid oak.*

**Eichhörnchen, das** [EI*SH*herrn*sh*ən] *n.* • squirrel
Auf dem Baum sitzt ein graues Eichhörnchen.
*There is a grey squirrel in the tree.*

**Eidechse, die** [EIdeksə] *n.* • lizard
Die Eidechse schläft auf dem Stein.
*The lizard is sleeping on the rock.*

**eifersüchtig** [EIferz*uesh*tish] *adj.* • jealous
Unsere Katze ist auf unser neues Kätzchen eifersüchtig.
*Our cat is jealous of our new kitten.*

**eigene, -r, -s** [EIgenə] *adj.* • own
Dieses ist meine eigene Kamera.
*This is my very own camera.*

**Eile, die** [EIlə] *n.* • hurry
**es eilig haben** • to be in a hurry
Es hat keine Eile.
*There is no hurry.*

**Eimer, der** [EImer] *n.* • pail; bucket
Er gießt Wasser aus dem Eimer.
*He pours water from the pail.*

Ich trage Wasser in einem Eimer.
*I carry water in a bucket.*

**ein; eine** [EIN; EInə] *indef. art.* • a; an
Dies ist ein alter Film.
*This is an old movie.*

Ich habe eine Tochter und einen Sohn.
*I have a daughter and a son.*

**ein, -s** [EIN] *adj.; pron.* • one; the one
**derjenige, der; diejenige, die; dasjenige, das** • the one who
**der (die, das) dort** • that one
**einer nach dem andern** • one by one
Möchtest du einen Keks oder zwei?
*Do you want one cookie or two?*

Geben Sie mir bitte den einen dort in der Ecke.
*Please give me that one in the corner.*

**Eingang, der** [EINgahng] *n.* • entrance
Der Eingang zum Flur ist durch die rote Tür.
*The entrance to the hall is through the red door.*

**eingießen** [EINgeesən] *v.* • to pour
Mutter gießt allen Kaffee ein.
*Mom pours coffee for everyone.*

**einige** [EInigə] *adj.* • several
Laßt uns noch einige Minuten auf ihn warten.
*Let's wait for him several more minutes.*

**einkaufen** [EINkaufən] *v.* • to shop
**einkaufen gehen** • to go shopping
Ich muß heute Lebensmittel einkaufen.
*I have to shop for groceries today.*

**einladen** [EINlahdən] *v.* • to invite
**Einladung, die** *n.* • invitation
Wir laden alle unsere Freunde zur Party ein.
*We're inviting all our friends to the party.*

**einmal** [EINmahl] *adv.* • once
**es war einmal** • once upon a time
**noch einmal** • once again
**auf einmal** • all at once
Zeig es mir nur einmal, und ich weiß wie man es macht.
*Show me just once and I'll know how to do it.*

**Eintrittskarte, die** [EINtritskahrtə] *n.* • ticket
Hast du die Entrittskarten für den Zoo?
*Do you have the tickets for the zoo?*

**einzig** [EINtsi*sh*] *adj.* • only
Sie ist die einzige Person, die hier Französisch spricht.
*She is the only person who speaks French here.*

**Eis, das** [EIS] *n.* • ice
**Eis (Speiseeis), das** *n.* • ice cream
**Eiswürfel, der** *n.* • ice cube
Es gibt Eis im Gefrierfach.
*There is ice in the freezer.*

**Eisen, das** [EIzən] *n.* • iron
**aus Eisen** • made of iron
Der Zaun ist aus Eisen.
*The fence is made of iron.*

**Eisenbahn, die** [EIzənbahn] *n.* • railroad
Ich fahre gern mit der Eisenbahn.
*I like to travel on the railroad.*

**Eislaufen, das** [EISlaufən] *n.* • ice skating
**Eisläufer, der (-in, f.)** *n.* • skater
**eislaufen** *v.* • to skate
Siehst du gern das Eislaufen?
*Do you like to watch ice skating?*

**elastisch** [eLAHStish] *adj.* • elastic
Der Gummiband ist elastisch.
*The rubber band is elastic.*

**Elefant, der** [eleFAHNT] *n.* • elephant
Diese Elefanten kommen aus Afrika.
*These elephants come from Africa.*

**elektrisch** [eLEKtrish] *adj.* • electric
Benutzt du einen elektrischen Rasierer?
*Do you shave with an electric razor?*

**elf** [ELF] *adj.* • eleven
Eine Mannschaft beim Amerikanischen Fußball hat elf Spieler.
*There are eleven players on an American football team.*

**Ellbogen, der** [ELbohgən] *n.* • elbow
Bitte nimm die Ellbogen vom Tisch.
*Please keep your elbows off the table!*

**Eltern, die** [ELtern] *n.* • parents
Meine Eltern feiern ihren Hochzeitstag.
*My parents are celebrating their wedding anniversary.*

**Ende, das** [ENDə] *n.* • end
Der Held stirbt am Ende der Geschichte.
*The hero dies at the end of the story.*

**endlich** [ENTli*sh*] *adv.* • finally
Ich bin endlich mit meinem Projekt fertig.
*I'm finally done with my project.*

**energisch** [eNERgish] *adj.* • energetic
**Energie, die** *n.* • energy
Er ist sehr energisch bei seiner Arbeit!
*He is very energetic in his work!*

**eng** [ENG] *adj.* • narrow; tight
Diese alten Straßen sind eng.
*These old streets are narrow.*

Diese Schuhe sind zu eng.
*These shoes are too tight.*

**Engel, der** [ENGəl] *n.* • angel
Marie singt wie ein Engel.
*Marie sings like an angel.*

**England** [ENGlahnt] *n.* • England
**Engländer, der (-in, f.)** *n.* • English (person)
**Englisch, das (Sprache)** *n.* • English (language)
London und Manchester sind Städte in England.
*London and Manchester are cities in England.*

**Enkel, der** [ENGkəl] *n.* • ankle
Ich habe meinen Enkel verstaucht.
*I sprained my ankle.*

**Enkelin, die** [ENGkəlin] *n.* • granddaughter
**Enkel, der** *n.* • grandson
Ihre Enkelin ist zwei Jahre alt.
*Her granddaughter is two years old.*

**entdecken** [entDEKən] *v.* • to discover
**Entdeckung, die** *n.* • discovery
Wir entdeckten einen neuen Weg in die Stadt.
*We discovered a new way to get to town.*

**Ente, die** [ENtə] *n.* • duck
Es gibt einige Enten auf diesem Teich.
*There are some ducks on the pond.*

**entfernen** [entFERnən] *v.* • to remove

| | |
|---|---|
| entferne | entfernen |
| entfernst | entfernt |
| entfernt | entfernen |

Wir müssen heute abend den Schmuck entfernen.
*We must remove the decorations tonight.*

**Entfernung, die** [entFERnung] *n.* • distance
**entfernt** *adj.* • distant
Die Entfernung zwischen New York und Paris beträgt ungefähr 3.500 Meilen.
*The distance between New York and Paris is about 3,500 miles.*

**entgegen** [entGAIgən] *prep.* • toward
Der Hund kommt mir entgegen.
*The dog is coming toward me.*

**enthalten** [entHAHLtən] *v.* • to contain; to hold

| | |
|---|---|
| enthalte | enthalten |
| enthältst | enthaltet |
| enthält | enthalten |

Dieses Buch enthält viele interessante Tatsachen.
*This book contains many interesting facts.*

**entlang** [entLAHNG] *prep.* • along
**neben** *prep.* • alongside; next to
Die Bäume wachsen entlang der Allee.
*Trees grow all along the avenue.*

**entmutigt** [entMOOti*sh*t] *adj.* • discouraged
Die Mannschaft war entmutigt, nachdem sie das Spiel verloren hatte.
*The team was discouraged after losing the game.*

**Entscheidung, die** [entSHEIdung] *n.* • decision
Es war eine schwere Entscheidung, von meiner Familie wegzuziehen.
*Moving away from my family was a difficult decision.*

**entschuldigen** [entSHULdigən] *v.* • to excuse

| | |
|---|---|
| entschuldige | entschuldigen |
| entschuldigst | entschuldigt |
| entschuldigt | entschuldigen |

Entschuldigen Sie bitte meine Verspätung.
*Please excuse me for being late.*

**entsetzlich** [entZETSli*sh*] *adj.* • horrible
**Entsetzen, das** *n.* • horror
Das war ein entsetzlicher Film!
*That was a horrible movie!*

**er** [AIR] *pron.* • he
Er ist der Mann mit dem roten Pullover.
*He is the man with the red sweater.*

**Erbsen, die** [ERBsən] *n. pl.* • peas
Diese Erbsen schmecken gut.
*These peas taste good.*

**Erdbeere, die** [ERDbairə] *n.* • strawberry
Hier ist etwas Erdbeermarmelade für dein Brot.
*Here is some strawberry jam for your bread.*

**Erde, die** [ERdə] *n.* • earth; ground
**Erdbeben, das** *n.* • earthquake
**Erdgeschoß, das** *n.* • ground floor

Die Erde ist der dritte Planet von der Sonne.
*The Earth is the third planet from the sun.*

Sie säen den Samen in die Erde.
*They plant the seeds in the ground.*

**Erdnuß, die** [ERDnus] *n.* • peanut
**Erdnußbutter, die** *n.* • peanut butter
Meine Schwester ist gegen Erdnüsse allergisch.
*My sister is allergic to peanuts.*

**Ereignis, das** [erEIGnis] *n.* • event
Die Eröffnung der Olympischen Spiele ist immer ein großes Ereignis.
*The opening of the Olympic Games is always a big event.*

**Erfahrung, die** [erFAHRung] *n.* • experience
Er hat drei Jahre Erfahrung mit dieser Arbeit.
*He has three years of experince on this job.*

**Erfolg haben** [erFAWLK hahbən] *v.* • to succeed
**Erfolg, der** *n.* • success
Sie hat Erfolg bei ihrer Arbeit.
*She succeeds at her work.*

**erfreut** [erFROIT] *adj.* • glad; delighted
Ich bin sehr erfreut, dich zu sehen.
*I am very glad to see you.*

Sie ist erfreut über ihren neuen Job.
*She is delighted with her new job.*

**erinnern, sich** [erINern; Z*ISH*] *v.* • to remember
**erinnern** *v.* • to remind
Ich erinnere mich noch an meine alte Telefonnummer.
*I still remember my old phone number.*

Erinnere mich bitte daran, meine Medizin zu nehmen.
*Please remind me to take my medicine.*

**Erkältung, die** [erKAILtung] *n.* • cold; chill (sickness)
**Erkältung bekommen, eine** • to catch a cold
Meine Tochter hat eine Erkältung.
*My daughter has a cold.*

**erklären** [erKLAIrən] *v.* • to explain

| | |
|---|---|
| erkläre | erklären |
| erklärst | erklärt |
| erklärt | erklären |

Erklären Sie uns bitte, warum Sie das getan haben.
*Please explain to us why you did that.*

**erlauben** [erLAUbən] *v.* • to permit
Der Lehrer erlaubt uns nicht, im Unterricht zu sprechen.
*The teacher doesn't permit us to talk in class.*

**Erlaubnis, die** [erLAUPnis] *n.* • permission
Wir brauchen die Erlaubnis unserer Eltern, um die Reise zu machen.
*We need our parent's permission to go on the trip.*

**ernst** [ERNST] *adj.* • serious; sincere
Hört auf zu kichern und seid ein bißchen ernst!
*Stop giggling and be serious!*

Sie nimmt die Tierliebe ernst.
*She is sincere about her love for animals.*

**Ernte, die** [ERNtə] *n.* • harvest
Die Bauern haben dieses Jahr eine gute Ernte.
*The farmers have a good harvest this year.*

**erröten** [erR*ER*tən] *v.* • to blush
Wenn alle Richard anschauen, errötet er.
*When everyone looks at Richard, he blushes.*

**erschrecken** [erSHREkən] *v.* • to scare; to be frightened

erschrecke erschrecken
erschrickst erschreckt
erschrickt erschrecken

Der bellende Hund erschreckte das Baby.
*The barking dog scared the baby.*

**ersetzen** [erZETSən] *v.* • to replace
Ich habe die zerbrochene Fensterscheibe ersetzt.
*I replaced the broken window.*

**erst** [ERST] *adj.* • first
Es ist das erste Mal, daß sie mit einem Düsenflugzeug fliegt.
*It's the first time she has flown on a jet.*

**erstaunen** [erSHTAUnən] *v.* • to amaze
**erstaunlich** *adj.* • amazing
Deine schnelle Verbesserung erstaunt mich.
*Your quick improvement amazes me.*

**erwachsen** [erVAHKsən] *adj.* • mature
Meine Mutter sagt, daß ich für mein Alter schon erwachsen bin.
*My mother says that I am mature for my age.*

**erzählen** [erTSAIlən] *v.* • to tell

erzähle erzählen
erzählst erzählt
erzählt erzählen

Großvater erzählt uns jeden Abend eine Geschichte.
*Grandfather tells us a story every night.*

**es** [ES] *pron.* • it
**es ist** • it is
**sein; ihr** *pron.* • its
Wo ist es? Ich sehe es nicht.
*Where is it? I don't see it.*

**Esel, der** [AIzəl] *n.* • donkey
Der Esel hat längere Ohren als das Pferd.
*A donkey has longer ears than a horse.*

**essen** [ESən] *v.* • to dine; to eat
**etwas zu essen haben** • to have something to eat
**Essen, das (Abendessen)** *n.* • dinner

| | |
|---|---|
| esse | essen |
| ißt | eßt |
| ißt | essen |

Wir essen heute abend bei unseren Freunden.
*We are dining at our friends' house tonight.*

Ich esse jeden Tag einen Apfel.
*I eat an apple every day.*

**etwas** [ETvahs] *adj.* • some; any
**etwas** *pron.* • something
**etwas zu essen haben** • to have something to eat
Möchtest du etwas Kuchen?
*Do you want some cake?*

Haben Sie etwas Milch?
*Do you have any milk?*

**euch** See *dich*.

**euer** See *dein*.

**Eule, die** [OIlə] *n.* • owl
Eine Eule lebt in diesem Baum.
*An owl lives in this tree.*

**Europa** [oiROHpah] *n.* • Europe
**Europäer, der (-in, f.)** *n.* • European (person)
**europäisch** *adj.* • European
Sie werden diesen Sommer durch Europa reisen.
*They will travel through Europe this summmer.*

**ewig** [AIvi*sh*] *adv.* • forever
Ich werde diese Erinnerung ewig bewahren.
*I will keep this memory forever.*

**Examen, das** [eksAHmən] *n.* • exam
Der Lehrer gab am Ende des Kurses ein Examen.
*The teacher gave an exam at the end of the course.*

**extrem** [eksTRAIM] *adj.* • extreme
Die Wetterverhältnisse auf dem Mt. Everest sind extrem.
*Weather conditions on Mt. Everest are extreme.*

# F

**Fabrik, die** [faBREEK] *n.* • factory
Was wird in dieser Fabrik produziert?
*What do they make in this factory?*

**Faden, der** [FAHdən] *n.* • thread
Man braucht einen Faden, um zu nähen.
*You need thread to sew.*

**Fahne, die** [FAHnə] *n.* • flag
Die amerikanische Fahne ist rot, weiß, und blau.
*The American flag is red, white, and blue.*

**fahren** [FAHrən] *v.* • to go; to leave for; to ride; to drive; to run
**Führerschein, der** *n.* • driver's license
**Fahrrad fahren** • to ride a bike
**Fahrer, der** *n.* • driver

| | |
|---|---|
| fahre | fahren |
| fährst | fahrt |
| fährt | fahren |

Sie fahren nächsten Monat nach Europa zurück.
*They're going back to Europe next month.*

Wir fahren für das Wochenende weg.
*We're going away for the weekend.*

Morgen fahren wir nach Paris.
*Tomorrow we're going to Paris.*

Laßt uns mit dem Bus in die Stadt fahren.
*Let's ride the bus downtown.*

Das Auto fährt mit Benzin.
*The car runs on gasoline.*

Sie fährt ungefähr fünf Meilen zur Arbeit.
*She drives about five miles to work.*

**Fahrrad, das** [FAHRraht] *n.* • bicycle
**radfahren** *v.* • to ride a bicycle
Laß dein Fahrrad nicht draußen stehen, wenn es regnet.
*Don't leave your bicycle outside when it's raining.*

**fallen** [FAHLən] *v.* • to fall

| | |
|---|---|
| falle | fallen |
| fällst | fallt |
| fällt | fallen |

Fall nicht auf dem Eis.
*Don't fall on the ice.*

**fallen lassen** [FAHLən LAHSsən] *v.* • to drop
Sei vorsichtig! Laß das Tablett nicht fallen!
*Be careful, don't drop the tray!*

**falls** [FAHLS] *prep.* • in case of
Er trägt einen Schirm, falls es regnet.
*He carries an umbrella in case of rain.*

**Fallschirm, der** [FAHLshirm] *n.* • parachute
Eines Tages werde ich Fallschirm springen.
*One day, I'm going to make a parachute jump.*

**falsch** [FAHLSH] *adj.* • incorrect; false; wrong
Ich habe drei falsche Antworten in dieser Prüfung.
*I have three incorrect answers on this test.*

Ist die Antwort richtig oder falsch?
*Is the answer true or false?*

Deine Addition hier ist falsch.
*Your addition here is wrong.*

**Familie, die** [fahMEELyə] *n.* • family
Die ganze Familie ist an den Feiertagen zusammen.
*The whole family is together for the holidays.*

**fangen** [FAHNGən] *v.* • to catch

| | |
|---|---|
| fange | fangen |
| fängst | fangt |
| fängt | fangen |

Ich werde den Ball werfen und Michael wird ihn fangen.
*I am going to throw the ball and Michael is going to catch it.*

**Farbe, die** [FAHRbə] *n.* • color
**Welche Farbe hat---? Was für eine Farbe hat---?** • What color is ---?
Welche Farben hat der Regenbogen?
*What are the colors of the rainbow?*

**Farbstift, der** [FAHRPshtift] *n.* • crayon
Das Kind zeichnet mit ihren Farbstiften.
*The child is drawing with her crayons.*

**fast** [FAHST] *adv.* • almost
**fast niemals** • hardly ever
Der Zug kam fast eine Stunde zu spät an.
*The train arrived almost an hour late.*

**faul** [FAUL] *adj.* • lazy
Diese Katze ist so faul! Sie schläft den ganzen Tag.
*This cat is so lazy! She sleeps all day.*

**Februar, der** [FAIbruahr] *n.* • February
Der Februar ist der kürzeste Monat.
*February is the shortest month.*

**Feder, die** [FAIdər] *n.* • feather
Der Papagei hat bunte Federn.
*The parrot has colorful feathers.*

**Federhalter, der** [FAIdərhahltər] *n.* • pen
Darf ich deinen Federhalter benutzen, um die Adresse aufzuschreiben?
*May I use your pen to write down the address?*

**Fee, die** [FAI] *n.* • fairy
In dieser Geschichte kommt eine gute Fee vor.
*A good fairy appears in this story.*

**fegen** [FAIgən] *v.* • to sweep
Meine Schwester fegt den Boden.
*My sister is sweeping the floor.*

**Fehler, der** [FAIlər] *n.* • error; mistake
In meiner Hausaufgabe sind keine Fehler.
*There aren't any errors in my homework.*

Er macht Fehler, wenn er nicht vorsichtig ist.
*He makes mistakes when he's not careful.*

**Feier, die** [FEIər] *n.* • celebration
**feiern** *v.* • to celebrate
Wir hatten eine Feier, als meine Schwester wieder nach Hause kam.
*We had a celebration when my sister came back home.*

**Feiertag, der** [FEIərtahk] *n.* • holiday
An Feiertagen haben wir schulfrei.
*We have no school on holidays.*

**Feld, das** [FELT] *n.* • field
Die Schafe sind auf dem Feld.
*The sheep are in the field.*

**Feldahorn, der** [FELTəhawrn] *n.* • maple
Ist dieses Blatt von einem Feldahorn oder von einer Eiche?
*Is this leaf from a maple or an oak?*

**Fell, das** [FEL] *n.* • fur
Das Fell des Kaninchens ist sehr weich.
*The rabbit's fur is very soft.*

**Fels, der** [FELS] *n.* • rock
Laßt uns auf diesen großen Felsen klettern.
*Let's climb this big rock.*

**Fenster, das** [FENStə*r*] *n.* • window
**Fensterauslage, die** *n.* • window display
**Fensterscheibe, die** *n.* • window pane
**Schaufenster, das** *n.* • store window
Schau aus dem Fenster und sieh, ob er da ist.
*Look out the window and see if he's here.*

**Ferien, die** [FAIriən] *n.* • vacation
**Ferien machen** • to take a vacation
**in Ferien** • on vacation
Wir machen jeden Sommer Ferien.
*We take a vacation every summer.*

**Fernsehen, das** [FERNzaiyən] *n.* • television
**Fernsehgerät, das** *n.* • television set
**Fernsehkanal, der** *n.* • T.V. channel
**Fernsehnachrichten, die** *n.* • T.V. news
Siehst du viel Fernsehen am Abend?
*Do you watch much television at night?*

**fertig** [FERti*sh*] *adv.* • finished
Er ist jetzt fertig mit seiner Arbeit.
*He is finished with his work now.*

**fest** [FEST] *adj.* • solid
Das Eis auf dem See ist fest.
*The ice on the lake is solid.*

**Fett, das** [FET] *n.* • fat
Sport treiben hilft, Fett abzubauen.
*Exercise will help you lose fat.*

**feucht** [FOI*SH*T] *adj.* • damp; humid
Diese Tücher sind feucht.
*These towels are damp.*

Im Sommer sind die Tage heiß und feucht.
*The days are hot and humid in summer.*

**Feuer, das** [FOIər] *n.* • fire
**Feuerwehrmann, der** *n.* • fireman
**Feuerwerke, die** *n.* • fireworks
**Feuerwehrwagen, der** *n.* • firetruck
Ich habe das Feuer mit einem Streichholz angezündet.
*I started the fire with a match.*

**Fieber, das** [FEEbər] *n.* • fever
Man bekommt oft Fieber bei Grippe.
*Often you get a fever with the flu.*

**Film, der** [FILM] *n.* • film; movie
Ein alter Film läuft im Kino.
*An old film is playing at the theater.*

Wir gehen ins Kino, um einen neuen Film zu sehen.
*We're going to the theater to see a new movie.*

**finden** [FINdən] *v.* • to find
**sich befinden** • to be located

| | |
|---|---|
| finde | finden |
| findest | findet |
| findet | finden |

Ich kann meine Handschuhe nicht finden.
*I can't find my gloves!*

**Finger, der** [FINGər] *n.* • finger
**Fingernagel, der** *n.* • fingernail
Iß nicht mit den Fingern!
*Don't eat with your fingers!*

**Fisch, der** [FISH] *n.* • fish
**Goldfisch, der** *n.* • goldfish
Gibt es Fisch auf der Speisekarte?
*Is there fish on the menu?*

**Flasche, die** [FLAHshə] *n.* • bottle
Wein wird gewöhnlich in Flaschen verkauft.
*Wine is usually sold in bottles.*

**Fleck, der** [FLEK] *n.* • stain; spot
**befleckt** *adj.* • spotted
Nancy versucht, den Fleck aus ihrer Bluse herauszubekommen.
*Nancy is trying to get the stain out of her blouse.*

Er hat einen Fleck auf seinem Hemd.
*He has a spot on his shirt.*

**Fleisch, das** [FLEISH] *n.* • meat
Das Fleisch brät schon seit einer Stunde im Ofen.
*The meat has been roasting in the oven for an hour.*

**Fleischer, der** [FLEIshər] *n.* • butcher
**Fleischerladen, der** *n.* • butcher shop
Wir kaufen Fleisch beim Fleischer.
*We buy meat from the butcher.*

**Fliege, die** [FLEEgə] *n.* • fly
Das Fliegengitter wird die Fliegen draußen lassen.
*The screen will keep the flies out.*

**fliegen** [FLEEgən] *v.* • to fly
**abfliegen** *v.* • to take off

| | |
|---|---|
| fliege | fliegen |
| fliegst | fliegt |
| fliegt | fliegen |

Ich möchte mit der Concorde fliegen.
*I want to fly on the Concorde.*

Das Flugzeug flog um 8 Uhr nach München ab.
*The plane took off at 8 o'clock for Munich.*

**Flöte, die** [FL*ER*tə] *n.* • flute
Meine Freundin spielt Flöte.
*My girlfriend plays the flute.*

**Flug, der** [FLOOK] *n.* • flight
**Flugbegleiter, der (-in, f.)** *n.* • flight attendant
**Fluglinie, die** *n.* • airline
Die Maschine mit der Flugnummer 507 ist eben am Ausgang angekommen.
*Flight 507 just arrived at the gate.*

**Flügel, der** [FL*UE*gəl] *n.* • wing
Der Vogel fliegt mit seinen Flügeln.
*The bird flies with its wings.*

**Flughafen, der** [FLOOKhahfən] *n.* • airport
Das Flugzeug landete pünktlich auf dem Flughafen.
*The plane landed at the airport on time.*

**Flugzeug, das** [FLOOKtsoik] *n.* • airplane
**in einem Flugzeug** • in an airplane
Wir fliegen mit dem Flugzeug nach Frankreich.
*We're going to France by airplane.*

**Fluß, der** [FLUS] *n.* • river
Das beste Ackerland liegt in der Nähe des Flusses.
*The best farmland is near the river.*

**Flußpferd, das** [FLUSpfert] *n.* • hippopotamus
Das Flußpferd steht im Fluß.
*The hippopotamus stands in the river.*

**folgen** [FAWLgən] *v.* • to follow

| | |
|---|---|
| folge | folgen |
| folgst | folgt |
| folgt | folgen |

Wir folgen immer den Anweisungen unseres Professors.
*We always follow our professor's directions.*

**Form, die** [FAWRM] *n.* • shape
Schau dir die Form dieser Wolke an!
*Look at the shape of that cloud!*

**fortbewegen, sich** [FAWRTbəvaigən, ZI*SH*] *v.* • to move
Der alte Mann bewegt sich langsam durch den Schnee fort.
*The old man is moving slowly through the snow.*

**fortfahren** [FAWRTfahrən] *v.* • to continue
Fahren wir mit dem Lesen fort, bis wir fertig sind.
*Let's continue reading until we finish.*

**fortlaufen** [FAWRTlaufən] *v.* • to run away
Wenn der Hund hereinkommt, läuft die Katze fort.
*When the dog comes in, the cat runs away.*

**Fortschritt, der** [FAWRTshrit] *n.* • progress
**Fortschritte machen** • to make progress
Machen Sie Fortschritte bei Ihrem Experiment?
*Are you making progress in your experiment?*

**Foto(grafie), das (die)** [FOHtoh; fawtohgraFEE] *n.* • photo(graph)
**Fotograf, der (-in, f.)** *n.* • photographer
Sie hat alte Fotos von unseren Urgroßeltern.
*She has old photos of our great-grandparents.*

**Frage, die** [FRAHgə] *n.* • question
Können Sie die Frage wiederholen?
*Can you repeat the question?*

**fragen** [FRAHgən] *v.* • to question

| | |
|---|---|
| frage | fragen |
| fragst | fragt |
| fragt | fragen |

Er fragte mich.
*He questioned me.*

**Frankreich** [FRAHNKrei*sh*] *n.* • France
**Franzose, der (-in, f.)** *n.* • French (person)
**französisch** *adj.* • French

Kannst du Dijon auf der Landkarte von Frankreich finden?
*Can you find Dijon on the map of France?*

**Frau, die** [FRAU] *n.* • woman; Mrs.
Diese Frau ist meine Lehrerin.
*This woman is my teacher.*

Darf ich Ihnen bitte meine Großmutter vorstellen, Frau Schmidt.
*Please meet my grandmother, Mrs. Smith.*

**Fräulein, das** [FROIlein] *n.* • young lady; Miss
Unsere Lehrerin heißt Fräulein Pasko.
*Our teacher is Miss Pasko.*

**frei** [FREI] *adj.* • free
**Freiheit, die** *n.* • freedom
Die Kinder haben heute nach der dritten Stunde frei.
*The children are free today after third period.*

Der Eintritt für das Museum ist Montags frei.
*Admission to the museum is free on Mondays.*

Religionsfreiheit ist ein Grundrecht.
*Freedom of religion is a basic right.*

**Freitag, der** [FREItahk] *n.* • Friday
Freitags fahren wir immer fürs Wochenende weg.
*On Fridays, we leave for the weekend.*

**fremd** [FREMT] *adj.* • strange
**Fremde, der** *n.* • stranger
Er ist ein Fremder in dieser Stadt.
*He is a stranger in this city.*

**Freude, die** [FROIdə] *n.* • joy
Das Kind war voller Freude, als es seine Mutter sah.
*The child was full of joy on seeing her mother.*

**Freund, der (-in, f.)** [FROINT] *n.* • friend
**Freundschaft, die** *n.* • friendship
**freundlich** *adj.* • friendly
Ich ging mit einem Freund ins Kino.
*I went to the movie with a friend.*

**frisch** [FRISH] *adj.* • fresh
Ist dieses Gemüse frisch?
*Are these vegetables fresh?*

**Frisur, die** [friZOOR] *n.* • hair style; hairdo
**beim Herrenfriseur** • at the barbershop
**Friseur, der (-in, f.)** *n.* • hairdresser
**Herrenfriseur, der** *n.* • barber
Meine Freundin hat eine neue Frisur.
*My girlfriend has a new hair style.*

**Frosch, der** [FRAWSH] *n.* • frog
Es gibt einige Frösche in diesem Teich.
*There are several frogs in this pond.*

**Frucht, die** [FRU*SH*T] *n.* • fruit
Früchte und Gemüse sind gut für die Gesundheit.
*Fruits and vegetables are good for your health.*

**früh** [FR*UE*] *adv.* • early
Sie stehen früh auf, um zur Schule zu gehen.
*They get up early to go to school.*

**Frühling, der** [FR*UE*ling] *n.* • spring
Im Frühling regnet es viel.
*It rains a lot in the spring.*

**Frühstück, das** [FR*UE*sht*ue*k] *n.* • breakfast
Essen Sie jeden Morgen Frühstück?
*Do you eat breakfast every morning?*

**Fuchs, der** [FUKS] *n.* • fox
Der Fuchs ist sehr schlau.
*The fox is very sly.*

**fühlen, sich** [F*UE*lən] *v.* • to feel

| | |
|---|---|
| fühle mich | fühlen uns |
| fühlst dich | fühlt euch |
| fühlt sich | fühlen sich |

Ich fühle mich schlecht, nachdem ich den ganzen Kuchen gegessen habe.
*I feel bad after eating the whole cake.*

**führen** [F*UE*rən] *v.* • to lead
**Führer, der (-in, f.)** *n.* • leader

| | |
|---|---|
| führe | führen |
| führst | führt |
| führt | führen |

Der Führer führt die Touristen durch das Schloß.
*The guide leads the tourists through the castle.*

**füllen** [F*UE*lən] *v.* • to fill

| | |
|---|---|
| fülle | füllen |
| füllst | füllt |
| füllt | füllen |

Sie füllt ihre Teller mit Nudeln.
*She fills their plates with noodles.*

**fünf** [F*UE*NF] *adj.* • five
Ein Nickel ist fünf Cent wert.
*A nickel is worth five cents.*

**fünfzehn** [F*UE*NFtsain] *adj.* • fifteen
Ich wohne fünfzehn Kilometer von hier.
*I live fifteen kilometers from here.*

**fünfzig** [F*UE*NFtsi*sh*] *adj.* • fifty
Fünfzig Dollar ist teuer für einen Pullover.
*Fifty dollars is expensive for a sweater.*

**für** [F*UE*R] *prep.* • for
**für sich** • by oneself
Dieses Geschenk ist für dich.
*This present is for you.*

**furchtbar** [FUR*SH*Tbahr] *adj.* • awful
Das Geräusch in der Fabrik ist furchtbar.
*The noise in the factory is awful.*

**fürchten, sich** [F*UE*R*SH*tən] *v.* • to fear
**Furcht, die** *n.* • fear

| | |
|---|---|
| fürchte mich | fürchten uns |
| fürchtest dich | fürchtet euch |
| fürchtet sich | fürchten sich |

Er fürchtet sich vor Spinnen.
*He is afraid of spiders.*

Fürchtest du dich vor großen Höhen?
*Are you afraid of heights?*

**furchterregend** [FUR*SH*Terraigənt] *adj.* • frightening
Glaubst du, daß Gespenster furchterregend sind?
*Do you think that ghosts are frightening?*

**Fuß, der** [FOOS] *n.* • foot
**Füße, die** *n. pl.* • feet
**Fußnagel, der** *n.* • toenail
**Tierfuß, der** *n.* • animal foot; paw
**zu Fuß** • on foot
Sie stehen auf meinem Fuß!
*You are stepping on my foot!*

Diese Schuhe tun meinen Füßen weh.
*These shoes make my feet hurt.*

**Fußball, der** [FOOSbahl] *n.* • football (soccer)
**amerikanische Fußball, der** • American football
**Fußball(spiel), das** *n.* • soccer
**Fußball spielen** • to play soccer
Mein Bruder hat einen neuen Fußball.
*My brother has a new football.*

Fußball wird in den U.S.A. beliebt.
*Soccer is becoming popular in the U.S.*

**Fußboden, der** [FOOSbohdən] *n.* • floor
Ich werde den Fußboden kehren.
*I am going to sweep the floor.*

# G

**Gabel, die** [GAHbəl] *n.* • fork
Hast du die Messer und Gabeln hingelegt?
*Did you put out the knives and forks?*

**Gans, die** [GAHNS] *n.* • goose
**Gänse, die** *n. pl.* • geese
Die Gans ist weiß.
*The goose is white.*

**Gänseblümchen, das** [GAINsəbl*ue*ms*h*ən] *n.* • daisy
Die Gänseblümchen blühen im Frühling.
*Daisies bloom in the spring.*

**ganz** [GANTS] *adj.; adv.* • entire; completely
**ganz egal!** • no matter!
Unsere ganze Familie ist am Feiertag zu Hause.
*Our entire family is home for the holiday.*

Ich habe die Anweisungen ganz gelesen.
*I read the instructions completely.*

**ganze, -r, -s** [GANtsə] *adj.* • whole
Er wird einen ganzen Monat bei uns bleiben.
*He is going to stay with us a whole month.*

**Garage, die** [gahRAHzhə] *n.* • garage
Vati parkt den Wagen in der Garage.
*Dad is parking the car in the garage.*

**Gardinen, die** [gahrDEEnən] *n. pl.* • curtains
Frau Schmidt hängt neue Gardinen auf.
*Mrs. Smith is hanging new curtains.*

**Garnelen, die** [gahrNELən] *pl.* • shrimp
Wenn wir in dieses Restaurant gehen, bestelle ich gewöhnlich Garnelen.
*When we go to this restaurant, I usually order shrimp.*

**Garten, der** [GAHRtən] *n.* • garden
Diese Blumen sind aus unserem Garten.
*These flowers are from our garden.*

**Gas, das** [GAHS] *n.* • gas
Wir haben einen Gasherd.
*We have a gas stove.*

**Gast, der** [GAHST] *n.* • guest
Wann kommen die Gäste an?
*When are the guests arriving?*

**Gebäck, das** [geBAIK] *n.* • pastry
Nancy kauft das Gebäck in der Bäckerei.
*Nancy is going to buy the pastries at the bakery.*

**Gebäude, das** [geBOIdə] *n.* • building
**Appartementgebäude, das** *n.* • apartment building
In diesem Gebäude sind Büros.
*There are offices in this building.*

**geben** [GAIbən] *v.* • to give
**zurückgeben** *v.* • to give back

| | |
|---|---|
| gebe | geben |
| gibst | gebt |
| gibt | geben |

Bitte geben Sie mir die Gelegenheit zu sprechen.
*Please give me a chance to speak.*

**Gebirge, das** [geBEERgə] *n.* • mountains; mountain range
**ins Gebirge** • to (in) the mountains
Wir fahren am Wochenende ins Gebirge.
*We're going to the mountains this weekend.*

**geboren** [geBOHrən] *v.* • to be born
Er ist in Paris geboren.
*He was born in Paris.*

**gebrauchen** [geBRAU*kh*ən] *v.* • to use
**Gebrauchtwagen, der** *n.* • used car

| | |
|---|---|
| gebrauche | gebrauchen |
| gebrauchst | gebraucht |
| gebraucht | gebrauchen |

Wir könnten deine Hilfe gebrauchen.
*We could use your help.*

**Geburtstag, der** [geBOORTStahk] *n.* • birthday
**Herzlichen Glückwunsch zum Geburtstag!** • Happy Birthday!
Wann hast du Geburtstag?
*When is your birthday?*

**Gedächtnis, das** [geDAI*SH*Tnis] *n.* • memory
**im Gedächtnis behalten** • to memorize
Sie hat ein ausgezeichnetes Namensgedächtnis.
*She has an excellent memory for names.*

**Gedicht, das** [geDI*SH*T] *n.* • poem
**Dichter, der (-in, f.)** *n.* • poet
Der Text dieses Liedes stammt von einem Gedicht.
*The words to this song are from a poem.*

Ich liebe die Gedichte William Shakespeares.
*I like William Shakespeare's poetry.*

**Gedränge, das** [geDRAINgə] *n.* • crowd
Es gibt ein großes Gedränge bei dem Spiel.
*There is a big crowd at the game.*

**Gefahr, die** [geFAHR] *n.* • danger
**gefährlich** *adj.* • dangerous
Die Soldaten waren während des Kampfes in großer Gefahr.
*The soldiers were in great danger during the battle.*

Ist Skilaufen gefährlich?
*Is skiing dangerous?*

**Gefängnis, das** [geFAINGnis] *n.* • prison
**Gefangene, der** *n.* • prisoner
Die Verbrecher sind im Gefängnis.
*The criminals are in prison.*

**gefrieren** [geFREErən] *v.* • to freeze
Im Winter gefriert der Regen auf den Straßen.
*In winter, the rain freezes on the roads.*

**gegen** [GAIgən] *prep.* • about; against
Es ist gegen drei Uhr.
*It's about three o'clock.*

Die andere Manschaft ist gegen uns.
*The other team is against us.*

**Gegend, die** [GAIgənt] *n.* • area; region
Diese Gegend ist sehr bergig.
*This area is very mountainous.*

Aus welcher Gegend Deutschlands kommst du?
*What region of Germany are you from?*

**Gegenstand, der** [GAIgənshtant] *n.* • subject
Was ist der Gegenstand dieser Diskussion?
*What is the subject of this discussion?*

**Gegenteil, das** [GAIgənteil] *n.* • opposite
Du sagst, daß du Hunde lieber magst als Katzen. Bei mir ist es genau das Gegenteil.
*You say that you prefer dogs to cats. For me it is exactly the opposite.*

**gegenüber** [gaigənUEbər] *prep.* • opposite; across (from)
Der Parkplatz liegt gegenüber dem Bahnhof.
*The parking lot is opposite the train station.*

Sie wohnen gegenüber der Schule.
*They live across from the school.*

**Geheimnis, das** [geHEIMnis] *n.* • secret; mystery
**geheimnisvoll** *adj.* • mysterious
Kannst du ein Geheimnis behalten?
*Do you know how to keep a secret?*

**gehen** [GAIyən] *v.* • to go; to walk
**ausgehen** *v.* • to go out (leave)
**Geh!** • Go!
**hinaufgehen** *v.* • to go up
**hineingehen** *v.* • to go into
**hinuntergehen** *v.* • to go down
**spazierengehen** *v.* • to go for a walk
**weggehen** *v.* • to go away
**zu Bett gehen** • to go to bed
**zurückgehen** *v.* • to go back

| | |
|---|---|
| gehe | gehen |
| gehst | geht |
| geht | gehen |

Wir gehen bald nach Hause.
*We'll be going home soon.*

**Gehirn, das** [geHIRN] *n.* • brain
Der Schädel schützt das Gehirn.
*The skull protects the brain.*

**gehorchen** [geHAWR*SH*ən] *v.* • to obey
**gehorsam** *adj.* • obedient
Dieser Hund gehorcht seinem Herrn.
*This dog obeys his master.*

**gehören** [geH*ER*rən] *v.* • to belong (to)
Dieser Koffer gehört meinem Vater.
*This suitcase belongs to my father.*

**Geige, die** [GEIgə] *n.* • violin
Magst du Geigenmusik?
*Do you like violin music?*

**Geist, der** [GEIST] *n.* • ghost
Glaubst du an Geister?
*Do you believe in ghosts?*

**geizig** [GEItsi*sh*] *adj.* • stingy
Er ist zu geizig, um sein Essen zu teilen.
*He is too stingy to share his food.*

**gelb** [GELP] *adj.* • yellow
Der Schulbus ist gelb.
*The school bus is yellow.*

**Geld, das** [GELT] *n.* • money
**Geldautomat, der** *n.* • automatic teller
Ich habe mein ganzes Geld ausgegeben.
*I have spent all my money.*

**Gemälde, das** [gəMAILdə] *n.* • picture (painting)
Das Gemälde ist von Monet.
*The painting is by Monet.*

**gemein** [geMEIN] *adj.* • mean
Der Junge war seiner Schwester gegenüber gemein.
*The boy was mean to his sister.*

**Gemüse, das** [geM*UE*zə] *n.* • vegetable
Welches Gemüse ißt du am liebsten?
*Which vegetables do you like best?*

**genug** [geNOO*SH*] *adj.* • enough
Danke, ich habe genug zu essen gehabt.
*Thank you, I have had enough to eat.*

**Geographie, die** [gaiohgrahFEE] *n.* • geography
Ich lernte etwas über Landkarten in der Geographieklasse.
*I learned about maps in geography class.*

**Geometrie, die** [gaiohmeTREE] *n.* • geometry
Ich mag Geometrie lieber als Algebra.
*I like geometry better than algebra.*

**Gepäck, das** [gePAIK] *n.* • luggage; baggage
Sie trugen ihr Gepäck in das Hotel.
*They carried their baggage into the hotel.*

**gerade** [geRAHdə] *adj.; adv.* • direct; just; straight
Er zeichnete eine gerade Linie.
*He drew a straight line.*

**gern haben** [GERN HAHbən] *v.* • to like
Wir haben gern jeden Abend Nachtisch.
*We like to have dessert every night.*

**Geschäft, das** [geSHAIFT] *n.* • business
**Geschäftsmann, der** *n.* • businessman
**Geschäftsfrau, die** *n.* • businesswoman
Dieser Laden hat im Sommer ein gutes Geschäft.
*This store does a lot of business in the summer.*

**geschehen** [geSHAIyən] *v.* • to happen
Ich weiß nicht, was geschah, nachdem ich gegangen war.
*I don't know what happened after I had left.*

**Geschenk, das** [geSHENGK] *n.* • gift; present
Man bekommt Geschenke an seinem Geburtstag.
*You get gifts on your birthday.*

Schaut euch nur alle die Geschenke unter dem Weihnachtsbaum an!
*Look at all the presents under the Christmas tree!*

**Geschichte, die** [geSHI*SH*tə] *n.* • history; tale; story
Die Geschichte der Menschheit ist faszinierend.
*The history of mankind is fascinating.*

Großmutter unterhielt die Kinder mit ihren Geschichten von anno dazumal.
*Grandma entertained the children with her tales of long ago.*

Erzähl mir die Geschichte, wie du sie kennengelernt hast.
*Tell me the story of how you met her.*

**Geschirr, das** [geSHIR] *n.* • dishes
Bitte, stell das Geschirr in den Schrank.
*Please puts the dishes in the cupboard.*

**Geschmack, der** [geSHMAHK] *n.* • flavor
Diese Suppe hat den Geschmack von Zwiebeln.
*This soup has the flavor of onions.*

**Gesellschaft,die** [geZELshahft] *n.* • company
Mein Vater arbeitet bei einer großen Gesellschaft.
*My father works for a large company.*

**Gesetz, das** [geZETS] *n.* • law
Man muß das Gesetz befolgen.
*You must obey the law.*

**Gesicht, das** [geZI*SH*T] *n.* • face
Ich wasche mir Morgens das Gesicht.
*I wash my face in the morning.*

**Gesundheit, die** [geZUNTheit] *n.* • health
Gehen ist gut für die Gesundheit.
*Walking is good for your health.*

**Getränk, das** [geTRAINK] *n.* • beverage; drink
**trinken** *v.* • to drink
Was für ein Getränk möchten Sie?
*What would you like for a beverage?*

Willst du zu deinem Essen etwas trinken?
*Do you want something to drink with your meal?*

**Gewehr, das** [geVAIR] *n.* • gun
Man muß mit Gewehren vorsichtig sein.
*You must be careful with guns.*

**gewinnen** [geVINən] *v.* • to win

| | |
|---|---|
| gewinne | gewinnen |
| gewinnst | gewinnt |
| gewinnt | gewinnen |

Ihr werdet oft gewinnen, wenn eure Mannschaft gut zusammenspielt.
*You will win often if your team plays well together.*

**Gewohnheit, die** [geVOHNheit] *n.* • habit; custom
Es ist eine gute Gewohnheit, früh aufzustehen.
*To get up early is a good habit.*

Er hat die Gewohnheit, ein Glas Milch zu trinken, ehe er ins Bett geht.
*It's his custom to drink a glass of milk before bedtime.*

**gewöhnlich** [geV*ER*Nli*sh*] *adj.* • common; usual
Diese Krankheit ist bei Kindern ziemlich gewöhnlich.
*This disease is quite common in children.*

Dieses ist nicht mein gewöhnlicher Platz.
*This isn't my usual seat.*

**Gift, das** [GIFT] *n.* • poison
Man benutzt Gift, um Ratten zu töten.
*You use poison to kill rats.*

**Giraffe, die** [giRAHFə] *n.* • giraffe
Giraffen haben sehr lange Hälse.
*Giraffes have very long necks.*

**Gitarre, die** [giTAHRrə] *n.* • guitar
**Gitarre spielen** • to play the guitar
Diese Gitarre hat sechs Saiten.
*This guitar has six strings.*

**Gladiole, die** [glahdiOHlə] *n.* • gladiola
Ihre Großmutter hatte schöne Gladiolen im Garten.
*Her grandmother had pretty gladiolas in her garden.*

**Glas, das** [GLAHS] *n.* • glass; jar
**aus Glas** • made of glass
Das Glas des Fensters ist zerbrochen.
*The glass in the window is broken.*

Steht ein Glas Oliven im Kühlschrank?
*Is there a jar of olives in the refrigerator?*

**glauben** [GLAUbən] *v.* • to believe
**glaubhaft** *adj.* • believable
**unglaublich** *adj.* • unbelievable

| | |
|---|---|
| glaube | glauben |
| glaubst | glaubt |
| glaubt | glauben |

Ich glaube, daß die Geschichte wahr ist.
*I believe that the story is true.*

**gleich** [GLEI*SH*] *adj.* • equal
Beide Hälften sind gleich.
*Both halves are equal.*

**gleiten** [GLEItən] *v.* • to slide

| | |
|---|---|
| gleite | gleiten |
| gleitest | gleitet |
| gleitet | gleiten |

Die Eisläufer gleiten über das Eis.
*The skaters slide across the ice.*

**Glocke, die** [GLAWKə] *n.* • bell
Es gibt eine Glocke im Kirchturm.
*There is a bell in the church's steeple.*

**Glück, das** [GL*UE*K] *n.* • luck; happiness
**Glück haben** • to be lucky
**Viel Glück!** • Good luck!
Hast du im Kasino Glück gehabt?
*Did you have any luck at the casino?*

**glücklich** [GL*UE*Kli*sh*] *adj.* • happy
Wenn ich eine gute Note bekomme, bin ich glücklich.
*I am happy when I get a good grade.*

**Glückwünsche, die** [GL*UE*Kv*ue*nshə] *n.* • congratulations
Herzliche Glückwünsche! Sie haben den Preis gewonnen!
*Congratulations! You won the prize!*

**Gold, das** [GAWLT] *n.* • gold
Ist diese Halskette aus Gold?
*Is this necklace made of gold?*

**Golfspiel, das** [GAWLFshpeel] *n.* • golf
**Golfplatz, der** *n.* • golf course
**Golf spielen** • to play golf
Wir spielen im Sommer Golf.
*We play golf in the summer.*

**Gorilla, der** [gawRILah] *n.* • gorilla
Dieser Gorilla erschreckt mich.
*This gorilla scares me!*

**grandios** [grahnDEEohs] *adj.* • splendid
Das Feuerwerk ist grandios!
*The fireworks are splendid!*

**Gras, das** [GRAHS] *n.* • grass
Das Gras auf diesem Feld ist sehr hoch.
*The grass in this field is very high.*

**grau** [GRAU] *adj.* • gray
Der Bart meines Großvaters ist grau.
*My grandfather's beard is gray.*

**grausam** [GRAUzahm] *adj.* • ferocious
Dieser Hund sieht grausam aus.
*This dog looks ferocious.*

**Griechenland** [GREE*sh*ənlant] *n.* • Greece
**Grieche, der (-in, f.)** *n.* • Greek (person)
**griechisch** *adj.* • Greek
Athen ist die Hauptstadt Griechenlands.
*Athens is the capital of Greece.*

**Grille, die** [GRILə] *n.* • cricket
Im Sommer hören wir abends Grillen.
*In the summertime we hear crickets at night.*

**grimmig** [GRImi*sh*] *adj.* • fierce
Wilde Tiere sind grimmig.
*Wild animals are fierce.*

**Grippe, die** [GRIpə] *n.* • flu
Es ist kein Spaß, Grippe zu haben.
*It's no fun to have the flu.*

**groß** [GROHS] *adj.* • large; big; tall
**größer** *adj.* • bigger
**Großartig!** *interj.* • Great!
Der Elefant ist ein sehr großes Tier.
*The elephant is a very large animal.*

Er muß schon groß sein, wenn er die Decke berühren kann.
*He must be tall if he can reach the ceiling.*

**Größe, die** [GR*ER*sə] *n.* • size
Ist dies die richtige Größe?
*Is this the right size?*

**Großeltern, die** [GROHSeltərn] *n.* • grandparents
Meine Großeltern sind aus Deutschland.
*My grandparents are from Germany.*

**großmütig** [GROHSm*ue*ti*sh*] *adj.* • generous
Meine Großeltern sind sehr großmütig.
*My grandparents are very generous.*

**Großmutter, die** [GROHSmutər] *n.* • grandmother
Meine Großmütter sind beide zu meiner Hochzeit gekommen.
*Both my grandmothers came to my wedding.*

**Großvater, der** [GROHSfahtər] *n.* • grandfather
Mein Großvater ist jetzt pensioniert.
*My grandfather is retired now.*

**grün** [GR*UE*N] *adj.* • green
**grüne Bohnen** • green beans
Tannenbäume sind das ganze Jahr lang grün.
*Pine trees are green all year long.*

**Grund, der** [GRUNT] *n.* • reason
Was ist der Grund dafür, daß du aufhören willst?
*What's your reason for wanting to quit?*

**Gruppe, die** [GRUpə] *n.* • group
Die Studenten verlassen die Klasse in Gruppen.
*The students leave class in groups.*

**Gummi, das** [GUmee] *n.* • rubber
**aus Gummi** • made of rubber
**Radiergummi, der** *n.* • eraser
Gummi ist ein wichtiges Exportprodukt für Brasilien.
*Rubber is an important export for Brazil.*

Diese Reifen sind aus Gummi.
*These tires are made of rubber.*

**Gurke, die** [GURkə] *n.* • cucumber
Meine Schwester liebt Gurkensalat.
*My sister likes cucumber salad.*

**Gürtel, der** [G*UE*Rtəl] *n.* • belt
Ich brauche einen Gürtel zu diesem Rock.
*I need a belt with this skirt.*

**gut** [GOOT] *adj.; adv.* • fine; well; good; kind
**gut aussehend** • good looking
**Guten Abend!** *interj.* • Good Evening
**Gute Nacht!** *interj.* • Good night
**Guten Tag!** *interj.* • Good day
**gut erzogen** • well-behaved
**so gut wie** • as well as
Es geht mir wieder gut.
*I am feeling fine now.*

Doreen spielt sehr gut Klavier.
*Doreen plays the piano very well.*

Sie bekommt immer gute Noten.
*She always gets good grades.*

Meine Großmutter ist gut und großzügig.
*My grandmother is kind and generous.*

Es geht mir gut.
*I am well.*

**Gymnasium, das** [gimNAHZyum] *n.* • high school
Mein ältester Sohn besucht das Gymnasium.
*My oldest son is in high school.*

# H

**Haar, das** [HAHR] *n.* • hair
**Haarbürste, die** *n.* • hairbrush
**die Haare waschen** • to wash one's hair
**Haarschnitt, der** *n.* • haircut
Meine Schwester hat lange Haare.
*My sister has long hair.*

**haben** [HAHbən] *v.* • to have
**Glück haben** • to have luck; to be lucky

| | |
|---|---|
| habe | haben |
| hast | habt |
| hat | haben |

Hast du Zeit, diesen Brief zu lesen?
*Do you have time to read this letter?*

Ich habe um sieben Uhr eine Verabredung.
*I have a date at seven.*

**Habicht, der** [HAHbi*sh*t] *n.* • hawk
Der Habicht frißt die Maus.
*The hawk is eating the mouse.*

**Hafen, der** [HAHfən] *n.* • port
Das Schiff fährt in den Hafen.
*The ship comes into port.*

**Hafer, der** [HAHfə*r*] *n.* • oats
Das Pferd frißt Hafer.
*The horse is eating oats.*

**Hahn, der** [HAHN] *n.* • rooster
Der Hahn weckt uns morgens auf.
*The rooster wakes us up in the morning.*

**Hälfte, die** [HAILFtə] *n.* • half
Möchtest du die Hälfte dieses Apfels?
*Do you want half of this apple?*

**Hallo** [HAHloh] *interj.* • Hello
Hallo, ich heiße Philip.
*Hello, my name is Philip.*

**Hals, der** [HAHLS] *n.* • neck; throat
**Halskette, die** *n.* • necklace
Dieses Hemd ist mir am Hals zu eng.
*This shirt is too tight around my neck.*

Richard hat eine Halsentzündung.
*Richard has a sore throat.*

**halten** [HAHLtən] *v.* • to hold; to stop

| | |
|---|---|
| halte | halten |
| hältst | haltet |
| hält | halten |

Die Mutter hält ihr Kind an der Hand.
*The mother holds her child's hand.*

**Hammer, der** [HAHm*ər*] *n.* • hammer
Der Zimmermann benutzt einen Hammer, um die Nägel einzuschlagen.
*The carpenter uses a hammer to drive nails.*

**Hand, die** [HAHNT] *n.* • hand
**Hände schütteln** • to shake hands
**linke Hand, die** • left hand
**rechte Hand, die** • right hand
Wenn Sie die Antwort wissen, heben Sie die Hand.
*If you know the answer, raise your hand.*

**Handschuh, der** [HAHNTshoo] *n.* • glove
Diese zwei Handschuhe passen nicht zusammen.
*These two gloves don't match.*

**Handtasche, die** [HAHNTtashə] *n.* • purse
Sie steckt ihr Portemonnaie in die Handtasche.
*She puts her billfold in her purse.*

**Handtuch, das** [HAHNTtoo*kh*] *n.* • towel
Ich brauche ein trockenes Handtuch.
*I need a dry towel.*

**hassen** [HAHsən] *v.* • to hate

| | |
|---|---|
| hasse | hassen |
| haßt | haßt |
| haßt | hassen |

Ich hasse Regenwetter!
*I hate rainy weather!*

**häßlich** [HAISl*ish*] *adj.* • ugly
Lila ist eine häßliche Farbe für ein Haus.
*Purple is an ugly color for a house.*

**Hauptstadt, die** [HAUPTshtat] *n.* • capital
Washington, D.C. ist die Hauptstadt der Vereinigten Staaten.
*Washington, D.C. is the capital of the United States.*

**Hauptstraße, die** [HAUPTshtrahsə] *n.* • highway; main street
Die Kirche liegt an der Hauptstraße.
*The church is on the main street.*

**Haus, das** [HAUS] *n.* • house
**Haus in Ordnung bringen, das** • to do housework
**im Haus** • indoors
**nach Hause kommen** • to come home
**zu Hause** • at home
Sie haben ein großes Haus mit zwölf Zimmern.
*They have a big house with twelve rooms.*

Wenn das Wetter schlecht ist, bleiben wir im Haus.
*When the weather is bad, we stay indoors.*

Fühlen Sie sich wie zu Hause.
*Make yourself at home.*

**Hausaufgaben, die** [HAUSaufgahbən] *n.* • homework
Wir machen unsere Hausaufgaben.
*We are doing our homework.*

**Hausschuh, der** [HAUSshoo] *n.* • slipper
Großmutter trägt zu Hause ihre Hausschuhe.
*Grandma wears her slippers at home.*

**Haustier, das** [HAUSteer] *n.* • pet
Hast du einen Hund als Haustier?
*Do you have a dog as a pet?*

**Haut, die** [HAUT] *n.* • skin
Das Baby hat eine weiche Haut.
*The baby has soft skin.*

**He!** [HAI] *interj.* • Hi!
He! Wie gehts?
*Hi! How are you?*

**heben** [HEIbən] *v.* • to lift; to raise

| | |
|---|---|
| hebe | heben |
| hebst | hebt |
| hebt | heben |

Wir heben unsere Hände in der Klasse, bevor wir etwas sagen.
*We raise our hands in class before speaking.*

**Heer, das** [HAIR] *n.* • army
Dieses Land hat ein mächtiges Heer.
*This country has a powerful army.*

**Heftmaschine, die** [HEFTməsheenə] *n.* • stapler
Die Heftmaschine ist im Büro.
*The stapler is in the office.*

**Heimat, die** [HEImaht] *n.* • homeland; hometown
**Heimweh haben** • to be homesick
Amerika ist meine Heimat.
*America is my home.*

**heiraten** [HEIrahtən] *v.* • to marry (to get married)

| | |
|---|---|
| heirate | heiraten |
| heiratest | heiratet |
| heiratet | heiraten |

Robert und Jane heiraten morgen.
*Robert and Jane are getting married tomorrow.*

**heiß** [HEIS] *adj.* • hot
**Es ist draußen heiß.** • It's hot (outside).
Sei vorsichtig! Der Herd ist heiß!
*Be careful! The oven is hot!*

**heißen** [HEIsən] *v.* • to be called (named)

| | |
|---|---|
| heiße | heißen |
| heißt | heißt |
| heißt | heißen |

Wie heißt dein Vetter?
*What is your cousin's name?*

**heiter** [HEItər] *adj.* • cheerful
Die Kinder waren heute in einer heiteren Stimmung.
*The children were in a cheerful mood today.*

**helfen** [HELfən] *v.* • to help
**Hilfe, die** *n.* • help
**Hilfe!** • Help!

| | |
|---|---|
| helfe | helfen |
| hilfst | helft |
| hilft | helfen |

Ich helfe meinem Vater bei der Vorbereitung des Abendessens.
*I help my father prepare dinner.*

Können Sie mir bitte helfen?
*Can you help me, please?*

**Helm, der** [HELM] *n.* • helmet
Man muß einen Sturzhelm tragen, wenn man Motorrad fährt.
*You must wear a helmet when riding a motorcycle.*

**Hemd, das** [HEMT] *n.* • shirt
Er trägt ein Hemd und eine Krawatte bei der Arbeit.
*He wears a shirt and tie to work.*

**Henne, die** [HENə] *n.* • hen
Diese Hennen schützen ihre Küken.
*These hens are protecting their chicks.*

**heraus** [herAUS] *adv.* • out
Kommen Sie bitte heraus, damit wir Sie besser sehen können.
*Please come out so we can see you better.*

**Herbst, der** [HERPST] *n.* • autumn; fall
Die Blätter sind schön im Herbst.
*The leaves are beautiful in autumn.*

**Herd, der** [HERT] *n.* • stove
Die Soße kocht auf dem Herd.
*The sauce is cooking on the stove.*

**hereinkommen** [herEINkawmən] *v.* • to come into
Sie kommen eben ins Klassenzimmer herein.
*They are coming into the classroom now.*

**Herr, der (mein)** [HER] *n.* • sir; mister (Mr.)
Darf ich Ihren Hut nehmen, mein Herr?
*May I take your hat, sir?*

Darf ich Ihnen meinen Nachbarn, Herr Stuart, vorstellen?
*I'd like you to meet my neighbor, Mr. Stuart.*

**herum** [herUM] *prep.* • around
Die Kinder sind alle um mich herum.
*The children are all around me.*

**Herz, das** [HERTS] *n.* • heart
Wenn man läuft, schlägt das Herz schneller.
*When you run, your heart beats faster.*

**Heu, das** [HOI] *n.* • hay
**Heufieber, das** n. • hay-fever
Die Rinder fraßen das Heu, das wir ihnen gegeben hatten.
*The cattle ate the hay we had given them.*

**Heuschrecke, die** [HOIshrekə] *n.* • grasshopper
Die Heuschrecke hüpfte vor der Katze weg.
*The grasshopper jumped away from the cat.*

**heute** [HOItə] *adv.* • today
Heute ist mein Geburtstag.
*Today is my birthday.*

**hier** [HEER] *adv.* • here
**hier ist; hier sind** • here is; here are
Hier ist das Buch, das du gesucht hast.
*Here is the book you were looking for.*

**Hilfe, die** See *helfen.*

**Himbeere, die** [HIMbairə] *n.* • raspberry
Ich esse sehr gern frische Himbeeren.
*I love to eat fresh raspberries.*

**Himmel, der** [HIMəl] *n.* • sky
Die Sonne scheint; der Himmel ist blau; das Wetter ist toll!
*The sun shines, the sky is blue, the weather is great!*

**hinauf** [hinAUF] *adv.* • up
**hinaufgehen** v. • to go up
Die Katze kletterte auf den Baum hinauf und blieb stecken.
*The cat climbed up the tree and got stuck.*

**hinaufsteigen** [hinAUFshteigən] *v.* • to climb
Willst du die Treppen hinaufsteigen oder den Fahrstuhl nehmen?
*Do you want to climb the steps or take the elevator?*

**hinaus** [hinAUS] *adv.* • out; outside
Wir gehen hinaus, um nachts die Sterne zu sehen.
*We go outside to see the stars at night.*

**hinter** [HINtər] *prep.* • behind
**Hintergrund, der** n. • background (theater)
Wer versteckt sich hinter dem Vorhang?
*Who is hiding behind the curtain?*

**hinunter** [hinUNtər] *adv.* • down
Die Skiläufer fahren den Berg hinunter.
*The skiers go down the mountain.*

**hinuntergehen** [hinUNtərgaiyən] *v.* • to go down
Sei vorsichtig, wenn du die Treppen hinuntergehst.
*Be careful when you go down the steps.*

**hinweisen auf** [HINveizən auf] *v.* • to point; to indicate
Der Führer weist auf die Türme von Notre Dame hin.
*The guide points to the towers of Notre Dame.*

Ich möchte Sie auf die richtige Lösung hinweisen.
*I would like to indicate the correct solution to you.*

**hinzufügen** [hinTSOOf*ue*gən] *v.* • to add
Wir werden für unseren Gast noch einen Platz am Tisch hinzufügen.
*We'll add a place setting at the table for our guest.*

**Hirte, der** [HIRtə] *n.* • shepherd
**Hirtin, die** n. • shepherdess
Der Hirte hütet die Schafe.
*The shepherd watches the sheep.*

**Hitze, die** [HITsə] *n.* • heat
Spürst du die Hitze des Feuers?
*Do you feel the heat of the fire?*

**Hobby, das** [HAWbee] *n.* • hobby
Was ist dein Lieblingshobby?
*What is your favorite hobby?*

**hoch** [HOH*KH*] *adj.* • high
Diese Berge sind hoch.
*These mountains are high.*

**Hochwild, das** [HOH*KH*vilt] *n.* • deer
In diesem Wald gibt es Hochwild.
*There are deer in these woods.*

**Hochzeit, die** [HAW*KH*tseit] *n.* • wedding
**Hochzeitsreise, die** n. • honeymoon
**Hochzeitstag, der** n. • anniversary (wedding)
In der Kirche findet heute eine Hochzeit statt.
*There is a wedding at the church today.*

Der Hochzeitstag meiner Eltern ist am 8. August.
*My parents' wedding anniversary is August 8.*

**Hockey(spiel), das** [HAWkee(shpeel)] *n.* • hockey
**Hockey spielen** • to play hockey
Wir spielen Hockey auf dem Teich, wenn er zugefroren ist.
*We play hockey on the pond when it's frozen.*

**hoffen** [HAWFən] *v.* • to hope
**hoffnungslos** adj. • hopeless
**hoffnungsvoll** adj. • hopeful

| | |
|---|---|
| hoffe | hoffen |
| hoffst | hofft |
| hofft | hoffen |

Ich hoffe, daß Sie kommen können!
*I hope you can come!*

**höflich** [H*ER*Fli*sh*] *adj.* • polite
Diese Kinder sind sehr höflich.
*These children are very polite.*

**Höhe, die** [H*ER*ə] *n.* • height
Die Höhe dieses Gebäudes ist beeindruckend.
*The height of this building is impressive.*

**Höhle, die** [H*ER*lə] *n.* • cave
Fledermäuse leben in Höhlen.
*Bats live in caves.*

**holen** [HOHlən] *v.* • to fetch; to take (down or out)
**einholen** *v.* • to catch up with
Der Hund will den Stock holen.
*The dog wants to fetch the stick.*

**Holland** [HAWlant] *n.* • Holland
**Holländer, der (-in, f.)** *n.* • Dutch (person)
**holländisch** *adj.* • Dutch
In Holland werden Tulpen gezüchtet.
*They grow tulips in Holland.*

Die holländische Sprache ist dem Deutschen ähnlich.
*The Dutch language is similar to German.*

**Holz, das** [HAWLTS] *n.* • wood
**hölzern** *adj.* • wooden
Die Möbel sind aus Holz gemacht.
*The furniture is made of wood.*

**Honig, der** [HOHnis*h*] *n.* • honey
Ich streiche Honig auf mein Brot.
*I put honey on my bread.*

**hören** [H*ER*rən] *v.* • to hear

| | |
|---|---|
| höre | hören |
| hörst | hört |
| hört | hören |

Wir hören den Wind in den Bäumen.
*We hear the wind blowing in the trees.*

**Hose, die** [HOHzə] *n.* • pants; trousers
Ich bügele meine Hose selbst.
*I'm ironing my pants myself.*

Ist diese Hose zu lang?
*Are these trousers too long?*

**Hotel, das** [hawTEL] *n.* • hotel
Unser Hotel ist sehr nahe am Bahnhof.
*Our hotel is very near the railway station.*

**hübsch** [H*UE*PSH] *adj.* • pretty
Was für ein hübsches Kleid!
*What a pretty dress!*

**Hubschrauber, der** [HOOPshraubə*r*] *n.* • helicopter
Siehst du den Hubschrauber über uns?
*Do you see the helicopter above us?*

**Hügel, der** [H*UE*gəl] *n.* • hill
Im Winter fahren wir auf diesem Hügel Schlitten.
*We go sledding on this hill in the winter.*

**Huhn, das** [HOON] *n.* • chicken
Wir haben ein gutes Rezept für Huhn.
*We have a good recipe for chicken.*

**Hummer, der** [HUMə*r*] *n.* • lobster
Dieser Hummer ist sehr köstlich.
*This lobster is absolutely delicious.*

**Hund, der** [HUNT] *n.* • dog
**Achtung! Bissiger Hund! Warnung vor dem Hund!** • beware of dog
**Hundehalsband, das** *n.* • dog collar
Wir haben einen Hund und eine Katze als Haustiere.
*We have a dog and a cat as pets.*

**hundert** [HUNdə*r*t] *adj.* • hundred
Er hat hundert Punkte in diesem Spiel erzielt
*He made one hundred points in this game.*

**Hunger, der** [HUNGə*r*] *n.* • hunger
**Hunger haben** • to be hungry
Ich habe Hunger.
*I am hungry.*

Unsere Katze hat immer Hunger.
*Our cat is hungry all the time.*

**husten** [HOOStən] *v.* • to cough
Manchmal hustet man, wenn man eine Erkältung hat.
*Sometimes you cough when you have a cold.*

**Hut, der** [HOOT] *n.* • hat
Er trägt einen Hut, um seinen Kopf zu bedecken.
*He wears a hat to cover his head.*

# I

**ich** [I*SH*] *pron.* • I
Ich möchte mit meinen Freunden ausgehen.
*I want to go out with my friends.*

**Idee, die** [iDAI] *n.* • idea
Es ist eine gute Idee, eine Landkarte zu benutzen.
*Using a map is a good idea.*

**ihn; ihm** [EEN; EEM] *pron.* • him
Diese neue Krawatte ist für ihn.
*This new tie is for him.*

**ihnen** [EEnən] *pron.* • them
Ich habe ihnen allen gesagt, ruhig zu sein.
*I told them all to be quiet.*

**ihr; ihre** [EER; EErə] *pron.* • her; your; their
Ist dies ihr eigenes Haus oder mieten sie es?
*Is this their own house or do they rent it?*

Sie vergißt immer ihre Schlüssel.
*She always forgets her keys.* see also *dein; sie*

**immer** [IMər] *adv.* • always
Wir essen immer um 6 Uhr abends.
*We always eat at six o'clock in the evening.*

**in** [IN] *prep.* • at; in; into
Sie lernt in der Bibliothek.
*She studies at the library.*

Sie steckt ihre Schlüssel in ihre Tasche.
*She puts her keys in her pocket.*

Tu die Butter in die Pfanne.
*Put the butter into the frying pan.*

**Industrie, die** [indusTREE] *n.* • industry
Hollywood ist das Zentrum der Filmindustrie in den U.S.A.
*Hollywood is the center of the U.S. movie industry.*

**Ingenieur, der** [inzheNY*UE*R] *n.* • engineer
Der Ingenieur hat einen akademischen Grad an der Universität Cal Tech erworben.
*The engineer has a degree from Cal Tech.*

**innerhalb** [INerhahlp] *prep.* • inside (of); within
Der Zug fährt innerhalb zehn Minuten aus dem Bahnhof.
*The train leaves the station within ten minutes.*

**Insekt, das** [inZEKT] *n.* • insect
Insekten haben sechs Beine.
*Insects have six legs.*

**Insel, die** [INzəl] *n.* • island
Hast du jemals eine der Karibischen Insel besucht?
*Have you ever visited a Caribbean island?*

**Inserate, die** [inzeRAHtə] *n.* • advertisements (want ads)
Ich habe die Inserate in der Zeitung gesehen.
*I saw the ads in the newspaper.*

**intelligent** [inteliGENT] *adj.* • intelligent
Welches Tier ist am intelligentesten?
*Which animal is the most intelligent?*

**Interesse, das** [intəRESə] *n.* • interest
**interessant** *adj.* • interesting
**interessieren für, sich** • to be interested in
Mein Bruder hat ein großes Interesse für Chemie.
*My brother has a keen interest in chemistry.*

**international** [internahtsyohNAHL] *adj.* • international
Eine internationale Konferenz findet Montag in Washington, D.C. statt.
*There is an international conference in Washington, D.C. Monday.*

**irgend** [EERgənt] *adv.* • any; at all
**irgend etwas** *pron.* • anything
**irgend jemand** *pron.* • anyone; somebody
**irgendwo** *adv.* • somewhere
Möchte irgend jemand Milch?
*Does anyone want milk?*

Ist irgend jemand hier?
*Is anyone here (at all)?*

**irren, sich** [IRən, ZI*SH*] *v.* • to be wrong
Sie haben sich bezüglich der Zeit der Schau geirrt.
*They were wrong about the time of the show.*

**Italien** [iTAHlyən] *n.* • Italy
**Italiener, der (-in, f.)** *n.* • Italian (person)
**italienisch** *adj.* • Italian
Auf der Landkarte sieht Italien einem Stiefel ähnlich.
*On a map, Italy is shaped like a boot.*

Ein italienisches Restaurant müßte Espresso haben.
*An Italian restaurant should have espresso.*

# J

**ja** [YAH] *adv.* • yes
Ja, ich möchte gern etwas Nachtisch!
*Yes, I would like some dessert!*

**Jacke, die** [YAHkə] *n.* • jacket
**Skijacke, die** *n.* • ski jacket
Es ist kühl; also nimm eine Jacke mit.
*It is cool, so take a jacket.*

**jagen** [YAHgən] *v.* • to hunt
**Jäger, der** *n.* • hunter
Manche Leute benutzen Pfeil und Bogen, um Hochwild zu jagen.
*Some people use a bow and arrow to hunt deer.*

**Jahr, das** [YAHR] *n.* • year
**Neujahrstag, der** *n.* • New Year's Day
Ich lerne im ersten Jahr Französisch.
*I am in my first year of French.*

**Jahreszeit, die** [YAHrəs-tseit] *n.* • season
Ist der Herbst deine Lieblingsjahreszeit?
*Is autumn your favorite season?*

**Januar, der** [YAHnuahr] *n.* • January
Wir haben hier Schnee im Januar.
*We have snow here in January.*

**Japan** [YAHpahn] *n.* • Japan
**Japaner, der (-in, f.)** *n.* • Japanese (person)
**japanisch** *adj.* • Japanese
Japan ist ein Land auf einer Insel in Asien.
*Japan is an island country in Asia.*

**Jargon, der** [YAHRgawn] *n.* • slang
Der Studentenjargon ist sehr lustig.
*Student slang is very funny.*

**Jeans, die** [DZHEENS (like English)] *n.* • jeans
Ich ziehe es vor, Jeans zu tragen, wenn ich reise.
*I prefer to wear jeans when I travel.*

**jede, -r, -s** [YAIdə; YAIdə*r*; YAIdəs] *adj.* • every; each; each one
**jeder(mann)** *pron.* • everyone; everybody
**jeden Tag** • every day
Jede Person nimmt einen Teller.
*Each person takes a plate.*

Ich war letzten Monat jeden Tag bei der Arbeit.
*I was at work every day last month.*

**jedoch** [yeDAW*KH*] *conj.; adv.* • however
Ich verliere immer; ich spiele jedoch weiter!
*I always lose; however, I keep playing!*

**jemals** [YAImahls] *adv.* • ever
Wenn du jemals Hilfe brauchst, ruf mich an!
*If you ever need help, call me.*

**jemand** [YAImahnt] *pron.* • someone; somebody
Jemand hat meine Brieftasche gestohlen.
*Someone stole my wallet.*

**jener, -e, -es** [YAInə*r*; YAInə; YAInəs] *adj.* • that; those
Geben Sie mir bitte jenes Buch dort drüben.
*Please pass me that book over there.*

Ich will jene Ohrringe.
*I want those earrings.*

**jetzt** [YETST] *adv.* • now
Die Lehrerin sagt, daß wir jetzt gehen können.
*The teacher says we can leave now.*

**Job, der** [DZHAWB (like English)] *n.* • job
Hast du für den Sommer einen Job gefunden?
*Have you found a job for the summer?*

**joggen** [ZHAWgən] *v.* • to jog
Dieselben Leute gehen jeden Morgen im Park joggen.
*The same people go jogging in the park every morning.*

**Juli, der** [YOOlee] *n.* • July
Der Vierte Juli ist ein großer Feiertag in den Vereinigten Staaten.
*The Fourth of July is a big holiday in the U.S.*

**jung** [YUNG] *adj.* • young
**Jugendliche, der (die)** *n.* • youth
Er ist zu jung, um Auto zu fahren.
*He is too young to drive.*

**Junge, der** [YUNGə] *n.* • boy
**junge Dame, die** • young lady
Dieser Junge ist der Sohn meines Nachbarn.
*This boy is my neighbor's son.*

**Jugendalter, das** [YOOgendahltər] *n.* • adolescence
**Jugendliche, der** *n.* • adolescent
Das Jugendalter ist eine Zeit zum Lernen und sich Entwickeln.
*Adolescence is a time to learn and mature.*

**Juni, der** [YOOnee] *n.* • June
Ihr Hochzeitstag ist im Juni.
*Their wedding anniversary is in June.*

**Juwel, der** [YOOvəl] *n.* • jewel
**Juwelier, der** *n.* • jeweler
Der Juwelier zeigte mir einen Diamantring.
*The jeweler showed me a diamond ring.*

# K

**Kaffee, der** [kahFAI] *n.* • coffee
**eine Tasse Kaffee** • a cup of coffee
Ich nehme Zucker in meinen Kaffee.
*I put sugar in my coffee.*

**Kaffeehaus, das** [KAHfaihaus] *n.* • café
Treffen wir uns im Kaffeehaus an der Ecke.
*Let's meet at the café on the corner.*

**Kalb, das** [KAHLP] *n.* • calf
Das Kalb folgt seiner Mutter.
*The calf follows its mother.*

**Kalender, der** [kahLENdə*r*] *n.* • calendar
Der Kalender vom vorigen Jahr hängt noch an der Wand.
*Last year's calendar is still hanging on the wall.*

**kalt** [KAHLT] *adj.* • cold
**Erkältung, die** *n.* • cold (illness)
Es ist draußen kalt.
*It's cold out.*

Im Winter ist es kalt.
*It's cold in the winter.*

**Kamel, das** [kahMAIL] *n.* • camel
Kamele können ohne Wasser in der Wüste leben.
*Camels can live without water in the desert.*

**Kamera, die** [KAHmerah] *n.* • camera
Diese Kamera macht gute Aufnahmen.
*This camera takes good pictures.*

**Kamerad, der** [kahmeRAHD] *n.* • pal
Er ist mein alter Kamerad.
*He is an old pal of mine.*

**Kamin, der** [kahMEEN] *n.* • chimney
**offene Kamin, der** • fireplace
Einige Vögel haben in unserem Kamin ihr Nest gebaut.
*Some birds have made their nest in our chimney.*

**Kamm, der** [KAHM] *n.* • comb
**sich kämmen** *v.* • to comb (oneself)
Ich habe meine Bürste, aber wo ist mein Kamm?
*I have my brush, but where is my comb?*

**Kanada** [KAnahdah] *n.* • Canada
**Kanadier, der (-in, f.)** *n.* • Canadian (person)
**kanadisch** *adj.* • Canadian
Kanada liegt nördlich der Vereinigten Staaten.
*Canada is north of the United States.*

**Känguruh, das** [KAINGgooroo] *n.* • kangaroo
Känguruhs leben in Australien.
*Kangaroos live in Australia.*

**Kaninchen, das** [kaNEEN*sh*ən] *n.* • rabbit
Das Kaninchen hat unseren ganzen Salat im Garten gefressen.
*The rabbit ate all our lettuce from the garden.*

**Kante, die** [KAHNtə] *n.* • edge
Schneide dich nicht an den scharfen Kanten.
*Don't cut yourself on the sharp edges.*

**Kardinal, der** [kahrdiNAHL] *n.* • cardinal (bird)
Der rote Kardinal sitzt auf dem Zweig.
*The red cardinal is sitting on the twig.*

**Karikatur, die** [kahrikahTOOR] *n.* • cartoon (animated)
**Karikaturstreifen, der** *n.* • comic strip
Ich liebe die Karikaturen von Gary Larson.
*I like Gary Larson's cartoons.*

**Karotte, die** [kahRAWtə] *n.* • carrot
Das Kaninchen frißt eine Karotte.
*The rabbit is eating a carrot.*

**Karriere, die** [kahREErə] *n.* • career
Was für eine Ausbildung braucht man für diese Karriere?
*What kind of education do you need for this career?*

**Karte, die** [KAHRtə] *n.* • card; ticket
**Kartenschalter, der** *n.* • ticket office
**Karten spielen** • to play cards
**Kreditkarte, die** *n.* • credit card
**Postkarte, die** *n.* • postcard
**Rückfahrkarte, die** *n.* • round trip ticket
Mein kleiner Bruder lernt Karten spielen.
*My little brother is learning to play cards.*

**Kartoffel, die** [kahrTAWfəl] *n.* • potato
Möchtest du eine gebackene Kartoffel zu deinem Steak?
*Would you like a baked potato with your steak?*

**Karussell, das** [kahruSEL] *n.* • merry-go-round
Fährst du gern Karussell?
*Do you like to ride the merry-go-round?*

**Käse, der** [KAIzə] *n.* • cheese
**gebratenes Käsebrot mit Schinken** • grilled ham and cheese
Gruyere ist mein Lieblingskäse.
*Gruyere is my favorite cheese.*

**Kassette, die** [kahSEtə] *n.* • tape recording
**Kassettenrekorder, der** *n.* • tape recorder
Er hört sich eine Kassette mit seinem Lieblingslied an.
*He is listening to a tape of his favorite song.*

**Kasten, der** [KAHStən] *n.* • box
Dieser Kasten ist für mein ganzes Spielzeug nicht groß genug.
*This box isn't big enough for all my toys.*

**Kätzchen, das** [KAITS*sh*ən] *n.* • kitten
**Kasse, die** *n.* • kitty
Unsere Katze hat vier Kätzchen.
*Our cat has four kittens.*

**Katze, die** [KAHTSə] *n.* • cat
Wir haben eine Katze als Haustier.
*We have a cat for a pet.*

**kaufen** [KAUFən] *v.* • to buy
**Kaufhaus, das** *n.* • department store

| | |
|---|---|
| kaufe | kaufen |
| kaufst | kauft |
| kauft | kaufen |

Wir kaufen unser Gemüse auf dem Markt.
*We buy our vegetables at the market.*

**kein** [KEIN] *adj.* • no
**keineswegs** • not at all
**Kein Eintritt!** • No admittance!
Sie hatte überhaupt kein Geld übrig.
*She had absolutely no money left.*

**Keks, der** [KAIKS] *n.* • cookie
Wir backten Kekse für unsere Gäste.
*We baked cookies for our guests.*

**Keller, der** [KELər] *n.* • cellar
Der Keller ist immer kühl und feucht.
*The cellar is always cool and damp.*

**Kellner, der** [KELnə*r*] *n.* • waiter
**Kellnerin, die** *n.* • waitress
Wir haben dem Kellner ein Trinkgeld gegeben.
*We gave a tip to the waiter.*

**kennen** [KENən] *v.* • to be acquainted with; to know (people)

| | |
|---|---|
| kenne | kennen |
| kennst | kennt |
| kennt | kennen |

Kennst du deine Nachbarn?
*Are you acquainted with your neighbors?*

Ich kenne ihre Eltern nicht gut, denn ich habe sie eben erst kennengelernt.
*I just met her parents, so I don't know them well.*

**Kerze, die** [KERtsə] *n.* • candle
Kannst du bitte die Kerzen anzünden?
*Can you light the candles, please?*

**kicken** [KIkən] *v.* • to kick
Er kickt den Fußball ins Tor.
*He is kicking the football into the goal.*

**Kilometer, der** [kilohMAItə*r*] *n.* • kilometer
Wie viele Kilometer lang ist die Strecke zwischen New York und Chicago?
*How many kilometers are there between New York and Chicago?*

**Kind, das** [KINT] *n.* • child
**Kinder, die** *n. pl.* • children
**Kinderwagen, der** *n.* • baby carriage
Wie heißt das Kind?
*What is the child's name?*

**Kindergarten, der** [KINdə*r*gahrtən] *n.* • kindergarten
Meine kleine Schwester geht in den Kindergarten.
*My little sister goes to kindergarten.*

**Kinn, das** [KIN] *n.* • chin
Paul hat eine Schramme an seinem Kinn.
*Paul has a bruise on his chin.*

**Kino, das** [KEEnoh] *n.* • movie theater
Wir gehen heute abend ins Kino.
*We're going to the movies tonight.*

Was wird heute abend im Kino gezeigt?
*What's playing at the movie theater tonight?*

**Kirche, die** [KIR*sh*ə] *n.* • church
Viele Leute gehen am Sonntag in die Kirche.
*Many people go to church on Sunday.*

**Kirsche, die** [KIRshə] *n.* • cherry
Wir pflückten Kirschen vom Baum.
*We picked cherries from the tree.*

**Klang, der** [KLAHNG] *n.* • sound
Dieses Instrument hat einen guten Klang.
*This instrument has a good sound.*

**klar** [KLAHR] *adj.* • clear
Deine Erklärung ist nicht klar.
*Your explanation is not clear.*

**Klarinette, die** [klahriNEtə] *n.* • clarinet
Meine Schwester spielt Klarinette.
*My sister plays the clarinet.*

**Klasse, die** [KLAHsə] *n.* • class
**Klassenzimmer, das** *n.* • classroom
Wie viele Studenten sind in dieser Klasse?
*How many students are in this class?*

**Klavier, das** [klahVEER] *n.* • piano
**Klavier spielen** • to play the piano
Dieses alte Klavier hat immer noch einen schönen Ton.
*This old piano still sounds nice.*

Sie spielt sehr gut Klavier.
*She plays the piano very well.*

**kleben** [KLAIbən] *v.* • to glue; to paste; to stick
**Klebstoff, der** *n.* • glue; paste

| | |
|---|---|
| klebe | kleben |
| klebst | klebt |
| klebt | kleben |

Wir klebten den Deckel wieder auf das Buch.
*We glued the cover back on the book.*

**Kleid, das** [KLEIT] *n.* • dress
**gut gekleidet** • well dressed
Das Mädchen trägt ein schönes Kleid.
*The girl is wearing a pretty dress.*

**Kleider, die** [KLEIdər] *n.* • clothes
**Kleidung, die** *n.* • clothing
Ich kaufte neue Kleider und Schuhe für meine Reise.
*I bought new clothes and shoes for my trip.*

**klein** [KLEIN] *adj.* • little; small; short
Dieses kleine Buch paßt in meine Tasche.
*This little book fits in my pocket.*

Diese Schuhe sind zu klein!
*These shoes are too small!*

Das kleine Mädchen ist zu klein, um das oberste Regal zu erreichen.
*The little girl is too short to reach the top shelf.*

**Klimaanlage, die** [KLEEmah-anlahgə] *n.* • air-conditioner
**klimatisiert** *adj.* • air-conditioned
**Klimatisierung, die** *n.* • air-conditioning
Dieses Kino hat eine Klimaanlage.
*This movie theater has an air-conditioner.*

**Klingel, die** [KLINGəl] *n.* • bell
**Türklingel, die** • doorbell
Die Klingel hat eben geläutet.
*The bell has just rung.*

**klopfen** [KLAWPfən] *v.* • to knock
**Anklopfen, das** *n.* • knock

| | |
|---|---|
| klopfe | klopfen |
| klopfst | klopft |
| klopft | klopfen |

Alan klopfte an die Tür, aber niemand kam.
*Alan knocked on the door, but no one came.*

**klug** [KLOOG] *adj.* • smart
Alle diese Studenten sind klug.
*All these students are smart.*

**Knie, das** [KNEE] *n.* • knee
Ich habe mein Knie beim Fußballspielen verletzt.
*I hurt my knee playing football.*

**Knochen, der** [KNAW*kh*ən] *n.* • bone
Der Hund vergräbt einen Knochen.
*The dog is burying a bone.*

**Knopf, der** [KNAWPF] *n.* • button
Ich nähe nicht gern Knöpfe an.
*I don't like to sew buttons.*

**kochen** [KAW*kh*ən] *v.* • to cook; to boil
**Koch, der (Köchin, die)** *n.* • cook (person)
**Kochherd, der** *n.* • range; stove

| | |
|---|---|
| koche | kochen |
| kochst | kocht |
| kocht | kochen |

Wir haben ein besonderes Essen zu deinem Geburtstag gekocht.
*We cooked a special dinner for your birthday.*

**Koffer, der** [KAWfər] *n.* • suitcase
**seinen Koffer packen** • to pack one's suitcase
Wie viele Koffer bringen sie mit?
*How many suitcases are they bringing?*

**Kofferraum, der** [KAWfər-raum] *n.* • trunk (of a car)
Der Kofferraum ist voll.
*The trunk (of the car) is full.*

**Kohl, der** [KOHL] *n.* • cabbage
Die Kaninchen fressen den Kohl in unserem Garten.
*Rabbits are eating the cabbage in our garden.*

**Kokosnuß, die** [KAWkawsnus] *n.* • coconut
Die Kokosnuß hat eine sehr harte Schale.
*The coconut has a very hard shell.*

**Kolonialwarenhändler, der** [kawlawniAHLvahrenhaindlər] *n.* • grocer
**Kolonialwarenladen, der** *n.* • grocery store
Der Kolonialwarenhändler verkauft Früchte und Gemüse.
*The grocer sells fruits and vegetables.*

Wir kaufen Lebensmittel im Kolonialwarenladen.
*We buy food at the grocery store.*

**kommen** [KAWmən] *v.* • to come
**zurückkommen** *v.* • to come back; to return

| | |
|---|---|
| komme | kommen |
| kommst | kommt |
| kommt | kommen |

Seine Tante kommt im Sommer auf Besuch.
*His aunt comes to visit in the summer.*

**Kompliment, das** [kawmpliMENT] *n.* • compliment
Jeder bekommt gern Komplimente.
*Everyone likes to receive compliments.*

**Konditorei, die** [kawnditoREI] *n.* • pastry shop
Man kann in dieser Konditorei Kuchen kaufen.
*You can buy cake in this pastry shop.*

**König, der** [K*ER*nis*h*] *n.* • king
Der König trägt eine Krone.
*The king wears a crown.*

**Königin, die** [K*ER*nigin] *n.* • queen
Die Königin lebt in einem Schloß.
*The queen lives in the castle.*

**Konkurrenz, die** [kawnkuRENTS] *n.* • competition
**in Konkurrenz stehen** • to compete
Unsere Mannschaft fürchtet keine Konkurrenz.
*Our team is not afraid of competition.*

**können** [K*ER*nən] *v.* • to be able (can)

| | |
|---|---|
| kann | können |
| kannst | könnt |
| kann | können |

Sie können dieses Problem lösen.
*They can solve this problem.*

**Kontinent, der** [kawntiNENT] *n.* • continent
Afrika und Asien sind riesige Kontinente.
*Africa and Asia are huge continents.*

**Konzert, das** [kawnTSERT] *n.* • concert
Ich gehe mit meiner Freundin ins Konzert.
*I am going to the concert with my girlfriend.*

**Kopf, der** [KAWPF] *n.* • head
**Kopfweh, das** *n.* • headache
Ich legte meinen Kopf auf das Kissen.
*I laid my head on the pillow.*

**Kopfkissen, das** [KAWPFkisən] *n.* • pillow
Ich legte das Kopfkissen auf mein Bett.
*I put the pillow on my bed.*

**Kopfsalat, der** [KAWPFsahlaht] *n.* • lettuce
Mein Salat besteht aus Kopfsalat und Tomaten.
*My salad is made with lettuce and tomatoes.*

**Kopfsprung, der** [KAWPFshprung] *n.* • dive
Der Schwimmer macht einen Kopfsprung ins Schwimmbad.
*The swimmer makes a dive into the swimming pool.*

**Kopie, die** [kawPEE] *n.* • copy
**Kopie machen, die** • to copy (photocopy)
Haben Sie eine Kopie von diesem Brief?
*Do you have a copy of this letter?*

**Korb, der** [KAWRP] *n.* • basket
Meine Mutter legt die Früchte in einen Korb.
*My mother is putting the fruits in a basket.*

**Korbballspiel, das** [KAWRPbalshpeel] *n.* • basketball
**Korbball spielen** • to play basketball
Willst du mit uns Korbball spielen?
*Do you want to play basketball with us?*

**Körper, der** [K*ER*pər] *n.* • body
Medizinstudenten studieren den menschlichen Körper.
*Medical students study the human body.*

**korrekt** [kawREKT] *adj.* • correct
**korrigieren** *v.* • to correct
Das ist die korrekte Antwort.
*That's the correct answer.*

**kostbar** [KAWSTbahr] *adj.* • precious
Diamanten sind kostbare Edelsteine.
*Diamonds are precious jewels.*

**kosten** [KAWStən] *v.* • to cost
**Kosten, die (pl.)** *n.* • cost
**teuer sein** • to be expensive

| | |
|---|---|
| koste | kosten |
| kostest | kostet |
| kostet | kosten |

Wieviel kostet diese Jacke?
*How much does this jacket cost?*

**köstlich** [K*ER*STlis*h*] *adj.* • delicious
Dieses Essen ist köstlich.
*This meal is delicious.*

**Kotelett, das** [kawtLET] *n.* • cutlet (chop)
Ich möchte bitte ein Schweinskotelett.
*I would like a pork cutlet, please.*

**Kragen, der** [KRAHgən] *n.* • collar
Dieser Kragen ist zu eng.
*This collar is too tight.*

**krank** [KRAHNGK] *adj.* • sick; ill
Ich bleibe im Bett, wenn ich krank bin.
*I stay in bed when I am sick.*

Wenn man krank ist, geht man zum Arzt.
*When you are ill, you go to the doctor.*

**Krankenhaus, das** [KRAHNGkənhaus] *n.* • hospital
Der Chirurg arbeitet im Krankenhaus.
*The surgeon works at the hospital.*

**Krankenschwester, die** [KRAHNGkənshvestə*r*] *n.* • nurse
Die Krankenschwester arbeitet im Krankenhaus.
*The nurse works in the hospital.*

**Krankenwagen, der** [KRAHNGkənvahgən] *n.* • ambulance

Der Krankenwagen bringt Kranke zum Krankenhaus.
*The ambulance takes sick people to the hospital.*

**Krankheit, die** [KRAHNGKheit] *n.* • disease; sickness
Ihre Krankheit kann mit dieser Medizin geheilt werden.
*Your disease can be cured with this medicine.*

**Krawatte, die** [kraVAHtə] *n.* • tie
Trägst du gern eine Krawatte?
*Do you like to wear a tie?*

**Kreide, die** [KREIdə] *n.* • chalk
Der Lehrer schreibt mit Kreide an die Tafel.
*The teacher writes on the blackboard with chalk.*

**Kreis, der** [KREIS] *n.* • circle
Andrew zeichnet einen Kreis auf das Papier.
*Andrew is drawing a circle on the paper.*

**kreuzen** [KROITSən] *v.* • to cross
**Kreuzworträtsel, das** *n.* • crossword puzzle
Unsere Wegen werden sich wieder kreuzen.
*Our paths will cross again.*

**Krieg, der** [KREEG] *n.* • war
Diese Leute demonstrieren gegen den Krieg.
*These people are demonstrating against war.*

**Kriminalroman, der** [krimiNAHLrohmahn] *n.* • detective novel
**Kriminalfilm, der** *n.* • detective film
Er liest gern Kriminalromane.
*He likes to read detective stories.*

**Krokodil, das** [krawkawDIL] *n.* • crocodile
Krokodile leben in der Nähe von Flüssen und Sümpfen.
*Crocodiles live near rivers and swamps.*

**Krone, die** [KROHnə] *n.* • crown
Die Königin trägt eine Krone.
*The queen wears a crown.*

**Krug, der** [KROOK] *n.* • pitcher
Die Milch ist in dem Krug dort drüben.
*The milk is in the pitcher over there.*

**Kruste, die** [KRUStə] *n.* • crust
Ich liebe die Kruste beim französischen Brot.
*I like the crust on French bread.*

**Küche, die** [K*UE*sh*ə*] *n.* • kitchen
Wir essen in der Küche zu Mittag.
*We eat lunch in the kitchen.*

**Kuchen, der** [KOO*kh*ən] *n.* • pie; cake
  **Apfelkuchen, der** *n.* • apple pie
Wir essen Kuchen zum Nachtisch.
*We'll have pie for dessert.*

Was für einen Kuchen möchtest du zu deinem Geburtstag?
*What kind of cake do you want for your birthday?*

**Kugelschreiber, der** [KOOgəlshreibə*r*] *n.* • ball-point pen
Ich ziehe es vor, mit einem Kugelschreiber zu schreiben.
*I prefer to write with a ball-point pen.*

**Kuh, die** [KOO] *n.* • cow
Kühe geben Milch.
*The cows give milk.*

**kühl** [K*UE*L] *adj.* • cool
Es ist draußen kühl.
*It's cool out.*

Ein kühles Getränk ist an einem warmen Tag angenehm.
*A cool drink is welcome on a hot day.*

**Kühlschrank, der** [K*UE*Lshrahnk] *n.* • refrigerator
Die Milch ist im Kühlschrank.
*The milk is in the refrigerator.*

**Kunst, die** [KUNST] *n.* • art
**Künstler, der (-in, f.)** *n.* • artist
Ballet ist eine Kunst.
*Ballet is an art.*

Mir gefallen die Zeichnungen dieses Künstlers.
*I like this artist's drawings.*

**Kürbis, der** [K*UE*Rbis] *n.* • pumpkin
Magst du Kürbiskuchen?
*Do you like pumpkin pie?*

**Kurs, der** [KOORS] *n.* • course
Welchen Kurs belegst du in der Schule?
*Which course are you taking in school?*

**kurz** [KURTS] *adj.* • short (length)
Mein Sohn hat kurze Haare.
*My son has short hair.*

**küssen** [K*UE*sən] *v.* • to kiss
**Kuß, ein** *n.* • kiss
Ich werde dich auf die Backe küssen.
*I'll kiss you on the cheek.*

**Küste, die** [K*UE*Stə] *n.* • shore
Sie leben (wohnen) in der Nähe der Küste.
*They live near the shore.*

# L

**lächeln** [LAI*sh*əln] *v.* • to smile
**Lächeln, das** *n.* • smile

| | |
|---|---|
| lächle | lächeln |
| lächelst | lächelt |
| lächelt | lächeln |

Wir sollten für das Bild lächeln.
*We ought to smile for the picture.*

**lachen** [LA*kh*ən] *v.* • to laugh

| | |
|---|---|
| lache | lachen |
| lachst | lacht |
| lacht | lachen |

Die Kinder lachen, wenn sie den Clown sehen.
*The children laugh when they see the clown.*

**Laden, der** [LAHdən] *n.* • store
**Buchladen, der** *n.* • book store
Hast du in dem neuen Laden eingekauft?
*Did you shop at the new store?*

**Lage, die** [LAHgə] *n.* • location
Der Laden an der Ecke hat eine gute Lage.
*The store on the corner has a good location.*

**Lager, das** [LAHgə*r*] *n.* • camp
Wo sollen wir unser Lager aufschlagen?
*Where should we make our camp?*

**Lamm, das** [LAHM] *n.* • lamb
**Lammschinken, der** *n.* • leg of lamb
Die Lämmer bleiben in der Nähe ihrer Mutter.
*The lambs stay close to their mothers.*

**Lampe, die** [LAHMpə] *n.* • lamp
Kannst du bitte die Lampe anmachen?
*Can you please turn on the lamp?*

**Land, das** [LAHNT] *n.* • land; country; countryside
**landen** *v.* • to land
**Landung, die** *n.* • landing
Die Vögel fliegen über das Land.
*The birds fly over the land.*

Mein Großvater wohnt auf dem Land.
*My grandfather lives in the country.*

Welche Länder haben Sie schon besucht?
*What countries have you visited?*

**Landkarte, die** [LAHNTkahrtə] *n.* • map
An der Wand hängt eine Landkarte von Frankreich.
*There is a map of France on the wall.*

**lang** [LAHNG] *adj.* • long
**eine lange Zeit** • a long time
Diese Schlange ist sehr lang.
*This snake is very long.*

**langsam** [LAHNGzahm] *adj.; adv.* • slow; slowly
Dieser langsame Zug wird uns verspätet ankommen lassen.
*This slow train will make us late.*

**langweilig** [LAHNGveili*sh*] *adj.* • boring
Dieses Buch ist zu langweilig, um es zu Ende zu lesen.
*This book is too boring to finish.*

**Lärm, der** [LAIRM] *n.* • noise
Wer macht den lauten Lärm?
*Who is making that loud noise?*

**lassen** [LAHsən] *v.* • to let; to leave; to allow
**allein lassen** • to let alone

| | |
|---|---|
| lasse | lassen |
| läßt | laßt |
| läßt | lassen |

Werden deine Eltern uns länger bleiben lassen?
*Will your parents let us stay longer?*

**Lastwagen, der** [LAHSTvahgən] *n.* • truck
**Lastwagenfahrer, der** *n.* • truck driver
Mein Onkel fährt einen Lastwagen.
*My uncle drives a truck.*

**laufen** [LAUFən] *v.* • to run

| | |
|---|---|
| laufe | laufen |
| läufst | lauft |
| läuft | laufen |

Lauf oder du verpaßt den Bus!
*Run or you'll miss the bus!*

**Laune, die** [LAUnə] *n.* • mood
**gute Laune, die** • good mood
**schlechte Laune, die** • bad mood
Meine Frau hat heute schlechte Laune.
*My wife is in a bad mood today.*

**laut** [LAUT] *adj.; adv.* • loud; aloud
**Lautsprecher, der** *n.* • loudspeaker
Er spricht zu laut.
*He speaks too loudly.*

Wiederholen Sie diese Sätze laut.
*Repeat these sentences aloud.*

**Leben, das** [LAIbən] *n.* • life
**leben** *v.* • to live
**lebhaft** *adj.* • lively
**seinen Lebensunterhalt verdienen** • to earn a living
Wasser ist notwendig für das Leben auf der Erde.
*Water is necessary for life on Earth.*

Tiere leben im Wald.
*Animals live in the forest.*

**Lebensmittel, die** [LAIbənsmitəl] *n. pl.* • food
**Lebensmittelgeschäft, das** *n.* • grocery store
Wir kaufen Lebensmittel im Lebensmittelgeschäft.
*We buy food at the grocery store.*

**leer** [LAIR] *adj.* • empty
Stellen Sie die leeren Flaschen auf den Ladentisch!
*Put the empty bottles on the counter.*

**legen** [LAIgən] *v.* • to lay; to put; to place

| | |
|---|---|
| lege | legen |
| legst | legt |
| legt | legen |

Marie legt ihre Bücher auf den Tisch.
*Marie lays her books on the table.*

**Legende, die** [leGENDə] *n.* • legend
Kennst du die Legende von König Arthur?
*Do you know the legend of King Arthur?*

**Lehnstuhl, der** [LAINshtool] *n.* • armchair
Setz' dich auf diesen bequemen Lehnstuhl!
*Sit down in this comfortable armchair.*

**lehren** [LAIrən] *v.* • to teach

| | |
|---|---|
| lehre | lehren |
| lehrst | lehrt |
| lehrt | lehren |

Meine Mutter lehrt an einem Gymnasium.
*My mother teaches high school.*

**Lehrer, der (-in, f.)** [LAIrər] *n.* • instructor; teacher
Mein Skilehrer ist großartig!
*My ski instructor is great!*

**leicht** [LEI*sh*T] *adj.* • easy; light
Diese Übungen sind zu leicht.
*These exercises are too easy.*

Der Koffer ist leicht.
*The suitcase is light.*

**leid tun** [LEIT toon] *v.* • to be sorry
Es tut mir leid, daß ich so spät komme.
*I am sorry I am late.*

**leider** [LEIdə*r*] *adv.* • unfortunately
Leider haben wir kein Auto.
*Unfortunately, we have no car.*

**leihen** [LEIən] *v.* • to lend

| | |
|---|---|
| leihe | leihen |
| leihst | leiht |
| leiht | leihen |

Kannst du mir einen Dollar leihen?
*Can you lend me a dollar?*

**leiten** [LEItən] *v.* • to direct
Der Polizist leitet den Verkehr.
*The police officer is directing traffic.*

**Leiter, die** [LEItə*r*] *n.* • ladder
Mein Vater steigt die Leiter hinauf.
*My father is climbing the ladder.*

**Lektion, die** [lekTSYOHN] *n.* • lesson
Verstehst du die Lektion?
*Do you understand the lesson?*

**Leopard, der** [laiohPAHRT] *n.* • leopard
Leoparden leben im Dschungel.
*Leopards live in the jungle.*

**lernen** [LERnən] *v.* • to learn
**auswendig lernen** • to learn by heart
**lernen wie . . .** • to learn how

lerne lernen
lernst lernt
lernt lernen

Man lernt viel, wenn man reist.
*You learn many things when you travel.*

**lesen** [LAIzən] *v.* • to read

lese lesen
liest lest
liest lesen

Welches Buch liest du gerade?
*What book are you reading?*

**letzt** [LETST] *adj.* • last
**Letzte (der, die, das)** *n.* • the last one

Ich steige an der letzten Bushaltestelle aus.
*I get off at the last stop on the bus line.*

**Leute, die** [LOItə] *n.* • people
**viele Leute** • a lot of people

Wo werden alle diese Leute sitzen?
*Where are all those people going to sit?*

**Licht, das** [LIS*H*T] *n.* • light

Ich brauche Licht, um zu lesen.
*I need light to read.*

**lieben** [LEEbən] *v.* • to love
**einander lieben** • to love each other
**Liebe, die** *n.* • love
**verliebt sein** • to be in love

liebe lieben
liebst liebt
liebt lieben

Wir lieben unsere Eltern.
*We love our parents.*

**lieber; liebe** [LEEbə*r*; LEEbə] *adj.* • dear

Der Brief fing an: “Liebe Mutti, ich vermisse dich.”
*The letter began, “Dear Mom, I miss you.”*

**Lieblings-** [LEEPlings] *comb. form* • favorite
Was ist deine Lieblingsfarbe?
*What is your favorite color?*

**Lied, das** [LEET] *n.* • song
Der Musiklehrer hat uns ein neues Lied beigebracht.
*The music teacher taught us a new song.*

**Lineal, das** [lineAHL] *n.* • ruler
Ich messe das Papier mit einem Lineal.
*I measure the paper with a ruler.*

**Linie, die** [LEENyə] *n.* • line
Schreiben Sie Ihren Namen auf die Linie.
*Write your name on the line.*

**linke, -r, -s** [LINGkə] *adj.* • left
**auf der linken Seite** • on the left-hand side
**linke Hand, die** • left hand
**links** *adv.* • on the left; to the left
Unser Haus steht auf der linken Seite der Straße.
*Our house is on the left side of the street.*

**Lippe, die** [LIPə] *n.* • lip
**Lippenstift, der** *n.* • lipstick
Im Winter habe ich trockene Lippen.
*I have dry lips in the winter.*

**Liste, die** [LIStə] *n.* • list
Ich habe eine lange Liste von Besorgungen zu machen.
*I have a long list of errands to run.*

**Loch, das** [LAW*KH*] *n.* • hole
Fall nicht in dieses Loch hinein!
*Don't fall in this hole!*

**Löffel, der** [L*ER*fəl] *n.* • spoon
Wie viele Löffel sind auf dem Tisch?
*How many spoons are there on the table?*

**Löwe, der** [L*ER*və] *n.* • lion
Es gibt Löwen in Afrika.
*There are lions in Africa.*

**Luft, die** [LUFT] *n.* • air
**mit Luftpost** • by air mail
Es ist zuviel Rauch in der Luft.
*There is too much smoke in the air.*

**lügen** [L*UE*gən] *v.* • to lie
**Lüge, die** *n.* • lie
**Lügner, der** *n.* • liar

| | |
|---|---|
| lüge | lügen |
| lügst | lügt |
| lügt | lügen |

Lügen Sie nicht! Sagen Sie mir die Wahrheit.
*Don't lie; tell me the truth.*

**Lutscher, der** [LUTshə*r*] *n.* • lollipop
Meine Kinder mögen Lutscher am liebsten.
*Lollipops are my children's favorite candy.*

# M

**machen** [MAH*kh*ən] *v.* • to do; to make; to take
**eine Reise machen** • to take a trip
**glücklich machen** • make happy

| | |
|---|---|
| mache | machen |
| machst | macht |
| macht | machen |

Wir werden unsere Arbeit machen.
*We are going to do our work.*

Sie machen einen Spaziergang im Wald.
*They are taking a walk in the woods.*

Ich mache jeden Morgen mein Bett.
*I make my bed every morning.*

**Mädchen, das** [MAIT*sh*ən] *n.* • girl
In diesem Zimmer sind drei Mädchen und zwei Jungen.
*There are three girls and two boys in the room.*

**Magen, der** [MAHgən] *n.* • stomach
**Magenschmerzen, die** *n.* • stomach ache
Mein Magen ist noch immer vom Abendessen voll.
*My stomach is still full from dinner.*

**mager** [MAHgə*r*] *adj.* • skinny; thin
Du siehst mager aus. Du solltest mehr essen.
*You look skinny. You should eat more.*

**Mahlzeit, die** [MAHLtseit] *n.* • meal
Wir haben unsere Hauptmahlzeit am Abend.
*We have our main meal in the evening.*

**Mai, der** [MEI] *n.* • May
Es gibt viele Blumen im Mai.
*There are many flowers in May.*

**Maiglöckchen, das** [maiGL*ER*K*sh*ən] *n.* • lily of the valley
Das Maiglöckchen blüht im Frühling.
*The lily of the valley blooms in the spring.*

**Mais, der** [MEIS] *n.* • corn
Dieser Mais kommt aus unserem Garten.
*This corn comes from our garden.*

**malen** [MAHlən] *v.* • to paint
**Maler, der (-in, f.)** *n.* • painter
**Gemälde, das** *n.* • painting

| | |
|---|---|
| male | malen |
| malst | malt |
| malt | malen |

Das Kind malt ein Bild.
*The child is painting a picture.*

**man** [MAHN] *indef. pron.* • you (one)
Man weiß nie.
*You never know.*

**manch** [MAHN*SH*] *adj.; pron.* • some; many
**manchmal** *adv.* • sometimes
Manche Leute spielen gern Tennis.
*Some people like to play tennis.*

Ich habe diese alte Geschichte so manches Mal gehört.
*I've heard that old story many times.*

**Mann, der** [MAHN] *n.* • man
Dieser Mann ist mein Onkel.
*This man is my uncle.*

**Mannschaft, die** [MAHNshahft] *n.* • team
Unsere Korbballmannschaft hat zwölf Spieler.
*Our basketball team has twelve players.*

**Mantel, der** [MAHNtəl] *n.* • coat
**Mäntel, die** *n. pl.* • coats
**Regenmantel, der** *n.* • raincoat
Dieser Mantel ist sehr warm.
*This coat is very warm.*

**Märchen, das** [MAIR*sh*ən] *n.* • fairy tale
Die Brüder Grimm sammelten viele Märchen.
*The Grimm brothers collected many fairy tales.*

**Marienkäfer, der** [mahREEənkaifər] *n.* • ladybug
Die Marienkäfer sind überall im Garten.
*The ladybugs are everywhere in the garden.*

**Markt, der** [MAHRKT] *n.* • market
Man kauft Früchte und Gemüse auf dem Markt.
*You buy fruits and vegetables at the market.*

**Marmelade, die** [mahrməLAHdə] *n.* • jam
Vincent streicht Marmelade auf sein Brot.
*Vincent puts jam on his bread.*

**März, der** [MAIRTS] *n.* • March
Der Frühling fängt im März an.
*Spring begins in March.*

**Maschine, die** [mahSHEEnə] *n.* • machine
**Nähmaschine, die** *n.* • sewing machine
**Waschmaschine, die** *n.* • washing machine
Kannst du die Waschmaschine reparieren?
*Can you fix the washing machine?*

**Mathematik, die** [mahtemahTEEK] *n.* • mathematics
Ingenieure müssen Mathematik studieren.
*Engineers need to study mathematics.*

**Maus, die** [MAUS] *n.* • mouse
Unsere Katze hat letzte Nacht eine Maus gefangen.
*Our cat caught a mouse last night.*

**Mechaniker, der** [me*SH*AHnikə*r*] *n.* • mechanic
Der Mechaniker repariert meinen Wagen.
*The mechanic repairs my car.*

**Medizin, die** [mediTSEEN] *n.* • medicine
Meine Großmutter kauft ihre Medizin in dieser Apotheke.
*My grandmother buys her medicine at this pharmacy.*

**Meer, das** [MAIR] *n.* • ocean
**Meerenge, die** *n.* • channel
**Meereskreuzer, der** *n.* • oceanliner
**Meeresküste, die** *n.* • seashore
Viele Schiffe fahren auf dem Meer.
*Many ships sail on the ocean.*

**Mehl, das** [MAIL] *n.* • flour
Man braucht Mehl, um Brot zu backen.
*You need flour to make bread.*

**mehr** [MAIR] *adj.* • more
**etwas mehr** • some more
**mehr oder weniger** • more or less
**mehr und mehr** • more and more
Geben Sie mir bitte etwas mehr Kaffee.
*Please let me have a little more coffee.*

**Meile, die** [MEIlə] *n.* • mile
Sie gehen täglich fünf Meilen.
*They walk five miles a day.*

**mein, -e** [MEIN, MEInə] *adj.* • my
Mein Bruder und meine Schwester kommen heute abend.
*My brother and sister are coming this evening.*

**meinen** [MEInən] *v.* • to mean

| | |
|---|---|
| meine | meinen |
| meinst | meint |
| meint | meinen |

Ich verstehe nicht, was Sie meinen.
*I don't understand what you mean.*

**Melone, die** [meLOHnə] *n.* • melon
Im Sommer essen wir Melonen aus unserem Garten.
*In the summer, we eat melons from our garden.*

**Messe, die** [MESə] *n.* • fair
Wir werden den Tag auf der Messe verbringen.
*We are going to spend the day at the fair.*

**messen** [MESən] *v.* • to measure

| | |
|---|---|
| messe | messen |
| mißt | meßt |
| mißt | messen |

Patrick mißt das Brett mit einem Lineal.
*Patrick is measuring the page with a ruler.*

**Messer, das** [MESər] *n.* • knife
**Taschenmesser, das** *n.* • pocket knife
Ich lege die Messer neben die Löffel.
*I put the knives next to the spoons.*

**Meter, der** [MAItər] *n.* • meter
Sie möchte zwei Meter von diesem Stoff kaufen.
*She would like to buy two meters of this material.*

**Mexiko** [MEKsikoh] *n.* • Mexico
**Mexikaner, der (-in, f.)** *n.* • Mexican (person)
**mexikanisch** *adj.* • Mexican
Mein Bruder fährt mit der Spanischklasse nach Mexiko.
*My brother is going to Mexico with the Spanish class.*

**mieten** [MEEtən] *v.* • to rent

| | |
|---|---|
| miete | mieten |
| mietest | mietet |
| mietet | mieten |

Mieten Sie dieses Haus oder gehört es Ihnen?
*Do you rent this home or own it?*

**Milch, die** [MIL*SH*] *n.* • milk
Das Kind trinkt Milch zu jeder Mahlzeit.
*The child drinks milk at each meal.*

**Million, die** [milYOHN] *n.* • million
Millionen von Sternen sind am Himmel.
*There are millions of stars in the sky.*

**minus** [MEEnus] *prep.* • minus
Vier minus zwei ist zwei.
*Four minus two is two.*

**Minute, die** [miNOOtə] *n.* • minute
Eine Minute hat sechzig Sekunden.
*There are sixty seconds in a minute.*

**mir** [MEER] *pron.* • me
Reichen Sie mir bitte das Buch.
*Hand me that book, please.*

**mischen** [MIshən] *v.* • to mix
Laut Rezept soll man alle Zutaten mischen.
*The recipe says one should mix all the ingredients.*

**mit** [MIT] *prep.* • with
  **mit dem Flugzeug** • by plane
  **mit dem Wagen** • by car
  **mit einem Boot** • by boat
  **mitgehen** *v.* • to go with
  **mit Luftpost** • by airmail
Joelle geht mit ihren Freunden tanzen.
*Joelle is going dancing with her friends.*

**mitbringen** [MITbringən] *v.* • to bring along
Er bringt seinen Freund zur Party mit.
*He is bringing his friend to the party.*

**Mitglied, das** [MITgleet] *n.* • member
Unser Club hat fünfzehn Mitglieder.
*There are fifteen members in our club.*

**Mittag, der** [MITahk] *n.* • noon; midday
Wir essen zu Mittag um 12 Uhr.
*We eat lunch at noon.*

**Mittagessen, das** [MITahkesən] *n.* • lunch
  **Mittagspause, die** *n.* • lunch time
  **zu Mittag essen** • to have lunch
Wir hatten Suppe und belegte Brote zum Mittagessen.
*We had soup and sandwiches for lunch.*

**Mitte, die** [MITə] *n.* • middle
Die Enten sind in der Mitte des Teichs.
*The ducks are in the middle of the lake.*

**mittel-** [MITəl] *adj.* • central; medium
  **Mitte, die** *n.* • center
  **Mittelamerika** *n.* • Central America
Er trägt einen mittelgroßen Pullover.
*He wears a medium sized sweater.*

**Mitternacht, die** [MITerna*kh*t] *n.* • midnight
Die Uhr schlägt zwölfmal um Mitternacht.
*The clock strikes twelve times at midnight.*

**Mittwoch, der** [MITvaw*kh*] *n.* • Wednesday
Mittwoch ist der dritte Tag der Arbeitswoche.
*Wednesday is the third day of the work week.*

**Möbel, die** [M*ER*bəl] *n. pl.* • furniture
Wir rückten die Möbel weg, um den Teppich zu reinigen.
*We moved the furniture to clean the rug.*

**Mode, die** [MOHdə] *n.* • fashion
Sind Hüte dieses Jahr in Mode?
*Are hats the fashion this year?*

**modern** [mawDERN] *adj.* • modern
Der neue Teil der Stadt hat moderne Gebäude.
*The new part of town has modern buildings.*

**mögen** [M*ER*gən] *v.* • to like
**Ich möchte** • I would like
**Wir möchten** • we would like

| | |
|---|---|
| mag | mögen |
| magst | mögt |
| mag | mögen |

Die Studenten mögen dieses Buch nicht.
*The students don't like this book.*

**Moment, der** [mawMENT] *n.* • moment
Wenn Sie einen Moment warten, werde ich Ihnen helfen.
*If you wait a moment I will help you.*

**Monat, der** [MOHnaht] *n.* • month
Der März ist der dritte Monat des Jahres.
*March is the third month of the year.*

**Mond, der** [MOHNT] *n.* • moon
Der Mond scheint heute nacht hell.
*The moon is shining brightly tonight.*

**Monster, das** [MAWNStər] *n.* • monster
In diesem Film gibt es ein Monster.
*There is a monster in this movie.*

**Montag, der** [MOHNtahk] *n.* • Monday
Montag ist der erste Arbeitstag der Woche.
*Monday is the first day of the work week.*

**Morgen, der** [MAWRgən] *n.* • morning
**Guten Morgen!** • Good morning!
**übermorgen** *adv.* • day after tomorrow
Ich lese jeden Morgen die Zeitung.
*I read the newspaper every morning.*

**morgens** [MAWRgəns] *adv.* • a.m.
Ich gehe um 8 Uhr morgens in die Schule.
*I go to school at 8 a.m.*

**Motor, der** [mohTOHR] *n.* • motor
**Motorrad, das** *n.* • motorcycle
Weißt du, wie ein Motor funktioniert?
*Do you know how a motor works?*

**Mücke, die** [M*UE*kə] *n.* • gnat; mosquito
Die Mücke hat mich gestochen.
*The gnat (mosquito) stung me.*

**müde** [M*UE*də] *adj.* • tired
Ich bin müde nach dem Spiel.
*I am tired after the game.*

**Müll, der** [M*UE*L] *n.* • garbage
**Mülleimer, der** *n.* • garbage can
Der Müll wird jeden Montag abgeholt.
*The trash is picked up every Monday.*

**Mund, der** [MUNT] *n.* • mouth
**Mund halten, den** • to shut up (person)
Der Zahnarzt bat mich, meinen Mund weit zu öffnen.
*The dentist told me to open my mouth wide.*

**Muschel, die** [MUshəl] *n.* • shell
Ich suche Muscheln am Strand.
*I look for shells on the beach.*

**Museum, das** [muTSAIum] *n.* • museum
Laßt uns heute zum Kunstmuseum gehen.
*Let's go to the art museum today.*

**Musik, die** [muZEEK] *n.* • music
**Musiker, der (-in, f.)** *n.* • musician
**Musikinstrumente, das** *n.* • musical instrument
Gefällt dir klassische Musik?
*Do you like classical music?*

**Muskel, der** [MUSkəl] *n.* • muscle
Welche Muskeln benutzt man, wenn man läuft?
*Which muscles do you use when you run?*

**müssen** [M*UE*sən] *v.* • to have to; must

| | |
|---|---|
| muß | müssen |
| mußt | müßt |
| muß | müssen |

Wir müssen sehr bald losfahren.
*We have to leave very soon.*

**mutig** [MOOti*sh*] *adj.* • courageous
Wir lasen eine Geschichte über einen mutigen Helden.
*We read a story about a courageous hero.*

**Mutter, die** [MUTə*r*] *n.* • mother
**Muttertag, der** *n.* • Mother's Day
**Mutti, die** *n.* • mama; mom
Wann haben deine Mutter und dein Vater geheiratet?
*When did your mother and father marry?*

Mutti (Mama) bittet mich immer, den Tisch zu decken.
*Mama always asks me to set the table.*

**Mütze, die** [M*UE*Tsə] *n.* • cap
Alle Mitglieder meiner Mannschaft tragen dieselben Mützen.
*All the members of my team wear the same caps.*

**mysteriös** [m*ue*steRY*ER*S] *adj.* • mysterious
Das ist wirklich eine mysteriöse Sache.
*That's really a mysterious thing.*

# N

**nach** [NAH*KH*] *prep.* • according to; after
**nach und nach** • little by little
Der Zeitung nach, wird es heute regnen.
*According to the newspaper, it is going to rain.*

Ich werde nach dir gehen.
*I'm going to leave after you.*

**Nachbar, der (-in, f.)** [NAH*KH*bahr] *n.* • neighbor
Unsere Nachbarn haben einen großen Hund.
*Our neighbors have a large dog.*

**Nachmittag, der** [NAH*KH*mitahk] *n.* • afternoon
Wir essen am frühen Nachmittag.
*We eat in the early afternoon.*

**Nachricht, die** [NAH*KH*ri*sh*t] *n.* • message
An der Tür hängt eine Nachricht.
*There is a message on the door.*

**Nachrichten, die** [NAH*KH*ri*sh*tən] *n. pl.* • news
**Fernsehnachrichten, die** *n. pl.* • T.V. news
Ich hoffe, daß die Nachrichten gut sind!
*I hope the news is good!*

**nächste; -r; -s** [NAIKStə; NAIKStə*r*; NAIKStəs] *adj.* • next
**nächstes Mal** • next time
Wer ist der nächste Teilnehmer?
*Who is the next participant?*

**Nacht, die** [NAH*KH*T] *n.* • night
**gestern nacht** • last night
**heute nacht** • tonight
**nächtlich; jede Nacht** • every night
**Nachttisch, der** *n.* • nightstand
Nachts ist der Himmel voller Sterne.
*At night the sky is full of stars.*

**Nachtisch, der** [NAH*KH*tish] *n.* • dessert
Dieser Nachtisch ist köstlich.
*This dessert is delicious.*

**Nadel, die** [NAHdəl] *n.* • needle
Die Näherin braucht eine Nähnadel und Zwirn.
*A seamstress needs a needle and thread.*

**Nagel, der** [NAHgəl] *n.* • nail
Hängen Sie das Bild an diesen Nagel.
*Hang the picture on that nail.*

**nahe** [NAHə] *adv.* • close
Ich wohne sehr nahe bei meinem Freund.
*I live very close to my friend.*

**Nähe, die** [NAIə] *n.* • neighborhood; proximity; vicinity
Wir wohnen in der Nähe des Flughafens.
*We live in the vicinity of the airport.*

**nähen** [NAIən] *v.* • to sew
**Nähmaschine, die** *n.* • sewing machine
Kannst du mir einen neuen Knopf annähen?
*Can you sew a new button on for me?*

**nähern, sich** [NAIern, zi*sh*] *v.* • to approach
Der Hund nähert sich der Katze.
*The dog is approaching the cat.*

**Name, der** [NAHmə] *n.* • name
**mein Name ist (or ich heiße)** • my name is...
**Nachname, der** *n.* • last name
**Vorname, der** *n.* • first name
Wiederholen Sie bitte Ihren Namen noch einmal.
*Please repeat your name again for me.*

**Nase, die** [NAHzə] *n.* • nose
Meine Nase ist verstopft, und ich kann nicht riechen.
*My nose is stuffed and I can't smell.*

**Nashorn, das** [NAHS-hawrn] *n.* • rhinoceros
Das Nashorn trägt ein Horn auf seiner Stirn.
*The rhinoceros has a horn on its head.*

**naß** [NAHS] *adj.* • wet
Meine Haare sind noch naß von der Dusche.
*My hair is still wet from the shower.*

**Nation, die** [nahtsYOHN] *n.* • nation
Die Geschichte dieser Nation ist sehr interessant.
*This nation's history is very interesting.*

**natürlich** [naht*UE*Rli*sh*] *adj.; adv.* • natural; naturally
**Natur, die** *n.* • nature
**natürlich nicht** • of course not
Ihre natürliche Schönheit bezauberte ihn.
*Her natural beauty facinated him.*

**Naturwissenschaft, die** [nahTOORvisənshahft] *n.* • natural science
Wir haben den Magnetismus im Naturwissenschaftsunterricht besprochen.
*We learned about magnetism in science class.*

**Nebel, der** [NAIbəl] *n.* • fog
Es ist schwer, bei diesem Nebel zu sehen.
*It's hard to see in this fog.*

**neben** [NAIbən] *prep.* • beside; next to
Mein Hund sitzt neben mir.
*My dog sits beside me.*

**necken** [NEKən] *v.* • to tease

| | |
|---|---|
| necke | necken |
| neckst | neckt |
| neckt | necken |

Necke deine Schwester nicht!
*Don't tease your sister!*

**Neffe, der** [NEFə] *n.* • nephew
Mein Neffe ist der Sohn meiner Schwester.
*My nephew is my sister's son.*

**nehmen** [NAImən] *v.* • to have (at mealtime); to take
**ein Bad nehmen** • to take a bath

| | |
|---|---|
| nehme | nehmen |
| nimmst | nehmt |
| nimmt | nehmen |

Ich nehme Eis zum Nachtisch.
*I'm having ice cream for dessert.*

Wir nahmen den Mittagszug.
*We took the train at noon.*

**nein** [NEIN] *adv.* • no
Nein, ich will noch nicht gehen.
*No, I don't want to leave yet.*

**Nelke, die** [NELkə] *n.* • carnation
Meine Mutter liebt rote Nelken.
*My mother likes red carnations.*

**nennen** [NENən] *v.* • to name; to call

nenne nennen
nennst nennt
nennt nennen

Das nennst du schön?
*You call that pretty?*

**Nest, das** [NEST] *n.* • nest
Ein Vogelnest ist im Baum.
*There is a bird's nest in the tree.*

**nett** [NET] *adj.* • nice
Sie hat immer ein nettes, freundliches Lächeln.
*She always has a nice, friendly smile.*

**neu** [NOI] *adj.* • new
Hast du neue Kleidung für die Schule gekauft?
*Did you buy any new clothes for school?*

**neugierig** [NOIgeeri*sh*] *adj.* • curious
Es wird behauptet, daß Katzen neugierig sind.
*They say that cats are curious.*

**neun** [NOIN] *adj.* • nine
Eine Baseballmannschaft hat neun Spieler.
*There are nine players on a baseball team.*

**neunzehn** [NOINtsain] *adj.* • nineteen
Wir sind neunzehn in unserem Französischclub.
*There are nineteen of us in the French club.*

**neunzig** [NOINtsi*sh*] *adj.* • ninety
Der Film dauerte neunzig Minuten lang.
*The movie lasted for ninety minutes.*

**nicht** [NI*SH*T] *adv.* • not
**nicht mehr** • no longer
**nicht wahr** • is it not?; isn't it?; right?

**noch nicht** • not yet
**selbstverständlich nicht** • of course not
**überhaupt nicht** • not at all
Die schlechten Nachrichten werden dir nicht gefallen.
*You're not going to like the bad news.*

**Nichte, die** [NI*SH*tə] *n.* • niece
Meine Nichte ist die Tochter meines Bruders.
*My niece is my brother's daughter.*

**nichts** [NI*SH*TS] *pron.* • nothing
Nichts ist wichtiger als gute Gesundheit.
*There's nothing more important than good health.*

**nie; niemals** [NEE; NEEmahls] *adv.* • never
**fast niemals** • hardly ever
**niemand** *pron.* • no one; nobody
Es regnet fast nie in der Wüste.
*It almost never rains in the desert.*

**Niederlande, die** [NEEderlandə] *n. pl.* • Netherlands
**Niederländer, der (-in, f.)** *n.* • person from the Netherlands
Ich habe einen Freund in den Niederlanden.
*I have a friend in the Netherlands.*

**niedlich** [NEETli*sh*] *adj.* • cute
Dieser junge Hund (Hündchen) ist so niedlich.
*This puppy is so cute.*

**niedrig** [NEETri*sh*] *adj.* • low
Neben der Straße ist eine niedrige Mauer.
*There is a low wall next to the street.*

**niemals** See *nie*.

**niemand** See *nie*.

**Nilpferd, das** [NEELPfert] *n.* • hippopotamus
Das Nilpferd ist ein großes Tier.
*The hippopotamus is a large animal.*

**noch** [NAW*KH*] *adv.* • still
**noch nicht** • not yet
Er erinnerte sich nach vielen Jahren noch an meinen Namen.
*He still remembered my name after many years.*

Sind sie noch nicht hier?
*Aren't they here yet?*

**noch ein; -e; -es** [NAW*KH* ein; einə; eints] *pron.* • another
**noch einmal** • once more
Ich brauche noch eine Stunde, um die Arbeit zu beenden.
*I need another hour to finish the work.*

**nördlich** [N*ER*Dli*sh*] *adv.* • north
Belgien liegt nördlich von Frankreich.
*Belgium is to the north of France.*

**Norwegen** [NAWRvaigən] *n.* • Norway
**Norweger, der (-in, f.)** *n.* • Norwegian (person)
**norwegisch** *adj.* • Norwegian
Wir gehen in Norwegen Ski laufen.
*We are going skiing in Norway.*

**Notizbuch, das** [nawTEETSboo*kh*] *n.* • notebook
**Notizblock, der** *n.* • notepad
Ich habe für jede Klasse ein Notizbuch.
*I have a notebook for each class.*

**notwendig** [NOHTvendi*sh*] *adj.* • necessary
Kalzium ist notwendig, um starke Knochen zu bekommen.
*Calcium is necessary for strong bones.*

**November, der** [nawFEMbər] *n.* • November
Der November ist der Monat vor Weihnachten.
*November is the month before Christmas.*

**Nudeln, die** [NOOdəln] *n.* • noodles
Laß uns Butter auf die Nudeln tun.
*Let's put butter on the noodles.*

**null** [NUL] *adj.* • zero
Zwei minus zwei ist null.
*Two minus two is zero.*

**Nummer, die** [NUMər] *n.* • number
Geben Sie mir bitte Ihre Telefonnummer.
*Please give me your phone number.*

**nur** [NOOR] *adv.* • only
Ich spreche nur Englisch.
*I can only speak English.*

**nützlich** See *benutzen.*

**nutzlos** See *benutzen.*

# O

**ob** [AWP] *conj.* • whether
  **als ob** • as if
Johann weiß nicht, ob er gehen kann oder nicht.
*John doesn't know whether he can go or not.*

**oben** [OHbən] *prep.* • up; upstairs; at the top
Unsere Schlafzimmer sind oben.
*Our bedrooms are upstairs.*

**oder** [OHdər] *conj.* • or
Willst du Fisch oder Huhn?
*Do you want fish or chicken?*

**öffentlich** [*ER*Fəntlis*h*] *adj.* • public
Dieses ist eine öffentliche Versammlung, und jeder ist willkommen.
*This is a public meeting and everyone is welcome.*

**öffnen** [*ER*Fnən] *v.* • to open
**offen** *adj.* • open
**Öffnung, die** *n.* • opening

| | |
|---|---|
| öffne | öffnen |
| öffnest | öffnet |
| öffnet | öffnen |

Öffne das Fenster und laß frische Luft herein.
*Open the window and let in the breeze.*

**oft** [AWFT] *adv.* • often
**Wie oft?** • How often?
Ich frage mich oft, wie es meinem alten Freund geht.
*I often wonder how my old friend is doing.*

**Ohr, das** [OHR] *n.* • ear
**Ohrring, der** *n.* • earring
Das laute Geräusch tat meinen Ohren weh.
*The loud noise hurt my ears.*

**O.K.** [awKAI] *interj.* • O.K.
O.K.! Du kannst mit mir kommen.
*O.K! You can come with me.*

**Oktober, der** [awkTOHbər] *n.* • October
Im Oktober haben wir Schule.
*We are in school during October.*

**Öl, das** [*ER*L] *n.* • oil
Um eine "Sauce Vinaigrette" zu machen, braucht man Öl und Essig.
*To make a vinaigrette sauce, you need oil and vinegar.*

**Omelett, das** [awmLET] *n.* • omelet
Wir brauchen Eier, um ein Omelett zu machen.
*We need eggs to make an omelet.*

**Omnibus, der** [AWMnibus] *n.* • bus (city bus; schoolbus)
Wir warten an der Haltestelle auf den Omnibus.
*We are waiting for the bus at the depot.*

**Onkel, der** [AWNGkəl] *n.* • uncle
Wo wohnen deine Tante und dein Onkel?
*Where do your aunt and uncle live?*

**Oper, die** [OHpə*r*] *n.* • opera
Kennst du die Bizet Oper "Carmen"?
*Do you know Bizet's opera "Carmen"?*

**Orange, die** [awRAWNzhə] *n.* • orange
**Orangensaft, der** *n.* • orange juice
Diese Orangen sind sehr saftig und süß.
*These oranges are very juicy and sweet.*

**Orchester, das** [awrKESTə*r*] *n.* • orchestra
Das Orchester gab heute abend ein Konzert.
*The orchestra gave a concert tonight.*

**organisieren** [awrgahniZEErən] *v.* • to organize
**Oranisation, die** *n.* • organization
Der Sportlehrer organisiert die Spiele.
*The physical education teacher organizes the games.*

**Original-** [awrigiNAHL] *comb. form* • original
**Originalität, die** *n.* • originality
Ist dies ein Originalgemälde?
*Is this an original painting?*

**Osten, der** [AWStən] *n.* • east
Die Sonne geht im Osten auf.
*The sun rises in the east.*

**Österreich** [*ER*Stəreis*h*] *n.* • Austria
**Österreicher, der (-in, f.)** *n.* • Austrian (person)
**österreichisch** *n.* • Austrian
Deutsch ist die Landessprache Österreichs.
*German is the national language of Austria.*

**Oval, das** [ohVAHL] *n.* • oval
Die Rennbahn ist in der Form eines Ovals.
*The racetrack is in the shape of an oval.*

**Ozean, der** [OHtseahn] *n.* • ocean
Man muß den Ozean überqueren, um von den U.S.A. nach Frankreich zu kommen.
*To go to France from the U.S., you must cross the Atlantic Ocean.*

# P

**Paar, das** [PAHR] *n.* • pair
Ich brauche ein Paar Stiefel.
*I need a pair of boots.*

**packen** [PAHKən] *v.* • to pack

| | |
|---|---|
| packe | packen |
| packst | packt |
| packt | packen |

Ich kann meine Koffer in einer Stunde packen.
*I can pack my bags in one hour.*

**Paket, das** [pahKAIT] *n.* • package
Ich habe das Paket, das du geschickt hast, bekommen.
*I received the package you sent in the mail.*

**Palast, der** [pahLAHST] *n.* • palace
Der Palast ist riesig!
*The palace is huge!*

**Pampelmuse, die** [PAHMpəlmoozə] *n.* • grapefruit
Ich esse gern Pampelmusen zu meinem Frühstück.
*I like grapefruit with my breakfast.*

**Panther, der** [PAHNtər] *n.* • panther
Der Panther ähnelt einem Leoparden, ist aber schwarz.
*The panther resembles a leopard but is black.*

**Papagei, der** [pahpahGEI] *n.* • parrot
Dieser Papagei ist ein schöner Vogel.
*This parrot is a beautiful bird.*

**Papier, das** [pahPEER] *n.* • paper
**Blatt Papier, ein** • a sheet of paper
**Papierkorb, der** *n.* • wastebasket
Ich brauche etwas Papier zum Zeichnen.
*I need some paper to draw on.*

**Papier (drachen), der** [pahPEERdrah*kh*ən] *n.* • kite
Es muß windig sein, um einen Papierdrachen fliegen zu lassen.
*It must be windy to fly a kite.*

**Paprika, der** [PAHprikah] *n.* • green pepper; paprika
Paprika schmeckt gut auf Pizza.
*Green pepper tastes good on pizza.*

**Parade, die** [pahRAHdə] *n.* • parade
Sie feiern jedes Jahr mit einer Parade.
*They celebrate every year with a big parade.*

**Parfüm, das** [pahrF*UE*M] *n.* • perfume
Dieses französische Parfüm hat einen herrlichen Duft.
*This French perfume smells lovely.*

**Park, der** [PAHRK] *n.* • park
Wir lassen unsere Drachen im Park fliegen.
*We are going to fly our kites in the park.*

**Party, die** [PAHRtee] *n.* • party
Wir haben heute abend eine Party.
*We are having a party tonight.*

**Paß, der** [PAHS] *n.* • passport
Ich brauche einen Paß, um zu reisen.
*I need a passport to travel.*

**Passagier, der (-in, f.)** [pahsahZHEER] *n.* • passenger
Die Passagiere sind im Zug.
*The passengers are on the train.*

**Paste, die** [PAHStə] *n.* • paste
Mit dieser neuen Zahnpaste werden meine Zähne ganz weiß.
*My teeth are getting really white with this new toothpaste.*

**Pazifik, der** [paTSIfik] *n.* • Pacific Ocean
Hawaii liegt in der Mitte des Pazifiks.
*Hawaii is in the middle of the Pacific Ocean.*

**perfekt** [perFEKT] *adj.* • perfect
Der Künstler arbeitete an der Skulptur, bis sie perfekt war.
*The artist worked on the sculpture till it was perfect.*

**Person, die** [perZOHN] *n.* • person
**Persönlichkeit, die** *n.* • personality
Wie heißt diese Person?
*What is this person's name?*

**Pfad, der** [PFAHT] *n.* • path
Führt dieser Pfad wirklich aus dem Wald heraus?
*Does this path really lead out of the woods?*

**Pfadfinder, der** [PFAHTfindər] *n.* • scout
Meine Brüder gehören zu den Pfadfindern.
*My brothers are Boy Scouts.*

**Pfanne, die** [PFAHNə] *n.* • pan
Vati brät Eier in einer Pfanne.
*Dad is frying eggs in a pan.*

**Pfannkuchen, der** [PFAHNkoo*kh*ən] *n.* • pancake
Ich esse gern Pfannkuchen zum Frühstück.
*I love pancakes for breakfast.*

**Pfeffer, der** [PFEFə*r*] *n.* • pepper (black)
Reichen Sie mir bitte den Pfeffer und das Salz.
*Please pass the pepper and salt.*

**Pfeife, die** [PFEIfə] *n.* • pipe
Mein Großvater raucht Pfeife.
*My grandfather smokes a pipe.*

**pfeifen** [PFEIfən] *v.* • to whistle

| | |
|---|---|
| pfeife | pfeifen |
| pfeifst | pfeift |
| pfeift | pfeifen |

Ich bringe meinem Bruder bei zu pfeifen.
*I am teaching my brother to whistle.*

**Pfeil, der** [PFEIL] *n.* • arrow
Johann schießt einen Pfeil auf die Zielscheibe.
*John is shooting an arrow at the target.*

**Pferd, das** [PFERT] *n.* • horse
**Pferderennen, das** *n.* • horse race
Ich ritt mit meinem Pferd aus der Scheune.
*I rode my horse out of the barn.*

**Pfirsich, der** [PFIRzi*sh*] *n.* • peach
Sind diese Pfirsiche reif?
*Are these peaches ripe?*

**Pflanze, die** [PFLAHNtsə] *n.* • plant
**pflanzen** *v.* • to plant
Die meisten Pflanzen brauchen Sonnenlicht.
*Most plants need sunlight.*

**Pflaume, die** [PFLAUmə] *n.* • plum
Es gibt in diesem Jahr nur wenige Pflaumen.
*Plums are very scarce this year.*

**pflücken** [PFL*UE*kən] *v.* • to pick
Ich pflücke nur ungern Erdbeeren.
*I don't like to pick strawberries.*

**Pfote, die** [PFOHtə] *n.* • paw
Der Hund hat eine entzündete Pfote.
*The dog has a sore paw.*

**Pfund, das** [PFUNT] *n.* • pound
Das deutsche Pfund und das amerikanische Pfund sind nicht identisch.
*The German pound and the American pound are not identical.*

**Physik, die** [F*UE*zik] *n.* • physics
Wir haben das Newtonsche Gesetz im Physikunterricht besprochen.
*We studied Newton's laws in physics class.*

**Picknick, das** [PIKnik] *n.* • picnic
**ein Picknick machen** • to go on a picnic
Ich hoffe, der Regen wird euer Picknick nicht ruinieren.
*I hope the rain doesn't spoil your picnic.*

**Pilot, der (in, f.)** [piLOHT] *n.* • pilot
Er ist Pilot bei der Air France.
*He is a pilot for Air France.*

**Pilz, der** [PILTS] *n.* • mushroom
Möchten Sie frische Pilze in ihrem Salat?
*Do you want fresh mushrooms on your salad?*

**Plan, der** [PLAHN] *n.* • schedule; plan
Wie sieht dein Plan für diese Woche aus?
*What is your schedule for this week?*

Habt ihr Pläne für das Wochenende?
*Do you have plans for the weekend?*

**Planet, der** [plahNAIT] *n.* • planet
Welcher Planet ist der Sonne am nächsten?
*Which planet is nearest the sun?*

**Plastik, das** [PLAHStik] *n.* • plastic
Dieses Spielzeug ist aus Plastik.
*This toy is made of plastic.*

**Platte, die** [PLAHTə] *n.* • plate; dish; record
**Plattenspieler, der** *n.* • record player
Wir brauchen eine große Platte für den Truthahn.
*We need a large plate for the turkey.*

**Platz, der** [PLAHTS] *n.* • place; seat; (town) square
Laßt uns einen ebenen, trockenen Platz für das Zelt suchen.
*Let's find a flat, dry place for the tent.*

Ist der Platz neben Ihnen besetzt?
*Is the seat next to you taken?*

**Platzdecke, die** [PLAHTSdekə] *n.* • placemat
Die Platzdecke ist auf dem Tisch.
*The placemat is on the table.*

**plötzlich** [PL*ER*TSli*sh*] *adv.* • suddenly; all at once
Plötzlich sprang er von seinem Sitz auf.
*Suddenly he jumped up from his seat.*

**Polen** [POHlən] *n.* • Poland
**Pole, der; Polin, die** *n.* • Pole
**polnisch** *adj.* • Polish
Warschau ist die Hauptstadt von Polen.
*Warsaw is the capital of Poland.*

**Polizei, die** [pawliTSAI] *n.* • police
**Polizeiamt, das** *n.* • police department
**Polizeibeamte, der (-in, f.)** *n.* • police official
**Polizeiwache, die** *n.* • police station
**Polizist, der; Polizistin, die** *n.* • police officer; policeman; policewoman
Der Polizist half uns, unser Hotel zu finden.
*The police officer helped us find our hotel.*

**Portugal** [PAWRtugahl] *n.* • Portugal
**Portugiese, der (-in, f.)** *n.* • Portuguese (person)
**portugiesisch** *adj.* • Portuguese
Wir werden unsere Ferien in Portugal verbringen.
*We are going to spend our vacation in Portugal.*

**Posaune, die** [pohZAUnə] *n.* • trombone
Sein Bruder spielt Posaune.
*His brother plays the trombone.*

**Post, die** [PAWST] *n.* • mail
**Postbote, der** *n.* • mail carrier
Habe ich heute Post bekommen?
*Did I get any mail today?*

**Postamt, das** [PAWSTahmt] *n.* • post office
Das Postamt liegt an derselben Straße wie das Rathaus.
*The post office is on the same street as the town hall.*

**Postkarte, die** [PAWSTkahrtə] *n.* • postcard
Ich habe während meiner Reise eine Postkarte nach Hause geschickt.
*I sent a postcard home during my trip.*

**prachtvoll** [PRAH*KH*Tfawl] *adj.* • magnificent
Diese Pferde sind prachtvoll!
*These horses are magnificent!*

**praktisch** [PRAHKtish] *adj.* • practical
Es ist nicht praktisch anzurufen, aber schreiben Sie uns bitte.
*It isn't be practical to call, but please write to us.*

**Präsident, der** [praiziDENT] *n.* • president
Der Präsident hält eine Rede im Fernsehen.
*The president is giving a speech on T.V.*

**Preis, der** [PREIS] *n.* • price; prize
Der Preis für dieses Fahrrad ist zu hoch.
*The price of this bike is too high.*

Der erste Preis ist ein neues Auto.
*The first prize is a new car.*

**Prinz, der** [PRINTS] *n.* • prince
**Prinzessin, die** *n.* • princess
Die Kinder eines Königs nennt man Prinz und Prinzessin.
*The prince and princess are the king's children.*

**privat** [priVAHT] *adj.* • private
Öffnen Sie diesen Brief nicht; er ist privat!
*Don't open this letter, it's private!*

**probieren** [prawBEErən] *v.* • to taste
Probiere diesen Käse! Er ist wirklich gut!
*Taste this cheese! It's really good!*

**Problem, das** [prohBLAIM] *n.* • problem
Lassen Sie mich beim Lösen des Problems helfen.
*Let me help you solve the problem.*

**Provinz, die** [prohVINTS] *n.* • province
Wie viele Provinzen hat Kanada?
*How many provinces are there in Canada?*

**prüfen** [PR*UE*fən] *v.* • to inspect
**Prüfung, die** *n.* • inspection
Er prüft seine Arbeit sorgfältig.
*He inspects his work with care.*

**Prüfung, die** [PR*UE*fung] *n.* • test; exam
**eine Prüfung ablegen** • to take an exam
**eine Prüfung bestehen** • to pass an exam
**eine Prüfung nicht bestehen; durch eine Prüfung fallen** • to fail an exam
Wir haben morgen drei Prüfungen!
*We have three tests tomorrow!*

**Psychologie, die** [ps*ue*kawlawGEE] *n.* • psychology
Meine Schwester studiert Psychologie an der Universität.
*My sister is studying psychology at the university.*

**Pullover, der** [PULohvə*r*] *n.* • sweater
Ich friere! Wo ist mein Pullover?
*I'm cold! Where is my sweater?*

**Puppe, die** [PUpə] *n.* • doll
**Puppenhaus, das** *n.* • dollhouse
Meine kleine Schwester legt ihre Puppen auf ihr Bett.
*My little sister puts her dolls on her bed.*

**Purpur, der** [PURpur] *n.* • purple
Man sagt, daß purpur die Farbe des Königtums sei.
*Purple is said to be the color of royalty.*

**Puzzle, das** [PAHzəl] *n.* • puzzle
Dieses Puzzle hat 1.000 Teile.
*This puzzle has 1000 pieces.*

# Q

**quadratisch** [kvaDRAHtish] *adj.* • square
Die Serviette ist quadratisch.
*The napkin is square.*

# R

**Rad, das** [RAHT] *n.* • wheel; bicycle; bike
**radfahren** *v.* • to ride a bicycle
**Steuerrad, das** *n.* • steering wheel
Ein Fahrrad hat zwei Räder.
*A bicycle has two wheels.*

Ich habe ein neues Rad zum Geburtstag bekommen.
*I got a new bike for my birthday.*

**Radio, das** [RAHdyoh] *n.* • radio
Sie hören Radio.
*They are listening to the radio.*

**Rakete, die** [rahKAItə] *n.* • rocket
Der Wettersatellit wurde von einer Rakete abgeschossen.
*The weather satellite was launched by a rocket.*

**Rasen, der** [RAHzən] *n.* • lawn
Ich mähe den Rasen, wenn das Gras zu lang wird.
*I mow the lawn when the grass gets too high.*

**rasieren, sich** [rahZEErən, zi*sh*] *v.* • to shave
Vater rasiert sich am Morgen.
*Father shaves in the morning.*

**Rasierer, der** [raZEErə*r*] *n.* • razor
Mein Bruder rasiert sich mit einem elektrischen Rasierer.
*My brother shaves with an electric razor.*

**raten** [RAHtən] *v.* • to guess; to advise

| | |
|---|---|
| rate | raten |
| rätst | ratet |
| rät | raten |

Kannst du raten, wie alt ich bin?
*Can you guess how old I am?*

**Ratgeber, der** [RAHTgaibə*r*] *n.* • adviser
Der Präsident hat mehrere Ratgeber.
*The president has several advisers.*

**Rathaus, das** [RAHThaus] *n.* • city hall
Das Rathaus liegt in der Stadmitte.
*City hall is in the middle of town.*

**Ratte, die** [RAHTə] *n.* • rat
Ich hasse Ratten, aber Mäuse machen mir nichts aus.
*I hate rats, but I don't mind mice.*

**rauben** [RAUbən] *v.* • to rob
**Räuber, der (-in, f.)** *n.* • robber
**Raubüberfall, der** *n.* • robbery
Der Mann hat mich rauben wollen.
*The man wanted to rob me.*

**Rauch, der** [RAU*KH*] *n.* • smoke
**rauchen** *v.* • to smoke
**Rauchen Verboten!** • no smoking
Heute gibt es viel Rauch am Himmel.
*There's a lot of smoke in the air today.*

**Raum, der** [RAUM] *n.* • space
**Raumschiff, das** *n.* • space ship
Der Satellit fliegt durch den Raum.
*The satellite flies through space.*

**Raupe, die** [RAUpə] *n.* • caterpillar
Die Raupe verwandelt sich in einen Schmetterling.
*A caterpillar changes into a butterfly.*

**Rechenmaschine, die** [RE*sh*ənmasheenə] *n.* • calculator
Heute verlassen sich die Leute auf die Rechenmaschine.
*Today people rely on the calculator.*

**Rechnung, die** [RE*SH*nung] *n.* • check (restaurant); bill
Der Kellner bringt die Rechnung nach dem Essen.
*The waiter brings the check after the meal.*

**rechte** [RE*SH*tə] *adj.* • right
**recht haben** • to be right (correct)
**rechte Hand, die** • the right hand
**rechts (von)** • to the right (of)
Die meisten Leute schreiben mit der rechten Hand.
*Most people write with their right hand.*

Ich weiß nicht, ob ich recht habe.
*I don't know if I'm right.*

**Rechteck, das** [RE*SH*tek] *n.* • rectangle
Ein Rechteck hat vier Seiten.
*A rectangle has four sides.*

**Rechtsanwalt, der (-wältin, f.)** [RE*SH*TSahnvahlt] *n.* • lawyer
Die Rechtsanwälte sind beim Gericht.
*The lawyers are at the court house.*

**Rede, die** [RAIdə] *n.* • speech
**eine Rede halten** • to give a speech
Deine Rede ist sehr klar und deutlich.
*Your speech is very clear and distinct.*

**reden** [RAIdən] *v.* • to talk
Der Junge redet zuviel.
*The boy talks too much.*

**Regal, das** [reGAHL] *n.* • shelf
Die Tassen stehen auf dem untersten Regal.
*The cups are on the bottom shelf.*

**Regel, die** [RAIgəl] *n.* • rule
Hast du die Spielregeln gelernt?
*Have your learned the rules of the game?*

**Regen, der** [RAIgən] *n.* • rain
  **es regnet** • it's raining
  **regnen** *v.* • to rain
  **Regenbogen, der** *n.* • rainbow
  **Regenmantel, der** *n.* • raincoat
  **Regenschirm, der** *n.* • umbrella
Das Gras ist naß vom Regen.
*The grass is wet from the rain.*

Es regnet! Wo ist der Regenschirm?
*It's raining! Where is the umbrella?*

**Regierung, die** [reGEErung] *n.* • government
Der Bürgermeister steht der Regierung der Stadt vor.
*The mayor is the head of the city's government.*

**Reh, das** [RAI] *n.* • deer
Das Reh steht im Wald.
*The deer is standing in the forest.*

**reich** [REI*SH*] *adj.* • rich
Mein reicher Onkel besitzt fünf Autos.
*My rich uncle owns five cars.*

**reichen** [REI*sh*ən] *v.* • to extend
Peter reicht Marie seine Hand.
*Peter extends his hand to Marie.*

**reif** [REIF] *adj.* • ripe
Ist diese Melone schon reif?
*Is this melon ripe yet?*

**Reifen, der** [REIfən] *n.* • tire
Das Auto hat einen platten Reifen!
*The car has a flat tire!*

**Reihe, die** [REIə] *n.* • row
Im Theater sind dreißig Sitzreihen.
*There are thirty rows of seats in the theater.*

**reinigen** [REInigən] *v.* • to clean
Wir reinigen das Haus jede Woche.
*We clean the house each week.*

**Reis, der** [REIS] *n.* • rice
Ich mag gern Huhn mit Reis.
*I like chicken with rice.*

**Reise, die** [REIzə] *n.* • trip; journey
**auf einer Reise** • on a trip
**eine Reise machen** • to take a trip
Wir brechen zu einer Reise auf.
*We are leaving on a trip.*

Er macht eine lange Reise durch Nordamerika.
*He is taking a long journey across North America.*

**reisen** [REIzən] *v.* • to travel
**Reisende, der (die, f.)** *n.* • traveler
Wir reisen übermorgen nach Italien.
*We're traveling to Italy the day after tomorrow.*

**reiten** [REItən] *v.* • to ride (a horse)

| | |
|---|---|
| reite | reiten |
| reitest | reitet |
| reitet | reiten |

Mein Sohn will dieses Pferd reiten.
*My son wants to ride this horse.*

**reparieren** [repahREErən] *v.* • to fix; to repair
Können Sie den platten Reifen reparieren?
*Can you fix the flat tire?*

**Restaurant, das** [restawRAHNT] *n.* • restaurant
Wir kennen ein gutes Restaurant, das nicht zu teuer ist.
*We know a good restaurant that's not too expensive.*

**retten** [REtən] *v.* • to save; to rescue

rette retten
rettest rettet
rettet retten

Der Feuerwehrmann rettete das Leben des Kindes.
*The fire fighter saved the child's life.*

**Rettich, der** [REti*sh*] *n.* • radish
Diese Rettiche sind aus unserem Garten.
*These radishes are from our garden.*

**Rezept, das** [reTSEPT] *n.* • recipe
Nach dem Rezept braucht man ein ganzes Huhn.
*The recipe calls for one whole chicken.*

**richten** [RI*SH*tən] *v.* • to adjust; to direct; to prepare; to judge

richte richten
richtest richtet
richtet richten

Können Sie mich auf den Bahnhof richten?
*Can you direct me to the train station?*

**Richter, der** [RI*SH*tə*r*] *n.* • judge
Der Richter unterweist die Geschworenen.
*The judge instructs the jury.*

**richtig** [RI*SH*ti*sh*] *adj.* • correct
Ist diese Antwort richtig?
*Is this answer correct?*

**riechen (an)** [REE*sh*ən] *v.* • to smell

rieche riechen
riechst riecht
riecht riechen

Die Dame riecht an den Blumen.
*The lady is smelling the flowers.*

**Riese, der** [REEzə] *n.* • giant
Es gibt einen Riesen in diesem Märchen.
*There is a giant in this fairy tale.*

**Rindfleisch, das** [RINTfleish] *n.* • beef
**der Rinderbraten** *n.* • roast beef
Ich ziehe Rindfleisch Huhn vor.
*I prefer beef to chicken.*

**Ring, der** [RING] *n.* • ring
Sie trägt einen Ehering an der linken Hand.
*She is wearing a wedding ring on her left hand.*

**Ritter, der** [RITər] *n.* • knight
Ich habe in der Bibliothek über Ritter und Rüstungen gelesen.
*I read about knights and armor at the library.*

**Rock, der** [RAWK] *n.* • skirt
Sie trägt einen neuen Rock für die Party.
*She is wearing a new skirt to the party.*

**roh** [ROH] *adj.* • raw
Man kann Karotten sowohl roh, als auch gekocht essen.
*You can eat carrots raw or cooked.*

**Rolle, die** [RAWLə] *n.* • role (theater)
**Hauptrolle, die** *n.* • the lead role
Welche Rolle spielst du in dem Stück?
*Which role do you have in the play?*

**rollen** [RAWLən] *v.* • to roll
**Rollschuh, der** *n.* • roller skate
**Rollstuhl, der** *n.* • wheel chair
**Rolltreppe, die** *n.* • escalator

| | |
|---|---|
| rolle | rollen |
| rollst | rollt |
| rollt | rollen |

Der Ball rollte auf die Straße.
*The ball rolled into the street.*

**Roman, der** [rohMAHN] *n.* • novel
**Detektivroman, der** *n.* • mystery novel
Ich kaufte einen Roman, um ihn im Flugzeug zu lesen.
*I bought a novel to read on the plane.*

**rosa** [ROHzah] *adj.* • pink
Das kleine Mädchen hat rosa Backen.
*The little girl has pink cheeks!*

**Rose, die** [ROHzə] *n.* • rose
Ich mag den Duft von Rosen.
*I love the smell of roses.*

**Rosine, die** [rawZEEnə] *n.* • raisin
Mutter hat einen Kuchen mit vielen Rosinen gebacken.
*Mom baked a cake with lots of raisins.*

**rot** [ROHT] *adj.* • red
**erröten; rot werden** *v.* • to turn red; to blush
**rothaarig** *adj.* • red-headed
Gleich nach Sonnenuntergang ist der Himmel ganz rot geworden.
*The sky turned red just after sunset.*

**Rücken, der** [R*UE*Kən] *n.* • back
Ich habe furchtbare Schmerzen im Rücken.
*I have awful pains in my back.*

**rufen** [ROOfən] *v.* • to call; to shout

| | |
|---|---|
| rufe | rufen |
| rufst | ruft |
| ruft | rufen |

Mutter ruft uns, wenn das Essen fertig ist.
*Mom calls us when dinner is ready.*

**Ruhe, die** [rooə] *n.* • silence
Der Lehrer bat die Klasse um Ruhe.
*The teacher asked the class for silence.*

**ruhig** [ROOi*sh*] *adj.* • quiet; silent
Wenn alle schlafen, ist das Haus ruhig.
*When everyone is sleeping the house is quiet.*

**ruhig sein** [ROOi*sh* zein] *v.* • to be quiet
Die Schüler sind ruhig, wenn der Lehrer ins Klassenzimmer kommt.
*The pupils are quiet when the teacher enters the classroom.*

**rund** [RUNT] *adj.* • round
Gib mir bitte das runde Tablett.
*Please hand me the round tray.*

**Rußland** [RUSlahnt] *n.* • Russia
**Russe, der (-in, f.)** *n.* • Russian (person)
**russisch** *adj.* • Russian
Rußland ist ein riesiges Land.
*Russia is a huge country.*

Das russische Ballett ist eine Woche lang in New York.
*The Russian ballet is in New York for a week.*

# S

**Saft, der** [ZAHFT] *n.* • juice
**Apfelsaft, der** *n.* • apple juice
Ich trinke gern Orangensaft zum Frühstück.
*I like to drink orange juice at breakfast.*

**sagen** [ZAHgən] *v.* • to say; to tell

| | |
|---|---|
| sage | sagen |
| sagst | sagt |
| sagt | sagen |

Kannst du “Hallo” auf Französisch sagen?
*Can you say “Hello” in French?*

**Sahne, die** [ZAHnə] *n.* • cream
Mein Vater trinkt seinen Kaffee mit Sahne.
*My father drinks his coffee with cream.*

**Salat, der** [zaLAHT] *n.* • salad
Julia ißt einen Salat zu Mittag.
*Julia has a salad for lunch.*

**Salz, das** [ZALTS] *n.* • salt
Die Suppe braucht etwas mehr Salz.
*The soup needs a little more salt.*

**Samen, der** [ZAHmən] *n.* • seed
Wir säen Blumensamen in unserem Garten.
*We plant flower seeds in our garden.*

**sammeln** [ZAHMəln] *v.* • to collect
Die Kinder sammeln Muscheln am Strand.
*The children are collecting shells on the beach.*

**Sammlung, die** [ZAHMlung] *n.* • collection
Mein Bruder hat eine Münzensammlung.
*My brother has a collection of coins.*

**Samstag, der** [ZAHMStahk] *n.* • Saturday
Wir gehen am Samstag ins Theater.
*We are going to the theater on Saturday.*

**Sand, der** [ZANT] *n.* • sand
Wir bauen eine Sandburg am Strand.
*We are building a sand castle on the beach.*

**Sandalen, die** [zahnDAHLən] *n.* • sandals
Ich brauche ein neues Paar Sandalen.
*I need a new pair of sandals.*

**sanft** [ZANFT] *adj.* • gentle; gently
Die Krankenschwester ist sehr sanft.
*The nurse is very gentle.*

**Satz, der** [ZATS] *n.* • sentence
Schreibt fünf Sätze auf französisch!
*Write five sentences in French.*

**sauber** [ZAUbə*r*] *adj.* • clean
Jeden Montag bezieht sie die Betten mit sauberen Bettüchern.
*Every Monday she puts clean sheets on the beds.*

**sauer** [ZAUə*r*] *adj.* • sour
Zitronensaft ist sauer.
*Lemon juice is sour.*

**Sauerkraut, das** [ZAUə*r*kraut] *n.* • sauerkraut
Sauerkraut wird aus Kohl hergestellt.
*Sauerkraut is made with cabbage.*

**Saxophon, das** [zahksawFOHN] *n.* • saxophone
Mein Bruder spielt Saxophon.
*My brother plays the saxophone.*

**Schachspiel, das** [SHAH*KH*shpeel] *n.* • chess
Das Schachspiel ist eines der ältesten Spiele der Welt.
*Chess is one of the oldest games in the world.*

**Schafe, die (pl.)** [SHAHfə] *n.* • sheep
Die Schafe folgen dem Hirten.
*The sheep are following the shepherd.*

**Schäfer, der** [SHAIfə*r*] *n.* • shepherd
**deutsche Schäferhund, der** *n.* • German shepherd (dog)
Der Schäfer hütet seine Herde.
*The shepherd tends his flock.*

**Schal, der** [SHAHL] *n.* • scarf
Ich trage im Winter einen Schal.
*I wear a scarf in the winter.*

**Schallplatte, die** [SHAHLplahtə] *n.* • record
Kannst du die Schallplatte bitte noch einmal spielen?
*Can you play the record again, please?*

**schämen, sich** [SHAImən, zi*sh*] *v.* • to be ashamed
Der kleine Junge schämt sich, wenn er ungezogen ist.
*The little boy is ashamed when he is naughty.*

**Schatten, der** [SHAHTən] *n.* • shade; shadow
Laßt uns im Schatten dieses Baumes sitzen.
*Let's sit in the shade of this tree.*

**schauen** [SHAUən] *v.* • to watch; to look; to see

| | |
|---|---|
| schaue | schauen |
| schaust | schaut |
| schaut | schauen |

Diese Frau kann in die Zukunft schauen.
*This woman can see into the future.*

**Schaufel, die** [SHAUfəl] *n.* • shovel
Der kleine Junge spielt mit einer Schaufel im Sand.
*The little boy plays in the sand with a shovel.*

**Schaukel, die** [SHAUkəl] *n.* • swing
Im Park sind Schaukeln für die Kinder.
*There are swings for the children in the park.*

**Schauspieler, der** [SHAUshpeelə*r*] *n.* • actor
**Schauspielerin, die** *n.* • actress
Wie heißt der Schauspieler in dem neuen Film?
*What's the name of the actor in that new film?*

**Scheck, der** [SHEK] *n.* • check (bank)
Herr Franke deponierte den Scheck auf seinem Konto.
*Mr. Franke deposited the check to his account.*

**Scheibe, die** [SHEIbə] *n.* • slice
Möchtest du eine Scheibe Schinken?
*Would you like a slice of ham?*

**scheinen** [SHEInən] *v.* • to appear; to seem; to shine
**Scheinwerfer, der** *n.* • headlight

| | |
|---|---|
| scheine | scheinen |
| scheinst | scheint |
| scheint | scheinen |

Sie scheint von der langen Reise erschöpft zu sein.
*She appears weary from the long trip.*

Die Sterne scheinen bei Nacht.
*The stars shine at night.*

**Schere, die** [SHAIrə] *n.* • scissors
Man braucht eine scharfe Schere, um Stoff durchzuschneiden.
*You need sharp scissors to cut through cloth.*

**Scherz, der** [SHERTS] *n.* • joke
**scherzen** *v.* • to joke
Mein Bruder erzählte uns einen lustigen Scherz.
*My brother told us a funny joke.*

**Scheune, die** [SHOInə] *n.* • barn
Eine Eule lebt in dieser alten Scheune.
*An owl lives in this old barn.*

**schieben** [SHEEbən] *v.* • to push

| | |
|---|---|
| schiebe | schieben |
| schiebst | schiebt |
| schiebt | schieben |

Schiebe bitte nicht so, sonst falle ich.
*Don't push, please, you'll make me fall.*

**schießen** [SHEEsən] *v.* • to shoot

| | |
|---|---|
| schieße | schießen |
| schießt | schießt |
| schießt | schießen |

Der Jäger schießt mit seinem Gewehr.
*The hunter shoots his gun.*

**Schiff, das** [SHIF] *n.* • ship
Das Schiff überquert den Ozean.
*The ship crosses the ocean.*

**Schildkröte, die** [SHILTkr*er*tə] *n.* • turtle
Wir sahen eine riesige Schildkröte im Zoo.
*We saw a giant turtle at the zoo.*

**Schinken, der** [SHINGkən] *n.* • ham
Ich möchte Schinken auf meinem belegten Brot (Sandwich).
*I would like ham on my sandwich.*

**Schirm, der** [SHIRM] *n.* • umbrella
Wegen des Regens, trage ich einen Schirm.
*Because of the rain, I'm carrying an umbrella.*

**Schlafanzug, der** [SHLAHFahntsuk] *n.* • pajamas
Ich habe vergessen, meinen Schlafanzug einzupacken.
*I forgot to pack my pajamas.*

**schlafen** [SHLAHFən] *v.* • to sleep; to be asleep
**einschlafen** • to fall asleep
**lange schlafen** • to sleep late
**Schlafsack, der** *n.* • sleeping bag
**Schlafzimmer, das** *n.* • bedroom
**schläfrig sein** • to be sleepy

| | |
|---|---|
| schlafe | schlafen |
| schläfst | schlaft |
| schläft | schlafen |

Hast du letzte Nacht gut geschlafen?
*Did you sleep well last night?*

Die Katze schläft auf dem Sofa.
*The cat is asleep on the couch.*

Wenn ich schläfrig bin, gehe ich zu Bett.
*If I am sleepy, I go to bed.*

**schlagen** [SHLAHgən] *v.* • to hit; to beat

schlage schlagen
schlägst schlagt
schlägt schlagen

Beim Tennis muß man den Ball schlagen.
*In tennis you have to hit the ball.*

Ihre Fußballmanschaft schlägt uns jedes Jahr.
*Their football team beats us every year.*

**Schlamm, der** [SHLAHM] *n.* • mud
Seine Schuhe sind mit Schlamm bedeckt.
*His shoes are covered with mud.*

**Schlange, die** [SHLAHNGə] *n.* • snake
Eine Kobra ist eine gefährliche Schlange.
*A cobra is a dangerous snake.*

**schlank** [SHLAHNGK] *adj.* • slim
Du siehst nach deiner Diät sehr schlank aus.
*You're looking very slim after your diet.*

**schlecht** [SHLE*SH*T] *adj.* • bad
Die Ernte ist wegen des trockenen Wetters schlecht.
*The harvest is bad because of the dry weather.*

**schleifen** [SHLEIfən] *v.* • to drag

schleife schleifen
schleifst schleift
schleift schleifen

Seine Hose schleift auf dem Fußboden.
*His trousers drag on the floor.*

**schließen** [SHLEEsən] *v.* • to close; to shut; to conclude

schließe schließen
schließt schließt
schließt schließen

Schließen Sie die Tür, bitte.
*Close the door, please.*

**Schlitten, der** [SHLITən] *n.* • sled
Mein Schlitten fährt schnell den Hügel hinunter.
*My sled goes down the hill fast.*

**Schlittschuh, der** [SHLITshoo] *n.* • ice skate
**Schlittschuhlaufen** *v.* • to ice skate
Meine Schlittschuhe sind schwarz.
*My ice-skates are black.*

Läufst du Schlittschuh im Winter?
*Do you ice-skate in the winter?*

**Schloß, das** [SHLAWS] *n.* • castle
Der König wohnte in einem großen Schloß.
*The king lived in a large castle.*

**Schlüssel, der** [SHL*UE*səl] *n.* • key
Ohne einen Schlüssel kann ich die Tür nicht öffnen.
*I can't open the door without a key.*

**Schlußverkauf, der** [SHLUSferkauf] *n.* • sale
In diesem Laden gibt es einen Schlußverkauf von Sommerkleidung.
*This store is having a sale on summer clothes.*

**schmelzen** [SHMELtsən] *v.* • to melt

| | |
|---|---|
| schmelze | schmelzen |
| schmilzt | schmelzt |
| schmilzt | schmelzen |

Der Schneemann schmilzt in der Sonne.
*The snowman is melting in the sun.*

**Schmerz, der** [SHMERTS] *n.* • pain
**schmerzhaft** *adj.* • painful
Der Tennisspieler hat Schmerzen in der Schulter.
*The tennis player has pains in his shoulder.*

**Schmetterling, der** [SHMETə*r*ling] *n.* • butterfly
Das Kind versucht, den Schmetterling zu fangen.
*The child tries to catch the butterfly.*

**schmücken** [SHM*UE*kən] *v.* • to decorate
Ich schmücke mein Zimmer mit Postern.
*I decorate my room with posters.*

**schmutzig** [SHMUtsi*sh*] *adj.* • dirty
**Schmutz machen** • to make a mess
Der Schlamm machte meine Stiefel schmutzig.
*The mud made my boots dirty.*

**Schnabel, der** [SHNAHbəl] *n.* • beak
Der Vogel knackt Samen mit seinem Schnabel.
*The bird cracks seeds with its beak.*

**Schnecke, die** [SHNEKə] *n.* • snail
Man kann in diesem Restaurant Schnecken bestellen.
*You can order snails in this restaurant.*

**Schnee, der** [SHNAI] *n.* • snow
**Es schneit** • It's snowing
**Schneemann, der** *n.* • snowman
**schneien** *v.* • to snow
Laß uns im Schnee spielen!
*Let's go play in the snow!*

**schneiden** [SHNEIdən] *v.* • to cut
**sich schneiden** • to cut oneself

| | |
|---|---|
| schneide | schneiden |
| schneidest | schneidet |
| schneidet | schneiden |

Er schneidet sein Fleisch mit einem Messer.
*He cuts his meat with a knife.*

**Schneider, der (in, f.)** [SHNEIdə*r*] *n.* • tailor
Der Schneider macht einen Anzug.
*The tailor is making a suit.*

**schnell** [SHNEL] *adj.; adv.* • fast; quick; quickly; hurry
Dieses ist ein schneller Zug.
*This is a fast train.*

**Schnur, die** [SHNOOR] *n.* • string
Ich brauche eine Schnur für meinen Drachen.
*I need some string for my kite.*

**Schnurrbart, der** [SHNURbahrt] *n.* • mustache
Mein Vater hat einen Schnurrbart.
*My father has a mustache.*

**Schokolade, die** [shawkawLAHdə] *n.* • chocolate
Diese Süßigkeit ist aus Schokolade.
*This candy is made of chocolate.*

**schon** [SHAWN] *adv.* • already
Mein Bruder ist schon erwachsen.
*My brother is already grown up.*

**schön** [SH*ER*N] *adj.* • beautiful; handsome; nice; fine
Schauen Sie sich die schönen Blumen im Garten an!
*Look at the beautiful flowers in the garden!*

Es ist schön draußen.
*It's nice out.*

Wir hatten einen schönen Tag am Strand.
*We had a fine day at the beach.*

**Schottland** [SHAWTlant] *n.* • Scotland
**Schotte, der (-in, f.)** *n.* • a person from Scotland (Scot)
**schottisch** *adj.* • Scottish
Schottland liegt nördlich von England.
*Scotland is north of England.*

**Schrank, der** [SHRAHNK] *n.* • cupboard
Ich stellte das Geschirr in den Schrank.
*I put the dishes away in the cupboard.*

**schrecklich** [SHREKli*sh*] *adj.* • dreadful; horrible; terrible
Das Ungeheuer in der Geschichte ist schrecklich.
*The monster in the story is dreadful.*

**schreiben** [SHREIbən] *v.* • to write
**Kugelschreiber, der** *n.* • ball-point pen

| | |
|---|---|
| schreibe | schreiben |
| schreibst | schreibt |
| schreibt | schreiben |

Janine schreibt einen Brief an ihre Brieffreundin.
*Janine is writing a letter to her pen pal.*

**Schreibtisch, der** [SHREIPtish] *n.* • desk
Die Papiere sind im Schreibtisch.
*The papers are in the desk.*

**schreien** [SHREIən] *v.* • to scream; to shout

| | |
|---|---|
| schreie | schreien |
| schreist | schreit |
| schreit | schreien |

Ich schrie vor Schmerzen, als ich mir den Arm brach.
*I screamed in pain when I broke my arm.*

**Schritt, der** [SHRIT] *n.* • step
Wie viele Schritte enthalten die Anweisungen?
*How many steps are there in the directions?*

**schüchtern** [SH*UESH*tern] *adj.* • shy
Nicole ist schüchtern bei fremden Leuten.
*Nicole is shy around strange people.*

**Schuh, der** [SHOO] *n.* • shoe
Ich habe ein neues Paar Schuhe gekauft.
*I bought a new pair of shoes.*

**Schuld, die** [SHULT] *n.* • fault
Es ist meine Schuld, daß wir zu spät sind.
*It is my fault that we are late.*

**schuldig** [SHULdi*sh*] *adj.* • guilty
Die Geschworenen entscheiden, ob der Angeklagte schuldig ist.
*The jury decides if the defendant is guilty.*

**Schule, die** [SHOOlə] *n.* • school
Wie heißt deine Schule?
*What's the name of your school?*

**Schüler, der (-in, f.)** [SH*UE*lə*r*] *n.* • pupil
**Schülertisch, der** *n.* • student's desk
Die Schüler heben ihre Hände, bevor sie etwas sagen.
*The pupils raise their hands before speaking.*

**Schulter, die** [SHULtə*r*] *n.* • shoulder
Martine hat eine steife Schulter.
*Martine has a sore shoulder.*

**Schürze, die** [SH*UE*Rtsə] *n.* • apron
Meine Großmutter trägt eine Schürze, wenn sie kocht.
*My grandmother wears an apron when she cooks.*

**Schüssel, die** [SH*UE*Səl] *n.* • bowl
Ich tat die Frucht in eine Schüssel auf dem Tisch.
*I put the fruit in a bowl on the table.*

**schütteln** [SH*UE*Təln] *v.* • to shake
**Hände schütteln** • to shake hands
Der Hund schüttelte sich nach dem Bad.
*The dog shook himself after the bath.*

**schwach** [SHVAH*KH*] *adj.* • weak
Die jungen Vögel sind schwach.
*The baby birds are weak.*

**Schwamm, der** [SHVAHM] *n.* • sponge
Man reinigt die Badewanne mit einem Schwamm.
*You clean the bathtub with a sponge.*

**Schwan, der** [SHVAHN] *n.* • swan
Der Schwan schwimmt auf dem Teich.
*The swan is swimming in the pond.*

**Schwanz, der** [SHVAHNTS] *n.* • tail
Der Hund wedelt mit dem Schwanz, wenn er froh ist.
*The dog wags his tail when he is happy.*

**schwarz** [SHVAHRTS] *adj.* • black
Er trägt seine schwarzen Schuhe.
*He is wearing his black shoes.*

**Schweden** [SHVAIdən] *n.* • Sweden
**Schwede, der (-in, f.)** *n.* • Swede
**schwedisch** *adj.* • Swedish
Wir fahren in diesem Sommer nach Schweden.
*We're going to Sweden this Summer.*

**Schwein, das** [SHVEIN] *n.* • pig; hog
**Sparschwein, das** *n.* • piggy bank
**Schweinebraten, der** *n.* • pork roast
Es gibt Schweine und Pferde auf dem Bauernhof.
*There are pigs and horses on the farm.*

**Schweinefleisch, das** [SHVEInəfleish] *n.* • pork
Möchtest du Schweine- oder Rindfleisch zum Abendessen?
*Do you want pork or beef for dinner?*

**Schweiz, die** [SHVEITS] *n.* • Switzerland
**Schweizer, der (-in, f.)** *n.* • Swiss (person)
**schweizerisch** *adj.* • Swiss
Bern ist die Hauptstadt der Schweiz.
*Bern is the capital of Switzerland.*

**schwer** [SHVAIR] *adj.* • hard; heavy
Holz zu spalten ist eine sehr schwere Arbeit.
*Chopping wood is very hard work.*

**schwerfällig** [SHVAIRfaili*sh*] *adj.* • dull
Dieser Vortrag ist sehr schwerfällig.
*This lecture is very dull.*

**Schwertlilie, die** [SHVAIRTlilee] *n.* • iris (flower)
Diese Schwertlilien brauchen viel Wasser.
*These irises need a lot of water.*

**Schwester, die** [SHVESt*ər*] *n.* • sister
Deine Schwester scheint ein nettes Mädchen zu sein.
*Your sister seems like a nice girl.*

**schwierig** [SHVEEri*sh*] *adj.* • difficult
Die Aufgabe ist schwierig.
*This assignment is difficult.*

**Schwimmbecken, das** [SHVIMbekən] *n.* • pool (swimming)
Wollen wir ins Schwimmbecken gehen!
*Let's go swimming in the pool!*

**schwimmen** [SHVIMən] *v.* • to swim
**Schwimmen, das** *n.* • swimming

| | |
|---|---|
| schwimme | schwimmen |
| schwimmst | schwimmt |
| schwimmt | schwimmen |

Ich habe im Sommerlager schwimmen gelernt.
*I learned to swim at summer camp.*

**schwindeln** [SHVINdəln] *v.* • to cheat
Ich spiele mit diesen Kindern nicht mehr, weil sie schwindeln.
*I don't play with these children anymore because they cheat.*

**sechs** [ZEKS] *adj.* • six
Ich war im ersten Schuljahr sechs Jahre alt.
*I was six years old in first grade.*

**sechzehn** [ZE*SH*tsain] *adj.* • sixteen
Viele Leute lernen mit sechzehn, Auto zu fahren.
*Many people learn to drive at sixteen.*

**sechzig** [ZE*SH*tsi*sh*] *adj.* • sixty
Eine Stunde hat sechzig Minuten.
*There are sixty minutes in an hour.*

**See, der** [ZAI] *n.* • lake; sea
Wir gehen im See schwimmen.
*We are going swimming in the lake.*

**Seeman, der** [ZAImahn] *n.* • sailor
Der Seeman arbeitet auf dem Schiff.
*The sailor works on the ship.*

**Segelboot, das** [ZAIgəlboht] *n.* • sailboat
Schau dir nur die Segelboote auf dem See an!
*See the sailboats on the lake!*

**sehen** [ZAIYən] *v.* • to see; to realize
**wiedersehen** *v.* • to see again

| | |
|---|---|
| sehe | sehen |
| siehst | seht |
| sieht | sehen |

Ich sehe besser mit meiner neuen Brille.
*I see better with my new glasses.*

**sehr** [ZAIR] *adj.; adv.* • very
**sehr viel** • very much
Diese Suppe ist sehr gut!
*This soup is very good!*

**seid** See *sein.*

**Seife, die** [ZEIfə] *n.* • soap
Ich wasche mir die Hände vor jedem Essen mit Seife.
*I wash my hands with soap before every meal.*

**Seil, das** [ZEIL] *n.* • rope
Dieses Seil wird benutzt, um Boote festzumachen.
*This rope is used to tie up boats.*

**sein** [ZEIN] *poss. pron.* • his; her; its
Mein Vater brachte seine Kleidung zur Reinigung.
*My father took his clothes to the cleaner.*

**sein** [ZEIN] *v.* • to be
**früh sein** • to be early
**geboren sein** • to be born
**spät sein** • to be late

| | |
|---|---|
| bin | sind |
| bist | seid |
| ist | sind |

Es ist schön draußen.
*It is nice out.*

Sind wir zu spät für den Bus?
*Are we late for the bus?*

Es geht mir gut.
*I am fine. (well)*

**seit** [ZEIT] *prep.* • since
**seit wann?** • since when?
Ich bin schon seit vier Uhr hier.
*I've been here since four o'clock.*

**Seite, die** [ZEItə] *n.* • side; page
Er wohnt auf der anderen Seite der Straße.
*He lives on the other side of the street.*

Schlagen Sie ihr Buch auf Seite 36 auf.
*Turn to page 36 in your book.*

**Sekretär, der (-in, f.)** [zekreTAIR] *n.* • secretary
Meine Sekretärin beantwortet das Telefon.
*My secretary answers the phone.*

**selbst** [ZELPST] *pron.* • myself
Ich habe das Kleid selbst gemacht.
*I made the dress myself.*

**Sellerie, der** [ZELeree] *n.* • celery
Meine Mutter kauft Sellerie im Supermarkt.
*My mother buys celery at the supermarket.*

**selten** [ZELtən] *adj.* • rare
Hast du seltene Briefmarken?
*Do you have any rare stamps?*

**seltsam** [ZELTsahm] *adj.* • odd; strange
Das ist seltsam! Sie kommt nie zu spät zur Arbeit.
*That's odd! She is never late for work.*

**Senf, der** [ZENF] *n.* • mustard
Ich möchte etwas Senf auf meinem Sandwich.
*I would like some mustard on my sandwich.*

**September, der** [zepTEMbər] *n.* • September
Im September gehen wir wieder zurück zur Schule.
*We go back to school again in September.*

**Service, der** [SERvis] *n.* • service
Der Service ist sehr gut in diesem Restaurant.
*The service is very good in this restaurant.*

**Serviette, die** [zervyETə] *n.* • napkin
Sie legt die Serviette auf den Schoß.
*She puts the napkin on her lap.*

**Sessel, der** [ZESəl] *n.* • armchair
Dieser Sessel ist sehr bequem.
*This armchair is very comfortable.*

**Schachspiel, das** [SHAH*KH*shpeel] *n.* • chess
**Schach spielen** • to play chess
Ich habe ein neues Schachspiel bekommen.
*I received a new chess game.*

**Shampoo, das** [shahmPOO] *n.* • shampoo
Das Shampoo läßt mein Haar frisch duften.
*The shampoo makes my hair smell clean.*

**Shorts, die** [SHAWRTS] *n. pl.* • shorts
Wir tragen Shorts, wenn es heiß ist.
*We wear shorts when it's hot.*

**sich** [ZI*SH*] *pron.* • herself; himself
Sie sah sich im Spiegel an.
*She looked at herself in the mirror.*

**sicher** [ZI*SH*ər] *adj.* • certain; sure
Ich bin sicher, daß sie heute abend kommen
*I'm certain that they are coming this evening.*

**Sicherheit, die** [ZI*SH*ərheit] *n.* • safety
**Sicherheitsgurt, der** *n.* • safety-belt
Der Bademeister ist für die Sicherheit der Schwimmer verantwortlich.
*The lifeguard is responsible for the safety of the swimmers.*

**sie; Sie** [ZEE] *pron.* • she, her, it, they, them; you
Sie ist die Schwester meiner Mutter.
*She is my mother's sister.*

Ist die Milch weiß? Ja, sie ist weiß.
*Is the milk white? Yes, it is white.*

Sie lernen lesen in der Schule.
*They learn to read in school.*

Wie viele Bücher haben Sie?
*How many books do you have?*

Ich liebe sie, und sie lieben mich.
*I love them and they love me.* see also *dich; ihr*

**sieben** [ZEEbən] *adj.* • seven
Die Woche hat sieben Tage.
*There are seven days in the week.*

**siebzehn** [ZEEPtsain] *adj.* • seventeen
Ich war erst siebzehn, als ich anfing zu studieren.
*I was only seventeen when I started college.*

**siebzig** [ZEEPtsi*sh*] *adj.* • seventy
Mein Großvater ist siebzig Jahre alt.
*My grandfather is seventy years old.*

**Silber, das** [ZILbə*r*] *n.* • silver
**aus Silber gemacht** • made of silver
Meine Mutter hat einen Ring aus Silber.
*My mother has a silver ring.*

**sind** See *sein*.

**singen** [ZINGən] *v.* • to sing
**Sänger, der (-in, f.)** *n.* • singer

| | |
|---|---|
| singe | singen |
| singst | singt |
| singt | singen |

Die Klasse sang ein Lied, um die Show zu beenden.
*The class sang a song to end the show.*

**Sinn, der** [ZIN] *n.* • sense
Diese Aufgabe macht überhaupt keinen Sinn.
*This assignment makes no sense at all.*

**sitzen** [ZITSən] *v.* • to sit
**sitzen bleiben** • to remain seated

| | |
|---|---|
| sitze | sitzen |
| sitzt | sitzt |
| sitzt | sitzen |

Er sitzt immer auf diesem Stuhl.
*He always sits in this chair.*

**Skelett, das** [skeLET] *n.* • skeleton
Wie viele Knochen hat ein Skelett?
*How many bones are in a skeleton?*

**Ski, der** [SHEE] *n.* • ski
**Skilaufen, das** *n.* • skiing
**Ski laufen** • to ski
**Wasserski laufen** • to water ski
Hast du meinen anderen Ski gesehen?
*Have you seen my other ski?*

**so** [ZOH] *adv.* • so
**so viel (viele)** • so much (many)
**so-so** • so-so
**und so weiter** • and so on
Dieser Koffer ist so leicht.
*This suitcase is so light.*

**so . . . wie** [ZOH . . . VEE] *adv.; conj.* • as . . . as
**sobald wie** • as soon as
Sie geht so langsam wie eine Schildkröte.
*She walks as slow as a turtle!*

**Socke, die** [ZAWkə] *n.* • sock
Passen diese beiden Socken zusammen?
*Do these two socks go together?*

**Sofa, das** [ZOHfah] *n.* • sofa; couch
Setzen Sie sich auf das Sofa.
*Sit down on the couch.*

**sofort** [zohFAWRT] *adv.* • immediately
Ich werde sofort kommen, wenn du Hilfe brauchst.
*I will come immediately if you need help.*

**Sohn, der** [ZOHN] *n.* • son
Großvater und Großmutter haben sechs Söhne.
*Grandfather and grandmother have six sons.*

**Soldat, der** [zawlDAHT] *n.* • soldier
Die Soldaten warten auf ihre Befehle.
*The soldiers are waiting for their orders.*

**Sommer, der** [ZAWmər] *n.* • summer
Diesen Sommer verbringen wir unsere Ferien in Kanada.
*This summer we're spending our vacation in Canada.*

**Sonne, die** [ZAWnə] *n.* • sun
**Sonnenbad, das** *n.* • sunbath
**Sonnenblume, die** *n.* • sunflower
**Sonnenbrille, die** *n.* • sunglasses
Die Katze schläft in der Sonne.
*The cat is sleeping in the sun.*

**Sonntag, der** [ZAWNtahk] *n.* • Sunday
Wir gehen am Sonntag zu Großmutter.
*We are going to Grandma's on Sunday.*

**Sorte, die** [ZAWRtə] *n.* • sort
Was für eine Sorte Kuchen ist das?
*What sort of cake is this?*

**Soße, die** [ZOHsə] *n.* • gravy; sauce
Möchtest du Soße zu deinem Rinderbraten?
*Do you want gravy with your roast beef?*

**Sozialkunde, die** [sawTSYAHLkundə] *n.* • social studies
Wer ist dein Lehrer in Sozialkunde?
*Who is your social studies teacher?*

**Spanien** [SHPAHNyən] *n.* • Spain
**Spanier, der (-in, f.)** *n.* • Spaniard
**spanisch** *adj.* • Spanish
Meine Freunde haben ihre Ferien in Spanien verbracht.
*My friends spent their vacation in Spain.*

**sparen** [SHPAHrən] *v.* • to save; to economize
**Geld sparen** • to save money

| | |
|---|---|
| spare | sparen |
| sparst | spart |
| spart | sparen |

Ich muß mein Geld sparen.
*I have to save my money.*

**Spargel, der** [SHPAHRgəl] *n.* • asparagus
Der Spargel ist ein Frühlingsgemüse.
*Asparagus is a spring vegetable.*

**Spaß, der** [SHPAHS] *n.* • fun
Dieses Spiel macht viel Spaß.
*This game is lots of fun.*

**spät** [SHPAIT] *adj.; adv.* • late
**später** *adj.; adv.* • later
**sich verspäten; zu spät kommen** • to be late
Wie spät ist es?
*What time is it?*

Der Bus kommt heute spät.
*The bus is late today.*

**Spaziergang, der** [shpahTSEERgahng] *n.* • walk
**spazierengehen** *v.* • to take a walk
Wir wollten einen Spaziergang machen.
*We wanted to take a walk.*

**Speisekarte, die** [SHPEIzəkahrtə] *n.* • menu
**Speisezimmer, das** *n.* • dining room
Könnten Sie uns bitte die Speisekarte geben?
*Could you give us the menu, please?*

**Spiegel, der** [SHPEEgəl] *n.* • mirror
Ich sehe in den Spiegel, wenn ich mir die Haare kämme.
*I look in the mirror when I comb my hair.*

**Spiel, das** [SHPEEL] *n.* • game; play
**Karten spielen** *v.* • to play (cards)
**Spielkarten, die** *n.* • playing cards
**Spielplatz, der** *n.* • playground
**spielen** *v.* • to play (a game, a musical instrument)

Gehst du heute abend zum Basketballspiel?
*Are you going to the basketball game this evening?*

Die Kinder haben den Spielplatz im Park wirklich genossen.
*The children really enjoyed the playground in the park.*

**Spielzeug, das** [SHPEELtsoi*sh*] *n.* • toy
Das Kind möchte Spielzeug zu seinem Geburtstag.
*The child wants toys for his birthday.*

**Spinat, der** [shpiNAHT] *n.* • spinach
Der Salat ist mit Spinat gemacht.
*The salad is made with spinach.*

**Spinne, die** [SHPINə] *n.* • spider
Hast du Angst vor Spinnen?
*Are you afraid of spiders?*

**Spitze, die** [SHPITSə] *n.* • lace
Dieser Spitzenkragen ist elegant.
*This lace collar is elegant.*

**Sport, der** [SHPAWRT] *n.* • sports
**Sport treiben** • exercise
Hast du an der Universität Sport getrieben?
*Did you play sports in college?*

Ich treibe Sport, indem ich jeden Tag laufe.
*I exercise by running every day.*

**Sprache, die** [SHPRAH*kh*ə] *n.* • language
Wie viele Sprachen sprichst du?
*How many languages do you speak?*

**sprechen** [SHPRE*kh*ən] *v.* • to speak
**Gespräch, das** *n.* • talk
**gesprächig** *adj.* • talkative
**leiser sprechen** • to lower (voice)
**sprich!** *interj.* • say!

| | |
|---|---|
| spreche | sprechen |
| sprichst | sprecht |
| spricht | sprechen |

Ich werde nach dem Unterricht mit dem Lehrer sprechen.
*I will speak with the teacher after class.*

Wir sprechen leiser, wenn wir in die Kirche gehen.
*We lower our voices when we go into church.*

**Springbrunnen, der** [SHPRINGbrunən] *n.* • fountain
Es gibt einen schönen Springbrunnen in der Mitte des Dorfes.
*There is a pretty fountain in the middle of the village.*

**springen** [SHPRINGən] *v.* • to jump; to leap

| | |
|---|---|
| springe | springen |
| springst | springt |
| springt | springen |

Die Kinder springen ins Schwimmbad.
*The children are jumping into the pool.*

**Spritze, die** [SHPRITSə] *n.* • shot (injection)
Ich mag es nicht, wenn der Arzt mir eine Spritze gibt.
*I do not like it when the doctor gives me a shot.*

**Spülbecken, das** [SHP*UE*Lbekən] *n.* • sink
Wir spülen das Geschirr im Spülbecken.
*We wash the dishes in the sink.*

**Staat, der** [SHTAHT] *n.* • state
**Staatsangehörigkeit, die** *n.* • nationality
**Staats--** *adj.* • national
Die U.S.A. bestehen aus fünfzig Staaten.
*There are fifty states in the United States.*

**Stadion, das** [SHTAHdiawn] *n.* • stadium
Wir gehen zu einem Spiel im Stadion.
*We are going to a game at the stadium.*

**Stadt, die** [SHTAHT] *n.* • city; town
**in der Stadt** • in town
**Stadthalle, die** *n.* • town hall
Willst du in der Stadt oder auf dem Land wohnen?
*Do you want to live in the city or in the country?*

**stark** [SHTAHRK] *adj.* • strong
Dieser Athlet ist sehr stark.
*This athlete is very strong.*

**starten** [SHTAHRtən] *v.* • to start (a car)
Heute konnte ich meinen Wagen nicht starten.
*I couldn't start my car today.*

**Station, die** [shtatsYOHN] *n.* • station
**Polizeistation, die** *n.* • police station
Der Bus erreichte endlich die Station.
*The bus finally reached the station.*

**Statue, die** [shtaTUə] *n.* • statue
Die "Venus von Milo" ist eine berühmte Statue.
*The "Venus de Milo" is a famous statue.*

**Staub, der** [SHTAUP] *n.* • dust
Der Staub bringt mich zum Niesen.
*Dust makes me sneeze.*

**Staubsauger, der** [SHTAUPzaugər] *n.* • vacuum cleaner
**staubsaugen** • to vacuum
Der Staubsauger bekommt den Schmutz aus den Teppichen.
*The vacuum cleaner gets the dirt out of the rugs.*

Wer saugt bei euch Staub?
*Who vacuums at your house?*

**Steak, das** [SHTAIK] *n.* • steak
**Beefsteak, das** *n.* • beef steak
Ich möchte mein Steak gut durchgebraten.
*I would like my steak well done.*

**stechen** [SHTE*KH*ən] *v.* • to sting; to stab

| | |
|---|---|
| steche | stechen |
| stichst | stecht |
| sticht | stechen |

Diese Käfer stechen!
*These bugs sting!*

**Stechmücke, die** [SHTE*KH*m*ue*kə] *n.* • mosquito
Die Stechmücken sind diesen Sommer wirklich ärgerlich.
*The mosquitos are really annoying this summer.*

**Stecknadel, die** [SHTEKnahdəl] *n.* • pin
Man braucht Stecknadeln zum Nähen.
*You need pins when you sew.*

**stehen** [SHTAIYən] *v.* • to stand
**aufstehen** • to stand up

| | |
|---|---|
| stehe | stehen |
| stehst | steht |
| steht | stehen |

Die Verkäuferin steht den ganzen Tag.
*The saleswoman stands all day.*

**stehlen** [SHTAIlən] *v.* • to steal

| | |
|---|---|
| stehle | stehlen |
| stiehlst | stehlt |
| stiehlt | stehlen |

Der Fuchs stiehlt ein Huhn.
*The fox is stealing a chicken.*

**Stein, der** [SHTEIN] *n.* • stone
Laßt uns Steine in den See werfen.
*Let's throw stones in the lake.*

**stellen** [SHTELən] *v.* • to put; to place; to set

| | |
|---|---|
| stelle | stellen |
| stellst | stellt |
| stellt | stellen |

Ich stelle die Blumen in die Vase.
*I put the flowers in the vase.*

Stell die Kiste auf den Tisch!
*Set the box down on the table.*

**sterben** [SHTERbən] *v.* • to die

| | |
|---|---|
| sterbe | sterben |
| stirbst | sterbt |
| stirbt | sterben |

Der Held stirbt am Ende des Stückes.
*The hero dies at the end of the play.*

**Stern, der** [SHTERN] *n.* • star
Heute abend sind viele Sterne am Himmel.
*There are many stars in the sky tonight.*

**Steward, der (-ess, f.)** [SHTYOOahrt] *n.* • steward (flight attendant)
Der Steward bringt unsere Getränke.
*The steward brings our drinks.*

**Stiefel, der** [SHTEEFəl] *n.* • boot
Suzanne trägt Stiefel, wenn sie durch den Schnee geht.
*Suzanne wears boots when she walks in the snow.*

**Stiefmutter, die** [SHTEEFmutər] *n.* • stepmother
**Stiefvater, der** *n.* • stepfather
**Stiefsohn, der** *n.* • stepson
**Stieftochter, die** *n.* • stepdaughter
Darf ich Ihnen meine Stiefmutter vorstellen?
*May I introduce my stepmother to you?*

**still** [SHTIL] *adj.* • calm
Wenn alle schlafen, ist das Haus still.
*When everyone is asleep, the house is calm.*

**Stimme, die** [SHTIMə] *n.* • voice
Der Sänger hat eine schöne Stimme.
*The singer has a beautiful voice.*

**Stimmung, die** [SHTIMung] *n.* • mood
Ihre Stimmung ändert sich mit dem Wetter!
*Her mood changes with the weather!*

**Stirn, die** [SHTIRN] *n.* • forehead
Der Mann hat eine breite Stirn.
*The man has a broad forehead.*

**Stock, der** [SHTAWK] *n.* • floor (of a building)
Ich wohne im zweiten Stock.
*I live on the third floor.*

**stolz** [SHTAWLTS] *adj.* • proud
Wir sind stolz auf unsere Mannschaft.
*We are proud of our team.*

**stören** [SHT*ER*rən] *v.* • to disturb; to trouble; to upset

| | |
|---|---|
| störe | stören |
| störst | stört |
| stört | stören |

Stör Paul nicht; er schläft!
*Do not disturb Paul, he is asleep!*

**Strand, der** [SHTRANT] *n.* • beach
Wir können nach dem Essen am Strand spazierengehen.
*We can take a walk on the beach after dinner.*

**Straße, die** [SHTRAHsə] *n.* • road; street
**Straßencafé, das** *n.* • sidewalk cafe
**Straßenkehrer, der** *n.* • street cleaner
Führt diese Straße nach Paris?
*Does this road go to Paris?*

**Strauß, der** [SHTRAUS] *n.* • bouquet
Meine Lieblingsblumen sind in dem Strauß.
*My favorite flowers are in the bouquet.*

**streichen** [SHTREI*sh*ən] *v.* • to paint
**Anstreicher, der** *n.* • painter

| | |
|---|---|
| streiche | streichen |
| streichst | streicht |
| streicht | streichen |

Wer streicht euer Haus?
*Who is painting your house?*

**Streichholz, das** [SHTREI*sh*hawlts] *n.* • match
Hast du ein Streichholz, um das Feuer anzuzünden?
*Do you have a match to light the fire?*

**Streit, der** [SHTREIT] *n.* • quarrel
Die Brüder hatten Streit wegen des Spielzeugs.
*The brothers had a quarrel over the toy.*

**streiten** [SHTREItən] *v.* • to fight; to quarrel

| | |
|---|---|
| streite | streiten |
| streitest | streitet |
| streitet | streiten |

Meine kleinen Brüder streiten sich immer.
*My little brothers fight all the time.*

**streng** [SHTRENG] *adj.* • strict
Diese Regeln sind sehr streng.
*These rules are very strict.*

**stricken** [SHTRIKən] *v.* • to knit

| | |
|---|---|
| stricke | stricken |
| strickst | strickt |
| strickt | stricken |

Meine Mutter strickt mir einen Pullover.
*My mother is knitting me a sweater.*

**Stroh, das** [SHTROH] *n.* • straw
Die Tiere schlafen im Stroh.
*The animals sleep on the straw.*

**Strumpf, der** [SHTRUMPF] *n.* • stocking; sock
Sind diese Strümpfe trocken?
*Are these stockings dry?*

**Stück, das** [SHT*UE*K] *n.* • piece
Es sind noch drei Stück Kuchen übrig.
*There are three pieces of pie left.*

**Student, der (-in, f.)** [shtuDENT] *n.* • student
Diese Studenten gehen zur Universität.
*These students go to the university.*

**studieren** [shtuDEERən] *v.* • to study

| | |
|---|---|
| studiere | studieren |
| studierst | studiert |
| studiert | studieren |

Wir studieren Französisch.
*We are studying French.*

**Stufe, die** [SHTUfə] *n.* • stair; step
Vorsicht Stufe!
*Mind the step!*

**Stuhl, der** [SHTOOL] *n.* • chair
**Lehnstuhl, der** *n.* • armchair; easy chair
Sechs Stühle stehen um den Tisch.
*There are six chairs around the table.*

**Stunde, die** [SHTUNdə] *n.* • hour
**halbe Stunde, die** • half an hour
Ich warte schon eine Stunde auf meinen Freund.
*I have been waiting for my friend for an hour.*

**stur** [SHTUR] *adj.* • stubborn
Man sagt, daß Ziegen stur sind.
*They say that goats are stubborn.*

**Sturm, der** [SHTURM] *n.* • storm
Der Sturm hat den Baum entwurzelt.
*The storm blew the tree down.*

**stürzen** [SHT*UE*Rtsən] *v.* • to overturn; to plunge

| | |
|---|---|
| stürze | stürzen |
| stürzt | stürzt |
| stürzt | stürzen |

Die Revolution stürzte die Regierung.
*The revolution overturned the government.*

**suchen** [ZOO*kh*ən] *v.* • to look for; to search for

| | |
|---|---|
| suche | suchen |
| suchst | sucht |
| sucht | suchen |

Wir suchen eine Wohnung.
*We are looking for an apartment.*

**Süden, der** [Z*UE*dən] *n.* • south
**Südamerika** *n.* • South America
Wir sind in den Süden Mexikos gereist.
*We traveled into the south of Mexico.*

**Supermarkt, der** [ZOOpermahrkt] *n.* • supermarket
Dieser Supermarkt hat eine eigene Bäckerei.
*This supermarket has its own bakery.*

**Suppe, die** [ZUPə] *n.* • soup
Heiße Suppe ist etwas Gutes im Winter.
*Hot soup is good in the winter.*

**süß** [Z*UE*S] *adj.* • sweet
Dieser Nachtisch ist zu süß.
*This dessert is too sweet.*

**Süßigkeit, die** [*ZUE*sis*h*keit] *n.* • candy
**Süßwarengeschäft, das** *n.* • candy store
Iß nicht zu viele Süßigkeiten vor dem Abendessen.
*Don't eat too much candy before dinner.*

# T

**Tafel, die** [TAHfəl] *n.* • blackboard
Der Lehrer schreibt an die Tafel.
*The teacher writes on the blackboard.*

**Tag, der** [TAHK] *n.* • day
**den Tag freihaben** • day off
**jeden Tag** • every day
**Neujahrstag, der** *n.* • New Year's day
Es ist Tag.
*It's daytime.*

An welchem Tag wird sie ankommen?
*What day is she going to arrive?*

**Taille, die** [TEILyə] *n.* • waist
Sie trägt Gürtel, um ihre enge Taille zu zeigen.
*She wears belts to show off her small waist.*

**Tal, das** [TAHL] *n.* • valley
Es gibt ein hübsches Tal in den Bergen.
*There is a pretty valley between the mountains.*

**Tankstelle, die** [TAHNKshtelə] *n.* • gas station
Die Tankstelle liegt nicht weit von hier.
*The gas station is not far from here.*

**Tante, die** [TAHNTə] *n.* • aunt
Meine Tante heißt Sophia.
*My aunt's name is Sophia.*

**tanzen** [TAHNtsən] *v.* • to dance

| | |
|---|---|
| tanze | tanzen |
| tanzt | tanzt |
| tanzt | tanzen |

Wir nahmen Unterricht, um tanzen zu lernen.
*We took classes to learn to dance.*

**tapfer** [TAHPfər] *adj.* • brave
Polizisten sind sehr tapfer.
*Police officers are very brave.*

**Tasche, die** [TAHshə] *n.* • pocket; bag
**Handtasche, die** *n.* • pocketbook
**Taschenbuch, das** *n.* • paperback book
**Taschenmesser, das** *n.* • pocketknife
**Taschenlampe, die** *n.* • flashlight
Was hast du in deiner Tasche?
*What do you have in your pocket?*

Diese Tasche mit Lebensmitteln ist sehr schwer.
*This bag of groceries is very heavy.*

**Tasse, die** [TAHSə] *n.* • cup
**eine Tasse Kaffee** • a cup of coffee
**Kaffeetasse, die** *n.* • coffee cup
Bitte geben Sie mir eine Tasse Kaffee.
*Please give me a cup of coffee.*

**taub** [TAUP] *adj.* • deaf
Meine Großmutter fängt an, taub zu werden.
*My grandmother is starting to go deaf.*

**täuschen** [TOIshən] *v.* • to deceive
Der Mann täuschte die Polizei mit seiner Geschichte.
*The man deceived the police with his story.*

**tausend** [TAUzənt] *adj.* • thousand
Mein Bruder hat tausend Dollar in bar.
*My brother has a thousand dollars cash!*

**Taxi, das** [TAHKSee] *n.* • taxi
**Taxifahrer, der (in, f.)** *n.* • taxi driver
**Taxistand, der** *n.* • taxi stand
Wir nehmen ein Taxi zum Hotel.
*We'll take a taxi to the hotel.*

**Tee, der** [TAI] *n.* • tea
Ich hätte gern etwas Milch in meinen Tee, bitte.
*I would like some milk in my tea, please.*

**Teenager, der** [TEENaizhər] *n.* • teenager
Sein Sohn ist ein Teenager, der zum Gymnasium geht.
*His son is a teenager in high school.*

**Teich, der** [TAI*sh*] *n.* • pond
Es gibt Frösche im Teich.
*There are frogs in the pond.*

**Teil, der** [TEIL] *n.* • part
**teilen** *v.* • to divide
**teilen, sich** *v.* • to share
**Teil sein, ein** • to be part of
Hier ist ein Teil der Zeitung.
*Here is one part of the newspaper.*

Literatur ist ein Teil meines Studiums.
*Literature is part of my studies.*

Wir teilen uns die Süßigkeiten.
*We are dividing the candy among us.*

Wir können uns dieses Stück Kuchen teilen.
*We can share this serving of cake.*

**Telefon, das** [teləFOHN] *n.* • telephone; phone
**Telefonnummer, die** *n.* • telephone number
**Telefonzelle, die** *n.* • telephone booth

Benutz das Telefon im Gang, um deinen Bruder anzurufen.
*Use the phone in the hall to call your brother.*

**Teller, der** [TELə*r*] *n.* • plate
Wir tun das Essen auf unsere Teller.
*We put food on our plates.*

**Tennisspielen, das** [TENis-shpeelən] *n.* • tennis
**Tennis spielen** • to play tennis
Er spielt sehr gut Tennis.
*He plays tennis very well.*

**Teppich, der** [TEPi*sh*] *n.* • carpet; rug
Irgend jemand muß den Teppich reinigen.
*Someone must clean the carpet.*

**Termin, der** [terMEEN] *n.* • appointment
Ich habe um 9 Uhr einen Termin beim Arzt.
*I have a doctor's appointment at 9 o'clock.*

**teuer** [TOIə*r*] *adj.* • expensive
Diamanten sind teuer.
*Diamonds are expensive.*

**Theater, das** [teAHtə*r*] *n.* • theater
Wir sehen uns ein Schauspiel im Theater an.
*We see a play at the theater.*

**Theaterstück, das** [teAHtə*r*sht*ue*k] *n.* • play (theater)
**ein Theaterstück darbieten** • to put on a play
Wir gingen ins Theater, um das Stück zu sehen.
*We went to the theater to see the play.*

Das Theaterstück von Brecht hat uns gut gefallen.
*We enjoyed the play by Brecht.*

**Thunfisch, der** [TOONfish] *n.* • tuna
Kaufe eine Dose Thunfisch, damit wir belegte Brote machen können.
*Buy a can of tuna to make sandwiches.*

**tief** [TEEF] *adj.* • deep
Dieser See ist ziemlich tief in der Mitte.
*This lake is quite deep in the middle.*

**Tier, das** [TEER] *n.* • animal
**Tierarzt, der (-in, f.)** *n.* • veterinarian
**Tierfuß, der** *n.* • paw
Ein Tierarzt kümmert sich um Tiere.
*A veterinarian takes care of animals.*

**Tiger, der** [TEEgər] *n.* • tiger
Im Zoo sind Tiger.
*There are (some) tigers at the zoo.*

**Tinte, die** [TINtə] *n.* • ink
Mein Füller hat keine Tinte mehr!
*There's no more ink in my pen!*

**tippen** [TIPən] *v.* • to type
**Typist, der (-in, f.)** *n.* • typist
Ich habe tippen gelernt, als ich 16 Jahre alt war.
*I learned to type when I was 16 years old.*

**Tisch, der** [TISH] *n.* • table
**den Tisch decken** • to set the table
**Tischdecke, die** *n.* • tablecloth
Der Tisch ist im Eßzimmer.
*The table is in the dining room.*

**Toastbrot, das** [TOHSTbroht] *n.* • toast
Helen streicht Butter auf ihr Toastbrot.
*Helen puts butter on her toast.*

**Tochter, die** [TAW*KH*tər] *n.* • daughter
Mutter und Tochter sehen sich sehr ähnlich.
*The mother and daughter look very much alike.*

**Toilette, die** [toiLETə] *n.* • toilet; bathroom
**Toilettenpapier, das** *n.* • toilet paper
Die Toilette ist am Ende des Ganges.
*The toilet is at the end of the hallway.*

**Tomate, die** [tohMAHtə] *n.* • tomato
Tomaten schmecken gut mit Basilikum.
*Tomatoes taste good with basil.*

**Tonband, das** [TOHNbahnt] *n.* • tape (recording)
Er hat verschiedene Sorten von Musik auf Tonband.
*He has different kinds of music on tape.*

**Tornado, der** [tawrNAHdoh] *n.* • tornado
Im Sommer gibt es oft Tornados.
*There are often tornadoes in the summer.*

**töten** [T*ER*tən] *v.* • to kill
**tot** *adj.* • dead

| | |
|---|---|
| töte | töten |
| tötest | tötet |
| tötet | töten |

In der Geschichte tötet der Held den Riesen.
*In the story, the hero kills the giant.*

Mein Großvater ist schon sieben Jahre tot.
*My grandfather has been dead for seven years.*

**Tour, die** [TOOR] *n.* • tour
**Tourismus, der** *n.* • tourism
**Tourist, der (-in, f.)** *n.* • tourist
Wir machten eine Tour durch Schottland.
*We took a tour through Scotland.*

**tragen** [TRAHgən] *v.* • to wear; to carry

| | |
|---|---|
| trage | tragen |
| trägst | tragt |
| trägt | tragen |

Er trägt seinen blauen Pullover.
*He is wearing his blue sweater.*

Ich werde meinen Koffer auf mein Zimmer tragen.
*I'm going to carry my suitcase to my room.*

**Trainer, der (in, f.)** [TRAInər] *n.* • coach
Unser Trainer hat den Spielplan.
*Our coach has the game schedule.*

**Träne, die** [TRAInə] *n.* • tear
Sie hat Tränen in ihren Augen.
*She has tears in her eyes.*

**Transporter, der** [transPAWRtər] *n.* • van; panel truck
Wir benutzen unseren eigenen Transporter, um die Ware auszuliefern.
*We take our own van to deliver the merchandise.*

**Traube, die** [TRAUbə] *n.* • grape
Wir haben Trauben zum Nachtisch.
*We are having grapes for dessert.*

**Traum, der** [TRAUM] *n.* • dream
**träumen** *v.* • to dream
**Alptraum, der** *n.* • nightmare
Morgens kann ich mich an meinen Traum nicht erinnern.
*In the mornings I can't remember my dream.*

**traurig** [TRAUri*sh*] *adj.* • sad
Sie ist sehr traurig über den Verlust ihrer Katze.
*She is very sad about the loss of her cat.*

**treffen** [TREFən] *v.* • to meet

treffe treffen
triffst trefft
trifft treffen

Manchmal treffe ich Freunde in diesem Café.
*Sometimes I meet friends at this cafe.*

**Treppe(n), die** [TREPə(n)] *n.* • stairs
**Rolltreppe, die** *n.* • escalator
Wir steigen die Treppen hinauf.
*We climb the stairs.*

**Trickfilm, der** [TRIKfilm] *n.* • cartoon (animated)
Walt Disney hat viele Trickfilme geschaffen.
*Walt Disney created many cartoons.*

**Trinkgeld, das** [TRING(K)gelt] *n.* • tip
Wir lassen der Kellnerin ein Trinkgeld.
*We leave a tip for the waitress.*

**trocken** [TRAWkən] *adj.* • dry
**abtrocknen (das Geschirr)** *v.* • to dry (dishes)
**trocknen** *v.* • to dry
**Trockner, der** *n.* • clothes dryer
Holen Sie ein trockenes Handtuch aus dem Schrank.
*Get a dry towel from the closet.*

**Trommel, die** [TRAWməl] *n.* • drum
Wie lange spielst du schon Trommel?
*How long have you played the drum?*

**Trompete, die** [trawmPAItə] *n.* • trumpet
Mein Freund spielt Trompete.
*My friend plays the trumpet.*

**Truhe, die** [TROOə] *n.* • trunk
Laßt uns Großmutters alte Truhe öffnen!
*Let's open Grandma's old trunk!*

**Truthahn, der** [TROOThahn] *n.* • turkey
Wir essen an Feiertagen Truthahn.
*We eat turkey on holidays.*

**Tuch, das** [TOO*KH*] *n.* • towel
**Badetuch, das** *n.* • bath towel
Has du ein frisches Handtuch für mich?
*Do you have a clean hand towel for me?*

**Tür, die** [T*UE*R] *n.* • door
**Türgriff, der** *n.* • doorknob
**Türklingel, die** *n.* • doorbell
Bitte öffnen Sie die Tür für unsere Gäste.
*Please open the door for our guests.*

**Turm, der** [TURM] *n.* • tower
Der Eiffelturm ist sehr berühmt.
*The Eiffel Tower is very famous.*

**Turnhalle, die** [TURNhahlə] *n.* • gymnasium
**Turner, der (in, f.)** *n.* • gymnast
**Turnen, das** *n.* • gymnastics
Wir spielen Basketball in der Turnhalle.
*We play basketball in the gymnasium.*

**typisch** [T*UE*pish] *adj.; adv.* • typical; typically
Kaltes Wetter ist nicht typisch für den Sommer.
*Cold weather in not typical of summer.*

# U

**über** [*UE*bər] *adj.; prep.* • all; above; over
**überall** *adj.* • everywhere; all over.
Mein Zimmer ist über der Küche.
*My room is above the kitchen.*

**übereinstimmen** [*ue*bə*r*EINshtimən] *v.* • to agree
Sie stimmen in allem überein.
*They agree on everything.*

**überholen** [*ue*bə*r*HOHlən] *v.* • to pass (a car)
Man soll ein Auto nicht von der rechten Seite überholen.
*You should not pass a car on the right.*

**Überraschung, die** [*ue*bə*r*RAHSHung] *n.* • surprise
**überraschend** *adj.* • surprising
Erzähl es niemandem, denn es ist eine Überraschung!
*Don't tell anyone because it's a surprise!*

**überschreiten** [*ue*bə*r*SHREITən] *v.* • to cross
Kinder müssen die Straße mit einem Erwachsenen überschreiten.
*Children must cross the street with an adult.*

**übersetzen** [*ue*bə*r*ZETSən] *v.* • to translate
Er übersetzte einen englischen Text ins Deutsche.
*He translated an English text into German.*

**Uhr, die** [OOR] *n.* • clock; watch
Die Uhr an der Wand ist sehr genau.
*The clock on the wall is very accurate.*

**um** [UM] *prep.* • in order to
Er will nach Deutschland fahren, um Deutsch zu lernen.
*He wants to go to Germany in order to learn German.*

**Umleitung, die** [UMleitung] *n.* • detour
Wir folgten den Schildern der Umleitung.
*We followed the signs for the detour.*

**umrühren** [UMr*ue*rən] *v.* • to stir
Vater rührt die Suppe um.
*Father is stirring the soup.*

**unbekannt** [OONbəkahnt] *adj.* • unknown
Die Identität des Diebes war unbekannt.
*The thief's identity was unknown.*

**unbequem** [OONbəkvaim] *adj.* • uncomfortable
Dieser Stuhl ist unbequem.
*This chair is uncomfortable.*

**und** [UNT] *conj.* • and
Paul und Veronique gehen zum Jahrmarkt.
*Paul and Veronique are going to the fair.*

**unehrlich** [OONairlis*h*] *adj.* • dishonest
Der unehrliche Junge erzählte noch eine Lüge.
*The dishonest boy told another lie.*

**unerwartet** [OONervahrtət] *adj.* • unexpected
Diese Einladung kommt unerwartet.
*This invitation is unexpected.*

**ungeduldig** [OONgeduldis*h*] *adj.* • impatient
Wenn Johann es eilig hat, ist er ungeduldig.
*When John is in a hurry, he is impatient.*

**ungeschickt** [OONgeshikt] *adj.* • awkward; clumsy
Das Baby machte seine ersten ungeschickten Schritte.
*The baby took its first awkward steps.*

**ungewöhnlich** [OONgeve*r*nlis*h*] *adj.* • unusual
Knoblauch ist eine ungewöhnliche Geschmackssorte für Eis.
*Garlic is an unusual flavor for ice cream.*

**ungezogen** [OONgətsohgən] *adj.* • naughty
Dieser kleine Junge ist manchmal ungezogen.
*This little boy is naughty sometimes.*

**unglaublich** [oonGLAUPli*sh*] *adj.* • unbelievable
Das ist eine unglaubliche Geschichte.
*That's an unbelievable story.*

**Unglück, das** [OONgl*ue*k] *n.* • disaster
Der Flugzeugabsturz war ein großes Unglück.
*The plane crash was a great disaster.*

**unglücklich** [OONgl*ue*kli*sh*] *adj.* • unhappy
Sie ist unglücklich, wenn sie allein ist.
*She is unhappy when she is alone.*

**unhöflich** [OONh*er*fli*sh*] *adj.* • impolite
Es war unhöflich, mich deinem Freund nicht vorzustellen.
*It was impolite not to introduce me to your friend.*

**Universität, die** [universiTAIT] *n.* • university
In meiner Heimatstadt gibt es eine Universität.
*There is a university in my home town.*

**uns** [UNS] *pron.* • us
Dieses Geschenk ist für uns beide.
*This present is for both of us.*

**unschuldig** [OONshuldi*sh*] *adj.* • innocent
Obwohl sie unschuldig ist, wurde sie bestraft.
*She was punished, even though she is innocent.*

**unser, -e, -es** [UNsə*r*] *adj.; pron.* • our
Das ist unser Haus neben dem Park.
*That's our house next to the park.*

**unten** [UNtən] *adv.* • down; below
**da unten** • down there
Unten steht ein Mann und spielt Gitarre.
*There's a man down (stairs, below) playing guitar.*

**unter** [UNtə*r*] *prep.* • below; beneath; under
Die Geschäfte befinden sich unter den Wohnungen.
*The stores are below the apartments.*

**unterbrechen** [untə*r*BRE*SH*ən] *v.* • to interrupt

| | |
|---|---|
| unterbreche | unterbrechen |
| unterbrichst | unterbrecht |
| unterbricht | unterbrechen |

Er unterbricht immer unsere Unterhaltungen.
*He always interrupts our conversations.*

**Untergrundbahn, die (U-Bahn)** [UNtə*r*gruntbahn] *n.* • subway
Willst du mit der U-Bahn fahren?
*Do you want to ride the subway?*

**unterhalten** [untə*r*HAHLtən] *v.* • to amuse

| | |
|---|---|
| unterhalte | unterhalten |
| unterhältst | unterhaltet |
| unterhält | unterhalten |

Der Clown unterhält das kleine Mädchen.
*The clown amuses the little girl.*

**Unterhaltung, die** [untə*r*HAHLtung] *n.* • conversation
Ich hatte gestern eine Unterhaltung mit Maria am Telefon.
*I had a conversation with Mary on the phone yesterday.*

**unterschiedlich** [untə*r*SHEEDli*sh*] *adj.* • different
Seine Ideen sind von meinen sehr unterschiedlich.
*His ideas are very different from mine.*

**Unterschrift, die** [UNtə*r*shrift] *n.* • signature
Man kann seine Unterschrift kaum lesen.
*You can hardly read his signature.*

**Untertasse, die** [UNtərtahsə] *n.* • saucer
Stell die Tassen auf die Untertassen.
*Put the cups on the saucers.*

**unvollendet** [OONfawlendet] *adj.* • incomplete
Schubert schrieb eine unvollendete Symphonie.
*Schubert wrote an incomplete symphony.*

**uralt** [OORahlt] *adj.* • ancient
Wir werden die uralten Ruinen in Rom besuchen.
*We're going to visit the ancient ruins in Rome.*

# V

**Vanille, die** [fahNILə] *n.* • vanilla
Großmutter möchte etwas Vanilleeis.
*Grandma wants some vanilla ice cream.*

**Vase, die** [VAHzə] *n.* • vase
Stell die Blumen in die Vase.
*Put the flowers in the vase.*

**Vater, der** [FAHtər] *n.* • father
**Vati, der (Väterchen)** *n.* • dad; daddy
Mein Vater half mir bei meiner Hausaufgabe.
*My father helped me with my homework.*

Wo arbeitet dein Vati?
*Where does your dad work?*

**Veilchen, das** [FEIL*sh*ən] *n.* • violet
Das kleine Mädchen pflückt ein paar Veilchen.
*The little girl is picking some violets.*

**Ventilator, der** [fentiLAHtawr] *n.* • fan
Der Ventilator wird das Zimmer schnell kühlen.
*The fan will cool the room quickly.*

**Verantwortung, die** [ferAHNTvawrtung] *n.*
• responsibility
Mit dieser Entscheidung haben wir eine schwere Verantwortung übernommen.
*By making this decision, we took on a big responsibility.*

**verbinden** [ferBINdən] *v.* • to connect
Man verbindet die zwei Teile auf diese Weise.
*You connect the two parts like this.*

**verbrennen** [ferBRENən] *v.* • to burn
Im Herbst verbrennen wir das Laub.
*We burn leaves in autumn.*

**verbringen (Zeit)** [ferBRINGən] *v.* • to spend (time)
Paul verbringt einen Monat im Sommerlager.
*Paul spends a month at summer camp.*

**verdienen** [ferDEENən] *v.* • to earn

| | |
|---|---|
| verdiene | verdienen |
| verdienst | verdient |
| verdient | verdienen |

Ich suche eine Arbeit, um Geld zu verdienen.
*I am looking for a job to earn money.*

**vereinigen; vereinen** [ferEINigən; ferEINən] *v.* • to unite
**vereinigt; vereint** *adj.* • united
**Vereinigten Staaten, die** *n.* • United States
**Vereinten Nationen, die** *n.* • United Nations

| | |
|---|---|
| vereinige | vereinigen |
| vereinigst | vereinigt |
| vereinigt | vereinigen |

Meine Familie wohnt in den Vereinigten Staaten.
*My family lives in the United States.*

Wir sind vereint in unserem Wunsch nach Frieden.
*We are united in our desire for peace.*

**Vergangenheit, die** [ferGAHNGənheit] *n.* • past
In der Vergangenheit bin ich oft mit dem Zug nach Berlin gefahren.
*In the past, I often went to Berlin by train.*

**vergessen** [ferGESən] *v.* • to forget

| | |
|---|---|
| vergesse | vergessen |
| vergißt | vergeßt |
| vergißt | vergessen |

Vergiß nicht, deine Hausaufgabe zu machen!
*Don't forget to do your homework!*

**vergnügen, sich** [ferGN*UE*gən] *v.* • to enjoy; to have a good time
**mit Vergnügen!** • with pleasure!
**Vergnügen, das** *n.* • pleasure
**zum Vergnügen** • for fun
Wir vergnügen uns am Strand.
*We have a good time at the beach.*

Es ist mir ein besonderes Vergnügen, sie kennenzulernen.
*It is a special pleasure for me to meet them.*

**verhaften** [ferHAHFtən] *v.* • to arrest
Der Polizist verhaftet den Verbrecher.
*The policeman arrests the criminal.*

**Verhandlung, die** [ferHAHNDlung] *n.* • trial
Der Richter legte die Verhandlung für den 8. November fest.
*The judge set the trial for November 8.*

**Verkauf, der** [ferKAUF] *n.* • sale
**im Schlußverkauf sein** • *to be on sale*
**Verkäufer, der (-in, f.)** *n.* • salesman, saleswoman
Mein Cousin (Vetter) ist Verkäufer in diesem Geschäft.
*My cousin is a salesman in this store.*

In unserer Straße steht ein Haus zum Verkauf.
*There's a house for sale on our street.*

Ich kaufe nur Schuhe, wenn sie im Schlußverkauf sind.
*I only buy shoes when they're on sale.*

**verkaufen** [ferKAUfən] *v.* • to sell

| | |
|---|---|
| verkaufe | verkaufen |
| verkaufst | verkauft |
| verkauft | verkaufen |

Mein Bruder verkauft Autos.
*My brother sells cars.*

**Verkehr, der** [ferKAIR] *n.* • traffic
**Verkehrsampel, die** *n.* • traffic light
Achte auf den Verkehr, wenn du die Straße überquerst!
*Watch out for the traffic when you cross the street!*

**verlangsamen** [ferLAHNGzahmən] *v.* • to slow down
Sie mußten die Geschwindigkeit des Autos verlangsamen.
*They had to slow the car down.*

**verlassen** [ferLASən] *v.* • to leave
Wir verlassen die Schule am Ende des Tages.
*We leave school at the end of the day.*

**Verlegenheit bringen, in** [ferLAIgənheit BRINGən] *v. phrase* • to embarrass
Wenn ihn jemand in Verlegenheit bringt, wird er rot.
*When someone embarrasses him, he blushes.*

**verletzen** [ferLETsən] *v.* • to injure
**Verletzte, der (die, f.)** *n.* • injured (person); casualty
**verletzt sein** • to be hurt
Sie verletzte ihr Knie beim Fußballspielen.
*She injured her knee playing soccer.*

**verlieren** [ferLEErən] *v.* • to lose

| | |
|---|---|
| verliere | verlieren |
| verlierst | verliert |
| verliert | verlieren |

Ich habe meine Brieftasche im Flughafen verloren.
*I lost my wallet in the airport.*

**verlobt sein** [ferLOHPT zein] *v. phrase* • to be engaged
**Verlobte, die** *n.* • fiancé(e)
Sie war ein Jahr lang verlobt, bevor sie heiratete.
*She was engaged for a year before she married.*

Meine Verlobte möchte im Juni heiraten.
*My fiancé wants to have the wedding in June.*

**vermeiden** [ferMEIdən] *v.* • to avoid
Mein Bruder vermeidet es zu arbeiten, sooft er kann.
*My brother avoids working whenever he can.*

**Vernunft, die** [ferNUNFT] *n.* • sense
**vernünftig** *adj.* • sensible; reasonable
Hast du die Vernunft verloren?
*Have you lost your senses?*

**verpassen** [ferPAHSən] *v.* • to miss
Schnell! Wir verpassen den Zug!
*Hurry! We are going to miss the train!*

**verreisen** [ferREIzən] *v.* • to travel
Ich verreise jeden Sommer mit meiner Familie.
*I travel with my family every summer.*

**verrückt** [ferR*UE*KT] *adj.* • crazy; mad (insane)
Du bist wohl verrückt! Es ist zu kalt, um schwimmen zu gehen.
*You are crazy! It's too cold to go swimming.*

**versagen** [ferZAHgən] *v.* • to fail; to refuse

versage versagen
versagst versagt
versagt versagen

Die Beine haben ihm im Wettlauf versagt.
*His legs failed him in the race.*

**versammeln** [ferZAHMəln] *v.* • to gather
Die Gäste versammeln sich im Garten.
*The guests gather in the garden.*

**versäumen** [ferZOIMən] *v.* • to fail (to do something)
Ich versäumte es, die Aufgabe rechtzeitig zu beenden.
*I failed to finish the assignment on time.*

**verschicken** [ferSHIKən] *v.* • to send
Wir verschicken zu Weihnachten viele Pakete.
*We send many packages at Christmas.*

**verschütten** [ferSH*UE*Tən] *v.* • to spill
Das Kind hat die Milch verschüttet.
*The child spilled her milk.*

**verschwinden** [ferSHVINdən] *v.* • to disappear
Die Sterne verschwinden, wenn die Sonne aufgeht.
*The stars disappear when the sun comes up.*

**Versicherung, die** [ferZI*SH*ərung] *n.* • insurance
Wir haben eine Versicherung für das Haus und den Wagen.
*We have insurance for the house and the car.*

**versprechen** [ferSHPRE*SH*ən] *v.* • to promise
**Versprechen, das** *n.* • promise
Wir versprechen, vorsichtig zu sein.
*We promise to be careful!*

**Verstand, der** [ferSHTAHNT] *n.* • mind
**gesunde Menschenverstand, der** • good sense; common sense
Er hat einen wachen Verstand.
*He has a quick mind.*

**verstecken** [ferSHTEKən] *v.* • to hide
**Verstecken spielen** • to play hide and seek
Die Dame versteckt ihren Schmuck.
*The lady hides her jewelry.*

**verstehen** [ferSHTAIən] *v.* • to understand

| | |
|---|---|
| verstehe | verstehen |
| verstehst | versteht |
| versteht | verstehen |

Ich verstehe Deutsch, aber ich kann es nicht schreiben.
*I understand German, but I can't write it.*

**versuchen** [ferZOO*KH*ən] *v.* • to try

| | |
|---|---|
| versuche | versuchen |
| versuchst | versucht |
| versucht | versuchen |

Ich versuche, einen Brief auf französisch zu schreiben.
*I am trying to write a letter in French.*

**verzeihen** [ferTSEIən] *v.* • to forgive; to pardon
**Verzeihung!** • Pardon me.

| | |
|---|---|
| verzeihe | verzeihen |
| verzeihst | verzeiht |
| verzeiht | verzeihen |

Wirst du meine Verspätung verzeihen?
*Will you forgive me for being late?*

**Vetter, der** [FETə*r*] *n.* • cousin
Mein Vetter ist so alt wie ich.
*My cousin is the same age as I am.*

**Videorekorder, der** [VIdaiyohrekohrdə*r*] *n.* • video cassette recorder (VCR)

**Videocassette, die** *n.* • video cassette
**Videokamera, die** *n.* • video camera
Wir haben uns den Film auf dem Videorekorder angesehen.
*We watched the movie on the VCR.*

**viel** [FEEL] *adj.* • much; many; a lot (of)
**sehr viel** • very much
**so viel** • so much
**so viele wie** • as many as
**wieviel?** • how much?
**wie viele?** • how many?
Ich habe viel Arbeit zu erledigen.
*I have a lot of work to do.*

Meine Eltern haben viele Freunde.
*My parents have many friends.*

Wir haben diesen Winter viel Schnee.
*We have a lot of snow this winter.*

**vielleicht** [feeLEI*SH*T] *adv.* • perhaps
Vielleicht können Sie mir helfen, den richtigen Weg zu finden.
*Perhaps you can help me find the right way.*

**vier** [FEER] *adj.* • four
Der Tisch hat vier Beine.
*The table has four legs.*

**Viereck, das** [FEERek] *n.* • square
Ein Viereck hat gleiche Winkel.
*A square has equal angles.*

**Viertel, das** [FEERtəl] *n.* • quarter
Laßt uns den Apfel in vier Viertel schneiden.
*Let's cut the apple into four quarters.*

**vierzehn** [FEERtsain] *adj.* • fourteen
Die meisten Schüler sind vierzehn Jahre alt.
*Most of the pupils are fourteen years old.*

**vierzig** [FEERtsi*sh*] *adj.* • forty
Der Bus kann vierzig Passagiere befördern.
*The bus can carry forty passengers.*

**Vogel, der** [FOHgəl] *n.* • bird
Die Vögel bauen ihre Nester in den Bäumen.
*The birds make their nests in the trees.*

**voll** [FAWL] *adj.* • full
Meine Taschen sind voll.
*My pockets are full.*

**Volleyballspiel, das** [VAWlaibahlshpeel] *n.* • volleyball
**Volleyball spielen** • to play volleyball
Wir spielten am Strand Volleyball.
*We played volleyball on the beach.*

**von** [FAWN] *prep.* • of
Francine möchte gern ein Stück von dem Kuchen mit den Mandeln.
*Francine would like a piece of the cake with the almonds.*

**vor** [FOHR] *prep.* • ahead of; in front of; before
Sie kommt immer vor mir an.
*She always arrives ahead of me.*

Der Lehrer steht vor der Klasse.
*The teacher is standing in front of the class.*

Sie gingen vor Tagesanbruch los.
*They left before dawn.*

**Vorabend, der** [FOHRahbənt] *n.* • eve
Am Vorabend unserer Reise gehen wir früh zu Bett.
*On the eve of our trip, we're going to go to bed early.*

**vorbereiten** [FOHRbəreitən] *n.* • to prepare
Meine Schwester bereitet heute abend das Essen vor.
*My sister is preparing dinner tonight.*

**Vorbereitung, die** [FOHRbəreitung] *n.* • preparation
Wir treffen Vorbereitungen für unsere Reise.
*We are making preparations for our trip.*

**Vorfahr, der (die, f.)** [FOHRfahr] *n.* • ancestor
Meine Vorfahren kommen aus Irland.
*My ancestors come from Ireland.*

**Vorhang, der** [FOHRhahng] *n.* • curtain
Nachts zieht man gewöhnlich die Vorhänge zu.
*At night, you usually pull the curtains.*

**Vorort, der** [FOHRawrt] *n.* • suburb
Mein Freund lebt in einem Vorort von Paris.
*My friend lives in a suburb of Paris.*

**Vorsicht!** [FOHRzi*sh*t] *interj.* • Be careful! (watch out)
Vorsicht! Der Hund beißt!
*Be careful! The dog bites!*

**vorsichtig** [FAWRzi*sh*ti*sh*] *adv.* • carefully
Wenn die Straßen naß sind, muß man vorsichtig fahren.
*When the roads are wet you must drive carefully.*

**Vorspeise, die** [FOHRshpeizə] *n.* • appetizer
Möchtest du eine Vorspeise vor deinem Hauptgericht?
*Would you like an appetizer before your main course?*

**vorstellen** [FOHRshtelən] *v.* • to introduce
**vorstellen, sich** • to imagine

| | |
|---|---|
| stelle vor | stellen vor |
| stellst vor | stellt vor |
| stellt vor | stellen vor |

Herr Braun, ich möchte Sie meinen Eltern vorstellen.
*Mr. Brown, I'd like to introduce you to my parents.*

Kannst du dir vorstellen, wie sie sich fühlt?
*Can you imagine how she must feel?*

**vorziehen** [FOHRtseeən] *v.* • to prefer
Ich ziehe Schokoladeneis einem Stück Torte vor.
*I prefer chocolate ice cream to a piece of cake.*

**Vulkan, der** [vulKAHN] *n.* • volcano
Auf dieser Insel gibt es Vulkane.
*There are volcanoes on this island.*

# W

**Wächter, der (in, f.)** [VAI*SH*tər] *n.* • guard
Die Bank hat einen Wächter an der Tür.
*The bank has a guard at the door.*

**wagen** [VAHgən] *v.* • to dare

| | |
|---|---|
| wage | wagen |
| wagst | wagt |
| wagt | wagen |

Wagst du es, die Lehrerin mit ihrem Vornamen anzusprechen?
*Do you dare to call the teacher by her first name?*

**Wagen, der** [VAHgən] *n.* • car
**Eisenbahnwagen, der** *n.* • railroad car
Sie haben einen neuen, roten Wagen.
*They have a new red car.*

**Wahl, die** [VAHL] *n.* • choice
Patricia will die richtige Wahl treffen.
*Patricia wants to make the right choice.*

**wählen** [VAILən] *v.* • to choose; to vote

| | |
|---|---|
| wähle | wählen |
| wählst | wählt |
| wählt | wählen |

Sie müssen den einen oder den anderen wählen.
*You have to choose one or the other.*

Hast du bei der letzten Wahl gewählt?
*Did you vote in the last election?*

**wahr** [VAHR] *adj.* • true
**wahrhaft** *adj.; adv.* • truthful; truly
Ist diese Geschichte wahr oder falsch?
*Is this story true or false?*

**während** [VAIrənt] *prep.; conj.* • during; while
Sprich nicht während der Rede!
*Don't talk during the speech!*

Sie spielt, während ich arbeite.
*She plays while I work.*

**Wahrheit, die** [VAHRheit] *n.* • truth
Erzählt sie die Wahrheit?
*Is she telling the truth?*

**wahrscheinlich** [vahrSHEINli*sh*] *adv.* • probably
Ich habe mich noch nicht entschieden, aber ich gehe wahrscheinlich mit euch.
*I haven't decided, but I'll probably go with you.*

**Wald, der** [VAHLT] *n.* • forest
Es gibt viele Tannenbäume im Wald.
*The forest has many pine trees.*

**Wand, die** [VAHNT] *n.* • wall
An der Wand hängt ein Spiegel.
*There is a mirror hanging on the wall.*

**Wandschrank, der** [VAHNTshrahngk] *n.* • closet
Er hängt seinen Mantel in den Wandschrank.
*He hangs his coat in the closet.*

**Wange, die** [VAHNGə] *n.* • cheek
Das Paar tanzte Wange an Wange.
*The couple danced cheek to cheek.*

**wann** [VAHN] *adv.* • when
Sag mir, wann du gehen willst.
*Tell me when you want to leave.*

**Warenhaus, das** [VAHRənhaus] *n.* • department store
Meine Mutter arbeitet in einem Warenhaus.
*My mother works in a department store.*

**warm** [VAHRM] *adj.* • warm
**es ist warm** • it is warm
**warmherzig sein** • to be warm (a person)
Es war ein schöner, warmer Sommertag.
*It was a nice, warm Summer day.*

**warten** [VAHRtən] *v.* • to wait
**Wartezimmer, das** *n.* • waiting room
Ich warte im Vorzimmer.
*I'm going to wait in the anteroom.*

**warum** [vahRUM] *adv.* • why
Warum bist du so traurig?
*Why are you so sad?*

**was** [VAHS] *pron.* • what
Was hast du gesagt?
*What did you say?*

Was ist los?
*What's wrong?*

**waschen** [VAHshən] *v.* • to wash
**sich waschen** • to wash oneself
**Waschbecken, das** *n.* • sink; basin
**Waschbär, der** *n.* • raccoon
**Wäsche, die** *n.* • laundry
**Waschmaschine, die** *n.* • washing machine

| | |
|---|---|
| wasche | waschen |
| wäschst | wascht |
| wäscht | waschen |

Wir müssen das schmutzige Auto waschen.
*We must wash the dirty car.*

**Wasser, das** [VAHSə*r*] *n.* • water
**Mineralwasser, das** *n.* • mineral water
**Sprudelwasser, das** *n.* • soda
**Wassermelone, die** *n.* • watermelon
Ich bin durstig. Darf ich ein Glas Wasser haben?
*I'm thirsty. May I have a glass of water?*

**wechseln** [VEKseln] *v.* • to change (money)

| | |
|---|---|
| wechsele | wechseln |
| wechselst | wechselt |
| wechselt | wechseln |

Können Sie bitte diesen Schein wechseln?
*Can you please change this bill?*

**Wecker, der** [VEKə*r*] *n.* • alarm clock
Mein Wecker klingelt zu laut.
*My alarm clock rings too loud.*

**Weg, der** [VAIK] *n.* • way
Wir haben denselben Weg; laßt uns zusammen gehen.
*We are going the same way; let's walk together.*

**wegen** [VAIgən] *prep.* • because of
Meine Tochter kommt wegen meines Geburtstags.
*My daughter is coming because of my birthday.*

**weh tun** [VAI toon] *v.* • to hurt
Ich kann nicht gehen, weil meine Füße weh tun.
*I can't walk because my feet hurt.*

**weich** [VEI*SH*] *adj.* • soft
Diese Decke ist weich.
*This blanket is soft.*

**Weihnachten, das** [VEInah*kh*tən] *n.* • Christmas
**Weihnachtsabend, der** *n.* • Christmas Eve
Weihnachten ist am 25. Dezember.
*Christmas is December 25.*

**weil** [VEIL] *conj.* • because
Johann kann nicht gehen, weil er arbeiten muß.
*John can't go because he has work to do.*

**Wein, der** [VEIN] *n.* • wine
Dieser rote Wein kommt aus Frankreich.
*This red wine comes from France.*

**weinen** [VEINən] *v.* • to cry; to weep

| | |
|---|---|
| weine | weinen |
| weinst | weint |
| weint | weinen |

Viele Leute weinten bei der Beerdigung.
*Many people cried during the funeral.*

**weise** [VEIzə] *adj.* • wise
Wir fragten den weisen, alten Mann um Rat.
*We asked advice of the wise old man.*

**weiß** [VEIS] *adj.* • white
Das Papier ist weiß.
*The paper is white.*

**weit** [VEIT] *adj.* • far
Wohnst du weit von hier?
*Do you live far from here?*

**Weizen, der** [VEItsən] *n.* • wheat
Das Brot ist aus Weizenmehl gemacht.
*The bread is made with wheat flour.*

**welche; -r; -s** [VEL*sh*ə; VEL*sh*ər; VEL*sh*əs] *adj.; pron.* • what; which

Welche Straße sollen wir nehmen?
*What street are we supposed to take?*

**Welle, die** [VELə] *n.* • wave
Riesige Wellen schlugen im Sturm an Land.
*Huge waves came ashore in the storm.*

**Wellensittich, der** [VELənzitish] *n.* • parakeet
Dieser Wellensittich ist ein sehr lauter Vogel!
*This parakeet is a very noisy bird!*

**Welpe, der** [VELpə] *n.* • puppy
Die Hündin hatte vier Welpen.
*The dog had four puppies.*

**Welt, die** [VELT] *n.* • world
Eines Tages möchte ich um die Welt reisen.
*Someday I want to travel around the world.*

**Weltraum, der** [VELTraum] *n.* • space
Möchtest du eines Tages in den Weltraum fliegen?
*Do you want to go into space one day?*

**wenige** [VAInigə] *adj.* • few
Es sind nur wenige Kekse übrig.
*There are only a few cookies left.*

**weniger** [VAInigər] *adv.* • less
Du solltest nächstes Mal etwas weniger Salz nehmen.
*You should use a little less salt the next time.*

**wenn** [VEN] *conj.* • if
Wenn ich nicht kommen kann, ruf ich dich an.
*If I can't come, I'll call you.*

**wer** [VER] *pron.* • who
Wer will Fußball spielen?
*Who wants to play soccer?*

**Werbung, die** [VERbung] *n.* • publicity
Die Firma hat für dieses Produkt viel Werbung gemacht.
*The company had lots of publicity for this new product.*

**werden** [VERdən] *v.* • to become

| | |
|---|---|
| werde | werden |
| wirst | werdet |
| wird | werden |

Dein Benehmen wird immer schlechter.
*Your behavior is becoming worse and worse.*

**werfen** [VERfən] *v.* • to throw

| | |
|---|---|
| werfe | werfen |
| wirfst | werft |
| wirft | werfen |

Werf den Ball an die Wand.
*Throw the ball against the wall.*

**Westen, der** [VEStən] *n.* • west
Kalifornien liegt im Westen der U.S.A.
*California is in the west of the U.S.*

**Wetter, das** [VETə*r*] *n.* • weather
Wie ist das Wetter heute?
*What is the weather like today?*

**Wettkampf, der** [VETkahmpf] *n.* • contest
Ich habe den ersten Preis im Wettkampf gewonnen.
*I won first prize in the contest.*

**wichtig** [VI*sh*tis*h*] *adj.* • important
Es ist wichtig, daß du nicht versagst.
*It's important that you do not fail.*

**wie** [VEE] *adv.* • how; like
**Wie alt bist du?** • How old are you?
**Wie bitte?** • What (did you say)?
**Wie gehts?** • How are things?
**Wie weit ist --?** • How far is --?
**Wieviel?** • How much?

**Wie viele?** • How many?
**wissen wie** • to know how
Jetzt verstehe ich, wie man das macht!
*Now I understand how you do that!*

Ich liebe ihn wie einen Bruder.
*I love him like a brother.*

**wieder** [VEEdər] *adv.* • again
**nie wieder** • never again
Besuchen Sie uns bitte wieder.
*Please come to visit us again.*

**wiederholen** [veedərHOHLən] *v.* • to repeat

| | |
|---|---|
| wiederhole | wiederholen |
| wiederholst | wiederholt |
| wiederholt | wiederholen |

Wiederholen Sie bitte, was Sie gesagt haben, aber etwas langsamer.
*Please repeat what you said but more slowly.*

**Wiege, die** [VEEgə] *n.* • cradle
Die Mutter legt ihr Kind in die Wiege.
*The mother puts her baby in the cradle.*

**wiegen** [VEEgən] *v.* • to weigh
**Gewicht, das** *n.* • weight

| | |
|---|---|
| wiege | wiegen |
| wiegst | wiegt |
| wiegt | wiegen |

Der Lebensmittelhändler wiegt das Obst.
*The grocer weighs the fruit.*

**wild** [VILT] *adj.* • wild
Es gibt viele wilde Tiere im Dschungel.
*There are many wild animals in the jungle.*

**Willkommen, das** [vilKAWMən] *n.* • welcome
**du bist willkommen** • you are welcome
Willkommen bei uns zu Hause!
*Welcome to our home!*

**Wind, der** [VINT] *n.* • wind
**Windmühle, die** *n.* • windmill
Der Wind weht von Norden her.
*The wind is blowing from the north.*

**Winter, der** [VINtə*r*] *n.* • winter
Im Winter gehen wir Ski laufen.
*In winter we go skiing.*

**Wippe, die** [VIPə] *n.* • seesaw
Im Park ist eine Wippe.
*There is a seesaw in the park.*

**wir** [VEER] *pron.* • we
Wir gehen zusammen zum Bahnhof.
*We are going to the train station together.*

**wirklich** [VIRKli*sh*] *adv.* • really
Glaubst du wirklich, daß dieses der richtige Weg ist?
*Do you really think this is the right way?*

**wissen** [VISən] *v.* • to know

| | |
|---|---|
| weiß | wissen |
| weißt | wißt |
| weiß | wissen |

Für die Prüfung müssen wir alles wissen.
*We have to know everything for the test.*

**Wissenschaft, die** [VISənshahft] *n.* • science; knowledge
**wissenschaftlich** *adj.* • scientific
**Wissenschaftler, der (-in, f.)** *n.* • scientist
Die Wissenschaft ist für mich ein schweres Fach.
*Science is a hard subject for me.*

**Witz, der** [VITS] *n.* • joke
Jeder lacht, wenn er einen Witz erzählt.
*Everyone laughs when he tells a joke.*

**wo** [VOH] *adv.* • where
**wo(hin) immer; irgendwo** *adv.* • anywhere; wherever
**woher** *adv.* • where from
Wo sind meine Schuhe?
*Where are my shoes?*

**Woche, die** [VO*kh*ə] *n.* • week
**Wochenende, das** *n.* • weekend
Wie heißen die Wochentage auf Französisch?
*What are the days of the week in French?*

**wohlhabend** [VOHLhahbent] *adj.* • wealthy
Diese wohlhabende Familie ist sehr großzügig.
*This wealthy family is very generous.*

**wohnen** [VOHNən] *v.* • to live
**Wohnzimmer, das** *n.* • living room

| | |
|---|---|
| wohne | wohnen |
| wohnst | wohnt |
| wohnt | wohnen |

Die ganze Familie wohnt zusammen.
*The whole family lives together.*

**Wohnung, die** [VOHNung] *n.* • apartment
Sie haben eine große Wohnung.
*They have a big apartment.*

**Wolf, der** [VAWLF] *n.* • wolf
Hast du Angst vor Wölfen?
*Are you afraid of wolves?*

**Wolke, die** [VAWLkə] *n.* • cloud
**bewölkt** *adj.* • cloudy
**Wolkenkratzer, der** *n.* • skyscraper
Sieh die Wolken an! Es wird regnen!
*Look at the clouds! It is going to rain!*

**Wolle, die** [VAWLə] *n.* • wool
**aus Wolle; wollen** *adj.* • woolen
Meine Tante hat mir einen Pullover aus reiner Wolle gestrickt.
*My aunt knitted me a sweater of pure wool.*

**wollen** [VAWLən] *v.* • to want

| | |
|---|---|
| will | wollen |
| willst | wollt |
| will | wollen |

Wir wollen mit dir kommen.
*We want to come with you.*

**Wort, das** [VAWRT] *n.* • word
**Wörterbuch, das** *n.* • dictionary
Ich werde dieses Wort im Wörterbuch nachschlagen.
*I am going to look up this word in the dictionary.*

**wunderbar** [VUNdərbahr] *adj.* • marvelous; wonderful
Dieser Karneval ist wunderbar!
*This carnival is marvelous!*

**wünschen** [V*UE*Nshən] *v.* • to wish
**ein Wunsch** *n.* • a wish
**gute Wünsche** • best wishes

| | |
|---|---|
| wünsche | wünschen |
| wünschst | wünscht |
| wünscht | wünschen |

Was wünschst du dir zu Weihnachten?
*What do you wish for Christmas?*

**Würfel, der** [V*UE*Rfəl] *n.* • cube
Dieses Haus sieht einem großen Würfel ähnlich!
*This house looks like a big cube!*

**Wurm, der** [VURM] *n.* • worm
**Regenwurm, der** *n.* • earthworm
Wir benutzen die Würmer als Köder.
*We use the worms for bait.*

**Wurst, die** [VOORST] *n.* • sausage
Wir kaufen Wurst im Feinkostgeschäft.
*We buy sausages at the delicatessen.*

**Wüste, die** [V*UE*Stə] *n.* • desert
Es ist sehr heiß in der Wüste.
*It is very hot in the desert.*

**wütend** [V*UE*tent] *adj.* • furious
Wenn ich mein Zimmer nicht putze, wird meine Mutter wütend sein.
*If I don't clean my room my mother will be furious.*

# X

**Xylophon, das** [ks*ue*lohFOHN] *n.* • xylophone
Das Xylophon wird mit einem Holzklöppel gespielt.
*A xylophone is played with a wooden mallet.*

# Z

**zählen** [TSAILən] *v.* • to count
**zahlreich** *adj.* • numerous
Meine kleine Schwester kann bis 100 zählen.
*My little sister can count to 100.*

**Zahn, der** [TSAHN] *n.* • tooth
**Zahnarzt, der** *n.* • dentist
**Zahnbürste, die** *n.* • toothbrush
**Zahnpasta, die** *n.* • toothpaste
**Zahnschmerzen haben** • to have a toothache
Der Zahnarzt heilte meinen entzündeten Zahn.
*The dentist fixed my sore tooth.*

**Zapfsäule, die** [TSAHPFzoilə] *n.* • gas pump
Die Tankstelle hat acht Zapfsäulen.
*The gas station has eight gas pumps.*

**Zauberei, die** [tsaubəREI] *n.* • magic
**Zauberer, der; Zauberin; die** *n.* • magician
Der Prinz ist durch Zauberei in einen Stein verwandelt worden.
*The prince was changed into a stone by magic.*

**Zebra, das** [TSAIbrah] *n.* • zebra
Zebras haben schwarze und weiße Streifen.
*Zebras have black and white stripes.*

**Zeh, der** [TSAI] *n.* • toe
Mein Zeh schmerzt von den engen Schuhen.
*My toe hurts from the tight shoes.*

**zehn** [TSAIN] *adj.* • ten
Ich wohne seit zehn Jahren in diesem Haus.
*I've lived in this house for ten years.*

**zeichnen** [TSEI*SH*nən] *v.* • to draw
**Zeichen, das** *n.* • sign
**Zeichnung, die** *n.* • drawing

| | |
|---|---|
| zeichne | zeichnen |
| zeichnest | zeichnet |
| zeichnet | zeichnen |

Kannst von dem, was du gesehen hast, ein Bild zeichnen?
*Can you draw a picture of what you saw?*

**zeigen** [TSEIgən] *v.* • to show

| | |
|---|---|
| zeige | zeigen |
| zeigst | zeigt |
| zeigt | zeigen |

Zeig mir dein neues Buch.
*Show me your new book.*

**Zeit, die** [TSEIT] *n.* • time
**eine lange Zeit** • a long time

Wieviel Zeit haben wir?
*How much time do we have?*

**Zeitschrift, die** [TSEITshrift] *n.* • magazine
Welche Zeitschrift liest du gern?
*Which magazine do you like to read?*

**Zeitung, die** [TSEItung] *n.* • newspaper
Viele Leute lesen die Zeitung im Zug.
*Many people read the newspaper on the train.*

**Zelt, das** [TSELT] *n.* • tent
Ich schlafe gern in einem Zelt.
*I like to sleep in a tent.*

**zelten** [TSELtən] *n.* • go camping
Ich gehe im August mit meiner Familie zelten.
*I go camping with my family in August.*

**zentral** [tsenTRAHL] *adj.* • central
Dieser Laden befindet sich in einer zentralen Lage.
*This store is in a central location.*

**zerbrechen** [tserBRE*sh*ən] *v.* • to break
Glas zerbricht sehr leicht.
*Glass breaks very easily.*

**zerdrücken** [tserDR*UE*kən] *v.* • to crush
Sei vorsichtig! Zerdrück die Eier nicht.
*Be careful! Don't crush the eggs!*

**zerreißen** [tserREIsən] *v.* • to tear
Zerreiß das Papier nicht!
*Don't tear the paper.*

**zerschlagen** [tserSHLAHgən] *v.* • to smash
Er zerschlug das Glas mit einem Hammer.
*He smashed the glass with a hammer.*

**zerstören** [tserSHT*ER*rən] *v.* • to destroy

zerstöre zerstören
zerstörst zerstört
zerstört zerstören

Ein Vulkan zerstörte die Stadt Pompeji.
*A volcano destroyed the city of Pompeii.*

**Ziege, die** [TSEEgə] *n.* • goat
Der Bauer züchtet Schafe und Ziegen.
*The farmer raises sheep and goats.*

**ziehen** [TSEEən] *v.* • to pull
**umziehen** *v.* • to move (furniture)

ziehe ziehen
ziehst zieht
zieht ziehen

Man muß an der Schnur ziehen, damit die Glocke klingelt.
*You pull the rope to ring the bell.*

**Ziel, das** [TSEEL] *n.* • goal
Was ist das Ziel dieses Projekts?
*What is the goal of this project?*

**ziemlich** [TSEEMli*sh*] *adv.* • quite; rather
Diese Abschlußprüfung ist ziemlich lang.
*This final exam is quite long.*

**Zigarette, die** [tseegahRETə] *n.* • cigarette
Man darf keine Zigaretten im Flugzeug rauchen.
*You can't smoke cigarettes on the plane.*

**Zimmer, das** [TSIMə*r*] *n.* • room
**Badezimmer, das** *n.* • bathroom
**Eßzimmer, das** *n.* • dining room
**Klassenzimmer, das** *n.* • classroom
**Schlafzimmer, das** *n.* • bedroom
**Wohnzimmer, das** *n.* • living room
Unser Haus hat acht Zimmer.
*Our house has eight rooms.*

**Zimmerleute, die** [TSIMərloitə] *n. pl.* • carpenters
Die Zimmerleute bauen ein Haus.
*The carpenters are building a house.*

**Zirkus, der** [TSIRkus] *n.* • circus
Der Zirkus ist eine Woche lang in der Stadt.
*The circus is in town for a week.*

**Zitrone, die** [tseeTROHnə] *n.* • lemon
Wir benutzten eine Zitrone für dieses Rezept.
*We used a lemon for this recipe.*

**zittern** [TSITərn] *n.* • to shake
Ich habe solche Angst, daß ich am ganzen Körper zittere.
*I'm so scared I'm shaking all over.*

**Zoo, der** [TSOH] *n.* • zoo
Man kann alle möglichen Arten von Tieren im Zoo sehen.
*You see all sorts of animals at the zoo.*

**zornig** [TSAWRnish] *adj.* • angry
Wenn Johann zornig ist, schreit er.
*When John is angry, he yells.*

**zu** [TSOO] *prep.* • to; too
Ich gehe heute zu meiner Schwester.
*I am going to my sister's today.*

**züchten** [TSUEshtən] *v.* • to grow
Ich züchte Gemüse in meinem Garten.
*I grow vegetables in my garden.*

**Zucker, der** [TSUkər] *n.* • sugar
Nimmst du Zucker in deinen Kaffee?
*Do you take sugar in your coffee?*

**zufrieden sein** [tsuFREEdən zein] *adj.* • to be content

Der Lehrer ist mit unserer Arbeit zufrieden.
*The teacher is content with our work.*

**Zug, der** [TSOOK] *n.* • train
Um wieviel Uhr kommt der Zug an?
*What time does the train arrive?*

**zugeben** [TSOOgaibən] *v.* • to admit; to acknowledge
Sie geben zu, daß sie einen Fehler gemacht haben.
*They admit that they made a mistake.*

**zuhören** [TSOOh*err*ən] *v.* • to listen
Wir hörten den Anweisungen genau zu.
*We listened carefully to the directions.*

**Zukunft, die** [TSOOkunft] *n.* • future
Die Zukunft dieses Geschäfts ist vielsprechend.
*The future of this business is promising.*

**Zunge, die** [TSUNGə] *n.* • tongue
Die Zunge des Hundes ist rosa.
*The dog's tongue is pink.*

**zurück** [tsuR*UE*K] *prep.* • back
**zurückgeben** *v.* • to give back
**zurückgehen** *v.* • to return (go back to)
Wann kommst du zurück?
*When are you coming back?*

**zurückkommen** [tsuR*UE*Kkawmən] *v.* • to return
Sie kommen von ihrer Reise zurück.
*They are returning from their trip.*

**zusammen** [tsuZAHMən] *adv.* • together
Die zwei Freunde sitzen zusammen.
*The two friends sit together.*

**zusammenlegen** [tsuZAHMənlaigən] *v.* • to fold
Ich lege die Handtücher zusammenehe ich sie weglege.
*I fold the towels before I put them away.*

**zwanzig** [TSVAHNtsi*sh*] *adj.* • twenty
Es dauert zwanzig Minuten, um in die Stadt zu gehen.
*It takes twenty minutes to go downtown.*

**zwei** [TSVEI] *adj.* • two
**zwei auf einmal** • two at a time
Unsere Familie besitzt zwei Autos.
*Our family owns two cars.*

**zweimal** [TSVEImahl] *adv.* • twice
Er ißt nur zweimal am Tag.
*He eats only twice a day.*

**zweite** [TSVEItə] *adj.* • second
Dieses ist ihre zweite Reise nach Frankreich.
*This is her second trip to France.*

**Zwiebel, die** [TSVEEbəl] *n.* • onion
Das Zwiebelschneiden läßt meine Augen tränen.
*Slicing onions makes my eyes water.*

**Zwilling, der (die, f.)** [TSVILing] *n.* • twin
Meine Schwester hat Zwillinge.
*My sister has twins.*

**zwischen** [TSVISHən] *prep.* • between
Ich setze mich zwischen meine zwei besten Freunde.
*I sit down between my two best friends.*

**Zwischenmahlzeit, die** [TSVISHənmahltseit] *n.* • snack
Wir haben eine Zwischenmahlzeit, wenn wir nach Hause kommen.
*We have a snack when we get home from school.*

**zwölf** [TSV*ER*LF] *adj.* • twelve
Mein Freund ist zwölf Jahre alt.
*My friend is twelve years old.*

# Illustrations/*die Abbildungen*

## Clothing—die Kleider

## Clothing—die Kleider

## Office Supplies—die Büroartikel

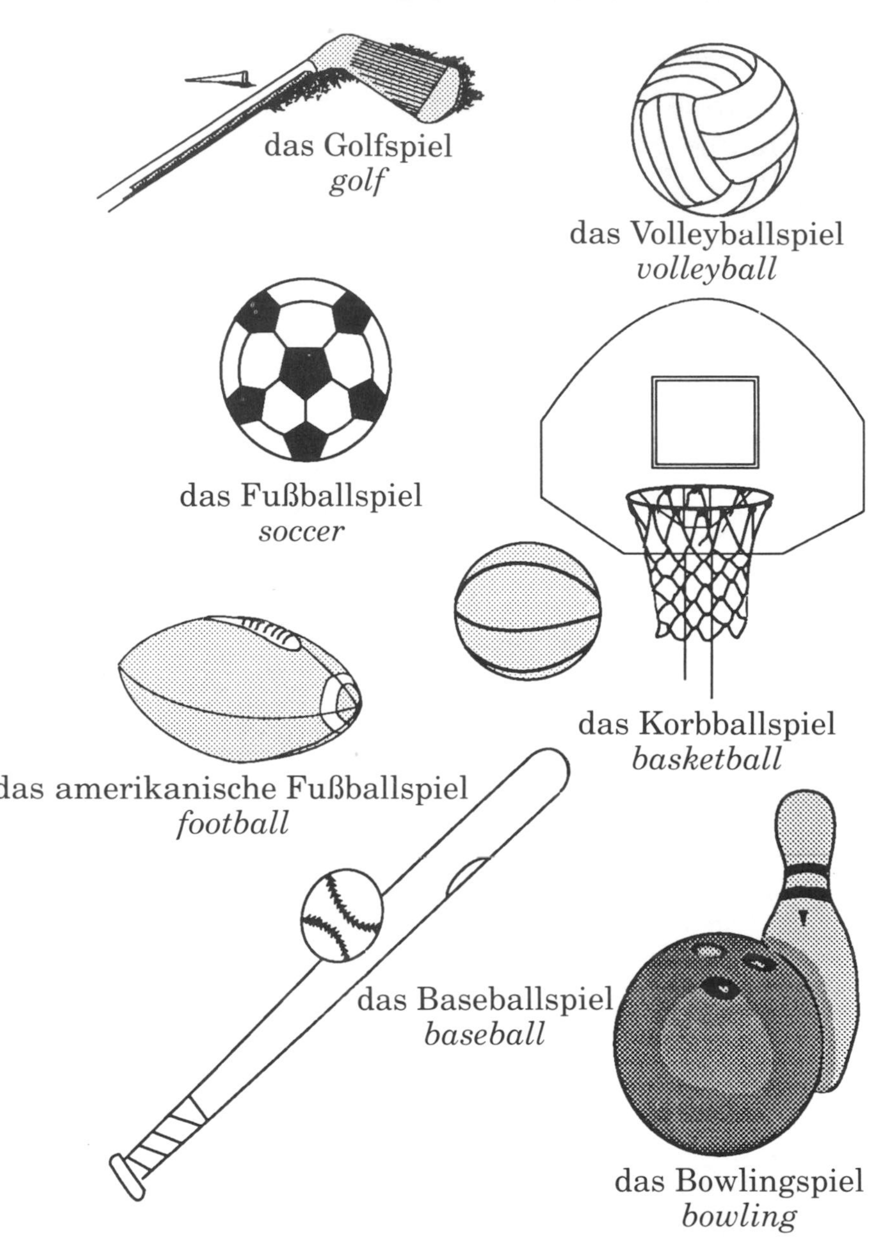


## Sports—die Sportarten

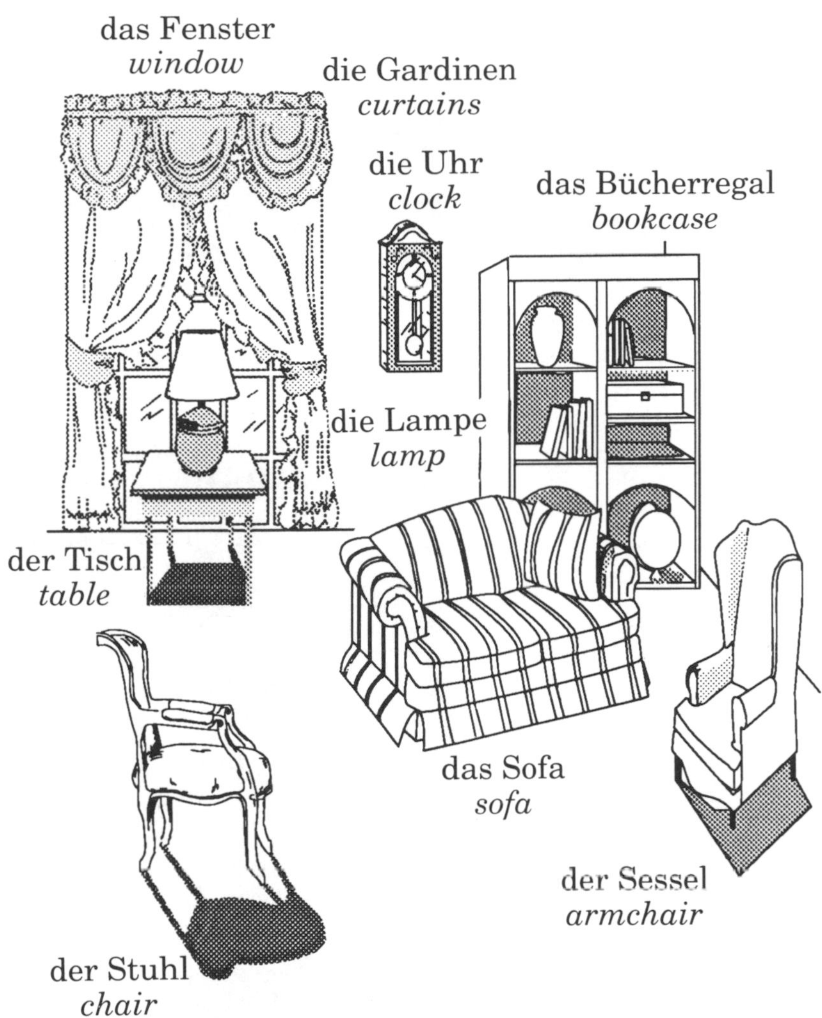


## Living Room—das Wohnzimmer

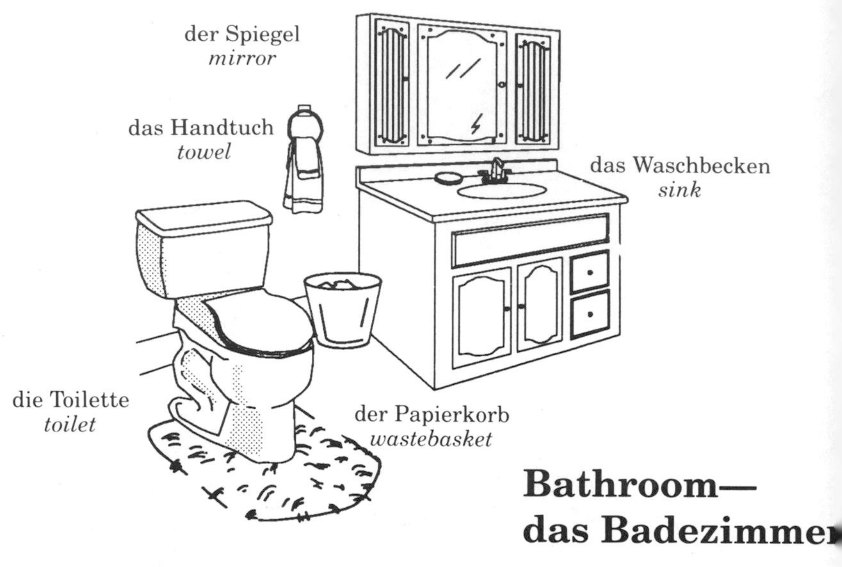


## Bathroom— das Badezimmer

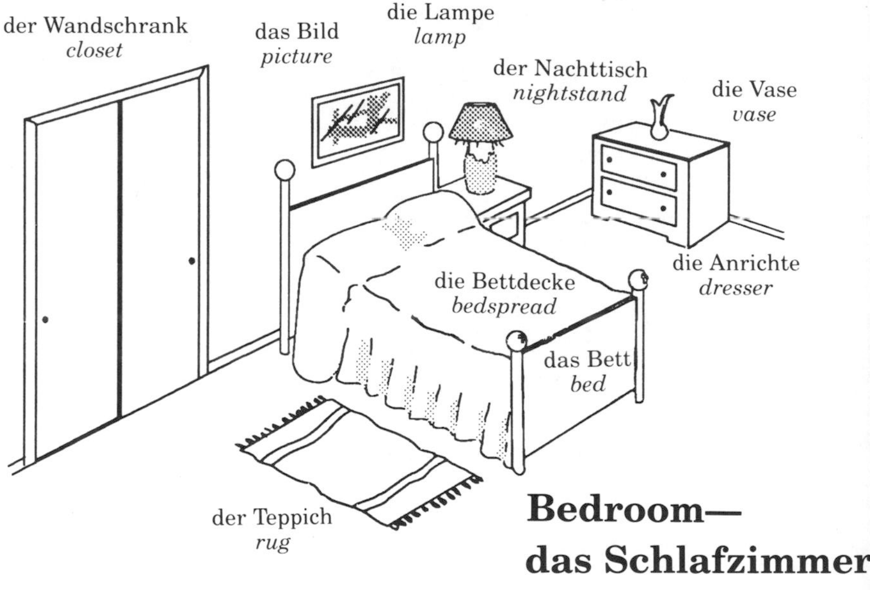


## Bedroom— das Schlafzimmer

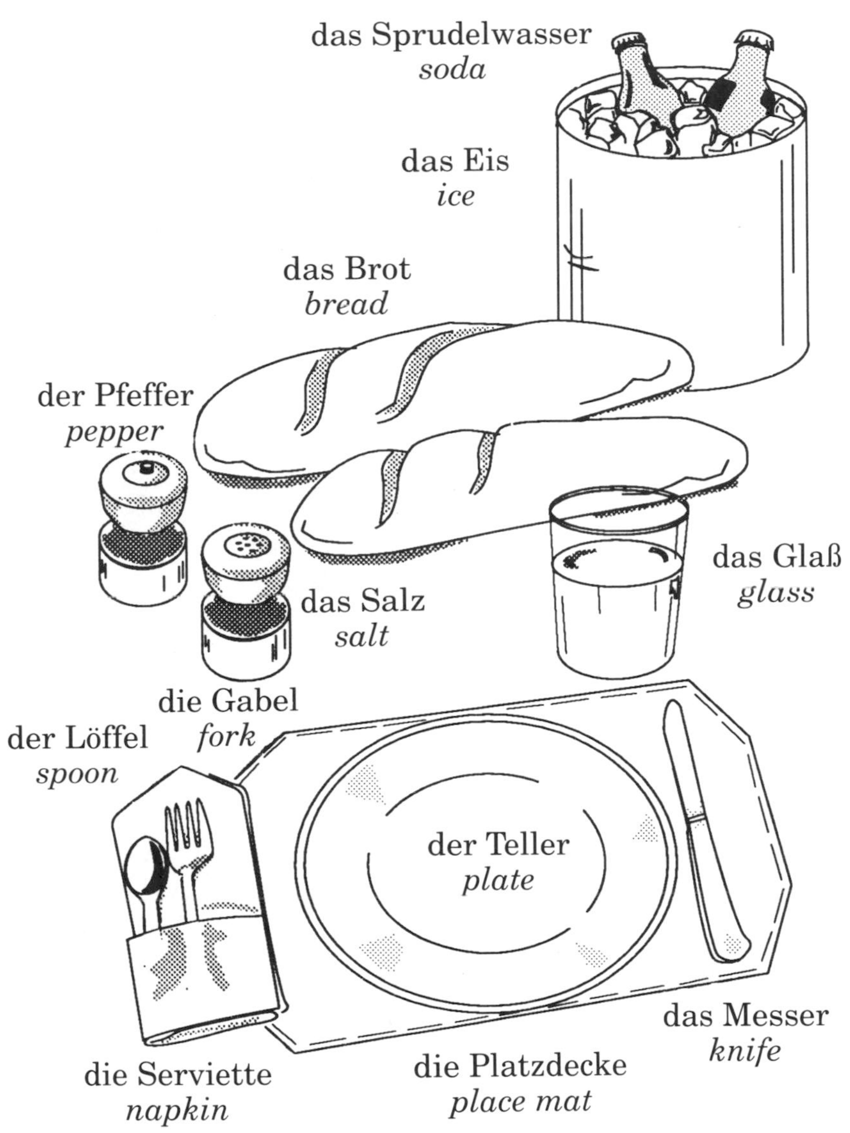


**Table—der Tisch**

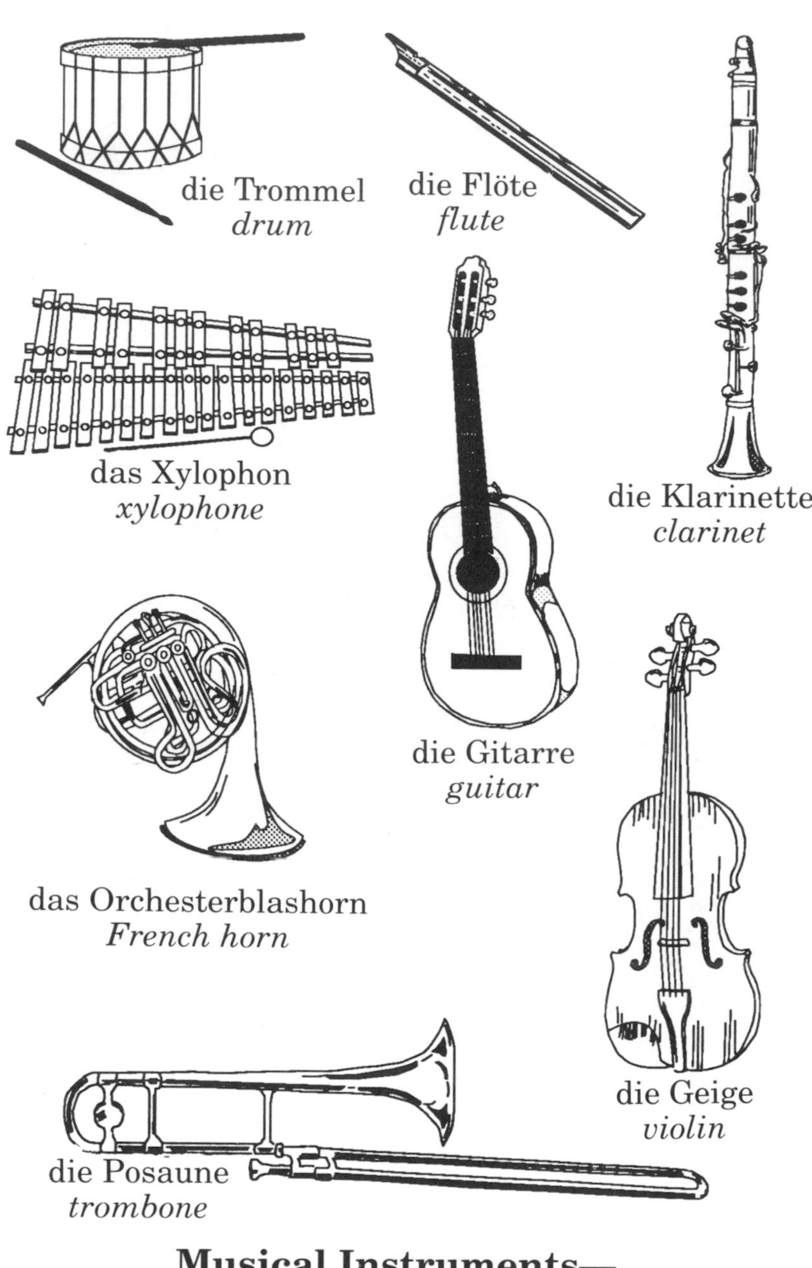


**Musical Instruments—Musikinstrumente**

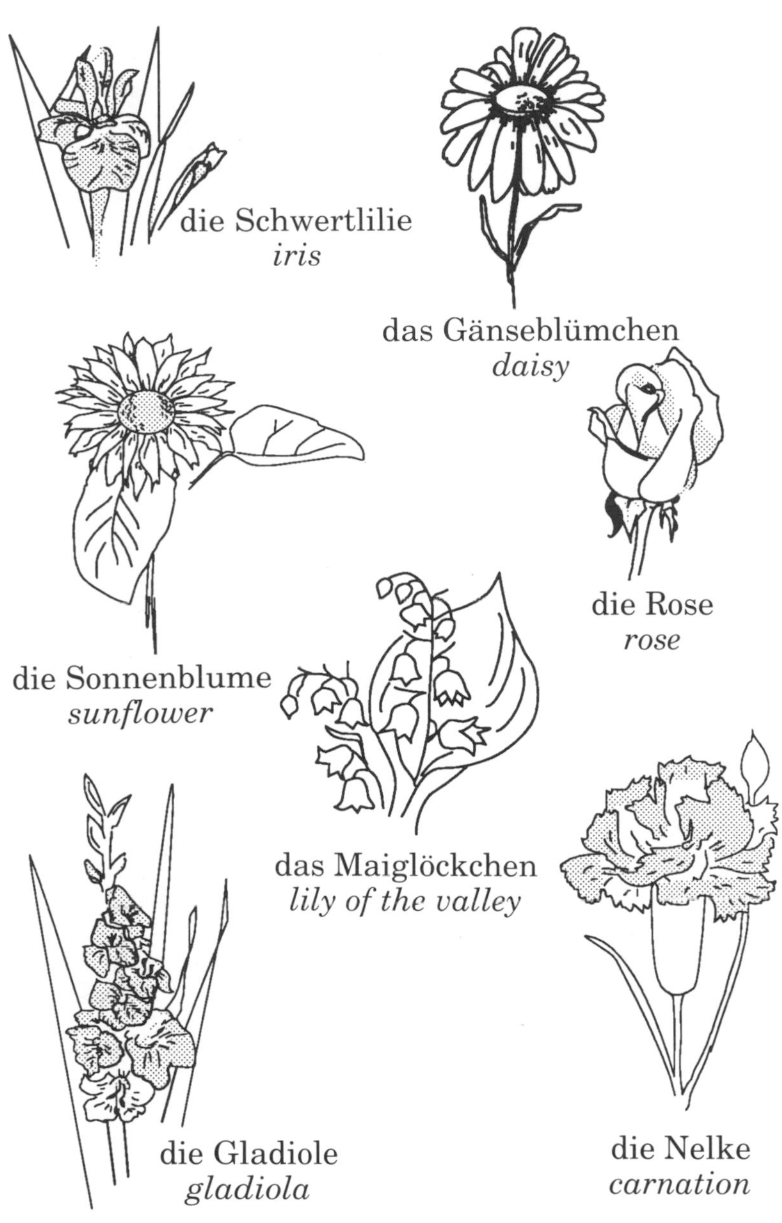


**Flowers—die Blumen**

**Vegetables—das Gemüse**

**Fruit—die Frucht**

**Farm animals—
Tiere auf dem Bauernhof**

**Birds—die Vögel**

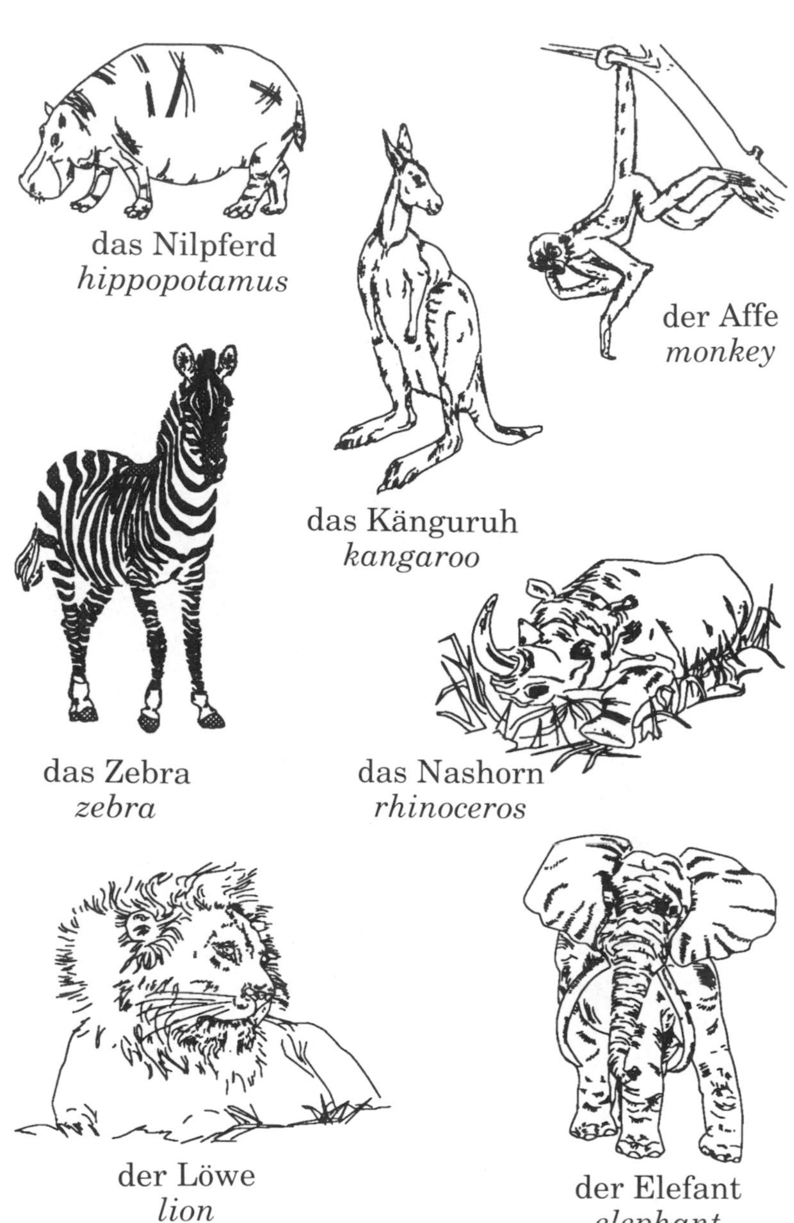


## Zoo Animals—Tiere im zoologischen Garten

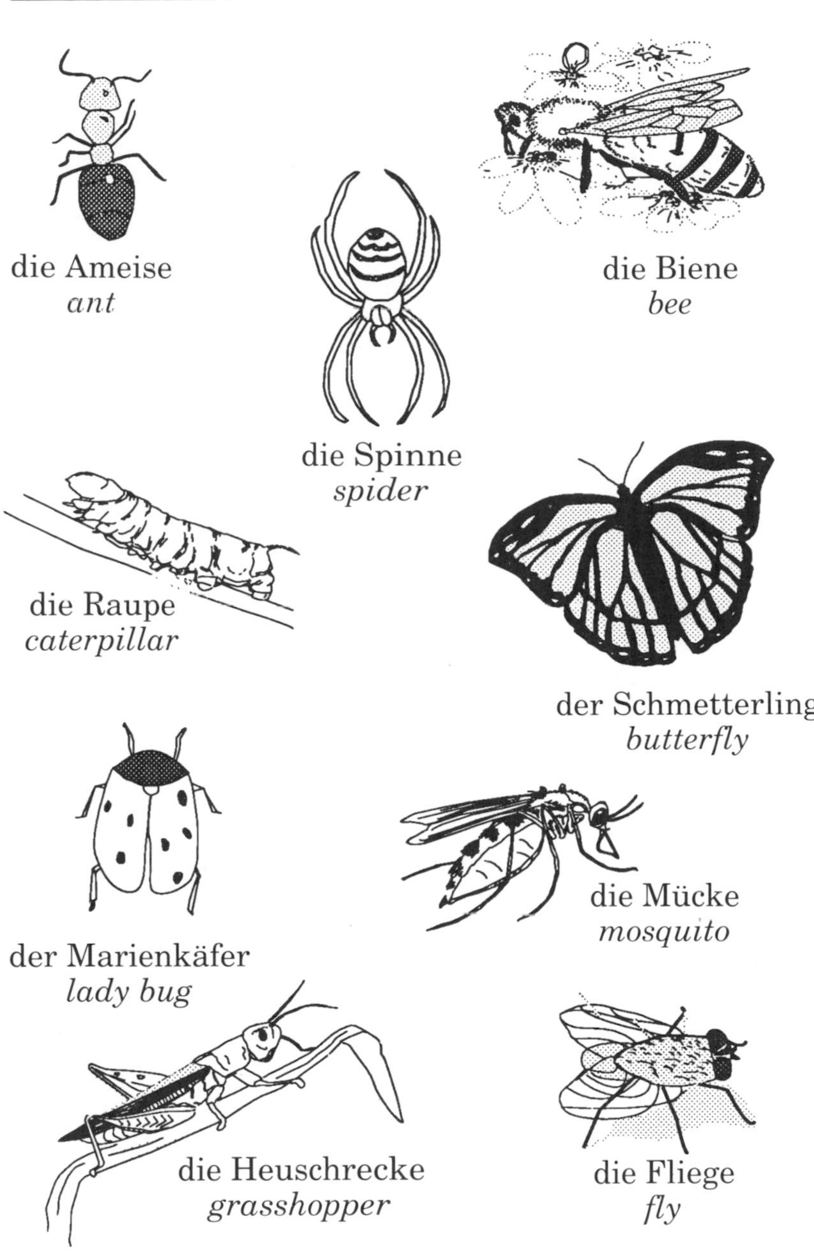


**Insects—die Insekten**

## Wild Animals—die Wildtiere

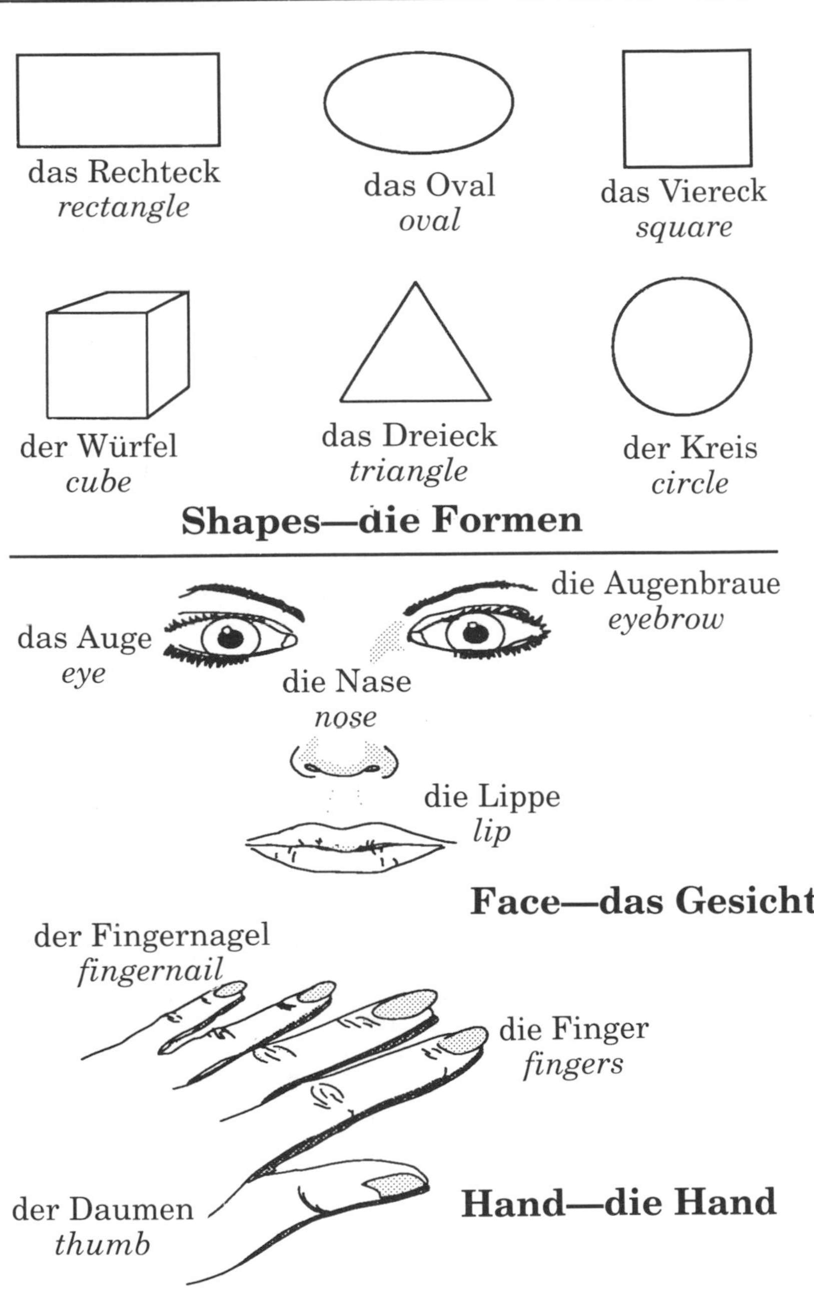
das Rechteck
rectangle
das Oval
oval
das Viereck
square
der Würfel
cube
das Dreieck
triangle
der Kreis
circle
Shapes—die Formen
die Augenbraue
eyebrow
das Auge
eye
die Nase
nose
die Lippe
lip
Face—das Gesicht
der Fingernagel
fingernail
die Finger
fingers
der Daumen
thumb
Hand—die Hand

der Fisch
*fish*

die Schlange
*snake*

die Schildkröte
*turtle*

die Maus
*mouse*

die Katze
*cat*

der Hund
*dog*

das Kaninchen
*rabbit*

**Pets—die Haustiere**

der Bus
*bus*

das Auto
*automobile*

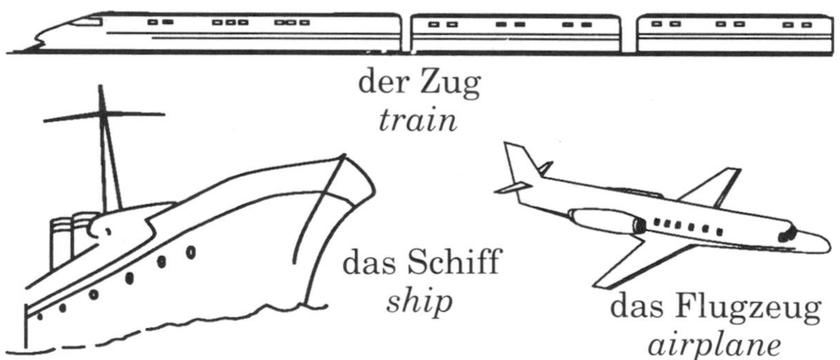

der Zug
*train*

das Schiff
*ship*

das Flugzeug
*airplane*

**Transportation—
die Verkehrsmittel**

# Englisch zu Deutsch/English to German

# A

**a; an** [*EJ*; ə; *A*N; əN] *indef. art.* • ein; eine
I have a daughter and a son.
*Ich habe eine Tochter und einen Sohn.*

This is an old movie.
*Dies ist ein alter Film.*

**able, to be (can)** [*EJ*bəl] *v.* • können
They are able to solve this problem.
*Sie können dieses Problem lösen.*

**about** [əBAUT] *adv.* • gegen
It's about three o'clock.
*Es ist gegen drei Uhr.*

**above** [əBə*V*] *prep.* • über
**above all** • vor allem
My room is above the kitchen.
*Mein Zimmer ist über der Küche.*

**absence** [*A*Bsəns] *n.* • Abwesenheit, die
His absence from class was seldom noticed.
*Seine Abwesenheit von der Klasse wurde selten bemerkt.*

**absent** [*A*Bsənt] *adj.* • abwesend
Half the class is absent today.
*Die Hälfte der Klasse ist heute abwesend.*

**accent** [*A*Ksent] *n.* • Betonung, die
The accent is on the first syllable.
*Die Betonung ist auf der ersten Silbe.*

**accept, to** [*a*kSEPT] *v.* • akzeptieren
The bank won't accept this check.
*Die Bank akzeptiert diesen Scheck nicht.*

**according to** [əK*AW*Rding t*oo*] *prep.* • nach
According to the newspaper, it is going to rain today.
*Der Zeitung nach, wird es heute regnen.*

**acquainted with, to be (to know)** [əK*WEJ*Ntəd *with*] *v.* • kennen
Are you acquainted with your neighbors?
*Kennst du deine Nachbarn?*

**across** [əKR*AW*S] *prep.* • über; hinüber; herüber
**across from** • gegenüber
He ran across the road.
*Er lief über die Straße.*

They live across from the school.
*Sie wohnen gegenüber der Schule.*

**actor; actress** [AKtə*r*; AKtrəs] *n.* • Schauspieler, der (-in, f.)
What's the name of the actor in that new film?
*Wie heißt der Schauspieler in dem neuen Film?*

**address** [ADres] *n.* • Adresse, die
What is your home address?
*Wie ist deine Adresse zu Hause?*

**add, to** [AD] *v.* • hinzufügen
We'll add a place setting at the table for our guest.
*Wir werden für unseren Gast noch einen Platz am Tisch hinzufügen.*

**admit** [*a*dMIT] *v.* • zugeben
They admit that they made a mistake.
*Sie geben zu, daß sie einen Fehler gemacht haben.*

**adolescence** [*a*dəLESənts] *n.* • Jugendalter, das
**adolescent** *n.* • Jugendliche, der (Heranwachsende)
Adolescence is a time to learn and mature.
*Das Jugendalter, ist eine Zeit zum Lernen und sich Entwickeln.*

**adopt, to** [əDAHPT] *v.* • adoptieren
The young couple is adopting a baby.
*Das junge Paar adoptiert ein kleines Kind.*

**adventure** [*a*dVEN*tsh*ə*r*] *n.* • Abenteuer, das
Our trip to Europe was a great adventure!
*Unsere Reise nach Europa war ein großes Abenteuer!*

**advertisement** [*a*d*v*ə*r*TEIZmənt] *n.* • Anzeige, die
**want ads** • Inserate, die
There are a lot of advertisements in this magazine.
*In dieser Zeitschrift gibt es viele Anzeigen.*

**adviser** [*a*dVEI*z*ə*r*] *n.* • Ratgeber, der
The president has several advisers.
*Der Präsident hat mehrere Ratgeber.*

**afraid** [əFR*EJ*D] *adj.* • sich fürchten
**to be afraid of** • sich vor etwas fürchten
He is afraid of spiders.
*Er fürchtet sich vor Spinnen.*

**after** [AFtə*r*] *prep.* • nach
I'm going to leave after you.
*Ich werde nach dir gehen.*

**afternoon** [*a*ftə*r*N*OO*N] *n.* • Nachmittag, der
We eat in the early afternoon.
*Wir essen am frühen Nachmittag.*

**air** [*EJ*R] *n.* • Luft, die
**airline** *n.* • Fluglinie, die
**airline steward (-ess, f.)** *n.* • Steward, der (-ess, f.)
**by air mail** • bei Luftpost
There is too much smoke in the air.
*Es gibt zuviel Rauch in der Luft.*

**airplane** [*EJ*Rpl*ej*n] *n.* • Flugzeug, das
We're going to France by airplane.
*Wir fliegen mit dem Flugzeug nach Frankreich.*

**airport** [*EJ*Rpohrt] *n.* • Flughafen, der
The plane landed at the airport on time.
*Das Flugzeug landete pünktlich auf dem Flughafen.*

**air-conditioned** [*EJ*Rkəndishənd] *adj.* • eine Klimaanlage haben
**air-conditioning** *n.* • Klimatisierung, die
This movie theater is air-conditioned.
*Dieses Kino hat eine Klimaanlage.*

**alarm clock** [əLAHRM KLAHK] *n.* • Wecker, der
My alarm clock rings too loud.
*Mein Wecker klingelt zu laut.*

**alike** [əLEIK] *adj.* • ähnlich
These dresses are too much alike.
*Diese Kleider sind zu ähnlich.*

**all** [*AW*L] *adj.* • ganz
**all at once** • plötzlich; auf einmal
**all over** • überall
**all right (OK)** • gut!; schön!; alles klar!
**not at all** • keineswegs; überhaupt nicht
All of my family is together on holidays.
*Meine ganze Familie ist an Feiertagen zusammen.*

**almost** [*AW*Lmohst] *adv.* • fast
The train arrived almost an hour late.
*Der Zug kam fast eine Stunde zu spät an.*

**alone** [əLOHN] *adj.* • allein
I felt alone in the strange city.
*Ich fühlte mich allein in der fremden Stadt.*

**along** [əL*AW*NG] *prep.* • entlang
**alongside** *adv.; prep.* • nebenan
Trees grow along the avenue.
*Die Bäume wachsen entlang der Allee.*

**aloud** [əLAUD] *adv.* • laut
Repeat these sentences aloud.
*Wiederholen Sie diese Sätze laut.*

**alphabet** [*A*Lfəbet] *n.* • Alphabet, das
Children begin to learn the alphabet in kindergarten.
*Kinder fangen im Kindergarten an, das Alphabet zu lernen.*

**already** [*aw*lREDie] *adv.* • schon
My brother is already grown up.
*Mein Bruder ist schon erwachsen.*

**also (too)** [*AW*Lsoh] *adv.* • auch
I also want to meet the students.
*Ich möchte auch die Studenten kennenlernen.*

**always** [*AW*L*wejz*] *adv.* • immer
We always eat at six o'clock in the evening.
*Wir essen immer um 6 uhr abends.*

**am** See *to be.*

**amaze, to** [əM*EJZ*] *v.* • erstaunen
**amazing** *adj.* • erstaunlich

Your quick improvement amazes me.
*Deine schnelle Verbesserung erstaunt mich.*

**ambassador** [*a*mBASədər] *n.* • Botschafter, der (-in, f.)
The ambassador works at the embassy.
*Der Botschafter arbeitet bei der Botschaft.*

**ambulance** [*A*Mbj*oo*ləns] *n.* • Krankenwagen, der
The ambulance takes sick people to the hospital.
*Der Krankenwagen bringt Kranke zum Krankenhaus.*

**America** [əMERikə] *n.* • Amerika
**American** *adj.* • amerikanisch
**American (person)** *n.* • Amerikaner, der, (-in, f.)
**Central America** *n.* • Mittelamerika
**North America** *n.* • Nordamerika
**South America** *n.* • Südamerika
Many people in America have ancestors from Europe.
*Viele Menschen in Amerika haben Vorfahren aus Europa.*

American music is popular around the world.
*Amerikanische Musik ist in der ganzen Welt populär.*

**amuse, to** [əMJ*OOZ*] *v.* • unterhalten
**amusing; fun** *adj.* • amüsant, belustigend
The clown amuses the little girl.
*Der Clown unterhält das kleine Mädchen.*

**an** See *a*.

**ancestor** [*A*Nsestər] *n.* • Vorfahr, der (die, f.)
My ancestors come from Ireland.
*Meine Vorfahren kommen aus Irland.*

**ancient** [*EJ*N*tsh*ənt] *adj.* • uralt
We're going to visit the ancient ruins in Rome.
*Wir werden die uralten Ruinen in Rom besuchen.*

**and** [*A*ND] *conj.* • und
Paul and Veronique are going to the fair.
*Paul und Veronique gehen zum Jahrmarkt.*

**angel** [*EJ*N*dzh*əl] *n.* • Engel, der
Marie sings like an angel.
*Marie singt wie ein Engel.*

**angry** [*A*NGgrie] *adj.* • zornig
When John is angry, he yells.
*Wenn Johann zornig ist, schreit er.*

**animal** [*A*Nimәl] *n.* • Tier, das
A veterinarian takes care of animals.
*Ein Tierarzt kümmert sich um Tiere.*

**anniversary (wedding)** [*a*nə*V*Ə*R*sərie] *n.* • Hochzeitstag, der
My parents' wedding anniversary is August 8.
*Der Hochzeitstag meiner Eltern ist am 8. August.*

**announce, to** [əNAUNS] *v.* • ankündigen
**announcement** *n.* • Anzeige, die
Should we announce our plans to your parents?
*Sollten wir deinen Eltern unsere Pläne ankündigen?*

**annoying** [əNEUjing] *adj.* • ärgerlich
It's annoying that we have to wait so long.
*Es ist ärgerlich, daß wir so lange warten müssen.*

**another** [əNƏ*dh*ə*r*] *adj.; pron.* • noch ein, -e, -es
I need another hour to finish the work.
*Ich brauche noch eine Stunde, um die Arbeit zu beenden.*

**answer, to** [*A*Nsə*r*] *v.* • beantworten
**answer** *n.* • Antwort, die
Answer questions 1-10 in your book.
*Beantworten Sie die Fragen 1-10 in ihrem Buch.*

**ant** [*A*NT] *n.* • Ameise, die
Ants are hard-working insects.
*Ameisen sind fleißige Insekten.*

**any** [ENie] *adj.; pron.* • etwas
**anyone** *pron.* • irgend jemand
**anything** *pron.* • irgend etwas
Do you have any milk?
*Haben Sie etwas Milch?*

Does anyone want milk?
*Möchte irgendjemand Milch?*

**apartment** [əPAHRTmənt] *n.* • Wohnung, die
**apartment building** *n.* •
Appartementgebäude, das
They have a big apartment.
*Sie haben eine große Wohnung.*

**appear, to** [əPIER] *v.* • scheinen
She appears weary from the long trip.
*Sie scheint von der langen Reise erschöpft zu sein.*

**appetite** [*A*Pəteit] *n.* • Appetit, der
After I exercise I have a big appetite.
*Nachdem ich Sport getreiben habe, habe ich großen Appetit.*

**appetizer** [*A*Pəteizə*r*] *n.* • Vorspeise, die
Would you like an appetizer before your main course?
*Möchtest du eine Vorspeise vor deinem Hauptgericht?*

**apple** [*A*Pəl] *n.* • Apfel, der
**apple juice** • Apfelsaft, der
Claude is making an apple pie.
*Claude macht einen Apfelkuchen.*

**appointment** [əPEUNTmənt] *n.* • Termin, der
I have a doctor's appointment at 9 o'clock.
*Ich habe um 9 Uhr einen Termin beim Arzt.*

**approach, to** [əPROH*TSH*] *v.* • sich nähern
The dog is approaching the cat.
*Der Hund nähert sich der Katze.*

**apricot** [*A*Prəkaht] *n.* • Aprikose, die
Apricots are like peaches but smaller.
*Aprikosen sind Pfirsichen ähnlich, nur kleiner.*

**April** [*EJ*prəl] *n.* • April, der
**April Fool** • Aprilnarr, der
My birthday is in April.
*Ich habe im April Geburtstag.*

**apron** [*EJ*prən] *n.* • Schürze, die
My grandmother wears an apron when she cooks.
*Meine Großmutter trägt eine Schürze, wenn sie kocht.*

**aquarium** [əK*W*ERie-əm] *n.* • Aquarium, das
The aquarium has many kinds of fish.
*Im Aquarium befindet sich eine große Vielfalt von Fischen.*

**are** see *to be*

**area** [ERie-ə] *n.* • Gegend, die
This area is very mountainous.
*Diese Gegend ist sehr bergig.*

**arithmetic** [əRI*TH*mətik] *n.* • Arithmetik, die
The children are studying arithmetic.
*Die Kinder lernen Arithmetik.*

**arm** [AHRM] *n.* • Arm, der
**arm in arm** • Arm in Arm
She is wearing five bracelets on her right arm.
*Sie trägt fünf Armbänder an ihrem rechten Arm.*

**armchair** [AHRM*tshej*r] *n.* • Lehnstuhl, der
Sit down in this comfortable armchair.
*Setz' dich auf diesen bequemen Lehnstuhl!*

**army** [AHRmie] *n.* • Heer, das
This country has a powerful army.
*Dieses Land hat ein mächtiges Heer.*

**around** [əRAUND] *prep.* • herum
The children are all around me.
*Die Kinder sind alle um mich herum.*

**arrange, to** [əR*EJ*N*DZH*] *v.* • arrangieren
Do you like to arrange flowers?
*Arrangieren Sie gern Blumen?*

**arrest, to** [əREST] *v.* • verhaften
The policeman arrests the criminal.
*Der Polizist verhaftet den Verbrecher.*

**arrival** [əREI*v*əl] *n.* • Ankunft, die
We are waiting for the plane's arrival.
*Wir erwarten die Ankunft des Flugzeugs.*

**arrive, to** [əREI*V*] *v.* • ankommen
Don't arrive too late!
*Komm' nicht zu spät an!*

**arrow** [*A*Roh] *n.* • Pfeil, der
John is shooting an arrow at the target.
*Johann schießt einen Pfeil auf die Zielscheibe.*

**art** [AHRT] *n.* • Kunst, die
Ballet is an art.
*Ballet ist eine Kunst.*

**artist** [AHRTist] *n.* • Künstler, der (-in, f.)
I like this artist's drawings.
*Mir gefallen die Zeichnungen dieses Künstlers.*

**as** [*AZ*] *adv.; conj.* • so; so . . . wie
Leave it as it is.
*Laß das so.*

She walks as slow as a turtle!
*Sie geht so langsam wie eine Schildkröte!*

**ashamed, to be** [əSH*E*J*MD] *v.* • sich schämen
The little boy is ashamed when he is naughty.
*Der kleine Junge schämt sich, wenn er ungezogen ist.*

**Asia** [*EJzh*ə] *n.* • Asien
My uncle often travels to Asia.
*Mein Onkel reist oft nach Asien.*

**ask (for), to** [*A*SK (fohr)] *v.* • bitten (um etwas)
Ask the waitress for some more coffee.
*Bitten Sie die Kellnerin um etwas mehr Kaffee.*

**asparagus** [əSPERəgəs] *n.* • Spargel, der
Asparagus is a spring vegetable.
*Der Spargel ist ein Frühlingsgemüse.*

**assignment** [əSEINmənt] *n.* • Aufgabe, die
The assignment for tomorrow is difficult.
*Die Aufgabe für morgen ist schwer.*

**assistant** [əSIStənt] *n.; adj.* • Assistent, der
Peter is an assistant in a laboratory.
*Peter ist Assistent in einem Labor.*

**astronaut** [*A*Strən*aw*t] *n.* • Astronaut, der
Astronauts are trained to endure space travel.
*Astronauten werden ausgebildet, um Weltraumfahrten zu bewältigen.*

**at** [*A*T] *prep.* • an; bei; in
**at last** • endlich
Er steht am (beim) Fenster.
*He stands at the window.*

She studies at the library.
*Sie lernt in der Bibliothek.*

**athlete** [*ATH*liet] *n.* • Athlet, der
**athletic** *adj.* • athletisch
You have to be a good athlete to play soccer.
*Man muß ein guter Athlet sein, um Fußball spielen zu können.*

**Atlantic (Ocean)** [*a*tLANtik] *n.* • Atlantik, der
I live near the Atlantic Ocean.
*Ich wohne in der Nähe des Atlantiks (am Atlantik).*

**attend** [əTEND] *v.* • besuchen
They are attending the concert tonight.
*Sie besuchen heute abend das Konzert.*

**attention** [əTENshən] *n.* • Achtgeben, das
**to pay attention (to)** • achtgeben
The students pay attention to the teacher.
*Die Studenten geben auf den Lehrer acht.*

**attic** [*A*Tik] *n.* • Dachgeschoß, das
My grandmother's house has a big attic.
*Das Haus meiner Großmutter hat ein großes Dachgeschoß.*

**attract, to** [əTRAKT] *v.* • anziehen
Sugar attracts flies.
*Zucker zieht Fliegen an.*

**August** [*AW*gəst] *n.* • August, der
My brother was born in August.
*Mein Bruder ist im August geboren.*

**aunt** [*A*NT; AHNT] *n.* • Tante, die
My aunt's name is Sophia.
*Meine Tante heißt Sophia.*

**Australia** [*aw*sTR*EJ*Ljə] *n.* • Australien
**Australian (person)** *n.* • Australier, der (-in, f.)
**Australian** *adj.* • australisch
Many unusual animals live in Australia.
*Viele außergewöhnliche Tiere leben in Australien.*

**Austria** [*AW*Strie-ə] *n.* • Österreich
**Austrian (person)** *n.* • Österreicher, der (-in, f.)
**Austrian** *adj.* • österreichisch
German is the national language of Austria.
*Deutsch ist die Landessprache Österreichs.*

**author** [*AWthər*] *n.* • Autor, der
My favorite author is a novelist.
*Mein Lieblingsautor ist ein Romanschriftsteller.*

**auto(mobile)** [*AW*toh; *aw*tohmohBIEL] *n.* • Auto, das; Wagen, der
The automobile is the standard mode of travel in America.
*Das Auto ist das Hauptfortbewegungsmittel in Amerika.*

**autumn** [*AW*təm] *n.* • Herbst, der
The leaves are beautiful in autumn.
*Die Blätter sind schön im Herbst.*

**avenue** [*AV*ənj*oo*] *n.* • Allee, die
The avenue is very wide near the city center.
*Die Allee ist in der Nähe des Stadtzentrums sehr breit.*

**avoid, to** [ə*V*EUD] *v.* • vermeiden
My brother avoids working whenever he can.
*Mein Bruder vermeidet es zu arbeiten, sooft er kann.*

**awful** [*AW*ful] *adj.* • furchtbar
The noise in the factory is awful.
*Das Geräusch in der Fabrik ist furchtbar.*

**awkward** [*AW*K*w*ərd] *adj.* • ungeschickt
The baby took its first awkward steps.
*Das Baby machte seine ersten ungeschickten Schritte.*

**a.m.** [*EJ* EM] *n.* • morgens
I go to school at 8 a.m.
*Ich gehe um 8 Uhr morgens in die Schule.*

# B

**baby** [B*EJ*bie] *n.* • Baby, das
**baby carriage** *n.* • Kinderwagen, der
**baby sitter** *n.* • Babysitter, der
What is your newborn baby's name?
*Wie heißt dein neugeborenes Baby?*

**back** [B*A*K] *n.* • Rücken, der
**back** *adv.* • zurück
**back and forth** • hin und her
**background (theater)** *n.* • Hintergrund, der
I have awful pains in my back.
*Ich habe furchtbare Schmerzen im Rücken.*

**bad** [B*A*D] *adj.* • schlecht
**badly** *adv.* • dringend
**that's too bad** • das ist zu dumm
The harvest is bad because of the dry weather.
*Die Ernte ist wegen des trockenen Wetters schlecht.*

**bag** [B*A*G] *n.* • Tasche, die
This bag of groceries is very heavy.
*Diese Tasche mit Lebensmitteln ist sehr schwer.*

**baggage** [B*A*Gi*dzh*] *n.* • Gepäck, das
They carried their baggage into the hotel.
*Sie trugen ihr Gepäck in das Hotel.*

**bake, to** [B*EJ*K] *v.* • backen
**baker** *n.* • Bäcker, der
**bakery** *n.* • Bäckerei, die
The baker bakes bread in his oven.
*Der Bäcker backt Brot in seinem Backofen.*

**ball** [B*A*WL] *n.* • Ball, der
The child throws the ball.
*Das Kind wirft den Ball.*

**balloon** [bəL*OO*N] *n.* • Ballon, der
The balloon is floating to the ceiling.
*Der Ballon fliegt an die Zimmerdecke.*

**ball-point pen** [B*AW*Lpeunt pen] *n.* • Kugelschreiber, der
I prefer to write with a ball-point pen.
*Ich ziehe es vor, mit einem Kugelschreiber zu schreiben.*

**banana** [bəN*A*nə] *n.* • Banane, die
The monkey is eating a banana.
*Der Affe ißst eine Banane.*

**bank** [B*A*NGK] *n.* • Bank, die
**banker** *n.* • Bankier, der (-in, f.)
Deposit your money at the bank on the corner.
*Zahlen Sie ihr Geld auf die Bank an der Ecke ein.*

**barn** [BAHRN] *n.* • Scheune, die
An owl lives in this old barn.
*Eine Eule lebt in dieser alten Scheune.*

**baseball** [B*EJ*Sb*aw*l] *n.* • Baseballspiel, das
Do we have enough players to play baseball?
*Haben wir genügend Spieler, um Baseball zu spielen?*

**basket** [B*A*Skət] *n.* • Korb, der
My mother is putting the fruit in a basket.
*Meine Mutter legt die Früchte in einen Korb.*

**basketball** [B*A*Skətb*aw*l] *n.* • Korbballspiel, das
Do you want to play basketball with us?
*Willst du mit uns Korbball spielen?*

**bath** [B*ATH*] *n.* • Bad, das
**bathing suit** *n.* • Badeanzug, der
**bathroom** *n.* • Badezimmer, das
**bathroom sink** *n.* • Waschbecken, das
**bathtub** *n.* • Badewanne, die
**sunbath** *n.* • Sonnenbad, das
She took a long bath to relax after work.
*Nach der Arbeit nahm sie ein langes Bad, um sich zu entspannen.*

**be, to** [BIE] *v.* • sein
**to be early** • früh sein
**to be late** • spät sein
**to be lucky** • Glück haben
**to be part of** • von etwas ein Teil sein
**to be right** • recht haben
**to be sleepy** • schläfrig (müde) sein
**to be wrong** • sich irren
I am fine (well).
*Es geht mir gut.*

I am hungry.
*Ich habe Hunger.*

It is nice out.
*Es ist schön draußen.*

Are we late for the bus?
*Sind wir zu spät für den Bus?*

I don't know if I'm right.
*Ich weiß nicht, ob ich Recht habe.*

Anyone can be wrong (make a mistake).
*Jeder kann sich mal irren.*

**Be careful!** [BIE K*EJ*Rful] *v. phr.* • Vorsicht!
Be careful! The dog bites!
*Vorsicht! Der Hund beißt!*

**beach** [BIE*TSH*] *n.* • Strand, der
We can take a walk on the beach after dinner.
*Wir können nach dem Essen am Strand spazierengehen.*

**beak** [BIEK] *n.* • Schnabel, der
The bird cracks seeds with its beak.
*Der Vogel knackt Samen mit seinem Schnabel.*

**beans** [BIENZ] *n. pl.* • Bohnen, die
**green beans** • grüne Bohnen
We are having green beans with dinner.
*Es gibt grüne Bohnen zum Essen.*

**bear** [B*EJ*R] *n.* • Bär, der
The fire will keep the bears away from our camp.
*Das Feuer wird die Bären von unserem Lager fern halten.*

**beard** [BIERD] *n.* • Bart, der
My dad has a beard.
*Mein Vater trägt einen Bart.*

**beast (animal)** [BIEST] *n.* • Tier, das
Wild beasts do not make good pets.
*Wilde Tiere sind keine guten Haustiere.*

**beat, to** [BIET] *v.* • schlagen
Their football team beats us every year.
*Ihre Fußballmanschaft schlägt uns jedes Jahr.*

**beautiful** [BJ*OO*tifəl] *adj.* • schön
Look at the beautiful flowers in the garden!
*Schauen Sie sich die schönen Blumen im Garten an!*

**beaver** [BIE*vər*] *n.* • Biber, der
Beavers build dams across the river.
*Die Biber bauen Deiche über den Fluß.*

**because** [bieK*AW*Z] *conj.* • weil; denn
**because of** *prep.* • wegen
John can't go because he has work to do.
*Johann kann nicht gehen, weil er arbeiten muß (denn er hat Arbeit zu tun).*

**become, to** [bieKƏM] *v.* • werden
Your behavior is becoming worse and worse.
*Dein Benehmen wird immer schlechter.*

**bed** [BED] *n.* • Bett, das
**bedroom** *n.* • Schlafzimmer, das
**to go to bed** • zu Bett gehen
**to make the bed** • Bett machen, das
My bed has a comfortable mattress.
*Mein Bett hat eine bequeme Matratze.*

**bee** [BIE] *n.* • Biene, die
Bees make honey.
*Bienen machen Honig.*

**beef** [BIEF] *n.* • Rindfleisch, das
**beef steak** • Beefsteak, das
**roast beef** • Rinderbraten, der
I prefer beef to chicken.
*Ich ziehe Rindfleisch Huhn vor.*

**before** [bieFOHR] *adv.; prep.* • vor
They left before dawn.
*Sie gingen vor Tagesanbruch los.*

**begin, to** [bieGIN] *v.* • anfangen
**beginning** *n.* • Anfang, der
What time does the movie begin?
*Um wieviel Uhr fängt der Film an?*

**behave, to** [bieH*EJV*] *v.* • sich benehmen
**Behave!** • Benimm dich!
**behavior** *n.* • Benehmen, das
**to behave badly** • sich schlecht benehmen
**to behave well** • sich gut benehmen
These children know how to behave in a restaurant.
*Diese Kinder wissen, wie man sich in einem Restaurant benimmt.*

**behind** [bieHEIND] *prep.* • hinter
Who is hiding behind the curtain?
*Wer versteckt sich hinter dem Vorhang?*

**Belgium** [BEL*dzh*əm] *n.* • Belgien
**Belgian (person)** *n.* • Belgier, der (-in, f.)
**Belgian** *adj.* • belgisch
They speak French and Flemish in Belgium.
*Man spricht Französisch und Flämisch in Belgien.*

**believe, to** [bieLIEV] *v.* • glauben
**believable** *adj.* • glaubhaft
**unbelievable** *adj.* • unglaublich
I believe that the story is true.
*Ich glaube, daß die Geschichte wahr ist.*

**bell** [BEL] *n.* • Glocke, die
**doorbell** *n.* • Türklingel, die
There is a bell in the church's steeple.
*Es gibt eine Glocke im Kirchturm.*

**belong (to), to** [bieL*A*WNG] *v.* • gehören
This suitcase belongs to my father.
*Dieser Koffer gehört meinem Vater.*

**below** [bieLOH] *prep.* • unter
The stores are below the apartments.
*Die Geschäfte befinden sich unter den Wohnungen.*

**belt** [BELT] *n.* • Gürtel, der
I need a belt with this skirt.
*Ich brauche einen Gürtel zu diesem Rock.*

**bench** [BEN*TSH*] *n.* • Bank, die
They sit down on a bench in the park.
*Sie setzen sich auf eine Bank im Park.*

**beneath** [bieNIE*TH*] *prep.* • unter
I put my books beneath my chair.
*Ich lege meine Bücher unter meinen Stuhl.*

**beside** [bieSEID] *prep.* • neben
My dog sits beside me.
*Mein Hund sitzt neben mir.*

**best** [BEST] *adj.* • bester, beste, bestes
**the best** *n.* • Beste (der, die, das)
He is my best friend.
*Er ist mein bester Freund.*

**better** [BEDə*r*] *adj.* • besser
This cake tastes better than that one.
*Dieser Kuchen schmeckt besser als jener.*

**between** [bieT*W*IEN] *prep.* • zwischen
I sit down between my two best friends.
*Ich setze mich zwischen meine zwei besten Freunde.*

**beverage** [BE*V*ri*dzh*] *n.* • Getränk, das
What would you like as a beverage?
*Was für ein Getränk möchten Sie?*

**bicycle** [BEIsikəl] *n.* • Fahrrad, das
**to ride a bicycle** • radfahren
Don't leave your bicycle outside when it's raining.
*Laß dein Fahrrad nicht draußen stehen, wenn es regnet.*

**big** [BIG] *adj.* • groß
**bigger** *adj.* • größer
**biggest** *adj.* • größte
The elephant is a very big animal.
*Der Elefant ist ein sehr großes Tier.*

**bike** [BEIK] *n.* • Rad, das
I got a new bike for my birthday.
*Ich habe ein neues Rad zum Geburtstag bekommen.*

**bill (restaurant)** [BIL] *n.* • Rechnung, die
The waiter brings us the bill.
*Der Kellener bringt uns die Rechnung.*

**billfold** [BILfohld] *n.* • Brieftasche, die
I keep my money in my billfold.
*Ich bewahre mein Geld in meiner Brieftasche auf.*

**biology** [beiAHLə*dzh*ie] *n.* • Biologie, die
My sister studies biology at the university.
*Meine Schwester studiert Biologie an der Universität.*

**bird** [Bə*R*D] *n.* • Vogel, der
The birds make their nests in the trees.
*Die Vögel bauen ihre Nester in den Bäumen.*

**birthday** [Bə*RTH*de*j*] *n.* • Geburtstag, der
**Happy Birthday!** • Herzlichen Glückwunsch zum Geburtstag!
When is your birthday?
*Wann hast du Geburtstag?*

**bite** [BEIT] *v.* • beißen
I am afraid of animals that bite.
*Ich habe Angst vor Tieren, die beißen.*

**black** [BL*A*K] *adj.* • schwarz
He is wearing his black shoes.
*Er trägt seine schwarzen Schuhe.*

**blackboard** [BL*A*Kbohrd] *n.* • Tafel, die
The teacher writes on the blackboard.
*Der Lehrer schreibt an die Tafel.*

**blanket** [BL*A*NGkət] *n.* • Decke, die
This blanket is warm.
*Diese Decke ist warm.*

**blind** [BLEIND] *adj.* • blind
My grandmother is almost blind.
*Meine Großmutter ist fast blind.*

**blond** [BLAHND] *adj.* • blond
The two little boys are blond.
*Die zwei kleinen Jungen sind blond.*

**blood** [BLƏD] *n.* • Blut, das
He gives blood at the hospital.
*Er spendet Blut im Krankenhaus.*

**blouse** [BLAUS] *n.* • Bluse, die
Does this blouse go with this skirt?
*Paßt diese Bluse zu diesem Rock?*

**blow, to** [BLOH] *v.* • blasen (löschen)
Blow out the candle!
*Blas' die Kerze aus!*

**blue** [BL*OO*] *adj.* • blau
My father is wearing a blue suit today.
*Mein Vater trägt heute einen blauen Anzug.*

**blush, to** [BLƏSH] *v.* • erröten
When everyone looks at Richard, he blushes.
*Wenn alle Richard anschauen, errötet er.*

**boat** [BOHT] *n.* • Boot, das
**by boat** • mit einem Boot
**sailboat** *n.* • Segelboot, das
We take a boat to go fishing.
*Wir nehmen ein Boot, um fischen zu gehen.*

**body** [BAHDie] *n.* • Körper, der
Medical students study the human body.
*Medizinstudenten studieren den menschlichen Körper.*

**bone** [BOHN] *n.* • Knochen, der
**fishbone** *n.* • Gräte, die

The dog is burying a bone.
*Der Hund vergräbt einen Knochen.*

**book** [BUK] *n.* • Buch, das
**bookstore** *n.* • Buchhandlung, die
I read two new books during my vacation.
*Ich las zwei neue Bücher während meiner Ferien.*

**boot** [B*OO*T] *n.* • Stiefel, der
Suzanne wears boots when she walks in the snow.
*Suzanne trägt Stiefel, wenn sie durch den Schnee geht.*

**boring** [BOHRing] *adj.* • langweilig
This book is too boring to finish.
*Dieses Buch ist zu langweilig, um es zu Ende zu lesen.*

**born** [BOHRN] *adj.* • geboren (sein)
He was born in Paris.
*Er ist in Paris geboren.*

I was born in 1952.
*Ich bin in 1952 geboren.*

**borrow, to (from)** [B*AW*roh] *v.* • borgen
He always wants to borrow my car.
*Er will immer meinen Wagen borgen.*

**boss** [B*AW*S] *n.* • Chef, der
My boss called a meeting for this morning.
*Mein Chef hat für heute morgen eine Versammlung einberufen.*

**both** [BOH*TH*] *pron.* • beide
Maurice and Alan are both going to the movies.
*Maurice und Alan gehen beide ins Kino.*

**bottle** [BAHDl] *n.* • Flasche, die
Wine is usually sold in bottles.
*Wein wird gewöhnlich in Flaschen verkauft.*

**bottom** [BAHDm] *n.* • Boden, der
Put the heavier things in the bottom of the bag.
*Stell' die schwereren Sachen auf den Boden der Tasche.*

**boulevard** [BULə*v*ahrd] *n.* • Boulevard, der
Are you familiar with the Boulevard St-Michel in Paris?
*Kennst du den Boulevard St-Michel in Paris?*

**bouquet** [b*oo*K*EJ*] *n.* • Strauß, der (Blumen, der)
My favorite flowers are in the bouquet.
*Meine Lieblingsblumen sind in dem Strauß.*

**boutique** [b*oo*TIEK] *n.* • Boutique, die
My cousin is a salesclerk in this boutique.
*Meine Cousine ist Verkäuferin in dieser Boutique.*

**bowl** [BOHL] *n.* • Schüssel, die
I put the fruit in a bowl on the table.
*Ich tat die Frucht in eine Schüssel auf dem Tisch.*

**box** [BAHKS] *n.* • Kasten, der
This box isn't big enough for all my toys.
*Dieser Kasten ist für mein ganzes Spielzeug nicht groß genug.*

**boy** [BEU] *n.* • Junge, der
This boy is my neighbor's son.
*Dieser Junge ist der Sohn meines Nachbarn.*

**bracelet** [BR*EJ*Slət] *n.* • Armband, das
She is wearing several bracelets on her left arm.
*Sie trägt mehrere Armbänder an ihrem linken Arm.*

**brain** [BR*EJ*N] *n.* • Gehirn, das
The skull protects the brain.
*Der Schädel schützt das Gehirn.*

**branch** [BR*A*N*TSH*] *n.* • Ast, der
The tree branches are bare in winter.
*Die Äste der Bäume sind im Winter kahl.*

**brave** [BR*EJV*] *adj.* • tapfer
Police officers are very brave.
*Polizisten sind sehr tapfer.*

**bread** [BRED] *n.* • Brot, das
**bread and jam** *n.* • Brot und Marmelade
Most white bread is made from wheat flour.
*Das meiste Weißbrot wird aus Weizenmehl gemacht.*

**breakfast** [BREKfəst] *n.* • Frühstück, das
Do you eat breakfast every morning?
*Essen Sie jeden Morgen Frühstück?*

**break, to** [BR*EJ*K] *v.* • zerbrechen
**to break off** • abbrechen
Glass breaks very easily.
*Glas zerbricht sehr leicht.*

**bridge** [BRI*DZH*] *n.* • Brücke, die
The Golden Gate Bridge is in San Francisco.
*Die "Golden Gate"-Brücke ist in San Francisco.*

**briefcase** [BRIEFk*ej*s] *n.* • Aktentasche, die
She left her briefcase at the office.
*Sie hat ihre Aktentasche im Büro gelassen.*

**bring, to** [BRING] *v.* • bringen
**bring to an end** • zu Ende bringen
**to bring with** • mitbringen
He is bringing his friend to the party.
*Er bringt seinen Freund zur Party mit.*

**broad** [BR*AW*D] *adj.* • breit
The avenues of New York are very broad.
*Die Alleen in New York sind sehr breit.*

**brook** [BRUK] *n.* • Bach, der
The boy fishes in this little brook.
*Der Junge fischt in diesem kleinen Bach.*

**broom** [BR*OO*M] *n.* • Besen, der
He used a broom to sweep the floor.
*Er benutzte einen Besen, um den Boden zu kehren*

**brother** [BRƏ*dh*ər] *n.* • Bruder, der
I have an older brother who is in college.
*Ich habe einen älteren Bruder, der die Universität besucht.*

**brown** [BRAUN] *adj.* • braun
The brown coat looks good on her.
*Der braune Mantel steht ihr gut.*

**brunette** [br*oo*NET] *n.; adj* • brünett
My mother is a brunette.
*Meine Mutter ist brünett.*

**brush, to** [BRƏSH] *v.* • bürsten
**brush** *n.* • Bürste, die
**toothbrush** *n.* • Zahnbürste, die
I brush my hair every morning.
*Ich bürste mein Haar jeden Morgen.*

I use a brush on my hair.
*Ich nehme eine Bürste für mein Haar.*

**bucket** [BƏket] *n.* • Eimer, der
I carry water in a bucket.
*Ich trage Wasser in einem Eimer.*

**build, to** [BILD] *v.* • bauen
We are building a new house outside of town.
*Wir bauen außerhalb der Stadt ein neues Haus.*

**building** [BILding] *n.* • Gebäude, das
**apartment building** *n.* •
Appartementgebäude, das

There are offices in this building.
*In diesem Gebäude sind Büros.*

**burn, to** [BƏ*R*N] *v.* • verbrennen
We burn leaves in autumn.
*Im Herbst verbrennen wir das Laub.*

**bus** [BƏS] *n.* • Omnibus, der
**excursion bus** • Ausflugsbus, der
We are waiting for the bus at the depot.
*Wir warten an der Haltestelle auf den Omnibus.*

**business** [BIZnəs] *n.* • Geschäft, das
**businessman** *n.* • Geschäftsmann, der
**businesswoman** *n.* • Geschäftsfrau, die
This store does a lot of business in the summer.
*Dieser Laden hat im Sommer ein gutes Geschäft.*

**busy** [BIZie] *adj.* • beschäftigt
The secretary is very busy.
*Die Sekretärin ist sehr beschäftigt.*

**but** [BƏT] *conj.; prep* • aber
I would like some cake, but I am on a diet.
*Ich möchte gern etwas Kuchen, aber ich halte eine Diät.*

**butcher** [BU*tsh*ə*r*] *n.* • Fleischer, der
**butcher shop** • Fleischerladen, der
We buy meat from the butcher.
*Wir kaufen Fleisch beim Fleischer.*

**butter** [BƏdə*r*] *n.* • Butter, die
Peter puts butter on his bread.
*Peter streicht Butter auf sein Brot.*

**butterfly** [BƏdə*r*flei] *n.* • Schmetterling, der
The child tries to catch the butterfly.
*Das Kind versucht, den Schmetterling zu fangen.*

**button** [BƏTn] *n.* • Knopf, der
I don't like to sew buttons.
*Ich nähe nicht gern Knöpfe an.*

**buy, to** [BEI] *v.* • kaufen
We buy our vegetables at the market.
*Wir kaufen unser Gemüse auf dem Markt.*

**by** [BEI] *prep.* • bei
**by airmail** • per Luftpost
**by car** • mit dem Wagen
**by day** • bei Tag
**by oneself** • für sich, allein
**by plane** • mit dem Flugzeug
His parents live by a lake.
*Seine Eltern wohnen bei einem See.*

# C

**cabbage** [K*A*Bi*dzh*] *n.* • Kohl, der
Rabbits are eating the cabbage in our garden.
*Die Kaninchen fressen den Kohl in unserem Garten.*

**café** [k*a*F*EJ*] *n.* • Kaffeehaus, das
**sidewalk café** • Straßencafé, das
Let's meet at the café on the corner.
*Treffen wir uns im Kaffeehaus an der Ecke.*

**cake** [K*EJ*K] *n.* • Kuchen, der
What kind of cake do you want for your birthday?
*Was für einen Kuchen möchtest du zu deinem Geburtstag?*

**calculator** [K*A*Lkj*oo*l*ej*tər] *n.* •
Rechenmaschine, die
Today people rely on the calculator.
*Heute verlassen sich die Leute auf die Rechenmaschine.*

**calendar** [KALəndər] *n.* • Kalender, der
Last year's calendar is still hanging on the wall.
*Der Kalender vom vorigen Jahr hängt noch an der Wand.*

**calf** [KAF] *n.* • Kalb, das
The calf follows its mother.
*Das Kalb folgt seiner Mutter.*

**call, to** [KAWL] *v.* • rufen
Mom calls us when dinner is ready.
*Mutti ruft uns, wenn das Abendessen fertig ist.*

**calm** [KAHM] *adj.* • still
When everyone is asleep, the night is calm.
*Wenn alle schlafen, ist die Nacht still.*

**camel** [KAMəl] *n.* • Kamel, das
Camels can live without water in the desert.
*Kamele können ohne Wasser in der Wüste leben.*

**camera** [KAMrə] *n.* • Kamera, die
This camera takes good pictures.
*Diese Kamera macht gute Aufnahmen.*

**camp** [KAMP] *n.* • Lager, das
**to go camping** • zelten gehen
Where should we pitch our camp?
*Wo sollen wir unser Lager aufschlagen?*

I go camping with my family in August.
*Ich gehe im August mit meiner Familie zelten.*

**Canada** [KANədə] *n.* • Kanada
**Canadian (person)** *n.* • Kanadier, der (-in, f.)
**Canadian** *adj.* • kanadisch
Canada is north of the United States.
*Kanada liegt nördlich der Vereinigten Staaten.*

**candle** [KANdl] *n.* • Kerze, die
Can you light the candles, please?
*Kannst du bitte die Kerzen anzünden?*

**candy** [K*A*Ndie] *n.* • Süßigkeit, die
**candy store** • Süßwarengeschäft, das
Don't eat too much candy before dinner.
*Iß nicht zu viele Süßigkeiten vor dem Abendessen.*

**cap** [K*A*P] *n.* • Mütze, die
All the members of my team wear the same caps.
*Alle Mitglieder meiner Mannschaft tragen dieselben Mützen.*

**capital** [K*A*Pitəl] *n.* • Hauptstadt, die
**capital letter** • große Anfangsbuchstabe, der
Washington, D.C. is the capital of the United States.
*Washington, D.C. ist die Hauptstadt der Vereinigten Staaten.*

**car** [KAHR] *n.* • Wagen, der
**railroad car** • Eisenbahnwagen, der
They have a new red car.
*Sie haben einen neuen, roten Wagen.*

**card** [KAHRD] *n.* • Karte, die
**postcard** *n.* • Postkarte, die
**to play cards** • Karten spielen
My little brother is learning to play cards.
*Mein kleiner Bruder lernt Karten spielen.*

**career** [kəRIER] *n.* • Karriere, die
What kind of education do you need for this career?
*Was für eine Ausbildung braucht man für diese Karriere?*

**carefully** [K*EJ*Rfəlie] *adv.* • vorsichtig
When the roads are wet you must drive carefully.
*Wenn die Straßen naß sind, muß man vorsichtig fahren.*

**carpenters** [KAHRpəntə*rz*] *n.* • Zimmerleute, die
The carpenters are building a house.
*Die Zimmerleute bauen ein Haus.*

**carpet** [KAHRpət] *n.* • Teppich, der
Someone must clean the carpet.
*Irgend jemand muß den Teppich reinigen.*

**carrot** [K*A*Rət] *n.* • Karotte, die
The rabbit is eating a carrot.
*Das Kaninchen frißt eine Karotte.*

**carry, to** [K*A*Rie] *v.* • tragen
I'm going to carry my suitcase to my room.
*Ich werde meinen Koffer auf mein Zimmer tragen.*

**cartoon** [kahrT*OO*N] *n.* • Trickfilm, der
**cartoon (comic strip)** • Karikaturstreifen, der
Walt Disney created many cartoons.
*Walt Disney hat viele Trickfilme geschaffen.*

**castle** [K*A*Səl] *n.* • Schloß, das
The king lived in a large castle.
*Der König wohnte in einem großen Schloß.*

**cat** [K*A*T] *n.* • Katze, die
We have a pet cat.
*Wir haben eine Katze als Haustier.*

**catch, to** [K*A*TSH] *v.* • fangen
**to catch a cold** • Erkältung bekommen, eine
**to catch fire** • in Brand geraten
**to catch up with** • einholen
I am going to throw the ball and Michael is going to catch it.
*Ich werde den Ball werfen und Michael wird ihn fangen.*

**caterpillar** [K*A*Tərpilə*r*] *n.* • Raupe, die
A caterpillar changes into a butterfly.
*Die Raupe verwandelt sich in einen Schmetterling.*

**cauliflower** [K*AW*liflau*w*ə*r*] *n.* • Blumenkohl, der
Cauliflower is my favorite vegetable.
*Blumenkohl ist mein Lieblingsgemüse.*

**cave** [K*EJ*V] *n.* • Höhle, die
Bats live in caves.
*Fledermäuse leben in Höhlen.*

**ceiling** [SIEling] *n.* • Decke, die
There is a fly on the ceiling.
*An der Decke ist eine Fliege.*

**celebration** [seləBR*EJ*shən] *n.* • Feier, die
**to celebrate** *v.* • feiern
We had a celebration when my sister came back home.
*Wir hatten eine Feier, als meine Schwester wieder nach Hause kam.*

**celery** [SELrie] *n.* • Sellerie, der
My mother buys celery at the supermarket.
*Meine Mutter kauft Sellerie im Supermarkt.*

**cellar** [SELə*r*] *n.* • Keller, der
The cellar is always cool and damp.
*Der Keller ist immer kühl und feucht.*

**center** see *middle*

**central** [SENtrəl] *adj.* • zentral
**Central America** *n.* • Mittelamerika
This store is in a central location.
*Dieser Laden befindet sich in einer zentralen Lage.*

**certain** [Sə*R*tn] *adj.* • sicher
I'm certain that they are coming this evening.
*Ich bin sicher, daß sie heute abend kommen.*

**chair** [*TSHEJ*R] *n.* • Stuhl, der
**armchair; easy chair** *n.* • Lehnstuhl, der
There are six chairs around the table.
*Sechs Stühle stehen um den Tisch.*

**chalk** [*TSHA*WK] *n.* • Kreide, die
**(chalk) board** *n.* • Tafel, die

The teacher writes on the (chalk) board with chalk.
*Der Lehrer schreibt mit Kreide an die Tafel.*

**change, to** [*TSHEJ*NDZ*H*] *v.* • ändern
**to change (money)** *v.* • wechseln
He always changes his opinion.
*Er ändert immer seine Meinung.*

**cheap** [*TSH*IEP] *adj.* • billig
**cheaply** *adv.* • billig
We bought a cheap used car.
*Wir kauften einen billigen Gebrauchtwagen.*

**cheat, to** [*TSH*IET] *v.* • schwindeln
I don't play with these children anymore because they cheat.
*Ich spiele mit diesen Kindern nicht mehr, weil sie schwindeln.*

**check (restaurant)** [*TSH*EK] *n.* • Rechnung, die
**check (bank)** *n.* • Scheck, der
The waiter brings the check after the meal.
*Der Kellner bringt die Rechnung nach dem Essen.*

**checkers** [*TSH*EKə*rz*] *n.* • Damespiel, das
I like to play checkers with my little sister.
*Ich spiele gern Dame mit meiner kleinen Schwester.*

**cheek** [*TSH*IEK] *n.* • Backe, die
Martine always has rosy cheeks!
*Martine hat immer rote Backen!*

**cheerful** [*TSH*IERful] *adj.* • heiter
The children were in a cheerful mood today.
*Die Kinder waren heute in einer heiteren Stimmung.*

**cheese** [*TSH*IEZ] *n.* • Käse, der
Gruyere is my favorite cheese.
*Gruyere ist mein Lieblingskäse.*

**chemistry** [KEMəstrie] *n.* • Chemie, die
I teach chemistry and physics at the high school.
*Ich unterrichte Chemie und Physik am Gymnasium.*

**cherry** [*TSH*ERie] *n.* • Kirsche, die
We picked cherries from the tree.
*Wir pflückten Kirschen vom Baum.*

**chess** [*TSH*ES] *n.* • Schachspiel, das
**to play chess** • Schach spielen
Chess is one of the oldest games in the world.
*Das Schachspiel ist eines der ältesten Spiele der Welt.*

**chicken** [*TSH*IKən] *n.* • Huhn, das
We have a good recipe for chicken.
*Wir haben ein gutes Rezept für Huhn.*

**child** [*TSH*EILD] *n.* • Kind, das
**children** *n. pl.* • Kinder, die
What is the child's name?
*Wie heißt das Kind?*

**chimney** [*TSH*IMnie] *n.* • Kamin, der
Some birds have made their nest in our chimney.
*Einige Vögel haben in unserem Kamin ihr Nest gebaut.*

**chin** [*TSH*IN] *n.* • Kinn, das
Paul has a bruise on his chin.
*Paul hat eine Schramme an seinem Kinn.*

**China** [*TSH*EInə] *n.* • China
**Chinese (person)** *n.* • Chinese, der (-in, f.)
**Chinese** *adj.* • chinesisch
I hope to visit China someday.
*Ich hoffe, eines Tages China besuchen zu können.*

**chocolate** [*TSHAW*klət] *n.; adj.* • Schokolade, die
This candy is made of chocolate.
*Diese Süßigkeit ist aus Schokolade.*

**choice** [*TSHEUS*] *n.* • Wahl, die
Patricia wants to make the right choice.
*Patricia will die richtige Wahl treffen.*

**choir** [K*W*EIə*r*] *n.* • Chor, der
This choir sings very well.
*Dieser Chor singt sehr gut.*

**choose, to** [*TSHOOZ*] *v.* • wählen
You have to choose one or the other.
*Sie müssen den einen oder den anderen wählen.*

**Christmas** [KRISməs] *n.* • Weihnachten, das
**Christmas Eve** • Heilige Abend, der; Weihnachtsabend, der
Christmas is December 25.
*Weihnachten ist am 25. Dezember.*

**church** [*TSHƏRTSH*] *n.* • Kirche, die
Many people go to church on Sunday.
*Viele Leute gehen am Sonntag in die Kirche.*

**cigarette** [sigəRET] *n.* • Zigarette, die
You can't smoke cigarettes on the plane.
*Man darf keine Zigaretten im Flugzeug rauchen.*

**circle** [SƏ*R*kəl] *n.* • Kreis, der
Andrew is drawing a circle on the paper.
*Andrew zeichnet einen Kreis auf das Papier.*

**circus** [SƏ*R*kəs] *n.* • Zirkus, der
The circus is in town for a week.
*Der Zirkus ist eine Woche lang in der Stadt.*

**citizen** [SItəzən] *n.* • Bürger, der
I am a citizen of the United States.
*Ich bin Bürger der Vereinigten Staaten.*

**city** [SITie] *n.* • Stadt, die
**city hall** *n.* • Rathaus, das

Do you want to live in the city or in the country?
*Willst du in der Stadt oder auf dem Land wohnen?*

**clarinet** [klerəNET] *n.* • Klarinette, die
My sister plays the clarinet.
*Meine Schwester spielt Klarinette.*

**class** [KLAS] *n.* • Klasse, die
**classroom** *n.* • Klassenzimmer, das
How many students are in this class?
*Wie viele Studenten sind in dieser Klasse?*

**clean, to** [KLIEN] *v.* • reinigen (putzen)
**clean** *adj.* • sauber (frisch)
We clean the house each week.
*Wir reinigen (putzen) das Haus jede Woche.*

Every Monday she puts clean sheets on the beds.
*Jeden Montag bezieht sie die Betten mit sauberen Bettüchern.*

**clear** [KLIER] *adj.* • klar
Your explanation is not clear.
*Deine Erklärung ist nicht klar.*

**climb** [KLEIM] *v.* • hinaufsteigen
Do you want to climb the steps or take the elevator?
*Willst du die Treppen hinaufsteigen oder den Fahrstuhl nehmen?*

**clock** [KLAHK] *n.* • Uhr, die
**alarm clock** *n.* • Wecker, der
The clock on the wall is very precise.
*Die Uhr an der Wand ist sehr genau.*

**close** [KLOHS] *adv.* • nahe
I live very close to my friend.
*Ich wohne sehr nahe bei meinem Freund.*

**close, to** [KLOHZ] *v.* • schließen
Close the door, please.
*Schließen Sie die Tür, bitte.*

**closet** [KL*AW*z*ə*t] *n.* • Wandschrank, der
He hangs his coat in the closet.
*Er hängt seinen Mantel in den Wandschrank.*

**clothes** [KLOH*DHZ*; KLOHZ] *n.* • Kleider, die
I bought new clothes and shoes for my trip.
*Ich kaufte neue Kleider und Schuhe für meine Reise.*

**cloud** [KLAUD] *n.* • Wolke, die
**cloudy** *adj.* • bewölkt
Look at the clouds! It is going to rain!
*Sieh die Wolken an! Es wird regnen!*

**clown** [KLAUN] *n.* • Clown, der
I like the clowns at the circus.
*Ich liebe die Clowns im Zirkus.*

**clumsy** [KLƏM*z*ie] *adj.* • ungeschickt
The clumsy waiter dropped the tray.
*Der ungeschickte Kellner ließ das Tablett fallen.*

**coach** [KOH*TSH*] *n.* • Trainer, der (-in, f.)
Our coach has the game schedule.
*Unser Trainer hat den Spielplan.*

**coat** [KOHT] *n.* • Mantel, der (Mäntel, die [pl.])
**raincoat** *n.* • Regenmantel, der
This coat is very warm.
*Dieser Mantel ist sehr warm.*

**coconut** [KOHkənət] *n.* • Kokosnuß, die
The coconut has a very hard shell.
*Die Kokosnuß hat eine sehr harte Schale.*

**coffee** [K*AW*Fie] *n.* • Kaffee, der
**a cup of coffee** • Tasse Kaffee, eine
I put sugar in my coffee.
*Ich nehme Zucker in meinen Kaffee.*

**cold** [KOHLD] *adj.* • kalt
**cold (illness)** *n.* • Erkältung, die
**to be cold (person)** • nüchtern sein
It's cold out.
*Es ist kalt draußen.*

It's cold in the winter.
*Im Winter ist es kalt.*

**collar** [KAHLə*r*] *n.* • Kragen, der
**dog collar** *n.* • Hundehalsband, das
This collar is too tight.
*Dieser Kragen ist zu eng.*

**collection** [kəLEKshən] *n.* • Sammlung, die
My brother has a collection of coins.
*Mein Bruder hat eine Münzensammlung.*

**color** [KƏLə*r*] *n.* • Farbe, die
**What color is ---?** • Welche Farbe hat---?; Was für eine Farbe hat---?
What are the colors of the rainbow?
*Welche Farben hat der Regenbogen?*

**comb** [KOHM] *n.* • Kamm, der
**to comb (oneself)** *v.* • sich kämmen
I have my brush, but where is my comb?
*Ich habe meine Bürste, aber wo ist mein Kamm?*

**come, to (to arrive)** [KƏM] *v.* • kommen; ankommen
**to come back** • zurückkommen
**to come into** • hereinkommen
His aunt comes to visit in the summer.
*Seine Tante kommt im Sommer auf Besuch.*

The train comes at eleven o'clock.
*Der Zug kommt um 11 Uhr an.*

They are coming into the classroom now.
*Sie kommen eben ins Klassenzimmer herein.*

**comfortable** [KƏMfərtəbəl] *adj.* • bequem
This arm-chair is very comfortable.
*Dieser Lehnstuhl ist sehr bequem.*

**command** [kəMAND] *n.* • Befehl, der
The officer gives commands to the soldiers.
*Der Offizier gibt den Soldaten Befehle.*

**common** [KAHMən] *adj.* • gewöhnlich
This disease is quite common in children.
*Diese Krankheit ist bei Kindern ziemlich gewöhnlich.*

**company** [KƏMpənie] *n.* • Gesellschaft, die
My dad works for a large company.
*Mein Vater arbeitet bei einer großen Gesellschaft.*

**competition** [kahmpəTISHən] *n.* • Konkurrenz, die
**to compete** *v.* • in Konkurrenz stehen
Our team is not afraid of competition.
*Unsere Mannschaft fürchtet keine Konkurrenz.*

**complain, to** [kəmPL*EJ*N] *v.* • beklagen, sich
He is always complaining about the weather.
*Er beklagt sich immer über das Wetter.*

**completely** [kəmPLIETlie] *adv.* • ganz
I read the instructions completely.
*Ich habe die Anweisungen ganz gelesen.*

**compliment** [KAHMpləment] *n.* • Kompliment, das
Everyone likes to receive compliments.
*Jeder bekommt gern Komplimente.*

**computer** [kəmPJ*OO*tər] *n.* • Computer, der
You can entertain yourself with games on the computer.
*Am Computer kann man sich mit Spielen unterhalten.*

**concert** [KAHNsərt] *n.* • Konzert, das
I am going to the concert with my girlfriend.
*Ich gehe mit meiner Freundin ins Konzert.*

**congratulations** [kəngr*adzh*əL*EJ*shənz] *n.* • Glückwünsche, die
Congratulations! You won the prize!
*Herzliche Glückwünsche! Sie haben den Preis gewonnen!*

**connect, to** [kəNEKT] *v.* • verbinden
You connect the two parts like this.
*Man verbindet die zwei Teile auf diese Weise.*

**construct** [kənSTRƏKT] *v.* • bauen
The carpenters are constructing a new house.
*Die Zimmerleute bauen ein neues Haus.*

**contain, to** [kənT*EJ*N] *v.* • enthalten
This book contains many interesting facts.
*Dieses Buch enthält viele interessante Tatsachen.*

**content** [kənTENT] *adj.* • zufrieden sein
The teacher is content with our work.
*Der Lehrer ist mit unserer Arbeit zufrieden.*

**contest** [KAHNtest] *n.* • Wettkampf, der
I won first prize in the contest.
*Ich habe den ersten Preis im Wettkampf gewonnen.*

**continent** [KAHNtinənt] *n.* • Kontinent, der
Africa and Asia are huge continents.
*Afrika und Asien sind riesige Kontinente.*

**continue, to** [kənTINj*oo*] *v.* • fortfahren
Let's continue reading until we finish.
*Fahren wir mit dem Lesen fort, bis wir fertig sind.*

**conversation** [kahn*v*ərS*EJ*shən] *n.* • Unterhaltung, die

I had a conversation with Mary on the phone yesterday.
*Ich hatte gestern eine Unterhaltung mit Maria am Telefon.*

**cookie** [KUKie] *n.* • Keks, der
We baked cookies for our guests.
*Wir backten Kekse für unsere Gäste.*

**cook, to** [KUK] *v.* • kochen
**the cook** *n.* • Koch, der (Köchin, die [f.])
**(cooking) stove** *n.* • Kochherd, der
We cooked a special dinner for your birthday.
*Wir haben ein besonderes Abendessen zu deinem Geburtstag gekocht.*

**cool** [K*OO*L] *adj.* • kühl
It's cool out.
*Es ist kühl draußen.*

A cool drink is welcome on a hot day.
*Ein kühles Getränk ist an einem warmen Tag angenehm.*

**copy, to** [KAHPie] *v.* • abschreiben
**copy** *n.* • Kopie, die
We are copying the questions that are on the blackboard.
*Wir schreiben die Fragen von der Tafel ab.*

**corn** [KOHRN] *n.* • Mais, der
This corn comes from our garden.
*Dieser Mais kommt aus unserem Garten.*

**corner** [KOHRnə*r*] *n.* • Ecke, die
**on the corner** • an der Ecke
This table has a sharp corner.
*Dieser Tisch hat eine scharfe Ecke.*

**correct** [kəREKT] *adj.* • richtig
**to correct** *v.* • korrigieren
Is this answer correct?
*Ist diese Antwort richtig?*

**cost, to** [K*A*W*S*T] *v.* • kosten
**cost** *n.* • Kosten, die (pl.)
**to cost a lot (be expensive)** *v.* • teuer sein
How much does this jacket cost?
*Wieviel kostet diese Jacke?*

**cotton** [KAHTn] *n.* • Baumwolle, die
**made of cotton** • aus Baumwolle (gemacht)
The shirt was made of cotton.
*Das Hemd war aus Baumwolle.*

**couch** [KAU*TSH*] *n.* • Sofa, das
Sit down on the couch.
*Setzen Sie sich auf das Sofa.*

**cough, to** [K*AW*F] *v.* • husten
Sometimes you cough when you have a cold.
*Manchmal hustet man, wenn man eine Erkältung hat.*

**count, to** [KAUNT] *v.* • zählen
My little sister can count to 100.
*Meine kleine Schwester kann bis 100 zählen.*

**country** [KəNtrie] *n.* • Land, das
What countries have you visited?
*Welche Länder haben Sie schon besucht?*

My grandfather lives in the country.
*Mein Großvater wohnt auf dem Land.*

**courageous** [kəR*EJdzh*əs] *adj.* • mutig
We read a story about a courageous hero.
*Wir lasen eine Geschichte über einen mutigen Helden.*

**course** [KOHRS] *n.* • Kurs, der
**of course** • natürlich; selbstverständlich
**of course not** • natürlich nicht
Which course are you taking in school?
*Welchen Kurs belegst du in der Schule?*

**cousin** [KƏzn] *n.* • Vetter, der; Cousine, die
My cousin is the same age as I am.
*Mein Vetter ist so alt wie ich.*

**cover (lid)** [KƏ*v*ə*r*] *n.* • Deckel, der
**to cover** *v.* • bedecken
**cover (blanket)** *n.* • Decke, die
**covered** *adj.* • bedeckt
This pot has a cover (lid).
*Dieser Topf hat einen Deckel.*

**cow** [KAU] *n.* • Kuh, die
Cows give milk.
*Kühe geben Milch.*

**cradle** [KR*EJ*Dl] *n.* • Wiege, die
The mother puts her baby in the cradle.
*Die Mutter legt ihr Kind in die Wiege.*

**crayon** [KR*EJ*ən] *n.* • Farbstift, der
The child is drawing with her crayons.
*Das Kind zeichnet mit ihren Farbstiften.*

**crazy** [KR*EJ*zie] *adj.* • verrückt
You are crazy! It's too cold to go swimming.
*Du bist wohl verrückt! Es ist zu kalt, um schwimmen zu gehen.*

**cream** [KRIEM] *n.* • Sahne, die
My dad drinks his coffee with cream.
*Mein Vater trinkt seinen Kaffee mit Sahne.*

**cricket** [KRIKət] *n.* • Grille, die
In the summertime we hear crickets at night.
*Im Sommer hören wir abends Grillen.*

**crocodile** [KRAHKədeil] *n.* • Krokodil, das
Crocodiles live near rivers and swamps.
*Krokodile leben in der Nähe von Flüssen und Sümpfen.*

**cross, to** [KR*AWS*] *v.* • überschreiten
**crossword puzzle** • Kreuzworträtsel, das
Children must cross the street with an adult.
*Kinder müssen die Straße mit einem Erwachsenen überschreiten.*

**crowd** [KRAUD] *n.* • Gedränge, das
There is a big crowd at the game.
*Es gibt ein großes Gedränge bei dem Spiel.*

**crown** [KRAUN] *n.* • Krone, die
The queen wears a crown.
*Die Königin trägt eine Krone.*

**crush, to** [KRUSH] *v.* • zerdrücken
Be careful! Don't crush the eggs!
*Sei vorsichtig! Zerdrück die Eier nicht!*

**crust** [KRəST] *n.* • Kruste, die
I like the crust on French bread.
*Ich liebe die Kruste beim französischen Brot.*

**cry, to** [KREI] *v.* • weinen
Many people cried during the funeral.
*Viele Leute weinten bei der Beerdigung.*

**cup** [KəP] *n.* • Tasse, die
**coffee cup** *n.* • Kaffeetasse, die
Please give me a cup of coffee.
*Bitte geben Sie mir eine Tasse Kaffee.*

**cupboard** [Kəbərd] *n.* • Schrank, der
I put the dishes away in the cupboard.
*Ich stellte das Geschirr in den Schrank.*

**curious** [KJURie-əs] *adj.* • neugierig
They say that cats are curious.
*Es wird behauptet, daß Katzen neugierig sind.*

**curtain** [KURTn] *n.* • Vorhang, der
At night, you usually pull the curtains.
*Nachts zieht man gewöhnlich die Vorhänge zu.*

**custom** [KəStəm] *n.* • Gewohnheit, die
It's his custom to drink a glass of milk before bedtime.
*Er hat die Gewohnheit, ein Glas Milch zu trinken, ehe er ins Bett geht.*

**cut, to** [KəT] *v.* • schneiden
**to cut oneself** • sich schneiden
He cuts his meat with a knife.
*Er schneidet sein Fleisch mit einem Messer.*

**cute** [KJ*OO*T] *adj.* • niedlich
This puppy is so cute.
*Dieser junge Hund ist so niedlich.*

**cutlet (chop)** [KəTlət] *n.* • Kotelett, das
I would like a pork cutlet, please.
*Ich möchte bitte ein Schweinskotelett.*

# D

**dad; daddy** [DAD; DADie] *n.* • Vati, der; Väterchen, der
Where does your dad work?
*Wo arbeitet dein Vati?*

**damp** [DAMP] *adj.* • feucht
These towels are damp.
*Diese Tücher sind feucht.*

**dance, to** [DANTS] *v.* • tanzen
We took classes to learn to dance.
*Wir nahmen Unterricht, um tanzen zu lernen.*

**danger** [D*EJ*N*dzh*ər] *n.* • Gefahr, die
  **dangerous** *adj.* • gefährlich
The soldiers were in great danger during the battle.
*Die Soldaten waren während des Kampfes in großer Gefahr.*

Is skiing dangerous?
*Ist Skilaufen gefährlich?*

**dare, to** [D*EJ*R] *v.* • wagen
Do you dare to call the teacher by her first name?
*Wagst du es, die Lehrerin mit ihrem Vornamen anzusprechen?*

**dark** [DAHRK] *adj.* • dunkel
The sky grows dark after the sun sets.
*Der Himmel wird nach Sonnenuntergang dunkel.*

It's dark out.
*Es ist dunkel draußen.*

**date** [D*EJ*T] *n.* • Datum, das
What date is your appointment?
*An welchem Datum ist dein Termin?*

**daughter** [DA*W*Tə*r*] *n.* • Tochter, die
The mother and daughter look very much alike.
*Mutter und Tochter sehen sich sehr ähnlich.*

**day** [D*EJ*] *n.* • Tag, der
  **day off** • den Tag freihaben
  **every day** • jeden Tag
  **New Year's Day** • Neujahrstag, der
It's daytime.
*Es ist Tag.*

What day is she going to arrive?
*An welchem Tag wird sie ankommen?*

**dead** [DED] *adj.* • tot
My grandfather has been dead for seven years.
*Mein Großvater ist schon sieben Jahre tot.*

**deaf** [DEF] *adj.* • taub
My grandmother is starting to go deaf.
*Meine Großmutter fängt an, taub zu werden.*

**dear** [DIER] *adj.* • lieber, liebe
The letter began, "Dear Mom, I miss you."
*Der Brief fing an: "Liebe Mutti, ich vermisse dich."*

**deceive, to** [diSIEV] *v.* • täuschen
The man deceived the police with his story.
*Der Mann täuschte die Polizei mit seiner Geschichte.*

**December** [diSEMbə*r*] *n.* • Dezember, der
December is the last month of the year.
*Dezember ist der letzte Monat des Jahres.*

**decision** [diSI*ZH*ən] *n.* • Entscheidung, die
Moving away from my family was a difficult decision.
*Es war eine schwere Entscheidung, von meiner Familie wegzuziehen.*

**decorate, to** [DEKəre*j*t] *v.* • schmücken
I decorate my room with posters.
*Ich schmücke mein Zimmer mit Postern.*

**deep** [DIEP] *adj.* • tief
**deep (color)** *adj.* • dunkel
**deep (feeling)** *adj.* • inbrünstig
This lake is quite deep in the middle.
*Dieser See ist ziemlich tief in der Mitte.*

**deer** [DIER] *n.* • Hochwild, das
There are deer in these woods.
*In diesem Wald gibt es Hochwild.*

**delicious** [diLISHəs] *adj.* • köstlich
This meal is delicious.
*Dieses Essen ist köstlich*

**delighted** [diLEITəd] *adj.* • erfreut
She is delighted with her new job.
*Sie ist erfreut über ihren neuen Job.*

**Denmark** [DENmahrk] *n.* • Dänemark
**Dane** *n.* • Däne (der, die)
**Danish** *adj.* • dänisch
Denmark is a country in northern Europe.
*Dänemark ist ein Land in Nordeuropa.*

**dentist** [DENtist] *n.* • Zahnarzt, der
I go to the dentist twice a year.
*Ich gehe zweimal pro Jahr zum Zahnarzt.*

**department store** [diPAHRTmənt ST*OH*R] *n.* • Warenhaus, das
My mother works in a department store.
*Meine Mutter arbeitet in einem Warenhaus.*

**desert** [DE*Z*ərt] *n.* • Wüste, die
It is very hot in the desert.
*Es ist sehr heiß in der Wüste.*

**desk** [DESK] *n.* • Schreibtisch, der
**student's desk** • Schülertisch, der
The papers are in the desk.
*Die Papiere sind im Schreibtisch.*

**dessert** [di*Z*ə*R*T] *n.* • Nachtisch, der
This dessert is delicious.
*Dieser Nachtisch ist köstlich.*

**destroy, to** [diSTREU] *v.* • zerstören
A volcano destroyed the city of Pompeii.
*Ein Vulkan zerstörte die Stadt Pompeji.*

**detective** [diTEKti*v*] *n.* • Detektiv, der
**detective film** • Kriminalfilm, der
**detective novel** • Detektivgeschichte; Kriminalroman, der

My dad loves detective novels.
*Mein Vati liebt Detektivgeschichten.*

**detour** [DIE*too*r] *n.* • Umleitung, die
We followed the signs for the detour.
*Wir folgten den Schildern der Umleitung.*

**dictionary** [DIKshənerie] *n.* • Wörterbuch, das
I am going to look up this word in the dictionary.
*Ich werde dieses Wort im Wörterbuch nachschlagen.*

**die, to** [DEI] *v.* • sterben
The hero dies at the end of the play.
*Der Held stirbt am Ende des Stückes.*

**diet** [DEIət] *n.* • Diät, die
**to be on a diet** • eine Diät halten
Did you lose weight on your diet?
*Hast du bei deiner Diät abgenommen?*

**different** [DIFrənt] *adj.* • unterschiedlich
His ideas are very different from mine.
*Seine Ideen sind von meinen sehr unterschiedlich.*

**difficult** [DIFikəlt] *adj.* • schwierig
This assignment is difficult.
*Diese Aufgabe ist schwierig.*

**dim** [DIM] *adj.* • düster
The light in this room is too dim.
*Das Licht in diesem Zimmer ist zu düster.*

**dine, to** [DEIN] *v.* • essen
**dining room** *n.* • Speisezimmer, das
**dinner** *n.* • Essen, das (Abendessen)
We are dining at our friends' house tonight.
*Wir essen heute abend bei unseren Freunden.*

**direct, to** [diREKT] *v.* • leiten
**direct** *adj.* • gerade
The police officer is directing traffic.
*Der Polizist leitet den Verkehr.*

**dirty** [DəRtie] *adj.* • schmutzig
The mud made my boots dirty.
*Der Schlamm machte meine Stiefel schmutzig.*

**disappear** [disəPIER] *v.* • verschwinden
The stars disappear when the sun rises.
*Die Sterne verschwinden, wenn die Sonne aufgeht.*

**disaster** [diZASt*ər*] *n.* • Unglück, das
The plane crash was a great disaster.
*Der Flugzeugabsturz war ein großes Unglück.*

**discouraged** [disKəRi*dzh*d] *adj.* • entmutigt
The team was discouraged after losing the game.
*Die Mannschaft war entmutigt, nachdem sie das Spiel verloren hatte.*

**discover, to** [disKə*vər*] *v.* • entdecken
**discovery** *n.* • Entdeckung, die
We discovered a new way to get to town.
*Wir entdeckten einen neuen Weg in die Stadt.*

**disease** [diZIEZ] *n.* • Krankheit, die
Your disease can be cured with this medicine.
*Ihre Krankheit kann mit dieser Medizin geheilt werden.*

**dishes** [DISHə*z*] *n.* • Geschirr, das
Please put the dishes in the cupboard.
*Bitte, stell das Geschirr in den Schrank.*

**dishonest** [disAHNəst] *adj.* • unehrlich
The dishonest boy told another lie.
*Der unehrliche Junge erzählte noch eine Lüge.*

**distance** [DIStəns] *n.* • Entfernung, die
**distant** *adj.* • entfernt
The distance between New York and Paris is about 3,500 miles.
*Die Entfernung zwischen New York und Paris beträgt ungefähr 3.500 Meilen.*

**disturb** [disTƏ*R*B] *v.* • stören
Do not disturb Paul, he is asleep!
*Stör' Paul nicht; er schläft!*

**dive, to** [DEI*V*] *v.* • einen Kopfsprung machen
The swimmer dives into the swimming pool.
*Der Schwimmer macht einen Kopfsprung ins Schwimmbad.*

**divide, to** [di*V*EID] *v.* • teilen
We are dividing the candy among us.
*Wir teilen uns die Süßigkeiten.*

**doctor** [DAHKtə*r*] *n.* • Arzt, der; Ärtzin, die
See a doctor if you are not feeling well.
*Suchen Sie einen Arzt auf, wenn Sie sich nicht wohl fühlen.*

**dog** [D*A*WG] *n.* • Hund, der
**Beware of the dog!** • Achtung! Bissiger Hund!; Warnung vor dem Hund!
We have a dog and a cat as pets.
*Wir haben einen Hund und eine Katze als Haustiere.*

**doll** [DAHL] *n.* • Puppe, die
**dollhouse** *n.* • Puppenhaus, das
My little sister puts her dolls on her bed.
*Meine kleine Schwester legt ihre Puppen auf ihr Bett.*

**dollar** [DAHLə*r*] *n.* • Dollar, der
The newspaper costs one dollar.
*Die Zeitung kostet einen Dollar.*

**dominoes** [DAHminohz] *n.* • Dominospiel, das
Do you know how to play dominoes?
*Weißt du, wie man Domino spielt?*

**donkey** [DAWNGkie] *n.* • Esel, der
A donkey has longer ears than a horse.
*Der Esel hat längere Ohren als das Pferd.*

**door** [DOHR] *n.* • Tür, die
**doorbell** *n.* • Türklingel, die
**doorknob** *n.* • Türgriff, der
Please open the door for our guests.
*Bitte öffnen Sie die Tür für unsere Gäste.*

**down** [DAUN] *adv.* • hinunter
**down there** • da unten
**to go down** • hinuntergehen
The skiers go down the mountain.
*Die Skiläufer fahren den Berg hinunter.*

**dozen** [DəZən] *n.* • Dutzend, das
My brother is going to buy a dozen eggs.
*Mein Bruder wird ein Dutzend Eier kaufen.*

**do, to** [DOO] *v.* • machen (tun)
We are going to do our work.
*Wir werden unsere Arbeit machen (tun).*

**dragon** [DRAGən] *n.* • Drache, der
The knight is fighting a dragon.
*Der Ritter kämpft mit einem Drachen.*

**drag, to** [DRAG] *v.* • schleifen
His trousers drag on the floor.
*Seine Hose schleift auf dem Fußboden.*

**draw, to** [DRAW] *v.* • zeichnen
**drawing** *n.* • Zeichnung, die
Can you draw a picture of what you saw?
*Kannst du von dem, was du gesehen hast, ein Bild zeichnen?*

**dreadful** [DREDful] *adj.* • schrecklich
The monster in the story is dreadful.
*Das Monster in der Geschichte ist schrecklich.*

**dream** [DRIEM] *n.* • Traum, der
**to dream** *v.* • träumen
In the mornings I can't remember my dream.
*Morgens kann ich mich an meinen Traum nicht erinnern.*

**dress** [DRES] *n.* • Kleid, das
**to dress** *v.* • sich anziehen
**well-dressed** *adj.* • gut gekleidet
The girl is wearing a pretty dress.
*Das Mädchen trägt ein schönes Kleid.*

**drink, to** [DRINGK] *v.* • trinken
**drink** *n.* • Getränk, das
Do you want something to drink with your meal?
*Willst du zu deinem Essen etwas trinken?*

**drive, to** [DREIV] *v.* • fahren
**driver** *n.* • Fahrer, der
**driver's license** *n.* • Führerschein, der
She drives about five miles to work.
*Sie fährt ungefähr fünf Meilen zur Arbeit.*

**drop, to** [DRAHP] *v.* • fallen lassen
Be careful! Don't drop the tray!
*Sei vorsichtig! Laß das Tablett nicht fallen!*

**drugstore** [DRƏGstohr] *n.* • Drogerie, die
My grandmother buys her medicine at the drugstore.
*Meine Großmutter kauft ihre Medizin in der Drogerie.*

**drum** [DRƏM] *n.* • Trommel, die
How long have you played the drum?
*Wie lange spielst du schon Trommel?*

**dry** [DREI] *adj.* • trocken
**to dry** *v.* • trocknen
**to dry (dishes)** *v.* • abtrocknen (das Geschirr)

Get a dry towel from the closet.
*Holen Sie ein trockenes Handtuch aus dem Schrank.*

**duck** [DəK] *n.* • Ente, die
There are some ducks on the pond.
*Es gibt einige Enten auf diesem Teich.*

**dull** [DəL] *adj.* • schwerfällig
This lecture is very dull.
*Dieser Vortrag ist sehr schwerfällig.*

**dumb** [DəM] *adj.* • dumm
We all laughed at his dumb remarks.
*Wir lachten über seine dummen Bemerkungen.*

**during** [DJUring; DUring] *prep.* • während
Don't talk during the speech!
*Sprich nicht während der Rede!*

**dust** [DəST] *n.* • Staub, der
Dust makes me sneeze.
*Der Staub bringt mich zum Niesen.*

**Dutch** [Də*TSH*] *adj.* • holländisch
**Dutch (person)** *n.* • Holländer, der (-in, die)
The Dutch language is similar to German.
*Die holländische Sprache ist dem Deutschen ähnlich.*

# E

**each** [IE*TSH*] *adj.; pron.* • jede, -r, -s
Each person takes a plate.
*Jede Person nimmt einen Teller.*

**eagle** [IEgəl] *n.* • Adler, der
The eagle is a bird of prey.
*Der Adler ist ein Raubvogel.*

**ear** [IER] *n.* • Ohr, das
**earring** *n.* • Ohrring, der
The loud noise hurt my ears.
*Das laute Geräusch tat meinen Ohren weh.*

**early** [ə*R*lie] *adv.* • früh
They get up early to go to school.
*Sie stehen früh auf, um zur Schule zu gehen.*

**earn, to** [ə*R*N] *v.* • verdienen
I am looking for a job to earn money.
*Ich suche einen Job, um Geld zu verdienen.*

**earth** [ə*RTH*] *n.* • Erde, die
**earthquake** *n.* • Erdbeben, das
The Earth is the third planet from the sun.
*Die Erde ist der dritte Planet von der Sonne.*

**east** [IEST] *n.* • Osten, der
The sun rises in the east.
*Die Sonne geht im Osten auf.*

**easy** [IE*z*ie] *adj.* • leicht
These exercises are too easy.
*Diese Übungen sind zu leicht.*

**eat, to** [IET] *v.* • essen
**to have something to eat** • etwas zu essen haben
I eat an apple every day.
*Ich esse jeden Tag einen Apfel.*

**edge** [E*DZH*] *n.* • Kante, die
Don't cut yourself on the sharp edges.
*Schneide dich nicht an den scharfen Kanten.*

**egg** [EG] *n.* • Ei, das
**boiled egg** • gekochte Ei, das
**hard-boiled egg** • hart gekochte Ei, das
**scrambled egg** • Rührei, das
Carole would like two fried eggs for breakfast.
*Carole möchte zwei Spiegeleier zum Frühstück.*

**eight** [*EJ*T] *n.; adj.* • acht
There are eight people on the bus.
*Es sind acht Personen im Bus.*

**eighteen** [ejt-TIEN] *n.; adj.* • achtzehn
There are eighteen of us in this class.
*Wir sind achtzehn in dieser Klasse.*

**eighty** [*EJ*Tie] *n.; adj.* • achtzig
Many people now live to be eighty.
*Viele Leute werden jetzt achtzig Jahre alt.*

**elastic** [iL*A*Stik] *n.; adj.* • elastisch
The rubber band is elastic.
*Der Gummiband ist elastisch.*

**elbow** [ELboh] *n.* • Ellbogen, der
Please keep your elbows off the table!
*Bitte nimm die Ellbogen vom Tisch.*

**electric** [iLEKtrik] *adj.* • elektrisch
Do you shave with an electric razor?
*Benutzt du einen elektrischen Rasierer?*

**elephant** [ELəfənt] *n.* • Elefant, der
These elephants come from Africa.
*Diese Elefanten kommen aus Afrika.*

**eleven** [iLE*v*ən] *n.; adj.* • elf
There are eleven players on an American football team.
*Eine Mannschaft beim Amerikanischen Fußball hat elf Spieler.*

**embarrass** [imB*A*Rəs] *v.* • in Verlegenheit bringen
When someone embarrasses him, he blushes.
*Wenn ihn jemand in Verlegenheit bringt, wird er rot.*

**embassy** [EMbəsie] *n.* • Botschaft, die
Call the embassy if you lose your passport.
*Wenn Sie ihren Reisepaß verlieren, rufen Sie die Botschaft an.*

**employee** [impleuJIE; imPLEUjie] *n.* • Angestellte, der
The company has ten employees.
*Die Gesellschaft hat zehn Angestellte.*

**empty** [EMPtie] *adj.* • leer
Put the empty bottles on the counter.
*Stellen Sie die leeren Flaschen auf den Ladentisch!*

**end** [END] *n.* • Ende, das
The hero dies at the end of the story.
*Der Held stirbt am Ende der Geschichte.*

**energetic** [enə*rDZH*ETik] *adj.* • energisch
**energy** *n.* • Energie, die
He is very energetic in his work!
*Er ist sehr energisch bei seiner Arbeit!*

**engaged** [enG*EJDZH*d] *adj.* • verlobt sein
She was engaged for a year before she married.
*Sie war ein Jahr lang verlobt, bevor sie heiratete.*

**engineer** [en*dzh*iNIER] *n.* • Ingenieur, der
The engineer has a degree from Cal Tech.
*Der Ingenieur hat einen akademischen Grad an der Universität Cal Tech erworben.*

**England** [INGlənd] *n.* • England
**English (person)** *n.* • Engländer, der (-in, f.)
**English (language)** *adj.* • Englisch, das (Sprache)

London and Manchester are cities in England.
*London und Manchester sind Städte in England.*

**enough** [iNƏF] *adv.* • genug
Thank you, I have had enough to eat.
*Danke, ich habe genug zu essen gehabt.*

**enter, to** [ENtə*r*] *v.* • betreten
The teacher enters the classroom.
*Der Lehrer betritt das Klassenzimmer.*

**enthusiasm** [in*THOO*zie-*az*əm] *n.* • Begeisterung, die
**enthusiastic** *adj.* • begeistert
You show a lot of enthusiasm for new subjects.
*Du zeigst große Begeisterung für neue Fächer.*

**entire** [enTEIR] *adj.* • ganz
Our entire family is home for the holiday.
*Unsere ganze Familie ist am Feiertag zu Hause.*

**entrance** [ENtrəns] *n.* • Eingang, der
The entrance to the hall is through the red door.
*Der Eingang zum Flur ist durch die rote Tür.*

**envelope** [EN*v*əlohp] *n.* • Briefumschlag, der
Fold the letter and put it in an envelope, please.
*Falten Sie den Brief und tun Sie ihn bitte in einen Briefumschlag.*

**equal** [IEk*w*əl] *adj.* • gleich
Both halves are equal.
*Beide Hälften sind gleich.*

**erase, to** [iR*EJ*S] *v.* • ausradieren
**eraser** *n.* • Radiergummi, der
I erase my mistakes with an eraser.
*Ich radiere meine Fehler mit einem Radiergummi aus.*

**errand** [ERənd] *n.* • Besorgung, die
**to run errands** *v.* • Besorgungen machen
We have errands to run in town.
*Wir haben Besorgungen in der Stadt zu machen.*

**error** [ER*ə*r] *n.* • Fehler, der
There aren't any errors in my homework.
*In meiner Hausaufgabe sind keine Fehler.*

**especially** [eSPESHəlie] *adv.* • besonders
I like to swim, especially when it is hot.
*Ich schwimme gern, besonders wenn es warm ist.*

**Europe** [JUrəp] *n.* • Europa
**European (person)** *n.* • Europäer, der (-in, f.)
**European** *adj.* • europäisch
They will travel through Europe this summmer.
*Sie werden diesen Sommer durch Europa reisen.*

**eve** [IE*V*] *n.* • Vorabend, der
On the eve of our trip, we're going to go to bed early.
*Am Abend vor unserer Reise gehen wir früh zu Bett.*

**evening** [IE*V*ning] *n.* • Abend, der
**Good evening!** • Guten Abend!
**in the evening** • am Abend; abends
**last evening** • gestern Abend
I do my homework in the evening.
*Ich mache meine Hausaufgaben am Abend.*

**event** [i*V*ENT] *n.* • Ereignis, das
The opening of the Olympic Games is always a big event.
*Die Eröffnung der Olympischen Spiele ist immer ein großes Ereignis.*

**eight** [*EJ*T] *n.; adj.* • acht
There are eight people on the bus.
*Es sind acht Personen im Bus.*

**eighteen** [ejt-TIEN] *n.; adj.* • achtzehn
There are eighteen of us in this class.
*Wir sind achtzehn in dieser Klasse.*

**eighty** [*EJ*Tie] *n.; adj.* • achtzig
Many people now live to be eighty.
*Viele Leute werden jetzt achtzig.*

**ever** [E*V*ər] *adv.* • jemals
**hardly ever** • fast niemals
If you ever need help, call me.
*Wenn du jemals Hilfe brauchst, ruf mich an!*

**every** [E*V*rie] *adj.* • jede, -r, -s
**everybody** *pron.* • jeder(mann)
**every day** • jeden Tag
**everything** *pron.* • alles
**everywhere** *adv.* • überall
I was at work every day last month.
*Ich war letzten Monat jeden Tag bei der Arbeit.*

**exam** [ig*Z*AM] *n.* • Examen, das (Prüfung, die)
**to fail an exam** • eine Prüfung nicht bestehen (durchfallen)
**to pass an exam** *v.* • eine Prüfung bestehen
**to take an exam** • eine Prüfung ablegen
The teacher gave an exam at the end of the course.
*Der Lehrer gab am Ende des Kurses ein Examen.*

**example** [ig*Z*AMpəl] *n.* • Beispiel, das
**for example** • zum Beispiel
Your behavior sets an example for the others.
*Dein Benehmen gibt den anderen ein Beispiel.*

**excellent** [EKsələnt] *adj.* • ausgezeichnet
She was rewarded for her excellent work.
*Sie wurde für ihre ausgezeichnete Arbeit belohnt.*

**except** [ekSEPT] *prep.* • außer
Everyone else can leave except me!
*Außer mir, können alle andere gehen!*

**excuse** [eksKJ*OOZ*] *v.* • entschuldigen
Please excuse me for being late.
*Entschuldigen Sie bitte meine Verspätung.*

**exercise** [EKsə*r*sei*z*] *v.* • Sport treiben
I exercise by running every day.
*Ich treibe Sport, indem ich jeden Tag laufe.*

**exit** [EG*z*it] *n.* • Ausgang, der
**emergency exit** • Notausgang, der
The exits in the theater are clearly marked.
*Die Ausgänge im Theater sind klar gekennzeichnet.*

**expensive** [ekSPENsi*v*] *adj.* • teuer
**to be expensive** • teuer sein (kostspielig)
**to be inexpensive** • billig sein (nicht kostspielig)
Diamonds are expensive.
*Diamanten sind teuer.*

**experience** [ekSPIERie-əns] *n.* • Erfahrung, die
He has three years of experince on this job.
*Er hat drei Jahre Erfahrung mit dieser Arbeit.*

**explain, to** [eksPL*EJ*N] *v.* • erklären
Please explain to us why you did that.
*Erklären Sie uns bitte, warum Sie das getan haben.*

**extend, to** [eksTEND] *v.* • reichen
**to extend one's hand** • einem die Hand reichen
Peter extends his hand to Marie.
*Peter reicht Marie seine Hand.*

**exterior** [eksTIERie-ə*r*] *n.* • Äußere, das
He is painting the exterior of the house.
*Er streicht das Äußere des Hauses.*

**extraordinary** [ekSTR*A*Wrdinerie] *adj.* • außerordentlich
Marie plays the piano with extraordinary skill.
*Marie spielt mit außerordentlicher Begabung Klavier.*

**extreme** [eksTRIEM] *adj.* • extrem
Weather conditions on Mt. Everest are extreme.
*Die Wetterverhältnisse auf dem Mt. Everest sind extrem.*

**eye** [EI] *n.* • Auge, das
**eyebrows** *n. pl.* • Augenbrauen, die
**eyelashes** *n. pl.* • Augenwimpern, die
**eyelid** *n.* • Augenlid, das
Both my parents have brown eyes.
*Meine Eltern haben beide braune Augen.*

# F

**face** [F*EJ*S] *n.* • Gesicht, das
I wash my face in the morning.
*Ich wasche mir morgens das Gesicht.*

**factory** [F*A*Ktərie] *n.* • Fabrik, die
What do they make in this factory?
*Was wird in dieser Fabrik produziert.*

**fail, to** [F*EJ*L] *v.* • versäumen
**to fail (an exam)** • durchfallen
I failed to finish the assignment on time.
*Ich versäumte es, die Aufgabe rechtzeitig zu beenden.*

**fair** [F*EJ*R] *n.* • Messe, die
We are going to spend the day at the fair.
*Wir werden den Tag auf der Messe verbringen.*

**fairy** [F*EJ*Rie] *n.* • Fee, die
A good fairy appears in this story.
*In dieser Geschichte kommt eine gute Fee vor.*

**fall** [F*A*WL] *n.* • Herbst, der
The leaves are beautiful in the fall.
*Das Laub ist schön im Herbst.*

**fall, to** [F*A*WL] *v.* • fallen
Don't fall on the ice.
*Fall nicht auf dem Eis.*

**false** [F*A*WLS] *adj.* • falsch
Is the answer true or false?
*Ist die Antwort richtig oder falsch?*

**family** [F*A*Mlie] *n.* • Familie, die
The whole family is together for the holidays.
*Die ganze Familie ist an den Feiertagen zusammen.*

**famous** [F*EJ*məs] *adj.* • berühmt
This restaurant is famous for its seafood.
*Dieses Restaurant ist für Meeresfrüchte berühmt.*

**fan** [F*A*N] *n.* • Ventilator, der
The fan will cool the room quickly.
*Der Ventilator wird das Zimmer schnell kühlen.*

**far** [FAHR] *adj.; adv.* • weit
Do you live far from here?
*Wohnst du weit von hier?*

**farm** [FAHRM] *n.* • Bauernhof, der
This farm produces corn and wheat.
*Dieser Bauernhof baut Mais und Weizen an.*

**fashion** [F*A*SHən] *n.* • Mode, die
Are hats the fashion this year?
*Sind Hüte dieses Jahr in Mode?*

**fast** [FAST] *adj.* • schnell
This is a fast train.
*Dieses ist ein schneller Zug.*

**fat** [FAT] *n.* • Fett, das
Exercise will help you lose fat.
*Sport treiben hilft, Fett abzubauen.*

**father** [FAH*dhər*] *n.* • Vater, der
My father helped me with my homework.
*Mein Vater half mir bei meiner Hausaufgabe.*

**fault** [F*A*WLT] *n.* • Schuld, die
It is my fault that we are late.
*Es ist meine Schuld, daß wir zu spät sind.*

**favorite** [F*EJV*rit] *adj.* • Lieblings-
What is your favorite color?
*Was ist deine Lieblingsfarbe?*

**fear, to** [FIER] *v.* • Angst haben
**fear** *n.* • Angst, die; Furcht, die
I fear for my life when he is driving.
*Ich habe Angst um mein Leben, wenn er fährt.*

**feather** [FE*dhər*] *n.* • Feder, die
The parrot has colorful feathers.
*Der Papagei hat bunte Federn.*

**February** [FEBj*oo*erie; FEBr*oo*erie] *n.* • Februar, der
February is the shortest month.
*Der Februar ist der kürzeste Monat.*

**feel, to** [FIEL] *v.* • sich fühlen
I feel bad after having eaten the whole cake.
*Ich fühle mich schlecht, nachdem ich den ganzen Kuchen gegessen habe.*

**feet** See *foot.*

**ferocious** [fəROHshəs] *adj.* • grausam
This dog looks ferocious.
*Dieser Hund sieht grausam aus.*

**fever** [FIE*v*ər] *n.* • Fieber, das
Often you get a fever with the flu.
*Man bekommt oft Fieber bei Grippe (Influenza).*

**few** [FJ*OO*] *adj.; pron.* • wenige
There are only a few cookies left.
*Es sind nur wenige Kekse übrig.*

**fiancé (-e, f.)** [fieahnS*EJ*] *n.* • Verlobte, die
My fiancé wants to have the wedding in June.
*Meine Verlobte möchte im Juni heiraten.*

**field** [FIELD] *n.* • Feld, das
The sheep are in the field.
*Die Schafe sind auf dem Feld.*

**fierce** [FIERS] *adj.* • grimmig
Wild animals are fierce.
*Wilde Tiere sind grimmig.*

**fifteen** [fifTIEN] *n.; adj.* • fünfzehn
I live fifteen kilometers from here.
*Ich wohne fünfzehn Kilometer von hier.*

**fifty** [FIFtie] *n.; adj.* • fünfzig
Fifty dollars is expensive for a sweater.
*Fünfzig Dollar ist teuer für einen Pullover.*

**fight, to** [FEIT] *v.* • sich streiten
My little brothers fight all the time.
*Meine kleinen Brüder streiten sich immer.*

**fill, to** [FIL] *v.* • füllen
She fills their plates with noodles.
*Sie füllt ihre Teller mit Nudeln.*

**film** [FILM] *n.* • Film, der
An old film is playing at the theater.
*Ein alter Film läuft im Kino.*

**finally** [FEInəlie] *adj.* • endlich
I'm finally done with my project.
*Ich bin endlich mit meinem Projekt fertig.*

**find, to** [FEIND] *v.* • finden
I can't find my gloves!
*Ich kann meine Handschuhe nicht finden.*

**fine** [FEIN] *adj.; adv.* • schön; sehr gut
We had a fine day at the beach.
*Wir hatten einen schönen Tag am Strand.*

I am feeling fine now.
*Ich fühle mich sehr gut jetzt.*

**finger** [FINGgə*r*] *n.* • Finger, der
Don't eat with your fingers!
*Iß nicht mit den Fingern!*

**finish, to** [FINish] *v.* • beenden
I finished my homework at 10:00 p.m.
*Ich beendete meine Hausaufgabe um 10 Uhr abends.*

**fire** [FEIR] *n.* • Feuer, das
**fireman** *n.* • Feuerwehrmann, der
**fireplace** *n.* • Kamin, der offene
**fire truck** • Feuerwehrwagen, der
**fireworks** *n.* • Feuerwerke, die
I started the fire with a match.
*Ich habe das Feuer mit einem Streichholz angezündet.*

**first** [Fə*R*ST] *adj.* • erst
It's the first time she has flown on a jet.
*Es ist das erste Mal, daß sie mit einem Düsenflugzeug fliegt.*

**fish, to** [FISH] *v.* • angeln
**fish** *n.* • Fisch, der
**goldfish** *n.* • Goldfisch, der
**to go fishing** • angeln gehen
We like to fish in the summer.
*Wir angeln gern im Sommer.*

Is there fish on the menu?
*Gibt es Fisch auf der Speisekarte?*

**five** [FEIV] *n.; adj.* • fünf
A nickel is worth five cents.
*Ein Nickel ist fünf Cent wert.*

**fix, to** [FIKS] *v.* • reparieren
Can you fix the flat tire?
*Können Sie den platten Reifen reparieren?*

**flag** [FLAG] *n.* • Fahne, die
The American flag is red, white, and blue.
*Die amerikanische Fahne ist rot, weiß, und blau.*

**flat** [FLAT] *adj.* • eben
You need a flat surface to play this game.
*Man braucht eine ebene Oberfläche, um dieses Spiel zu spielen*

**flavor** [FL*EJ*vər] *n.* • Geschmack, der
This soup has the flavor of onions.
*Diese Suppe hat den Geschmack von Zwiebeln.*

**flight** [FLEIT] *n.* • Flug, der
**flight attendant** • Flugbegleiter, der (-in, f.)
Flight 507 just arrived at the gate.
*Die Maschine mit der Flugnummer 507 ist eben am Ausgang angekommen.*

**floor** [FLOHR] *n.* • Fußboden, der
**floor (of a building)** *n.* • Stock, der
**ground floor** • Erdgeschoß, das

I am going to sweep the floor.
*Ich werde den Fußboden kehren.*

**flour** [FLAUR] *n.* • Mehl, das
You need flour to make bread.
*Man braucht Mehl, um Brot zu backen.*

**flower** [FLAU*wər*] *n.* • Blume, die
These flowers grow in the woods.
*Diese Blumen wachsen im Wald.*

**flu** [FL*OO*] *n.* • Grippe, die
It's no fun to have the flu.
*Es ist kein Spaß, Grippe zu haben.*

**fly** [FLEI] *n.* • Fliege, die
The screen will keep the flies out.
*Das Fliegengitter wird die Fliegen draußen lassen.*

**fly, to** [FLEI] *v.* • fliegen
I want to fly on the Concorde.
*Ich möchte mit der Concorde fliegen.*

**fog** [F*A*WG] *n.* • Nebel, der
It's hard to see in this fog.
*Es ist schwer, bei diesem Nebel zu sehen.*

**fold, to** [FOHLD] *v.* • zusammenlegen
I fold the towels before I put them away.
*Ich lege die Handtücher zusammen, ehe ich sie weglege.*

**follow, to** [FAHLoh] *v.* • folgen
We always follow our professor's directions.
*Wir folgen immer den Anweisungen unseres Professors.*

**food** [F*OO*D] *n.* • Lebensmittel, die (pl.)
We buy food at the grocery store.
*Wir kaufen Lebensmittel im Lebensmittelgeschäft.*

**foolish** [F*OO*Lish] *adj.* • dumm
It is foolish to drive so fast.
*Es ist dumm, so schnell zu fahren.*

**foot (pl. feet)** [FUT (pl. FIET)] *n.* • Fuß, der (pl. Füße, die)
**foot (animal)** *n.* • Tierfuß, der
**on foot** • zu Fuß
You are stepping on my foot!
*Sie stehen auf meinem Fuß!*

These shoes make my feet hurt.
*Diese Schuhe tun meinen Füßen weh.*

**football** [FUTb*aw*l] *n.* • Fußball, der
**to play football** • Fußball spielen
My brother has a new football.
*Mein Bruder hat einen neuen Fußball.*

**for** [F*AW*R] *prep.* • für
This present is for you.
*Dieses Geschenk ist für dich.*

**foreigner** [F*AW*Rənə*r*] *n.* • Ausländer, der (-in, f.)
These foreigners are visiting the United States.
*Diese Ausländer besuchen die Vereinigten Staaten.*

**forest** [F*AW*Rəst] *n.* • Wald, der
The forest has many pine trees.
*Es gibt viele Tannenbäume im Wald.*

**forever** [f*aw*rE*V*ə*r*] *adv.* • ewig
I will keep this memory forever.
*Ich werde diese Erinnerung ewig bewahren.*

**forget, to** [f*aw*rGET] *v.* • vergessen
Don't forget to do your homework!
*Vergiß nicht, deine Hausaufgabe zu machen!*

**forgive, to** [f*aw*rGIV] *v.* • verzeihen
Will you forgive me for being late?
*Wirst du meine Verspätung verzeihen?*

**fork** [FAWRK] *n.* • Gabel, die
Did you put out the knives and forks?
*Hast du die Messer und Gabeln hingelegt?*

**forty** [F*A*WRdie] *n.; adj.* • vierzig
The bus can carry forty passengers.
*Der Bus kann vierzig Passagiere befördern.*

**fountain** [FAUNtən] *n.* • Springbrunnen, der
There is a pretty fountain in the middle of the village.
*Es gibt einen schönen Springbrunnen in der Mitte des Dorfe.*

**four** [F*A*WR] *n.; adj.* • vier
The table has four legs.
*Der Tisch hat vier Beine.*

**fourteen** [f*aw*rTIEN] *n.; adj.* • vierzehn
Most of the pupils are fourteen years old.
*Die meisten Schüler sind vierzehn Jahre alt.*

**fox** [FAHKS] *n.* • Fuchs, der
The fox is very sly.
*Der Fuchs ist sehr schlau.*

**France** [FRANS] *n.* • Frankreich
**French (person)** *n.* • Franzose, der (-in, f.)
**French (language)** *adj.* • französisch
Can you find Dijon on the map of France?
*Kannst du Dijon auf der Landkarte von Frankreich finden?*

**free** [FRIE] *adj.* • frei
Admission to the museum is free on Mondays.
*Der Eintritt für das Museum ist montags frei.*

The children are free today after third period.
*Die Kinder haben heute nach der dritten Stunde frei.*

**freedom** [FRIEdəm] *n.* • Freiheit, die
Freedom of religion is a basic right.
*Religionsfreiheit ist ein Grundrecht.*

**freeze, to** [FRIE*Z*] *v.* • gefrieren
In winter, the rain freezes on the roads.
*Im Winter gefriert der Regen auf den Straßen.*

**fresh** [FRESH] *adj.* • frisch
Are these vegetables fresh?
*Ist dieses Gemüse frisch?*

**Friday** [FREId*ej*] *n.* • Freitag, der
On Fridays, we leave for the weekend.
*Freitags fahren wir immer fürs Wochenende weg.*

**friend** [FREND] *n.* • Freund, der (-in, f.)
**friendly** *adj.* • freundlich
**friendship** *n.* • Freundschaft, die
I went to the movie with a friend.
*Ich ging mit einem Freund ins Kino.*

**frightening** [FREITning] *adj.* • furchterregend
Do you think that ghosts are frightening?
*Glaubst du, daß Gespenster furchterregend sind?*

**frog** [FR*AW*G] *n.* • Frosch, der
There are several frogs in this pond.
*Es gibt einige Frösche in diesem Teich.*

**from** [FRƏM] *prep.* • aus
They are coming from Chicago.
*Sie kommen aus Chicago.*

**front** [FRƏNT] *n.; adj.* • vor
The teacher is standing in front of the class.
*Der Lehrer steht vor der Klasse.*

**fruit** [FR*OO*T] *n.* • Frucht, die
Fruits and vegetables are good for your health.
*Früchte und Gemüse sind gut für die Gesundheit.*

**full** [FUL] *adj.* • voll; satt
**I am full.** • Ich bin satt.
My pockets are full.
*Meine Taschen sind voll.*

**fun** [FəN] *n.; adj.* • Spaß, der
**for fun** • zum Vergnügen
**to have fun** • sich vergnügen
This game is lots of fun.
*Dieses Spiel macht viel Spaß.*

We always have fun at the beach.
*Wir vergnügen uns immer am Strand.*

**fur** [Fə*R*] *n.* • Fell, das
The rabbit's fur is very soft.
*Das Fell des Kaninchens ist sehr weich.*

**furious** [FJUrie-əs] *adj.* • wütend
If I don't clean my room my mother will be furious.
*Wenn ich mein Zimmer nicht putze, wird meine Mutter wütend sein.*

**furniture** [Fə*R*ni*tsh*ər] *n.* • Möbel, die
We moved the furniture to clean the carpet.
*Wir rückten die Möbel weg, um den Teppich zu reinigen.*

**future** [FJ*OO*tsh*ə*r] *n.* • Zukunft, die
The future of this business is promising.
*Die Zukunft dieses Geschäfts ist vielsprechend.*

# G

**game** [G*EJ*M] *n.* • Spiel, das
Are you going to the basketball game this evening?
*Gehst du heute abend zum Basketballspiel?*

**garage** [gəRAHD*ZH*; gəRAHZ*H*] *n.* • Garage, die
Dad is parking the car in the garage.
*Vati parkt den Wagen in der Garage.*

**garbage** [GAHRbi*dzh*] *n.* • Abfall, der
**garbage can** • Mülleimer, der
Put the garbage into the can.
*Tu den Abfall in den Mülleimer.*

**garden** [GAHRDn] *n.* • Garten, der
These flowers are from our garden.
*Diese Blumen sind aus unserem Garten.*

**gas** [GAS] *n., adj.* • Gas, das
We have a gas stove.
*Wir haben einen Gasherd.*

**gas(oline)** [g*a*səLIEN] *n.* • Benzin, das
**gas(oline) pump** *n.* • Benzinpumpe, die
Our car needs gas(oline).
*Unser Auto braucht Benzin.*

**gather** [GA*dh*ə*r*] *v.* • versammeln
**gather (fruit)** *v.* • pflücken
The guests gather in the garden.
*Die Gäste versammeln sich im Garten.*

**general** [*DZH*ENə*r*əl] *adj.* • allgemein
I have general directions, but please give me details.
*Ich habe allgemeine Anweisungen, aber geben Sie mir bitte Einzelheiten.*

**generous** [*DZH*ENə*r*əs] *adj.* • großmütig
My grandparents are very generous.
*Meine Großeltern sind sehr großmütig.*

**gentle** [*DZH*ENtəl] *adj.* • sanft
**gentleman** *n.* • Herr, der

**gently** *adv.* • sanft
**Ladies and gentlemen!** • Meine Damen und Herren!
The nurse is very gentle.
*Die Krankenschwester ist sehr sanft.*

**geography** [*dzh*ieAHgrəfie] *n.* • Geographie, die
I learned about maps in geography class.
*Ich lernte etwas über Landkarten in der Geographieklasse.*

**geometry** [*dzh*ieAHmətrie] *n.* • Geometrie, die
I like geometry better than algebra.
*Ich mag Geometrie lieber als Algebra.*

**Germany** [*DZH*ə*R*mənie] *n.* • Deutschland
**German (person)** *n.* • Deutsche, der
**German (language)** *n.* • Deutsch, das
**German** *adj.* • deutsch
**German shepherd (dog)** • deutsche Schäferhund, der
My father's ancestors come from Germany.
*Die Vorfahren meines Vaters kommen aus Deutschland.*

**get, to** [GET] *v.* • bekommen
**to get dressed** • anziehen, sich
**to get rid of** • loswerden
**to get up** • aufstehen
If you study hard, you will get a good grade.
*Wenn du tüchtig arbeitest, bekommst du eine gute Note.*

**ghost** [GOHST] *n.* • Geist, der
Do you believe in ghosts?
*Glaubst du an Geister?*

**giant** [*DZH*EIənt] *n.* • Riese, der
There is a giant in this fairy tale.
*Es gibt einen Riesen in diesem Märchen.*

**gift** [GIFT] *n.* • Geschenk, das
**gifted** *adj.* • begabt
You get gifts on your birthday.
*Man bekommt Geschenke an seinem Geburtstag.*

**giraffe** [*dzh*əRAF] *n.* • Giraffe, die
Giraffes have very long necks.
*Giraffen haben sehr lange Hälse.*

**girl** [GƏ*R*L] *n.* • Mädchen, das
There are three girls and two boys in the room.
*In diesem Zimmer sind drei Mädchen und zwei Jungen.*

**give, to** [GI*V*] *v.* • geben
**to give back** • zurückgeben
Please give me a chance to speak.
*Bitte geben Sie mir die Gelegenheit zu sprechen.*

**glad** [GL*A*D] *adj.* • erfreut; froh
I am very glad to see you.
*Ich bin sehr erfreut, dich zu sehen.*

**glass** [GL*A*S] *n.* • Glas, das
**made of glass** • aus Glas
The glass in the window is broken.
*Das Glas des Fensters ist zerbrochen.*

**glasses (eyeglasses)** [GL*A*Sə*z*] *n.* • Brille, die
**sunglasses** *n. pl.* • Sonnenbrille, die
I need my glasses to read this.
*Ich brauche meine Brille, um dies zu lesen.*

**glove** [GLƏ*V*] *n.* • Handschuh, der
These two gloves don't match.
*Diese zwei Handschuhe passen nicht zusammen.*

**glue, to (to paste)** [GL*OO*] *v.* • kleben
**glue (paste)** *n.* • Klebstoff, der; Leim, der
We glued the cover back on the book.
*Wir klebten den Deckel wieder auf das Buch.*

**goal** [GOHL] *n.* • Ziel, das
What is the goal of this project?
*Was ist das Ziel dieses Projekts?*

**goat** [GOHT] *n.* • Ziege, die
The farmer raises sheep and goats.
*Der Bauer züchtet Schafe und Ziegen.*

**gold** [GOHLD] *n.* • Gold, das
Is this necklace made of gold?
*Ist diese Halskette aus Gold?*

**golf** [G*AW*LF] *n.; v.* • Golfspiel, das
**golf course** • Golfplatz, der
**to play golf** • Golf spielen
We play golf in the summer.
*Wir spielen im Sommer Golf.*

**good** [GUD] *adj.* • gut
**Good-bye** • Auf Wiedersehen!
**Good day** • Guten Tag!
**Good Evening** • Guten Abend!
**good-looking** *adj.* • gut aussehend, schön
**Good luck** • Viel Glück!
**Good night** • Gute Nacht!
She always gets good grades.
*Sie bekommt immer gute Noten.*

**goose** [G*OO*S] *n.* • Gans, die
**geese** *n. pl.* • Gänse, die
The goose is white.
*Die Gans ist weiß.*

**gorilla** [gəRILə] *n.* • Gorilla, der
This gorilla scares me!
*Dieser Gorilla erschreckt mich!*

**government** [GƏ*v*ərnmənt] *n.* • Regierung, die
The mayor is the head of the city's government.
*Der Bürgermeister steht der Regierung der Stadt vor.*

**go, to** [GOH] *v.* • gehen
**to go away** • gehen (weggehen)
**to go away (to travel)** • wegfahren
**to go back** • zurückgehen
**to go back to (to travel)** • zurückfahren nach
**to go down** • hinuntergehen
**to go into** • hineingehen
**to go near** • sich nähern
**to go to bed** • zu Bett gehen
**to go out (to leave)** • ausgehen
**to go to (to travel)** • fahren nach
**to go up** • hinaufgehen
We'll be going home soon.
*Wir gehen bald nach Hause.*

We're going to the store for groceries.
*Wir gehen zum Laden, um Lebensmittel zu kaufen.*

They're going back to Europe next month.
*Sie fahren nächsten Monat nach Europa zurück.*

Be careful when you go down the steps.
*Sei vorsichtig, wenn du die Treppen hinuntergehst.*

We're going away for the weekend.
*Wir fahren für das Wochenende weg.*

Tomorrow we're going to Paris.
*Morgen fahren wir nach Paris.*

**granddaughter** [GRANd*aw*tər] *n.* • Enkelin, die
**grandson** *n.* • Enkel, der
Her granddaughter is two years old.
*Ihre Enkelin ist zwei Jahre alt.*

**grandfather** [GRAN(d)fah*th*ər] *n.* • Großvater, der
My grandfather is retired now.
*Mein Großvater ist jetzt pensioniert.*

**grandmother** [GR*A*N(d)mə*th*ə*r*] *n.* • Großmutter, die
**grandparents** *n. pl.* • Großeltern, die
Both my grandmothers came to my wedding.
*Meine Großmütter sind beide zu meiner Hochzeit gekommen.*

**grape** [GR*EJ*P] *n.* • Traube, die
We are having grapes for dessert.
*Wir haben Trauben zum Nachtisch.*

**grapefruit** [GR*EJ*Pfr*oo*t] *n.* • Pampelmuse, die
I like grapefruit with my breakfast.
*Ich esse gern Pampelmusen zu meinem Frühstück.*

**grass** [GR*A*S] *n.* • Gras, das
The grass is very tall in this field.
*Das Gras auf diesem Feld ist sehr hoch.*

**grasshopper** [GR*A*Shahpə*r*] *n.* • Heuschrecke, die
The grasshopper jumped away from the cat.
*Die Heuschrecke hüpfte von der Katze weg.*

**gravy** [GR*EJv*ie] *n.* • Soße, die
Do you want gravy with your roast beef?
*Möchtest du Soße zu deinem Rinderbraten?*

**gray** [GR*EJ*] *adj.* • grau
My grandfather's beard is gray.
*Der Bart meines Großvaters ist grau.*

**great** [GR*EJ*T] *adj.* • bedeutend
**Great!** *interj.* • Großartig!
Abraham Lincoln was one of the greatest U.S. presidents.
*Abraham Lincoln war einer der bedeutendsten Präsidenten der U.S.A.*

**Greece** [GRIES] *n.* • Griechenland
**Greek (person)** *n.* • Grieche, der (-in, f.)
**Greek** *adj.* • griechisch
Athens is the capital of Greece.
*Athen ist die Hauptstadt Griechenlands.*

**green** [GRIEN] *adj.* • grün
**green beans** • grüne Bohnen
Pine trees are green all year long.
*Tannenbäume sind das ganze Jahr lang grün.*

**grocer** [GROHsər] *n.* • Kolonialwarenhändler, der
**grocery store** *n.* • Kolonialwarenladen, der
The grocer sells fruits and vegetables.
*Der Kolonialwarenhändler verkauft Früchte und Gemüse.*

**ground** [GRAUND] *n.* • Erde, die
**ground floor** • Erdgeschoß, das
They plant the seeds in the ground.
*Sie säen den Samen in die Erde.*

**group** [GR*OO*P] *n.* • Gruppe, die
The students leave class in groups.
*Die Studenten verlassen die Klasse in Gruppen.*

**grow, to** [GROH] *v.* • züchten
I grow vegetables in my garden.
*Ich züchte Gemüse in meinem Garten.*

**guard** [GAHRD] *n.* • Wächter, der (-in, f.)
**to guard** *v.* • bewachen
The bank has a guard at the door.
*Die Bank hat einen Wächter an der Tür.*

**guess, to** [GES] *v.* • raten
Can you guess how old I am?
*Kannst du raten, wie alt ich bin?*

**guest** [GEST] *n.* • Gast, der
When are the guests arriving?
*Wann kommen die Gäste an?*

**guilty** [GILtie] *adj.* • schuldig
The jury decides if the defendant is guilty.
*Die Geschworenen entscheiden, ob der Angeklagte schuldig ist.*

**guitar** [giTAHR] *n.* • Gitarre, die
**to play the guitar** • Gitarre spielen
This guitar has six strings.
*Diese Gitarre hat sechs Saiten.*

**gun** [GəN] *n.* • Gewehr, das
You must be careful with guns.
*Man muß mit Gewehren vorsichtig sein.*

**gymnasium** [*dzh*imN*EJz*ie-əm] *n.* • Turnhalle, die
**gymnast** *n.* • Turner, der (-in, f.)
**gymnastics** *n.* • Turnen, das
We play basketball in the gymnasium.
*Wir spielen Basketball in der Turnhalle.*

# H

**habit** [H*A*Bit] *n.* • Gewohnheit, die
To get up early is a good habit.
*Es ist eine gute Gewohnheit, früh aufzustehen.*

**hair** [H*EJ*R] *n.* • Haar, das
**hairbrush** *n.* • Haarbürste, die
**haircut** *n.* • Haarschnitt, der
**hairdresser** *n.* • Friseur, der (-in, f.)
**hair-style** *n.* • Frisur, die

My sister has long hair.
*Meine Schwester hat lange Haare.*

**half** [HAF] *adj.; n.* • Hälfte, die
**half an hour** • halbe Stunde, die
Do you want half of this apple?
*Möchtest du die Hälfte dieses Apfels?*

**ham** [HAM] *n.* • Schinken, der
I would like ham on my sandwich.
*Ich möchte Schinken auf meinem belegten Brot (Sandwich).*

**hammer** [HAMər] *n.* • Hammer, der
The carpenter uses a hammer to drive nails.
*Der Zimmermann benutzt einen Hammer, um die Nägel einzuschlagen.*

**hand** [HAND] *n.* • Hand, die
**left hand** • linke Hand, die
**right hand** • rechte Hand, die
**to shake hands** • Hände schütteln
If you know the answer, raise your hand.
*Wenn Sie die Antwort wissen, heben Sie die Hand.*

**handsome** [HANsəm] *adj.* • schön
Martine thinks your brother is handsome.
*Martine findet deinen Bruder schön.*

**happen, to** [HAPən] *v.* • geschehen
I don't know what happened after I had left.
*Ich weiß nicht, was geschah, nachdem ich gegangen war.*

**happy** [HAPie] *adj.* • glücklich
**happiness** *n.* • Glück, das
**Happy Birthday!** • Herzlichen Glückwunsch zum Geburtstag!
I am happy when I get a good grade.
*Wenn ich eine gute Note bekomme, bin ich glücklich.*

**hard** [HAHRD] *adj.* • schwer
Chopping wood is very hard work.
*Holz zu spalten ist eine sehr schwere Arbeit.*

**harvest** [HAHR*v*əst] *n.* • Ernte, die
The farmers have a good harvest this year.
*Die Bauern haben dieses Jahr eine gute Ernte.*

**hat** [H*A*T] *n.* • Hut, der
He wears a hat to cover his head.
*Er trägt einen Hut, um seinen Kopf zu bedecken.*

**hate, to** [H*EJ*T] *v.* • hassen
I hate rainy weather!
*Ich hasse Regenwetter!*

**have, to** [H*AV*] *v.* • haben
**to have a good time** • sich vergnügen
**to have food** • (essen) nehmen
I have a date at seven.
*Ich habe um sieben Uhr eine Verabredung.*

Do you have time to read this letter?
*Hast du Zeit, diesen Brief zu lesen?*

We have a good time at the beach.
*Wir vergnügen uns am Strand.*

I'm having ice cream for dessert.
*Ich nehme Eis zum Nachtisch.*

**have to, to (must)** [H*AV* too] *v.* • müssen
We have to leave very soon.
*Wir müssen sehr bald losfahren.*

**hay** [H*EJ*] *n.* • Heu, das
**hay-fever** *n.* • Heufieber, das
The cattle ate the hay we had given them.
*Die Rinder fraßen das Heu, das wir ihnen gegeben hatten.*

**he** [HIE] *pron.* • er
He is the man with the red sweater.
*Er ist der Mann mit dem roten Pullover.*

**head** [HED] *n.* • Kopf, der
**headache** *n.* • Kopfweh, das
**headlight** *n.* • Scheinwerfer, der
I laid my head on the pillow.
*Ich legte meinen Kopf auf das Kissen.*

**health** [HEL*TH*] *n.* • Gesundheit, die
Walking is good for your health.
*Gehen ist gut für die Gesundheit.*

**hear, to** [HIER] *v.* • hören
We hear the wind blowing in the trees.
*Wir hören den Wind in den Bäumen.*

**heart** [HAHRT] *n.* • Herz, das
When you run, your heart beats faster.
*Wenn man läuft, schlägt das Herz schneller.*

**heat** [HIET] *n.* • Hitze, die
Do you feel the heat of the fire?
*Spürst du die Hitze des Feuers?*

**heavy** [HE*V*ie] *adj.* • schwer
This box is too heavy for me.
*Dieser Kasten ist zu schwer für mich.*

**height** [HEIT] *n.* • Höhe, die
The height of this building is impressive.
*Die Höhe dieses Gebäudes ist beeindruckend.*

**helicopter** [HELəkahptə*r*] *n.* •
Hubschrauber, der
Do you see the helicopter above us?
*Siehst du den Hubschrauber über uns?*

**Hello** [həLOH] *interj.* • Hallo!
Hello, my name is Philip.
*Hallo, ich heiße Philip.*

**helmet** [HELmət] *n.* • Helm, der
**helmet (crash, motor)** *n.* • Sturzhelm, der
You must wear a helmet when riding a motorcycle.
*Man muß einen Sturzhelm tragen, wenn man Motorrad fährt.*

**help, to** [HELP] *v.* • helfen
**help** *n.* • Hilfe, die
**Help!** • Hilfe!
I help my dad prepare dinner.
*Ich helfe meinem Vater bei der Vorbereitung des Abendessens.*

**hen** [HEN] *n.* • Henne, die
These hens are protecting their chicks.
*Diese Hennen schützen ihre Küken.*

**her** [Hə*R*] *adj.; pron.* • ihr; sie
Grete always forgets her keys.
*Grete vergißt immer ihre Schlüssel.*

**here** [HIER] *adj.* • hier
**here is; here are** • hier ist; hier sind
Here is the book you were looking for.
*Hier ist das Buch, das du gesucht hast.*

**herself** [hə*r*SELF] *pron.* • sich
She looked at herself in the mirror.
*Sie sah sich im Spiegel an.*

**Hi!** [HEI] *interj.* • He!
Hi! How are you?
*He! Wie gehts?*

**hide, to** [HEID] *v.* • verstecken
**to play hide and seek** • Verstecken spielen
The lady hides her jewelry.
*Die Dame versteckt ihren Schmuck.*

**high** [HEI] *adj.* • hoch
**high school** • Gymnasium, das
**highway** *n.* • Hauptstraße, die
These mountains are high.
*Diese Berge sind hoch.*

**hill** [HIL] *n.* • Hügel, der
We go sledding on this hill in the winter.
*Im Winter fahren wir auf diesem Hügel Schlitten.*

**him** [HIM] *adj.; pron.* • ihm; ihn
This new tie is for him.
*Diese neue Krawatte ist für ihn.*

**himself** [himSELF] *pron.* • sich
Marc bought himself a new pair of shoes.
*Marc kaufte sich ein neues Paar Schuhe.*

**hippopotamus** [hipəPAHDəməs] *n.* • Flußpferd, das
The hippopotamus stands in the river.
*Das Flußpferd steht im Fluß.*

**his** [HIZ] *adj.; pron.* • sein
My father took his clothes to the cleaner.
*Mein Vater brachte seine Kleidung zur Reinigung.*

**history** [HIStərie] *n.* • Geschichte, die
The history of mankind is fascinating.
*Die Geschichte der Menschheit ist faszinierend.*

**hit, to** [HIT] *v.* • schlagen
In tennis you have to hit the ball.
*Beim Tennis muß man den Ball schlagen.*

**hitchhike, to** [HI*TSH*heik] *v.* • per Anhalter reisen
One summer my father hitchhiked through France.
*In einem Sommer reiste mein Vater per Anhalter durch Frankreich.*

**hobby** [HAHBie] *n.* • Hobby, das (Steckenpferd, das)
What is your favorite hobby?
*Was ist dein Lieblingshobby?*

**hockey** [HAHKie] *n.* • Hockey(spiel), das
**to play hockey** • Hockey spielen
We play hockey on the pond when it's frozen.
*Wir spielen Hockey auf dem Teich, wenn er zugefroren ist.*

**hog** [HAWG] *n.* • Schwein, das
The hogs are eating corn.
*Die Schweine fressen Mais.*

**hold, to** [HOHLD] *v.* • halten
The mother holds her child's hand.
*Die Mutter hält ihr Kind an der Hand.*

**hole** [HOHL] *n.* • Loch, das
Don't fall in this hole!
*Fall nicht in dieses Loch hinein!*

**holiday** [HAHLədej] *n.* • Feiertag, der
We have no school on holidays.
*An Feiertagen haben wir schulfrei.*

**Holland** [HAHLənd] *n.* • Holland
They grow tulips in Holland.
*In Holland werden Tulpen gezüchtet.*

**home; homeland** [HOHM; HOHMland] *n.* • Heim, das; Heimat, die
**at home** • zu Hause
**to be homesick** • Heimweh haben
**to come home** • nach Hause kommen
Make yourself at home.
*Fühlen Sie sich wie zuhause.*

America is my home.
*Amerika ist meine Heimat.*

**homework** [HOHM*w*ərk] *n.* • Hausaufgaben, die
We are doing our homework.
*Wir machen unsere Hausaufgaben.*

**honest** [AHnəst] *adj.* • ehrlich
The boy gave an honest answer.
*Der Junge gab eine ehrliche Antwort.*

**honey** [HƏNie] *n.* • Honig, der
I put honey on my bread.
*Ich streiche Honig auf mein Brot.*

**honeymoon** [HƏNiem*oo*n] *n.* • Hochzeitsreise, die
Where did you go for your honeymoon?
*Wohin seid ihr auf eure Hochzeitsreise gefahren?*

**hope, to** [HOHP] *v.* • hoffen
**hope** *n.* • Huffnung, die
**hopeful** *adj.* • hoffnungsvoll
**hopeless** *adj.* • hoffnungslos
I hope you can come!
*Ich hoffe, daß Sie kommen können!*

**horrible** [HA*W*Rəbəl] *adj.* • schrecklich
**horror** *n.* • Entsetzen, das
That movie was horrible!
*Dieser Film war schrecklich!*

**horse** [HA*W*RS] *n.* • Pferd, das
**horse race** *n.* • Pferderennen, das
**horse shoe** *n.* • Hufeisen, das
I rode my horse out of the barn.
*Ich ritt mit meinem Pferd aus der Scheune.*

**hospital** [HAHSpitəl] *n.* • Krankenhaus, das
The surgeon works at the hospital.
*Der Chirurg arbeitet im Krankenhaus.*

**hot** [HAHT] *adj.* • heiß
It's hot out.
*Es ist draußen heiß.*

Be careful! The oven is hot!
*Sei vorsichtig! Der Herd ist heiß!*

**hotel** [hohTEL] *n.* • Hotel, das
Our hotel is very near the railway station.
*Unser Hotel ist sehr nahe am Bahnhof.*

**hour** [AUə*r*] *n.* • Stunde, die
I have been waiting for my friend for an hour.
*Ich warte schon eine Stunde auf meinen Freund.*

**house** [HAUS] *n.* • Haus, das
**to do housework** • Haus in Ordnung bringen, das
They have a big house with twelve rooms.
*Sie haben ein großes Haus mit zwölf Zimmern.*

**how** [HAU] *adv.* • wie
**How are things?** • Wie gehts?
**How far is --?** • Wie weit ist --?
**how many** • wie viele
**how much** • wieviel
**How old are you?** • Wie alt bist du?
**to know how** • wissen wie
Now I understand how you do that!
*Jetzt verstehe ich, wie man das macht!*

**however** [hauE*V*ə*r*] *conj.* • jedoch
I always lose; however, I keep playing!
*Ich verliere immer; ich spiele jedoch weiter!*

**humid** [HJ*OO*mid] *adj.* • feucht
The days are hot and humid in summer.
*Im Sommer sind die Tage heiß und feucht.*

**hundred (one hundred)** [HƏNdrəd] *n.; adj.* • hundert
He made one hundred points in this game.
*Er hat hundert Punkte in diesem Spiel erzielt.*

**hungry** [HƏNGgrie] *adj.* • hungrig
**to be hungry** • Hunger haben
We were hungry after having missed lunch.
*Wir hatten Hunger, nachdem wir das Mittagessen verpaßt hatten.*

**hunt, to** [HƏNT] *v.* • jagen
**hunter** *n.* • Jäger, der
Some people use a bow and arrow to hunt deer.
*Manche Leute benutzen Pfeil und Bogen, um Hochwild zu jagen.*

**hurry, to** [HƏ*R*ie] *v.* • beeilen, sich
**Hurry!** • Schnell!
**Hurry up!** • Beeile dich!
**to be in a hurry** • es eilig haben
There is no hurry.
*Es hat keine Eile.*

We are hurrying to catch the train.
*Wir beeilen uns, um den Zug zu erreichen.*

**hurt, to** [HƏ*R*T] *v.* • weh tun
**to be hurt** • verletzt sein
I can't walk because my feet hurt.
*Ich kann nicht gehen, weil meine Füße weh tun.*

**husband** [HƏ*Z*bənd] *n.* • Ehemann, der
What is your husband's name?
*Wie heißt Ihr Ehemann?*

# I

**I** [EI] *pron.* • ich
I want to go out with my friends.
*Ich möchte mit meinen Freunden ausgehen.*

**ice** [EIS] *n.* • Eis, das
  **ice cream** • Eis, das (Speiseeis, das)
  **ice cube** • Eiswürfel, der
There is ice in the freezer.
*Es gibt Eis im Gefrierfach.*

We are having ice cream for dessert.
*Wir nehmen Eis zum Nachtisch.*

**ice-skate, to** [EISsk*ej*t] *v.* •
  Schlittschuhlaufen
  **ice skate** *n.* • Schlittschuh, der
Do you ice-skate in the winter?
*Läufst du Schlittschuh im Winter?*

**idea** [eiDIEə] *n.* • Idee, die
It's a good idea to use a map.
*Es ist eine gute Idee, eine Landkarte zu benutzen.*

**if** [IF] *conj.* • wenn
  **as if** • als ob
  **if not** • falls (wenn) nicht
If I can't come, I'll call you.
*Wenn ich nicht kommen kann, ruf ich dich an.*

**ill** [IL] *adj.* • krank
  **illness** *n.* • Krankheit, die
When you are ill, you go to the doctor's.
*Wenn man krank ist, geht man zum Arzt.*

**imagine, to** [i*MADZH*ən] *v.* • sich vorstellen
Can you imagine how she must feel?
*Kannst du dir vorstellen, wie sie sich fühlt?*

**immediately** [iMIEdie-ətlie] *adv.* • sofort
I will come immediately if you need help.
*Ich werde sofort kommen, wenn du Hilfe brauchst.*

**impatient** [imP*EJ*shənt] *adj.* • ungeduldig
When John is in a hurry, he is impatient.
*Wenn Johann es eilig hat, ist er ungeduldig.*

**impolite** [impəLEIT] *adj.* • unhöflich
It was impolite not to introduce me to your friend.
*Es war unhöflich, mich deinem Freund nicht vorzustellen.*

**important** [imP*AW*Rtənt] *adj.* • wichtig
It's important that you do not fail.
*Es ist wichtig, daß du nicht versagst.*

**in** [IN] *prep.* • in
**in case of** • falls
**in front of** • vor
**in order to** • um
She puts her keys in her pocket.
*Sie steckt ihre Schlüssel in ihre Tasche.*

**incomplete** [inkəmPLIET] *adj.* • unvollendet
Beethoven wrote an incomplete symphony.
*Beethoven schrieb eine unvollendete Symphonie.*

**incorrect** [inkəREKT] *adj.* • falsch
I have three incorrect answers on this test.
*Ich habe drei falsche Antworten in dieser Prüfung.*

**indicate, to** [INdik*ej*t] *v.* • hinweisen auf
I would like to indicate the correct solution to you.
*Ich möchte Sie auf die richtige Lösung hinweisen.*

**indoors** [inD*A*W*R*Z] *adv.* • im Haus
When the weather is bad, we stay indoors.
*Wenn das Wetter schlecht ist, bleiben wir im Haus.*

**industry** [INdəstrie] *n.* • Industrie, die
Hollywood is the center of the U.S. movie industry.
*Hollywood ist das Zentrum der Filmindustrie in den U.S.A.*

**inexpensive** [inekSPENsi*v*] *adj.* • billig
**to be inexpensive** • billig sein
I bought an inexpensive car.
*Ich habe einen billigen Wagen gekauft.*

**information** [infə*r*M*EJ*shən] *n.* • Auskunft, die
If you don't know, ask for information.
*Wenn Sie nicht Bescheid wissen, bitten Sie um Auskunft.*

**injure, to** [IN*dzh*ə*r*] *v.* • verletzen
**injury** *n.* • Verletzung, die
She injured her knee playing soccer.
*Sie verletzte ihr Knie beim Fußballspielen.*

**ink** [INGK] *n.* • Tinte, die
There's no more ink in my pen!
*Mein Füller hat keine Tinte mehr!*

**innocent** [INəsənt] *adj.* • unschuldig
She was punished, even though she is innocent.
*Obwohl sie unschuldig ist, wurde sie bestraft.*

**insect** [INsekt] *n.* • Insekt, das
Insects have six legs.
*Insekten haben sechs Beine.*

**inside** [inSEID] *adv., prep.* • darin
Here is an old trunk. What is inside it?
*Hier ist ein alter Reisekoffer. Was ist darin?*

**insist, to** [inSIST] *v.* • bestehen auf
He insists that he is right.
*Er besteht darauf, daß er recht hat.*

**inspect, to** [inSPEKT] *v.* • prüfen
**inspection** *n.* • Prüfung, die
**inspector** *n.* • Inspektor, der
He inspects his work with care.
*Er prüft seine Arbeit sorgfältig.*

**instant** [INstənt] *n.* • Augenblick, der
The light flashed for only an instant.
*Das Licht leuchtete nur einen Augenblick auf.*

**instead** [inSTED] *adv.* • anstatt
Instead of taking the train, we'll fly.
*Anstatt den Zug zu nehmen, fliegen wir.*

**instructor** [inSTRUKtə*r*] *n.* • Lehrer, der
My ski instructor is great!
*Mein Skilehrer ist großartig!*

**insurance** [inSHURəns] *n.* • Versicherung, die
We have insurance for the house and the car.
*Wir haben eine Versicherung für das Haus und den Wagen.*

**intelligent** [inTELi*dzh*ənt] *adj.* • intelligent
Which animal is the most intelligent?
*Welches Tier ist am intelligentesten?*

**interest** [INtrest] *n.* • Interesse, das
**interesting** *adj.* • interessant
**to be interested in** • sich interessieren für
My brother has a keen interest in chemistry.
*Mein Bruder hat ein großes Interesse für Chemie.*

**international** [intərNASHənəl] *adj.* • international
There is an international conference in Washington, D.C., Monday.
*Eine internationale Konferenz findet Montag in Washington, D.C., statt.*

**interpreter** [inTƏRpretər] *n.* • Dolmetscher, der (-in, f.)
She works as an interpreter at the United Nations.
*Sie arbeitet als Dolmetscherin bei der U.N.O.*

**interrupt, to** [intəRƏPT] *v.* • unterbrechen
He always interrupts our conversations.
*Er unterbricht immer unsere Unterhaltungen.*

**into** [INtoo] *prep.* • in
Put the butter into the frying pan.
*Tu die Butter in die Pfanne.*

**introduce, to** [intrəDOOS] *v.* • vorstellen
Mr. Brown, I'd like to introduce you to my parents.
*Herr Braun, ich möchte Sie meinen Eltern vorstellen.*

**invite, to** [inVEIT] *v.* • einladen
**invitation** *n.* • Einladung, die
We're inviting all our friends to the party.
*Wir laden alle unsere Freunde zur Party ein.*

**iron** [EIərn] *n.* • Eisen, das
**to iron (clothes)** *v.* • bügeln
**iron (appliance)** *n.* • Bügeleisen, das
**made of iron** • aus Eisen
You'll have to iron the shirt to get the wrinkles out.
*Du mußt das Hemd bügeln, um die Falten herauszubekommen.*

**island** [EIlənd] *n.* • Insel, die
Have you ever visited a Caribbean island?
*Hast du jemals eine der Karibischen Insel besucht?*

**it** [IT] *pron.* • es (er, sie, ihn, ihm, ihr)
**its** *pron.; adj.* • sein, ihr
**it is; it's** • es ist
Where is it? I don't see it.
*Wo ist es? Ich sehe es nicht.*

It's raining.
*Es regnet.*
That is the milk. It is white.
*Das ist die Milch. Sie ist weiß.*

She does not give it to me.
*Sie gibt ihn mir nicht.*

**Italy** [ITəlie] *n.* • Italien
**Italian (person)** *n.* • Italiener, der (-in, f.)
**Italian** *adj.* • italienisch
On a map, Italy is shaped like a boot.
*Auf der Landkarte sieht Italien einem Stiefel ähnlich.*

An Italian restaurant should have espresso.
*Ein italienisches Restaurant müßte Espresso haben.*

# J

**jacket** [*DZHA*Kət] *n.* • Jacke, die
**ski jacket** • Skijacke, die
It is cool, so take a jacket.
*Es ist kühl, also nimm eine Jacke mit.*

**jam** [*DZHA*M] *n.* • Marmelade, die
Vincent puts jam on his bread.
*Vincent streicht Marmelade auf sein Brot.*

**January** [*DZHA*Nj*oo*erie] *n.* • Januar, der
We have snow here in January.
*Wir haben hier Schnee im Januar.*

**Japan** [*dzh*əPAN] *n.* • Japan
**Japanese (person)** *n.* • Japaner, der (-in, f.)
**Japanese** *adj.* • japanisch
Japan is an island country in Asia.
*Japan ist ein Land auf einer Insel in Asien.*

**jar** [*DZH*AHR] *n.* • Glas, das
Is there a jar of olives in the refrigerator?
*Steht ein Glas Oliven im Kühlschrank?*

**jealous** [*DZH*Eləs] *adj.* • eifersüchtig
Our cat is jealous of our new kitten.
*Unsere Katze ist auf unser neues Kätzchen eifersüchtig.*

**jeans** [*DZH*IENZ] *n.* • Jeans, die
I prefer to wear jeans when I travel.
*Ich ziehe es vor, Jeans zu tragen, wenn ich reise.*

**jet** [*DZH*ET] *n.* • Düsenflugzeug, das
Jets are faster than propeller planes.
*Düsenflugzeuge sind schneller als Propellerflugzeuge.*

**jewel** [*DZHOO*əl] *n.* • Edelstein, der
**jeweler** *n.* • Juwelier, der
The queen's crown is covered with jewels.
*Die Krone der Königin ist mit Edelsteinen belegt.*

The jeweler showed me a diamond ring.
*Der Juwelier zeigte mir einen Diamantring.*

**job** [*DZH*AHB] *n.* • Job, der
Have you found a job for the summer?
*Hast du für den Sommer einen Job gefunden?*

**jog, to** [*DZH*AHG] *v.* • joggen
The same people go jogging in the park every morning.
*Dieselben Leute gehen jeden Morgen im Park joggen.*

**joke** [*DZH*OHK] *n.* • Witz, der
**to joke** *v.* • scherzen

Everyone laughs when he tells a joke.
*Jeder lacht, wenn er einen Witz erzählt.*

**journey** [*DZH*ə*R*nie] *n.* • Reise, die
He is taking a long journey across North America.
*Er macht eine lange Reise durch Nordamerika.*

**joy** [*DZH*EU] *n.* • Freude, die
The child was joyful when she saw her mother.
*Das Kind war voller Freude, als es seine Mutter sah.*

**judge** [*DZH*ə*DZH*] *n.* • Richter, der
The judge instructs the jury.
*Der Richter unterweist die Geschworenen.*

**juice** [*DZHOO*S] *n.* • Saft, der
I like to drink juice at breakfast.
*Ich trinke gern Saft zum Frühstück.*

**July** [*dzhoo*LEI] *n.* • Juli, der
The Fourth of July is a big holiday in the U.S.
*Der Vierte Juli ist ein großer Feiertag in den Vereinigten Staaten.*

**jump, to** [*DZH*əMP] *v.* • springen
The children are jumping into the pool.
*Die Kinder springen ins Schwimmbad.*

**June** [*DZHOO*N] *n.* • Juni, der
Their wedding anniversary is in June.
*Ihr Hochzeitstag ist im Juni.*

# K

**kangaroo** [k*a*nggəR*OO*] *n.* • Känguruh, das
Kangaroos live in Australia.
*Känguruhs leben in Australien.*

**keep, to** [KIEP] *v.* • behalten
**keepsake** *n.* • Andenken, das
I will keep your picture in my wallet.
*Ich werde dein Bild in meiner Brieftasche behalten.*

**key** [KIE] *n.* • Schlüssel, der
I can't open the door without a key.
*Ohne einen Schlüssel kann ich die Tür nicht öffnen.*

**kick, to** [KIK] *v.* • kicken
He is kicking the football into the goal.
*Er kickt den Fußball ins Tor.*

**kill, to** [KIL] *v.* • töten
In the story, the hero kills the giant.
*In der Geschichte tötet der Held den Riesen.*

**kilometer** [kəLAHmətər] *n.* • Kilometer, der
How many kilometers are there between New York and Chicago?
*Wie viele Kilometer lang ist die Strecke zwischen New York und Chicago?*

**kind** [KEIND] *adj.* • gut
My grandmother is kind and generous.
*Meine Großmutter ist gut und großzügig.*

**kind (sort)** [KEIND] *n.* • Art, die
What kind of tree is that?
*Welche Art von Baum ist das?*

**kindergarten** [KINdərgahrdn] *n.* • Kindergarten, der
My little sister goes to kindergarten.
*Meine kleine Schwester geht in den Kindergarten.*

**king** [KING] *n.* • König, der
The king wears a crown.
*Der König trägt eine Krone.*

**kiss, to** [KIS] *v.* • küssen
**kiss** *n.* • Kuß, der
I'll kiss you on the cheek.
*Ich werde dich auf die Backe küssen.*

**kitchen** [KI*TSH*ən] *n.* • Küche, die
We eat lunch in the kitchen.
*Wir essen in der Küche zu Mittag.*

**kite** [KEIT] *n.* • Papierdrachen, der
It must be windy to fly a kite.
*Es muß windig sein, um einen Papierdrachen fliegen zu lassen.*

**kitten** [KITn] *n.* • Kätzchen, das
Our cat has four kittens.
*Unsere Katze hat vier Kätzchen.*

**knee** [NIE] *n.* • Knie, das
I hurt my knee playing football.
*Ich habe mein Knie beim Fußballspielen verletzt.*

**knife** [NEIF] *n.* • Messer, das
**pocket knife** • Taschenmesser, das
I put the knives next to the spoons.
*Ich lege die Messer neben die Löffel.*

**knight** [NEIT] *n.* • Ritter, der
I read about knights and armor at the library.
*Ich habe in der Bibliothek über Ritter und Rüstungen gelesen.*

**knit, to** [NIT] *v.* • stricken
My mother is knitting me a sweater.
*Meine Mutter strickt mir einen Pullover.*

**knock, to** [NAHK] *v.* • klopfen
**knock** *n.* • Anklopfen, das
Alan knocked on the door, but no one came.
*Alan klopfte an die Tür, aber niemand kam.*

**know, to** [NOH] *v.* • kennen; wissen
**to know (facts)** *v.* • wissen
**to know (people)** *v.* • kennen
I just met her parents, so I don't know them well.
*Ich kenne ihre Eltern nicht gut, denn ich habe sie eben erst kennengelernt.*

# L

**laborer** [L*EJ*bər-ə*r*] *n.* • Arbeiter, der
The laborers work in the factory.
*Die Arbeiter arbeiten in der Fabrik.*

**lace** [L*EJ*S] *n.* • Spitze, die
This lace collar is elegant.
*Dieser Spitzenkragen ist elegant.*

**ladder** [L*A*Də*r*] *n.* • Leiter, die
My father is climbing the ladder.
*Mein Vater steigt die Leiter hinauf.*

**lady** [L*EJ*die] *n.* • Dame, die
**young lady** • junge Dame, die
**Ladies and gentlemen!** • Meine Damen und Herren!
She has the manners of a lady.
*Sie hat das Benehmen einer Dame.*

**lake** [L*EJ*K] *n.* • See, der
We are going swimming in the lake.
*Wir gehen im See schwimmen.*

**lamb** [L*A*M] *n.* • Lamm, das
**leg of lamb** *n.* • Lammschinken, der
The lambs stay close to their mothers.
*Die Lämmer bleiben in der Nähe ihrer Mutter.*

**lamp** [L*A*MP] *n.* • Lampe, die
Can you please turn on the lamp?
*Kannst du bitte die Lampe anmachen?*

**land** [L*A*ND] *n.* • Land, das
**to land** *v.* • landen
**landing** *n.* • Landung, die
The birds fly over the land.
*Die Vögel fliegen über das Land.*

**language** [L*A*NGg*w*i*dzh*] *n.* • Sprache, die
How many languages do you speak?
*Wie viele Sprachen sprichst du?*

**large** [LAHR*DZH*] *adj.* • groß
The elephant is a very large animal.
*Der Elefant ist ein sehr großes Tier.*

**last** [L*A*ST] *adj.* • letzt
**at last** • endlich
**last night** • gestern abend
**the last one** • Letzte (der, die, das)
I get off at the last stop on the bus line.
*Ich steige an der letzten Bushaltestelle aus.*

**late** [L*EJ*T] *adj.; adv.* • spät
**later** *adj.; adv.* • später
**to be late** • sich verspäten; zu spät kommen
**to sleep late** • lange schlafen
The bus is late today.
*Der Bus kommt heute spät.*

**laugh, to** [L*A*F] *v.* • lachen
The children laugh when they see the clown.
*Die Kinder lachen, wenn sie den Clown sehen.*

**law** [L*AW*] *n.* • Gesetz, das
You must obey the law.
*Man muß das Gesetz befolgen.*

**lawn** [L*AW*N] *n.* • Rasen, der
I mow the lawn when the grass gets too high.
*Ich mähe den Rasen, wenn das Gras zu lang wird.*

**lawyer** [LEUjə*r*] *n.* • Rechtsanwalt, der (-wältin, f.)
The lawyers are at the court house.
*Die Rechtsanwälte sind beim Gericht.*

**lay, to** [L*EJ*] *v.* • legen
Marie lays her books on the table.
*Marie legt ihre Bücher auf den Tisch.*

**lazy** [L*EJ*zie] *adj.* • faul
This cat is so lazy! She sleeps all day.
*Diese Katze ist so faul! Sie schläft den ganzen Tag.*

**lead, to** [LIED] *v.* • führen
**lead (in a play)** *n.* • Hauptrolle, die
**leader; guide** *n.* • Führer, der (-in, f.)
The guide leads the tourists through the castle.
*Der Führer führt die Touristen durch das Schloß.*

**leaf** [LIEF] *n.* • Blatt, das
The leaves are beautiful in the fall.
*Die Blätter sind schön im Herbst.*

**leap, to** [LIEP] *v.* • springen
The dog can leap over the fence.
*Der Hund kann über den Zaun springen.*

**learn, to** [Lə*R*N] *v.* • lernen
**to learn by heart** • auswendig lernen
**to learn how** • lernen wie . . .
You learn many things when you travel.
*Man lernt viel, wenn man reist.*

**leave, to** [LIE*V*] *v.* • verlassen
We leave school at the end of the day.
*Wir verlassen die Schule am Ende des Tages.*

**left** [LEFT] *adj.* • linke
**left hand** • linke Hand, die
**on the left side** • auf der linken Seite
**to the left** • links
Our house is on the left side of the street.
*Unser Haus steht auf der linken Seite der Straße.*

**leg** [LEG] *n.* • Bein, das
This dancer has beautiful legs.
*Diese Tänzerin hat schöne Beine.*

**legend** [LE*DZH*ənd] *n.* • Legende, die
Do you know the legend of King Arthur?
*Kennst du die Legende von König Arthur?*

**lemon** [LEMən] *n.* • Zitrone, die
We used a lemon for this recipe.
*Wir benutzten eine Zitrone für dieses Rezept.*

**lend, to** [LEND] *v.* • leihen
Can you lend me a dollar?
*Kannst du mir einen Dollar leihen?*

**leopard** [LEPə*r*d] *n.* • Leopard, der
Leopards live in the jungle.
*Leoparden leben im Dschungel.*

**less** [LES] *adv.* • weniger
You should use a little less salt the next time.
*Du solltest nächstes Mal etwas weniger Salz nehmen.*

**lesson** [LESən] *n.* • Lektion, die
Do you understand the lesson?
*Verstehst du die Lektion?*

**letter** [LETə*r*] *n.* • Brief, der
I put the letter in the mailbox.
*Ich warf den Brief in den Briefkasten.*

**lettuce** [LETəs] *n.* • Kopfsalat, der
My salad is made with lettuce and tomatoes.
*Mein Salat besteht aus Kopfsalat und Tomaten.*

**let, to** [LET] *v.* • lassen
**to let alone (leave alone)** • allein lassen
Will your parents let us stay longer?
*Werden deine Eltern uns länger bleiben lassen?*

**library** [LEIbrerie] *n.* • Bibliothek, die
I am going to take these books back to the library.
*Ich werde diese Bücher zur Bibliothek zurückbringen.*

**lie, to** [LEI] *v.* • lügen
**lie** *n.* • Lüge, die
**liar** *n.* • Lügner, der
Don't lie! Tell me the truth.
*Lügen Sie nicht! Sagen Sie mir die Wahrheit.*

**life** [LEIF] *n.* • Leben, das
Water is necessary for life on Earth.
*Wasser ist notwendig für das Leben auf der Erde.*

**light** [LEIT] *n.* • Licht, das
**traffic light** • Verkehrsampel, die
I need light to read.
*Ich brauche Licht, um zu lesen.*

**lightning** [LEITning] *n.* • Blitz, der
Lightning struck the tower in the storm.
*Der Turm wurde im Sturm vom Blitz getroffen.*

**like** [LEIK] *prep.* • wie
I love him like a brother.
*Ich liebe ihn wie einen Bruder.*

**like, to** [LEIK] *v.* • gern haben
**I would like** • ich möchte; ich hätte gern
**we would like** • wir möchten; wir hätten gern

We like to have dessert every night.
*Wir haben gern jeden Abend Nachtisch.*

**line** [LEIN] *n.* • Linie, die
Write your name on the line.
*Schreiben Sie Ihren Namen auf die Linie.*

**lion** [LEIən] *n.* • Löwe, der
There are lions in Africa.
*Es gibt Löwen in Afrika.*

**lip** [LIP] *n.* • Lippe, die
**lipstick** *n.* • Lippenstift, der
I have dry lips in the winter.
*Im Winter habe ich trockene Lippen.*

**list** [LIST] *n.* • Liste, die
I have a long list of errands to run.
*Ich habe eine lange Liste von Besorgungen zu machen.*

**listen** [LISən] *v.* • zuhören
We listened carefully to the directions.
*Wir hörten den Anweisungen genau zu.*

**little** [LITl] *adj.* • klein
**a little** • bißchen, ein
**little by little** • nach und nach
This little book fits in my pocket.
*Dieses kleine Buch paßt in meine Tasche.*

I would like a little more coffee, please.
*Ich möchte gern ein bißchen mehr Kaffee, bitte.*

**live, to** [LIV] *v.* • leben
**to live (reside)** *v.* • wohnen
**lively** *adj.* • lebhaft
**living room** • Wohnzimmer, das
**to earn a living** • einen Lebensunterhalt verdienen

Animals live in the Forest.
*Tiere leben im Wald.*

The whole family lives together.
*Die ganze Familie wohnt zusammen.*

**lizard** [LIZərd] *n.* • Eidechse, die
The lizard is sleeping on the rock.
*Die Eidechse schläft auf dem Stein.*

**lobster** [LAHBstər] *n.* • Hummer, der
This lobster is absolutely delicious.
*Dieser Hummer ist sehr köstlich.*

**location** [lohK*EJ*shən] *n.* • Lage, die
**to be located** • sich befinden
The store on the corner has a good location.
*Der Laden an der Ecke hat eine gute Lage.*

**lock, to** [LAHK] *v.* • abschließen
Do you lock your house when you leave?
*Schließen Sie Ihr Haus ab, wenn Sie es verlassen?*

**lollipop** [LAHliepahp] *n.* • Lutscher, der
Lollipops are my children's favorite candy.
*Meine Kinder mögen Lutscher am liebsten.*

**long** [L*A*WNG] *adj.* • lang
**a long time** • eine lange Zeit
This snake is very long.
*Diese Schlange ist sehr lang.*

**look, to** [LUK] *v.* • ansehen
**to look after** • aufpassen
**to look (for); to search** *v.* • suchen
**to look (like); to resemble** *v.* • aussehen wie
They're looking at the pictures.
*Sie sehen sich die Bilder an.*

We are looking for an apartment.
*Wir suchen eine Wohnung.*

She looks like her sister.
*Sie sieht wie ihre Schwester aus.*

**lose, to** [L*OOZ*] *v.* • verlieren
I lost my wallet in the airport.
*Ich habe meine Brieftasche im Flughafen verloren.*

**lot** [LAHT] *n.* • Los, das
**a lot (of)** • viel
**a lot of people** • viele Leute
**such a lot** • so viel
They drew lots to see who would begin.
*Sie losten aus, wer anfangen sollte.*

We have a lot of snow this winter.
*Wir haben diesen Winter viel Schnee.*

**loud** [LAUD] *adj.* • laut
**loudly** *adv.* • laut
**loudspeaker** *n.* • Lautsprecher, der
He speaks too loudly.
*Er spricht zu laut.*

**love, to** [LƏ*V*] *v.* • lieben
**love** *n.* • Liebe, die
**to be in love** • verliebt sein
**to love each other** • einander lieben
We love our parents.
*Wir lieben unsere Eltern.*

**low** [LOH] *adj.* • niedrig
**to lower (voice)** *v.* • leiser sprechen
There is a low wall next to the street.
*Neben der Straße ist eine niedrige Mauer.*

We lower our voices when we go into church.
*Wir sprechen leiser, wenn wir in die Kirche gehen.*

**luck** [LƏK] *n.* • Glück, das
**Good luck!** • Viel Glück!
**to be lucky** • Glück haben

Did you have any luck at the casino?
*Hast du im Kasino Glück gehabt?*

**luggage** [LəGi*dzh*] *n.* • Gepäck, das
Please help me put my luggage in the car.
*Bitte helfen sie mir, mein Gepäck in den Wagen zu packen.*

**lunch** [LəN*TSH*] *n.* • Mittagessen, das
**lunchtime** *n.* • Mittagspause, die
**to have lunch** • zu Mittag essen
We had soup and sandwiches for lunch.
*Wir hatten Suppe und belegte Brote zum Mittagessen.*

# M

**machine** [məSHIEN] *n.* • Maschine, die
**copying machine** • der Kopierer
**washing machine** • Waschmaschine, die
Can you fix the sewing machine?
*Kannst du die Nähmaschine reparieren?*

**mad (crazy)** [M*A*D] *adj.* • verrückt
Are you mad? That's dangerous!
*Bist du verrückt? Das ist gefährlich!*

**made (of)** [M*EJ*D ə*V*] *adj.* • aus
This sweater is made of wool.
*Dieser Pullover ist aus Wolle.*

**magazine** [M*A*Gəzien] *n.* • Zeitschrift, die
Which magazine do you like to read?
*Welche Zeitschrift liest du gern?*

**magic** [M*ADZH*ik] *n.* • Zauberei, die
**magician** *n.* • Zauberer, der; die Zauberin

The prince was changed into a stone by magic.
*Der Prinz ist durch Zauberei in einen Stein verwandelt worden.*

**magnificent** [m*a*gNIFisənt] *adj.* • prachtvoll
These horses are magnificent!
*Diese Pferde sind prachtvoll!*

**maid** [M*EJ*D] *n.* • Dienstmädchen, das
The maid does the housework.
*Das Dienstmädchen macht die Hausarbeit.*

**mail** [M*EJ*L] *n.* • Post, die
**mailbox** *n.* • Briefkasten, der
**mail carrier** • Postbote, der; Briefträger, der
Did I get any mail today?
*Habe ich heute Post bekommen?*

**make, to (do)** [M*EJ*K] *v.* • machen
**make happy** • glücklich machen
**makeup** *n.* • Makeup, das
I make my bed every morning.
*Ich mache jeden Morgen mein Bett.*

**mama** [MAHMə] *n.* • Mutti, die (Mama)
Mama always asks me to set the table.
*Mutti (Mama) bittet mich immer, den Tisch zu decken.*

**man** [MAN] *n.* • Mann, der
This man is my uncle.
*Dieser Mann ist mein Onkel.*

**many** [MENie] *adj.; pron.* • viele
**as many as** • so viele wie
**how many?** • wie viele?
**so many** • so viele
**too many** • zu viele
My parents have many friends.
*Meine Eltern haben viele Freunde.*

**map** [M*A*P] *n.* • Landkarte, die
There is a map of France on the wall.
*An der Wand hängt eine Landkarte von Frankreich.*

**maple** [M*EJ*pl] *n.* • Feldahorn, der
Is this leaf from a maple or an oak?
*Ist dieses Blatt von einem Feldahorn oder von einer Eiche?*

**March** [MAHR*TSH*] *n.* • März, der
Spring begins in March.
*Der Frühling fängt im März an.*

**market** [MAHRkət] *n.* • Markt, der
You buy fruits and vegetables at the market.
*Man kauft Früchte und Gemüse auf dem Markt.*

**marry, to** [M*A*Rie] *v.* • heiraten
Robert and Jane are getting married tomorrow.
*Robert und Jane heiraten morgen.*

**marvelous** [MAHR*v*ələs] *adj.* • wunderbar
This carnival is marvelous!
*Dieser Karneval ist wunderbar!*

**match** [M*ATSH*] *n.* • Streichholz, das
Do you have a match to light the fire?
*Hast du ein Streichholz, um das Feuer anzuzünden?*

**mathematics** [m*ath*əMATiks] *n.* • Mathematik, die
Engineers need to study mathematics.
*Ingenieure müssen Mathematik studieren.*

**mature** [mə*TSHƏR*; məTJUR] *adj.* • erwachsen
My mother says that I am mature for my age.
*Meine Mutter sagt, daß ich für mein Alter schon erwachsen bin.*

**may** [M*EJ*] *v.* • dürfen
**maybe** *adv.* • vielleicht
May I help you?
*Darf ich Ihnen helfen?*

**May** [M*EJ*] *n.* • Mai, der
There are many flowers in May.
*Es gibt viele Blumen im Mai.*

**mayor** [M*EJ*ə*r*] *n.* • Bürgermeister, der
The office of the mayor is in city hall.
*Das Büro des Bürgermeisters ist im Rathaus.*

**me** [MIE] *pron.* • mir, mich
Hand me that book, please.
*Reichen Sie mir bitte das Buch.*

**meal** [MIEL] *n.* • Mahlzeit, die
We have our main meal in the evening.
*Wir haben unsere Hauptmahlzeit am Abend.*

**mean** [MIEN] *adj.* • gemein
The boy was mean to his sister.
*Der Junge war seiner Schwester gegenüber gemein.*

**mean, to** [MIEN] *v.* • meinen
I don't understand what you mean.
*Ich verstehe nicht, was Sie meinen.*

**measure, to** [ME*zh*ə*r*] *v.* • messen
Patrick is measuring the board with a ruler.
*Patrick mißt das Brett mit einem Lineal.*

**meat** [MIET] *n.* • Fleisch, das
The meat has been roasting in the oven for an hour.
*Das Fleisch brät schon seit einer Stunde im Ofen.*

**mechanic** [məKANik] *n.* • Mechaniker, der
The mechanic repairs my car.
*Der Mechaniker repariert meinen Wagen.*

**medicine** [MEDəisən] *n.* • Medizin, die
My grandmother buys her medicine at this pharmacy.
*Meine Großmutter kauft ihre Medizin in dieser Apotheke.*

**meet, to** [MIET] *v.* • treffen
Sometimes I meet friends at this cafe.
*Manchmal treffe ich Freunde in diesem Cafè.*

**melon** [MELən] *n.* • Melone, die
In the summer, we eat melons from our garden.
*Im Sommer essen wir Melonen aus unserem Garten.*

**melt, to** [MELT] *v.* • schmelzen
The snowman is melting in the sun.
*Der Schneemann schmilzt in der Sonne.*

**member** [MEMbə*r*] *n.* • Mitglied, das
There are fifteen members in our club.
*Unser Club hat fünfzehn Mitglieder.*

**memory** [MEMə*r*ie] *n.* • Gedächtnis, das
**to memorize** *v.* • im Gedächtnis behalten
She has an excellent memory for names.
*Sie hat ein ausgezeichnetes Namensgedächtnis.*

**menu** [MENj*oo*] *n.* • Speisekarte, die
Could you give us the menu, please?
*Könnten Sie uns bitte die Speisekarte geben?*

**merry-go-round** [MERie-goh-raund] *n.* • Karussell, das
Do you like to ride the merry-go-round?
*Fährst du gern Karussell?*

**mess** [MES] *n.* • Durcheinander, das
**to make a mess** • Schmutz machen
Please clean up the mess in your room.
*Räum bitte das Durcheinander in deinem Zimmer auf.*

**message** [MESi*dzh*] *n.* • Nachricht, die
There is a message on the door.
*An der Tür hängt eine Nachricht.*

**meter** [MIEtər] *n.* • Meter, der
She would like to buy two meters of this material.
*Sie möchte zwei Meter von diesem Stoff kaufen.*

**Mexico** [MEKsikoh] *n.* • Mexiko
**Mexican (person)** *n.* • Mexikaner, der (-in, f.)
**Mexican** *adj.* • mexikanisch
My brother is going to Mexico with the Spanish class.
*Mein Bruder fährt mit der Spanischklasse nach Mexiko.*

**middle** [MIDl] *n.* • Mitte, die
The ducks are in the middle of the pond.
*Die Enten sind in der Mitte des Teichs.*

**midnight** [MIDneit] *n.* • Mitternacht, die
The clock strikes twelve times at midnight.
*Die Uhr schlägt zwölfmal um Mitternacht.*

**mile** [MEIL] *n.* • Meile, die
They walk five miles a day.
*Sie gehen täglich fünf Meilen.*

**milk** [MILK] *n.* • Milch, die
The child drinks milk at each meal.
*Das Kind trinkt Milch zu jeder Mahlzeit.*

**million** [MILjən] *n.* • Million, die
There are millions of stars in the sky.
*Millionen von Sternen sind am Himmel.*

**mind** [MEIND] *n.* • Verstand, der
He has a quick mind.
*Er hat einen wachen Verstand.*

**minus** [MEInəs] *prep.* • minus
Four minus two is two.
*Vier minus zwei ist zwei.*

**minute** [MINət] *n.* • Minute, die
There are sixty seconds in a minute.
*Eine Minute hat sechzig Sekunden.*

**mirror** [MIRə*r*] *n.* • Spiegel, der
I look in the mirror when I comb my hair.
*Ich sehe in den Spiegel, wenn ich mir die Haare kämme.*

**Miss** [MIS] *n.* • Fräulein, das
**Misses; young ladies** • junge Damen (Frauen)
Our teacher is Miss Pasko.
*Unsere Lehrerin heißt Fräulein Pasko.*

**miss, to** [MIS] *v.* • verpassen
Hurry! We are going to miss the train!
*Schnell! Wir verpassen den Zug!*

**mistake** [misT*EJ*K] *n.* • Fehler, der
He makes mistakes when he's not careful.
*Er macht Fehler, wenn er nicht vorsichtig ist.*

**mister** [MIStə*r*] *n.* • Herr, der
I'd like you to meet my neighbor, Mr. Stuart.
*Darf ich Ihnen meinen Nachbarn, Herr Stuart, vorstellen?*

**mix, to** [MIKS] *v.* • mischen
The recipe says, "Mix the ingredients."
*Laut Rezept soll man alle Zutaten mischen.*

**modern** [MAHdə*r*n] *adj.* • modern
The new part of town has modern buildings.
*Der neue Teil der Stadt hat moderne Gebäude.*

**mom** [MAHM] *n.* • Mutti, die (Mutter)
My mom helped me learn to read.
*Meine Mutti half mir, lesen zu lernen.*

**moment** [MOHMənt] *n.* • Moment, der
If you wait a moment I will help you.
*Wenn Sie einen Moment warten, werde ich Ihnen helfen.*

**Monday** [MƏNd*ej*] *n.* • Montag, der
Monday is the first day of the work week.
*Montag ist der erste Arbeitstag der Woche.*

**money** [MƏNie] *n.* • Geld, das
I have spent all my money.
*Ich habe mein ganzes Geld ausgegeben.*

**monkey** [MƏNGkie] *n.* • Affe, der
I like to watch the monkeys at the zoo.
*Ich beobachte gern die Affen im Zoo.*

**monster** [MAHNstə*r*] *n.* • Monster, das
There is a monster in this movie.
*In diesem Film gibt es ein Monster.*

**month** [MƏN*TH*] *n.* • Monat, der
March is the third month of the year.
*Der März ist der dritte Monat des Jahres.*

**mood** [M*OO*D] *n.* • Stimmung, die
**bad mood** • schlechte Laune, die
**good mood** • gute Laune, die
Her mood changes with the weather!
*Ihre Stimmung ändert sich mit dem Wetter!*

**moon** [M*OO*N] *n.* • Mond, der
The moon is shining brightly tonight.
*Der Mond scheint heute nacht hell.*

**more** [MOHR] *adj.; adv.* • mehr
**more and more** • mehr und mehr
**more or less** • mehr oder weniger
**once more** • noch einmal
**some more** • etwas mehr

Please let me have some more coffee.
*Geben Sie mir bitte etwas mehr Kaffee.*

**morning** [M*AW*Rning] *n.* • Morgen, der
**Good morning!** • Guten Morgen!
I read the newspaper every morning.
*Ich lese jeden Morgen die Zeitung.*

**mosquito** [məsKIEtoh] *n.* • Stechmücke, die
The mosquitos are really annoying this summer.
*Die Stechmücken sind diesen Sommer wirklich ärgerlich.*

**mother** [MƏ*DH*ər] *n.* • Mutter, die
**Mother's Day** • Muttertag, der
When did your mother and father marry?
*Wann haben deine Mutter und dein Vater geheiratet?*

**motor** [MOHtər] *n.* • Motor, der
**motorcycle** *n.* • Motorrad, das
Do you know how a motor works?
*Weißt du, wie ein Motor funktioniert?*

**mountain** [MAUNtən] *n.* • Berg, der
**to go mountain climbing** • Bergsteigen gehen
**to (in) the mountains** • ins Gebirge
It's always cool in the mountains.
*In den Bergen ist es immer kühl.*

**mouse** [MAUS] *n.* • Maus, die
Our cat caught a mouse last night.
*Unsere Katze hat letzte Nacht eine Maus gefangen.*

**mouth** [MAU*TH*] *n.* • Mund, der
The dentist told me to open my mouth wide.
*Der Zahnarzt bat mich, meinen Mund weit zu öffnen.*

**move, to** [M*OO*V] *v.* • sich fortbewegen
**move (furniture)** *v.* • umziehen
The old man is moving slowly through the snow.
*Der alte Mann bewegt sich langsam durch den Schnee fort.*

**movie** [M*OO*Vie] *n.* • Film, der
**movies** *n. pl.* • Film, der
**movie theater** • Kino, das
We're going to the theater to see a new movie.
*Wir gehen ins Kino, um einen neuen Film zu sehen.*

**Mr.** See *mister*.

**Mrs.** [MISə*z*] *n.* • Frau, die
Please meet my grandmother, Mrs. Smith.
*Darf ich Ihnen bitte meine Großmutter vorstellen, Frau Schmidt.*

**much** [Mə*TSH*] *adj.* • viel
**as much as** • so viel wie
**how much?** • wieviel?
**so much** • so viel
**too much** • zuviel
**very much** • sehr viel
I have much work to do.
*Ich habe viel Arbeit zu erledigen.*

**mud** [MəD] *n.* • Schlamm, der
His shoes are covered with mud.
*Seine Schuhe sind mit Schlamm bedeckt.*

**muscle** [MəSəl] *n.* • Muskel, der
Which muscles do you use when you run?
*Welche Muskeln benutzt man, wenn man läuft?*

**museum** [mj*oo*ZIEəm] *n.* • Museum, das
Let's go to the art museum today.
*Laßt uns heute zum Kunstmuseum gehen.*

**mushroom** [MəSHr*oo*m] *n.* • Pilz, der
Do you want fresh mushrooms on your salad?
*Möchten Sie frische Pilze in Ihrem Salat?*

**music** [MJ*OO*zik] *n.* • Musik, die
**musician** *n.* • Musiker, der (-in, f.)

Do you like classical music?
*Gefällt dir klassische Musik?*

**must** [MəST] *v.* • müssen
We must leave at eight o'clock.
*Wir müssen um acht Uhr gehen.*

**mustache** [MəSt*a*sh] *n.* • Schnurrbart, der
My father has a mustache.
*Mein Vater hat einen Schnurrbart.*

**mustard** [MəStərd] *n.* • Senf, der
I would like some mustard on my sandwich.
*Ich möchte etwas Senf auf meinem Sandwich.*

**my** [MEI] *adj.; pron.* • mein; -e
My brother and sister are coming this evening.
*Mein Bruder und meine Schwester kommen heute abend.*

**myself** [meiSELF] *pron.* • selbst
I made the dress myself.
*Ich habe das Kleid selbst gemacht.*

**mysterious** [misTIERie-əs] *adj.* • mysteriös
**mystery** *n.* • Geheimnis, das
That's really a mysterious thing.
*Das ist wirklich eine mysteriöse Sache.*

# N

**nail** [N*EJ*L] *n.* • Nagel, der
Hang the picture on that nail.
*Hängen Sie das Bild an diesen Nagel.*

**name** [N*EJ*M] *n.* • Name, der
**first name** • Vorname, der
**last name** • Nachname, der
**my name is . . .** • ich heiße . . .; mein Name ist . . .
**named** *adj.* • genannt
**to be called; to be named** • heißen
Please repeat your name again for me.
*Wiederholen Sie bitte Ihren Namen noch einmal.*

What is your name?
*Wie heißen Sie? (formal) Wie heißt du? (familiar)*

What is your cousin's name?
*Wie heißt dein Vetter?*

**napkin** [N*A*Pkin] *n.* • Serviette, die
She puts the napkin on her lap.
*Sie legt die Serviette auf den Schoß.*

**narrow** [N*A*Roh] *adj.* • eng
These old streets are narrow.
*Diese alten Straßen sind eng.*

**nation** [N*EJ*shən] *n.* • Nation, die
**national** *adj.* • Staats--
**nationality** *n.* • Staatsangehörigkeit, die
This nation's history is very interesting.
*Die Geschichte dieser Nation ist sehr interessant.*

**natural** [N*ATSH*ərəl] *adj.* • angeboren
**naturally** *adv.* • natürlich
**nature** *n.* • Natur, die
He has a natural gift for music.
*Er hat ein angeborenes Talent für Musik.*

**naughty** [N*AW*tie] *adj.* • ungezogen
This little boy is naughty sometimes.
*Dieser kleine Junge ist manchmal ungezogen.*

**near** [NIER] *adv.* • nahe
**nearly** *adv.* • fast
We live near the airport.
*Wir wohnen in der Nähe des Flughafens.*

**necessary** [NESəserie] *adj.* • notwendig
Calcium is necessary for strong bones.
*Kalzium ist notwendig, um starke Knochen zu bekommen.*

**neck** [NEK] *n.* • Hals, der
**necklace** *n.* • Halskette, die
**necktie** *n.* • Krawatte, die
This shirt is too tight around my neck.
*Dieses Hemd ist mir am Hals zu eng.*

**need, to** [NIED] *v.* • brauchen
The little boy needs help getting dressed.
*Der kleine Junge braucht Hilfe, um sich anzuziehen.*

**needle** [NIEDl] *n.* • Nadel, die
A seamstress needs a needle and thread.
*Die Näherin braucht eine Nähnadel und Zwirn.*

**neighbor** [N*EJ*bər] *n.* • Nachbar, der (-in, f.)
Our neighbors have a large dog.
*Unsere Nachbarn haben einen großen Hund.*

**nephew** [NEFj*oo*] *n.* • Neffe, der
My nephew is my sister's son.
*Mein Neffe ist der Sohn meiner Schwester.*

**nest** [NEST] *n.* • Nest, das
There is a bird's nest in the tree.
*Ein Vogelnest ist im Baum.*

**Netherlands** [NE*DH*ərləndz] *n.* • Niederlande, die
**Netherlander (person)** *n.* • Niederländer, der (-in, f.)

I have a friend in the Netherlands.
*Ich habe einen Freund in den Niederlanden.*

**never** [NE*V*ər] *adv.* • nie
It almost never rains in the desert.
*Es regnet fast nie in der Wüste.*

**new** [N(J)*OO*] *adj.* • neu
Did you buy any new clothes for school?
*Hast du neue Kleidung für die Schule gekauft?*

**news** [N(J)*OOZ*] *n.* • Nachrichten, die
**T.V. news** • Fernsehnachrichten, die
I hope the news is good!
*Ich hoffe, daß die Nachrichten gut sind!*

**newspaper** [N(J)*OO*Spe*j*pər] *n.* • Zeitung, die
Many people read the newspaper on the train.
*Viele Leute lesen die Zeitung im Zug.*

**next** [NEKST] *adj.* • nächste, -r, -s
**next to** • neben
Who is the next participant?
*Wer ist der nächste Teilnehmer?*

**nice** [NEIS] *adj.* • nett
**It's nice out.** • Es ist schön draußen.
She always has a nice, friendly smile.
*Sie hat immer ein nettes, freundliches Lächeln.*

**niece** [NIES] *n.* • Nichte, die
My niece is my brother's daughter.
*Meine Nichte ist die Tochter meines Bruders.*

**night** [NEIT] *n.* • Nacht, die
**every night** • jede Nacht; nächtlich
**last night** • gestern nacht (abend)
**nightmare** *n.* • Alptraum, der
**tonight** *n.; adv.* • heute nacht (abend)

## nine

At night the sky is full of stars.
*Nachts ist der Himmel voller Sterne.*

**nine** [NEIN] *n.; adj.* • neun
There are nine players on a baseball team.
*Eine Baseballmannschaft hat neun Spieler.*

**nineteen** [neinTIEN] *n.; adj.* • neunzehn
There are nineteen of us in the French club.
*Wir sind neunzehn in unserem Französischclub.*

**ninety** [NEINtie] *n.; adj.* • neunzig
The movie lasted for ninety minutes.
*Der Film dauerte neunzig Minuten lang.*

**no** [NOH] *adv.* • nein
**No admittance** • Kein Eintritt
**no doubt** • ohne Zweifel
**no longer** • nicht mehr (länger)
**no matter!** • ganz egal!
**no one** • niemand
**No smoking** • Rauchen Verboten
No, I don't want to leave yet.
*Nein, ich will noch nicht gehen.*

**noise** [NEUZ] *n.* • Lärm, der
Who is making that loud noise?
*Wer macht den lauten Lärm?*

**noodles** [N*OO*Dlz] *n.* • Nudeln, die
Let's put butter on the noodles.
*Laß' uns Butter auf die Nudeln tun!*

**noon** [N*OO*N] *n.* • Mittag, der
We eat lunch at noon.
*Wir essen zu Mittag um 12 Uhr.*

**north** [N*AW*R*TH*] *n.* • Norden, der
**North America** *n.* • Nordamerika

Belgium is to the north of France.
*Belgien liegt nördlich von Frankreich.*

**Norway** [N*A*W*R*we*j*] *n.* • Norwegen
**Norwegian (person)** *n.* • Norweger, der (-in, f.)
**Norwegian** *adj.* • norwegisch
We are going skiing in Norway.
*Wir gehen in Norwegen Skilaufen.*

**nose** [NOHZ] *n.* • Nase, die
My nose is stuffed and I can't smell.
*Meine Nase ist verstopft, und ich kann nicht riechen.*

**not** [NAHT] *adv.* • nicht
**not at all** • überhaupt nicht
**not yet** • noch nicht
**of course not** • selbstverständlich nicht
You're not going to like the bad news.
*Die schlechten Nachrichten werden dir nicht gefallen.*

**notebook** [NOHTbuk] *n.* • Notizbuch, das (Heft, das)
I have a notebook for each class.
*Ich habe für jede Klasse ein Notizbuch (Heft).*

**nothing** [Nə*TH*ing] *pron.* • nichts
There's nothing more important than good health.
*Nichts ist wichtiger als gute Gesundheit.*

**notice, to** [NOHTis] *v.* • bemerken
She notices every detail.
*Sie bemerkt jedes Detail.*

**novel** [NAH*V*əl] *n.* • Roman, der
**mystery novel** • Detektivroman, der
I bought a novel to read on the plane.
*Ich kaufte einen Roman, um ihn im Flugzeug zu lesen.*

**November** [nohVEMbər] *n.* • November, der
November is the month before Christmas.
*Der November ist der Monat vor Weihnachten.*

**now** [NAU] *adv.* • jetzt
**right now** • sofort
The teacher says we can leave now.
*Die Lehrerin sagt, daß wir jetzt gehen können.*

**number** [NƏMbər] *n.* • Nummer, die
**numerous** *adj.* • zahlreich
Please give me your phone number.
*Geben Sie mir bitte Ihre Telefonnummer.*

**nurse** [NƏRS] *n.* • Krankenschwester, die
The nurse works in the hospital.
*Die Krankenschwester arbeitet im Krankenhaus.*

# O

**oak** [OHK] *n.* • Eiche, die
The table is made of solid oak.
*Der Tisch ist ganz aus Eiche gemacht.*

**oats** [OHTS] *n.* • Hafer, der
The horse is eating oats.
*Das Pferd frißt Hafer.*

**obey, to** [ohBEJ] *v.* • gehorchen
**obedient** *adj.* • gehorsam
This dog obeys his master.
*Dieser Hund gehorcht seinem Herrn.*

**occupation** [ahkjooPEJshən] *n.* • Beruf, der
**occupied (busy)** *adj.* • besetzt
What occupation are you going to choose?
*Welchen Beruf wirst du ergreifen?*

**ocean** [OHshən] *n.* • Ozean, der
**oceanliner** *n.* • Meereskreuzer, der
To go to France from the U.S., you must cross the Atlantic Ocean.
*Man muß den Ozean überqueren, um von den U.S.A. nach Frankreich zu kommen.*

**October** [ahkTOHbər] *n.* • Oktober, der
We are in school during October.
*Im Oktober haben wir Schule.*

**odd** [AHD] *adj.* • seltsam
That's odd! She is never late for work.
*Das ist seltsam! Sie kommt nie zu spät zur Arbeit.*

**of** [əV] *prep.* • von
Francine would like a piece of the cake with the almonds.
*Francine möchte gern ein Stück von dem Kuchen mit den Mandeln.*

**offer, to** [AWFər] *v.* • anbieten
Mr. Peters is offering us a present.
*Herr Peters bietet uns ein Geschenk an.*

**office** [AWFis] *n.* • Büro, das
**post office** *n.* • Post, die
My dad's office is in this building.
*Das Büro meines Vaters ist in diesem Gebäude.*

**often** [AWFən] *adv.* • oft
**How often?** • wie oft?
I often wonder how my old friend is doing.
*Ich frage mich oft, wie es meinem alten Freund geht.*

**oil** [EUL] *n.* • Öl, das
To make a vinaigrette sauce, you need oil and vinegar.
*Um eine "Sauce Vinaigrette" zu machen, braucht man Öl und Essig.*

**OK** [OH K*EJ*] *interj.* • OK
OK! You can come with me.
*OK! Du kannst mit mir kommen.*

**old** [OHLD] *adj.* • alt
**old pal** *n.* • alte Kamerad, der
How old are you?
*Wie alt bist du?*

I like old movies from the 1930s.
*Ich liebe alte Filme aus den dreißiger Jahren.*

**omelet** [AHMlet] Omelett, das *n.* •
We need eggs to make an omelet.
*Wir brauchen Eier, um ein Omelett zu machen.*

**on** [*A*WN] *prep.* • auf
He put his books on the desk.
*Er stellte seine Bücher auf den Schreibtisch.*

**once** [*W*əNS] *adv.* • einmal
**all at once** • plötzlich
**once again** • noch einmal
**once upon a time** • es war einmal
Show me just once and I'll know how to do it.
*Zeig es mir nur einmal, und ich weiß wie man es macht.*

**one** [*W*əN] *adj.; pron.* • ein, -s
**one by one** • einer nach dem andern
**someone** *pron.* • jemand
**that one** • dort (der, die, das)
**the one who** • derjenige, der; diejenige, die; dasjenige, das
**this one** • diese, -r, -s (da)
Do you want one cookie or two?
*Möchtest du einen Keks oder zwei?*

Please give me the one in the corner.
*Geben Sie mir bitte den einen dort in der Ecke.*

**onion** [əNjən] *n.* • Zwiebel, die
Slicing onions makes my eyes water.
*Das Zwiebelschneiden läßt meine Augen tränen.*

**only** [OHNlie] *adj.* • einzig
**only** *adv.* • nur
She is the only person who speaks French here.
*Sie ist die einzige Person, die hier Französisch spricht.*

I can only speak English.
*Ich spreche nur Englisch.*

**open, to** [OHPən] *v.* • öffnen
**opening** *n.* • Öffnung, die (Er-)
Open the window and let in the breeze.
*Öffne das Fenster und laß frische Luft herein.*

**opera** [AHPrə] *n.* • Oper, die
Do you know Bizet's opera "Carmen"?
*Kennst du die Bizet Oper "Carmen"?*

**opposite** [AHPəzit] *n.* • Gegenteil, das
**opposite** *prep.* • gegenüber
You say that you prefer dogs to cats. For me it is exactly the opposite.
*Du sagst, daß du Hunde lieber magst als Katzen. Bei mir ist es genau das Gegenteil.*

The parking lot is opposite the train station.
*Der Parkplatz liegt gegenüber dem Bahnhof.*

**or** [AWR] *conj.* • oder
Do you want fish or chicken?
*Willst du Fisch oder Huhn?*

**orange** [AWR(ə)ndzh] *n.* • Orange, die
**orange juice** • Orangensaft, der
These oranges are very juicy and sweet.
*Diese Orangen sind sehr saftig und süß.*

**orchestra** [*AW*Rkəstrə] *n.* • Orchester, das
The orchestra gave a concert tonight.
*Das Orchester gab heute abend ein Konzert.*

**order, to** [*AW*Rdər] *v.* • bestellen
**in order that** • damit
I have just ordered our meal.
*Ich habe eben unser Essen bestellt.*

**organize, to** [*AW*Rgəneiz] *v.* • organisieren
**organization** *n.* • Organisation, die
The physical education teacher organizes the games.
*Der Sportlehrer organisiert die Spiele.*

**original** [əRI*DZH*inəl] *adj.* • Original-
**originality** *n.* • Originalität, die
Is this an original painting?
*Ist dies ein Originalgemälde?*

**other** [ə*DH*ər] *adj.* • andere, -r, -s
**otherwise** *adv.* • sonst
This book is mine; the other is yours.
*Dieses Buch gehört mir; das andere gehört dir.*

**our** [AUR] *adj.* • unser, -e, -es
That's our house next to the park.
*Das ist unser Haus neben dem Park.*

**out** [AUT] *adv.* • heraus
**outside** *adv.* • hinaus; im Freien, draußen
**to get out of** • aussteigen
**to go out** • ausgehen
Please come out so we can see you better.
*Kommen Sie bitte heraus, damit wir Sie besser sehen können.*

We go outside to see the stars at night.
*Wir gehen hinaus, um nachts die Sterne zu sehen.*

**oven** [əVən] *n.* • Backofen, der
The bread is in the oven.
*Das Brot ist im Backofen.*

**over** [OHV*ər*] *prep.* • über
**overcoat** *n.* • Mantel, der
**over there** • drüben
I'm going over the bridge.
*Ich gehe über die Brücke.*

**overturn, to** [oh*vər*TƏ*R*N] *v.* • stürzen
The revolution overturned the government.
*Die Revolution stürzte die Regierung.*

**owl** [AUL] *n.* • Eule, die
An owl lives in this tree.
*Eine Eule lebt in diesem Baum.*

**own, to** [OHN] *v.* • besitzen
**own** *adj.* • eigene, -r, -s
Our wealthy friends own several houses.
*Unsere wohlhabenden Freunde besitzen mehrere Häuser.*

This is my very own camera.
*Dieses ist meine eigene Kamera.*

**oyster** [EUSt*ər*] *n.* • Auster, die
Do you eat raw oysters?
*Essen Sie rohe Austern?*

# P

**Pacific Ocean** [pəSIFik OHshən] *n.* • Pazifik, der
Hawaii is in the middle of the Pacific Ocean.
*Hawaii liegt in der Mitte des Pazifiks.*

**package** [PAKi*dzh*] *n.* • Paket, das
I received the package you sent in the mail.
*Ich habe das Paket, das du geschickt hast, bekommen.*

**pack, to (one's bags)** [PAK] *v.* • packen
I can pack my bags in one hour.
*Ich kann meine Koffer in einer Stunde packen.*

**page** [P*EJDZH*] *n.* • Seite, die
Turn to page 36 in your book.
*Schlagen Sie ihr Buch auf Seite 36 auf.*

**pail** [P*EJ*L] *n.* • Eimer, der
He pours water from the pail.
*Er gießt Wasser aus dem Eimer.*

**pain** [P*EJ*N] *n.* • Schmerz, der
  **painful** *adj.* • schmerzhaft
The tennis player has pains in his shoulder.
*Der Tennisspieler hat Schmerzen in der Schulter.*

**paint, to** [P*EJ*NT] *v.* • streichen
  **paint** *n.* • Farbe, die
  **painter** *n.* • Maler, der (-in, f.)
  **painting** *n.* • Gemälde, das
Who is painting your house?
*Wer streicht euer Haus?*

**pair** [P*EJ*R] *n.* • Paar, das
I need a pair of boots.
*Ich brauche ein Paar Stiefel.*

**pajamas** [pəJAHMə*z*] *n.* • Schlafanzug, der
I forgot to pack my pajamas.
*Ich habe vergessen, meinen Schlafanzug einzupacken.*

**pal** [PAL] *n.* • Kamerad, der
He is an old pal of mine.
*Er ist mein alter Kamerad.*

**palace** [PA*L*əs] *n.* • Palast, der
The palace is huge!
*Der Palast ist riesig!*

**pan** [PA*N*] *n.* • Pfanne, die
Dad is frying eggs in a pan.
*Vati brät Eier in einer Pfanne.*

**pancake** [PANk*ej*k] *n.* • Pfannkuchen, der
I love pancakes for breakfast.
*Ich esse gern Pfannkuchen zum Frühstück.*

**panther** [PAN*th*ə*r*] *n.* • Panther, der
The panther resembles a leopard but is black.
*Der Panther ähnelt einem Leoparden, ist aber schwarz.*

**pants** [PANTS] *n.* • Hose, die
I'm ironing my pants myself.
*Ich bügele meine Hose selbst.*

**paper** [P*EJ*pə*r*] *n.* • Papier, das
**paperback (book)** *n.* • Taschenbuch, das
**sheet of paper** • Blatt Papier, ein
I need some paper to draw on.
*Ich brauche etwas Papier zum Zeichnen.*

**parachute** [PARəsh*oo*t] *n.* • Fallschirm, der
One day, I'm going to make a parachute jump.
*Eines Tages werde ich Fallschirm springen.*

**parade** [pəR*EJ*D] *n.* • Parade, die
They celebrate every year with a big parade.
*Sie feiern jedes Jahr mit einer Parade.*

**paragraph** [PARəgraf] *n.* • Absatz, der
Write two paragraphs from the book for tomorrow.
*Schreiben Sie für Morgen zwei Absätze aus dem Buch ab.*

**parakeet** [PARəkiet] *n.* • Wellensittich, der
This parakeet is a very noisy bird!
*Dieser Wellensittich ist ein sehr lauter Vogel!*

**pardon, to** [PAHRdən] *v.* • verzeihen
**Pardon me.** • Verzeihung! (Ich bitte um-)
I hope you will pardon my interruption.
*Ich hoffe, Sie werden mir die Unterbrechung verzeihen.*

**parents** [PARənts] *n.* • Eltern, die
My parents are celebrating their anniversary.
*Meine Eltern feiern ihren Hochzeitstag.*

**park** [PAHRK] *n.* • Park, der
We are going to fly our kites in the park.
*Wir lassen unsere Drachen im Park fliegen.*

**parrot** [PARət] *n.* • Papagei, der
This parrot is a beautiful bird.
*Dieser Papagei ist ein schöner Vogel.*

**part** [PAHRT] *n.* • Teil, der
**part (in a play)** *n.* • Rolle, die
Here is one part of the newspaper.
*Hier ist ein Teil der Zeitung.*

**party** [PAHRtie] *n.* • Party, die
We are having a party tonight.
*Wir haben heute abend eine Party.*

**pass, to (car)** [PAS] *v.* • überholen
**to pass a test** • eine Prüfung bestehen
You should not pass a car on the right.
*Man soll ein Auto nicht von der rechten Seite überholen.*

**passenger** [PASiən*dzh*ər] *n.* • Passagier, der (-in, f.)
The passengers are on the train.
*Die Passagiere sind im Zug.*

**past** [P*A*ST] *n.* • Vergangenheit, die
In the past, I often went to Berlin by train.
*In der Vergangenheit bin ich oft mit dem Zug nach Berlin gefahren.*

**paste** [P*EJ*ST] *n.* • Paste, die
**to paste** *v.* • (be)kleben
My teeth are getting really white with this new toothpaste.
*Mit dieser neuen Zahnpaste werden meine Zähne ganz weiß.*

**pastry** [P*EJ*Strie] *n.* • Gebäck, das
**pastry shop** • Konditorei, die
Nancy is going to buy the pastries at the bakery.
*Nancy kauft das Gebäck in der Bäckerei.*

**path** [P*ATH*] *n.* • Pfad, der (Weg, der)
Does this path really lead out of the woods?
*Führt dieser Pfad (Weg) wirklich aus dem Wald heraus?*

**paw** [P*AW*] *n.* • Pfote, die
The dog has a sore paw.
*Der Hund hat eine entzündete Pfote.*

**pay, to (for)** [P*EJ*] *v.* • bezahlen
My father is paying for the tickets.
*Mein Vater bezahlt die Karten.*

**peach** [PIE*TSH*] *n.* • Pfirsich, der
Are these peaches ripe?
*Sind diese Pfirsiche reif?*

**peanut** [PIEnət] *n.* • Erdnuß, die
**peanut butter** *n.* • Erdnußbutter, die
My sister is allergic to peanuts.
*Meine Schwester ist gegen Erdnüsse allergisch.*

**pear** [P*EJ*R] *n.* • Birne, die
The fruit bowl is full of pears and apples.
*Die Fruchtschale ist voller Birnen und Äpfel.*

**pen** [PEN] *n.* • Federhalter, der; Füller, der
**ball-point pen** *n.* • Kugelschreiber, der
May I use your pen to write down the address?
*Darf ich deinen Federhalter benutzen, um die Adresse aufzuschreiben?*

**pencil** [PENsəl] *n.* • Bleistift, der
I prefer to write with a pencil so I can erase my mistakes.
*Ich schreibe lieber mit einem Bleistift, damit ich meine Fehler ausradieren kann.*

**people** [PIEpəl] *n.* • Leute, die
**a lot of people** • viele Leute
Where are all those people going to sit?
*Wo werden alle diese Leute sitzen?*

**pepper (black)** [PEPə*r*] *n.* • Pfeffer, der
**pepper (green or sweet)** *n.* • Paprika, der
Please pass the pepper and salt.
*Reichen Sie mir bitte den Pfeffer und das Salz.*

**perfect** [Pə*R*fikt] *adj.* • perfekt
The artist worked on the sculpture until it was perfect.
*Der Künstler arbeitete an der Skulptur, bis sie perfekt war.*

**perfume** [pə*r*FJ*OO*M] *n.* • Parfüm, das
This French perfume smells lovely.
*Dieses französische Parfüm hat einen herrlichen Duft.*

**perhaps** [pə*r*HAPS] *adv.* • vielleicht
Perhaps you can help me find the right way.
*Vielleicht können Sie mir helfen, den richtigen Weg zu finden.*

**perm(anent)** [Pə*R*M(ənənt)] *n.* • Dauerwelle, die
She goes to the hairdresser's to get a perm.
*Sie geht zum Friseur, um sich eine Dauerwelle machen zu lassen.*

**permission** [pə*r*MISHən] *n.* • Erlaubnis, die
We need our parent's permission to go on the trip.
*Wir brauchen die Erlaubnis unserer Eltern, um die Reise zu machen.*

**permit, to** [pə*r*MIT] *v.* • erlauben
The teacher doesn't permit us to talk in class.
*Der Lehrer erlaubt uns nicht, im Unterricht zu sprechen.*

**person** [PƏ*R*sən] *n.* • Person, die
**personality** *n.* • Persönlichkeit, die
What is this person's name?
*Wie heißt diese Person?*

**pet** [PET] *n.* • Haustier, das
Do you have a dog as a pet?
*Hast du einen Hund als Haustier?*

**pharmacy** [FAHRməsie] *n.* • Apotheke, die
**pharmacist** *n.* • Apotheker, der (-in, f.)
My grandmother buys her medicine at this pharmacy.
*Meine Großmutter kauft ihre Medizin bei dieser Apotheke.*

**phone** [FOHN] *n.* • Telefon, das
Who is on the phone?
*Wer ist am Telefon?*

Use the phone in the hall to call your brother.
*Benutz das Telefon im Gang, um deinen Bruder anzurufen.*

**photo(graph)** [FOHtoh; FOHtəgr*a*f] *n.* • Foto(grafie), das (die); Bild, das
**photographer** *n.* • Fotograf, der (-in, f.)
She has old photos of our great-grandparents.
*Sie hat alte Fotos von unseren Urgroßeltern*

**physics** [FIZiks] *n.* • Physik, die
We studied Newton's laws in physics class.
*Wir haben das Newtonische Gesetz im Physikunterricht besprochen.*

**piano** [pi*A*Noh] *n.* • Klavier, das
**to play the piano** • Klavier spielen
This old piano still sounds nice.
*Dieses alte Klavier hat immer noch einen schönen Ton.*

She plays the piano very well.
*Sie spielt sehr gut Klavier.*

**pick, to** [PIK] *v.* • pflücken
I don't like to pick strawberries.
*Ich pflücke nur ungern Erdbeeren.*

**picnic** [PIKnik] *n.* • Picknick, das
**to go on a picnic** • ein Picknick machen
I hope the rain doesn't spoil your picnic.
*Ich hoffe, der Regen wird euer Picknick nicht ruinieren.*

**picture** [PIK*tshər*] *n.* • Bild, das
**picture (painting)** *n.* • Gemälde, das
I have a picture of my family on my desk.
*Ich habe ein Bild von meiner Familie auf dem Schreibtisch.*

**pie** [PEI] *n.* • Kuchen, der
**apple pie** • Apfelkuchen, der
We'll have pie for dessert.
*Wir essen Kuchen zum Nachtisch.*

**piece** [PIES] *n.* • Stück, das
There are three pieces of pie left.
*Es sind noch drei Stück Kuchen übrig.*

**pig** [PIG] *n.* • Schwein, das
**piggy bank** *n.* • Sparschwein, das
There are pigs and horses on the farm.
*Es gibt Schweine und Pferde auf dem Bauernhof.*

**pillow** [PILoh] *n.* • Kopfkissen, das
I put the pillow on my bed.
*Ich legte das Kopfkissen auf mein Bett.*

**pilot** [PEIlət] *n.* • Pilot, der (-in, f.)
He is a pilot for Air France.
*Er ist Pilot bei der Air France.*

**pin** [PIN] *n.* • Stecknadel, die
You need pins when you sew.
*Man braucht Stecknadeln zum Nähen.*

**pineapple** [PEIN*a*pəl] *n.* • Ananas, die
They grow pineapples in Hawaii.
*Auf Hawaii pflanzt man Ananas an.*

**pink** [PINGK] *adj.* • rosa
The little girl has pink cheeks!
*Das kleine Mädchen hat rosa Backen!*

**pipe** [PEIP] *n.* • Pfeife, die
My grandfather smokes a pipe.
*Mein Großvater raucht Pfeife.*

**pitcher** [PI*TSH*ər] *n.* • Krug, der
The milk is in the pitcher over there.
*Die Milch ist in dem Krug dort drüben.*

**place** [PL*EJ*S] *n.* • Platz, der
**to place** *v.* • hinstellen
Let's find a flat, dry place for the tent.
*Laßt uns einen ebenen, trockenen Platz für das Zelt suchen.*

**plan** [PL*A*N] *n.* • Plan, der
Do you have plans for the weekend?
*Habt ihr Pläne für das Wochenende?*

**plane** [PL*EJ*N] *n.* • Flugzeug, das
Our plane is on time.
*Unser Flugzeug ist pünktlich.*

**planet** [PL*A*Nət] *n.* • Planet, der
Which planet is nearest the sun?
*Welcher Planet ist der Sonne am nächsten?*

**plant** [PLANT] *n.* • Pflanze, die
**to plant** *v.* • pflanzen
Most plants need sunlight.
*Die meisten Pflanzen brauchen Sonnenlicht.*

**plastic** [PLAStik] *adj.* • Plastik, aus
This toy is made of plastic.
*Dieses Spielzeug ist aus Plastik.*

**plate** [PLEJT] *n.* • Teller, der
We still have to wash the plates.
*Wir müssen die Teller noch spülen.*

**play, to** [PLEJ] *v.* • spielen
**play (theatrical)** *n.* • Theaterstück
**playground** *n.* • Spielplatz, der
**playing cards** *n. pl.* • Spielkarten, die
**to play cards** • Karten spielen
**to play (a game)** *v.* • (ein Spiel) spielen
**to play (a musical instrument)** *v.* • (ein Musikinstrument) spielen
**to put on a play** • ein Theaterstück aufführen
The children play every day in the park.
*Die Kinder spielen jeden Tag im Park.*

We enjoyed the play by Brecht.
*Das Theaterstück von Brecht hat uns gut gefallen.*

The children enjoyed the playground in the park.
*Die Kinder haben sich auf den Spielplatz im Park vergnügt.*

**pleasant** [PLEZənt] *adj.* • angenehm
We had a pleasant evening at the theater.
*Wir hatten einen angenehmen Abend im Theater.*

**please** [PLIEZ] *v.* • bitte
May I have the salt, please?
*Kann ich bitte das Salz haben?*

**pleasure** [PLEZ*H*ər] *n.* • Vergnügen, das
**with pleasure!** • mit Vergnügen!
It is a special pleasure for me to meet them.
*Es ist mir ein besonderes Vergnügen, sie kennenzulernen.*

**plum** [PLƏM] *n.* • Pflaume, die
Plums are very scarce this year.
*Es gibt in diesem Jahr nur wenige Pflaumen.*

**p.m.** [PIE EM] *adj.* • nachmittags; abends
It's 6:00 p.m. and time for dinner.
*Es ist 6 Uhr abends und Zeit zum Essen.*

**pocket** [PAHKet] *n.* • Tasche, die
**pocketbook (handbag)** *n.* • Handtasche, die
**pocketknife** *n.* • Taschenmesser, das
What do you have in your pocket?
*Was hast du in deiner Tasche?*

**poem** [POHƏM] *n.* • Gedicht, das
**poet** *n.* • Dichter, der
**poetry** *n.* • Poesie, die
The words to this song are from a poem.
*Der Text dieses Liedes stammt von einem Gedicht.*

I love the poetry of the old masters.
*Ich liebe die Poesie der alten Meister.*

**point, to** [PEUNT] *v.* • hinweisen
**pointed** *adj.* • spitz
The guide points to the towers of Notre Dame.
*Der Führer weist auf die Türme von Notre Dame hin.*

**poison** [PEUZən] *n.* • Gift, das
You use poison to kill rats.
*Man benutzt Gift, um Ratten zu töten.*

**Poland** [POHlənd] *n.* • Polen
**Pole** *n.* • Pole, der; Polin, die
**Polish** *adj.* • polnisch

Warsaw is the capital of Poland.
*Warschau ist die Hauptstadt von Polen.*

**police (force)** [pəLIES] *n.* • Polizei, die
**police department** *n.* • Polizeiwache, die
**policeman; policewoman** *n.* • Polizist, der; Polizistin, die
**police officer** *n.* • Polizeibeamte, der (-in, f.)
The police officer helped us find our hotel.
*Der Polizeibeamte half uns, das Hotel zu finden.*

**polite** [pəLEIT] *adj.* • höflich
These children are very polite.
*Diese Kinder sind sehr höflich.*

**pond** [PAHND] *n.* • Teich, der
There are frogs in the pond.
*Im Teich sind Frösche.*

**pool (swimming)** [P*OO*L] *n.* • Schwimmbecken, das
The pool finally needs to be cleaned.
*Das Schwimmbecken muß endlich gereinigt werden.*

**poor** [PUR] *adj.* • arm
These poor people don't have enough money.
*Diese armen Leute haben nicht genug Geld.*

**pork** [P*AW*RK] *n.* • Schweinefleisch, das
**pork chops** • Kotelett, das
**pork roast** • Schweinebraten, der
Do you want pork or beef for dinner?
*Möchtest du Schweine- oder Rindfleisch zum Abendessen?*

**port** [P*AW*RT] *n.* • Hafen, der
The ship comes into port.
*Das Schiff fährt in den Hafen.*

**Portugal** [PAW*R*t*sh*əgəl] *n.* • Portugal
**Portuguese (person)** *n.* • Portugiese, der (-in, f.)
**Portuguese** *adj.* • portugiesisch
We are going to spend our vacation in Portugal.
*Wir werden unsere Ferien in Portugal verbringen.*

**post office** [POHST *AWF*is] *n.* • Postamt, das
The post office is on the same street as the town hall.
*Das Postamt liegt an derselben Straße wie das Rathaus.*

**postcard** [POHSTkahrd] *n.* • Postkarte, die
I sent a postcard home during my trip.
*Ich habe während meiner Reise eine Postkarte nach Hause geschickt.*

**potato** [pəT*EJ*toh] *n.* • Kartoffel, die
Would you like a baked potato with your steak?
*Möchtest du eine gebackene Kartoffel zu deinem Steak?*

**pound** [PAUND] *n.* • Pfund, das
The German pound and the American pound are not identical.
*Das deutsche Pfund und das amerikanische Pfund sind nicht identisch.*

**pour, to** [P*A*WR] *v.* • eingießen
Mother pours coffee for everyone.
*Mutter gießt allen Kaffee ein.*

**practical** [PRAKtikəl] *adj.* • praktisch
It isn't practical to call, but please write to us.
*Es ist nicht praktisch anzurufen, aber schreiben Sie uns bitte.*

**precious** [PRESHəs] *adj.* • kostbar
Diamonds are precious jewels.
*Diamanten sind kostbare Edelsteine.*

**prefer, to** [prieFƏ*R*] *v.* • vorziehen
I prefer chocolate ice cream to a piece of cake.
*Ich ziehe Schokoladeneis einem Stück Torte vor.*

**preparation** [prepəR*EJ*shən] *n.* • Vorbereitung, die
We are making preparations for our trip.
*Wir treffen Vorbereitungen für unsere Reise.*

**prepare, to** [prieP*EJ*R] *v.* • vorbereiten
My sister is preparing dinner tonight.
*Meine Schwester bereitet heute abend das Essen vor.*

**present** [PREZənt] *n.* • Geschenk, das
Look at all the presents under the Christmas tree!
*Schaut euch nur alle die Geschenke unter dem Weihnachtsbaum an!*

**president** [PREZidənt] *n.* • Präsident, der
The president is giving a speech on T.V.
*Der Präsident hält eine Rede im Fernsehen.*

**press, to (clothes)** [PRES] *v.* • bügeln
Can you press my pants, please?
*Kannst du bitte meine Hose bügeln?*

**pretty** [PRITie] *adj.* • hübsch
What a pretty dress!
*Was für ein hübsches Kleid!*

**price** [PREIS] *n.* • Preis, der
The price of this bike is too high.
*Der Preis für dieses Fahrrad ist zu hoch.*

**prince** [PRINS] *n.* • Prinz, der
**princess** *n.* • Prinzessin, die
A king's children are called prince and princess.
*Die Kinder eines Königs nennt man Prinz und Prinzessin.*

**principal** [PRINsipəl] *n.* • Direktor, der (-in, f.)
The school has a new principal this year.
*Die Schule hat in diesem Jahr einen neuen Direktor.*

**print, to** [PRINT] *v.* • drucken
This is where they print the newspaper.
*Hier wird die Zeitung gedruckt.*

**prison** [PRIZən] *n.* • Gefängnis, das
**prisoner** *n.* • Gefangene, der
The criminals are in prison.
*Die Verbrecher sind im Gefängnis.*

**private** [PREIvət] *adj.* • privat
Don't open this letter, it's private!
*Öffnen Sie diesen Brief nicht; er ist privat!*

**prize** [PREIZ] *n.* • Preis, der
The first prize is a new car.
*Der erste Preis ist ein neues Auto.*

**probably** [PRAHbəblie] *adv.* • wahrscheinlich
I haven't decided, but I'll probably go with you.
*Ich habe mich noch nicht entschieden, aber ich gehe wahrscheinlich mit euch.*

**problem** [PRAHbləm] *n.* • Problem, das
Let me help you solve the problem.
*Lassen Sie mich beim Lösen des Problems helfen.*

**profession** [prəFESHən] *n.* • Beruf, der
Doctors must study a long time before they can practice their profession.
*Ärzte müssen lange studieren, bevor sie ihren Beruf ausüben können.*

**progress** [PRAHgres] *n.* • Fortschritt, der
**to make progress** • Fortschritte machen
Are you making progress in your experiment?
*Machen Sie Fortschritte bei Ihrem Experiment?*

**promise, to** [PRAHmis] *v.* • versprechen
**promise** *n.* • Versprechen, das
We promise to be careful!
*Wir versprechen, vorsichtig zu sein.*

**pronounce, to** [prəNAUNS] *v.* • aussprechen
How do you pronounce this word?
*Wie spricht man dieses Wort aus?*

**protect, to** [prəTEKT] *v.* • beschützen
The cat protects her kittens.
*Die Katze beschützt ihre Jungen.*

**proud** [PRAUD] *adj.* • stolz
We are proud of our team.
*Wir sind stolz auf unsere Mannschaft.*

**province** [PRAH*v*ins] *n.* • Provinz, die
How many provinces are there in Canada?
*Wie viele Provinzen hat Kanada?*

**psychology** [seiKAHLə*dzh*ie] *n.* • Psychologie, die
My sister is studying psychology at the university.
*Meine Schwester studiert Psychologie an der Universität.*

**public** [PƏBlik] *adj.* • öffentlich
This is a public meeting and everyone is welcome.
*Dieses ist eine öffentliche Versammlung und jeder ist willkommen.*

**publicity** [pəbLISətie] *n.* • Werbung, die
The company had lots of publicity for this product.
*Die Firma hat für dieses Produkt viel Werbung gemacht.*

**pull, to** [PUL] *v.* • ziehen
You pull the rope to ring the bell.
*Man muß an der Schnur ziehen, damit die Glocke klingelt.*

**pumpkin** [PəMPkin] *n.* • Kürbis, der
Do you like pumpkin pie?
*Magst du Kürbiskuchen?*

**punish, to** [PəNish] *v.* • bestrafen
They are going to punish the criminal.
*Man wird den Verbrecher bestrafen.*

**pupil** [PJ*OO*pəl] *n.* • Schüler, der (-in, f.)
The pupils raise their hands before speaking.
*Die Schüler heben ihre Hände, bevor sie etwas sagen.*

**puppy** [PəPie] *n.* • Welpe, der
The dog had four puppies.
*Die Hündin hatte vier Welpen.*

**purple** [Pə*R*pəl] *n.; adj.* • Purpur, der
Purple is said to be the color of royalty.
*Man sagt, daß purpur die Farbe des Königtums sei.*

**purse (handbag)** [Pə*R*S] *n.* • Handtasche, die
She puts her billfold in her purse.
*Sie steckt ihr Portemonnaie in die Handtasche.*

**push, to** [PUSH] *v.* • schieben
Don't push, please, you'll make me fall.
*Schiebe bitte nicht so, sonst falle ich.*

**put, to** [PUT] *v.* • setzen; stellen; legen
**to put clothes on** • etwas anziehen
I put the flowers in the vase.
*Ich stelle die Blumen in die Vase.*

**puzzle** [PəZəl] *n.* • Puzzle, das
This puzzle has 1000 pieces.
*Dieses Puzzle hat 1.000 Teile.*

# Q

**quarrel** [KW*A*WRəl] *n.* • Streit, der
The brothers had a quarrel over the toy.
*Die Brüder hatten Streit wegen des Spielzeugs.*

**quarter** [KW*A*WRtə*r*] *n.* • Viertel, das
Let's cut the apple into four quarters.
*Laßt uns den Apfel in vier Viertel schneiden.*

**queen** [KW*I*EN] *n.* • Königin, die
The queen lives in the castle.
*Die Königin lebt in dem Schloß.*

**question, to** [KW*E*S*tsh*ən] *v.* • fragen
**question** *n.* • Frage, die
He questioned me.
*Er fragte mich.*

Can you repeat the question?
*Können Sie die Frage wiederholen?*

**quick** [KW*I*K] *adj.* • schnell
**quickly** *adv.* • schnell
I'll take a quick shower before I go.
*Ich dusche mich schnell, bevor ich gehe.*

Dad walks quickly when he is in a hurry.
*Vati geht immer schnell, wenn er in Eile ist.*

**quiet** [KW*E*Iət] *adj.* • ruhig
**to be quiet** • ruhig sein
When everyone is sleeping the house is quiet.
*Wenn alle schlafen, ist das Haus ruhig.*

**quite** [KW*EI*T] *adv.* • ziemlich
This final exam is quite long.
*Diese Abschlußprüfung ist ziemlich lang.*

# R

**rabbit** [R*A*Bit] *n.* • Kaninchen, das
The rabbit ate all our lettuce from the garden.
*Das Kaninchen hat unseren ganzen Salat im Garten gefressen.*

**radio** [R*EJ*die-oh] *n.* • Radio, das
They are listening to the radio.
*Sie hören Radio.*

**radish** [R*A*Dish] *n.* • Rettich, der
These radishes are from our garden.
*Diese Rettiche sind aus unserem Garten.*

**railroad** [R*EJ*Lrohd] *n.* • Eisenbahn, die
**railroad station** *n.* • Bahnhof, der
I like to travel on the railroad.
*Ich fahre gern mit der Eisenbahn.*

**rain** [R*EJ*N] *n.* • Regen, der
**it's raining** • es Regnet
**rainbow** *n.* • Regenbogen, der
**raincoat** *n.* • Regenmantel, der
**to rain** *v.* • regnen
The grass is wet from the rain.
*Das Gras ist naß vom Regen.*

**raise, to** [R*EJZ*] *v.* • heben
We raise our hands in class before speaking.
*Wir heben unsere Hände in der Klasse, bevor wir etwas sagen.*

**raisin** [R*EJ*z*ə*n] *n.* • Rosine, die
Mom baked a cake with lots of raisins.
*Mutti hat einen Kuchen mit vielen Rosinen gebacken.*

**rapid** [R*A*Pid] *adj.* • schnell (Schnell-)
This is a rapid train.
*Dieses ist ein Schnellzug.*

**rare** [R*EJ*R] *adj.* • selten
Do you have any rare stamps?
*Hast du seltene Briefmarken?*

**raspberry** [R*AZ*berie] *n.* • Himbeere, die
I love to eat fresh raspberries.
*Ich esse sehr gern frische Himbeeren.*

**rat** [R*A*T] *n.* • Ratte, die
I hate rats, but I don't mind mice.
*Ich hasse Ratten, aber Mäuse machen mir nichts aus.*

**rather** [R*Adhə*r] *adv.* • ziemlich
This movie is rather long.
*Dieser Film ist ziemlich lang.*

**raw** [R*AW*] *adj.* • roh
You can eat carrots raw or cooked.
*Man kann Karotten sowohl roh, als auch gekocht essen.*

**razor** [R*EJ*z*ə*r] *n.* • Rasierer, der
My brother shaves with an electric razor.
*Mein Bruder rasiert sich mit einem elektrischen Rasierer.*

**read, to** [RIED] *v.* • lesen
What book are you reading?
*Welches Buch liest du gerade?*

**ready** [REDie] *adj.* • bereit; fertig
We are ready to go.
*Wir sind bereit zu gehen.*

**really** [RIElie] *adv.* • wirklich
Do you really think this is the right way?
*Glaubst du wirklich, daß dieses der richtige Weg ist?*

**reason** [RIEZən] *n.* • Grund, der
**reasonable** *adj.* • vernünftig
What's your reason for wanting to quit?
*Was ist der Grund dafür, daß du aufhören willst?*

**receive, to** [rəSIEV] *v.* • bekommen
She receives a lot of compliments for her good manners.
*Sie bekommt viele Komplimente wegen ihres guten Benehmens.*

**recipe** [RESəpie] *n.* • Rezept, das
The recipe calls for one whole chicken.
*Nach dem Rezept braucht man ein ganzes Huhn.*

**record** [REKərd] *n.* • Schallplatte, die
**record player** *n.* • Plattenspieler, der
Can you play the record again, please?
*Kannst du die Schallplatte bitte noch einmal spielen?*

**record, to** [riKOHRD] *v.* • aufnehmen
**tape recorder** *n.* • Cassettenrekorder, der
The teacher records our conversations in class.
*Der Lehrer nimmt unsere Gespräche in der Klasse auf.*

**red** [RED] *adj.* • rot
**red-headed (red-haired)** *adj.* • rothaarig
**to redden; to blush** *v.* • erröten; rot werden
The sky turned red just after sunset.
*Gleich nach Sonnenuntergang ist der Himmel ganz rot geworden.*

**refrigerator** [riFRIDZHərejtər] *n.* • Kühlschrank, der
The milk is in the refrigerator.
*Die Milch ist im Kühlschrank.*

**region** [RIE*dzh*ən] *n.* • Gegend, die (Region, die)
What region of Germany are you from?
*Aus welcher Gegend Deutschlands kommst du?*

**remain, to** [riM*EJ*N] *v.* • bleiben
Remain in your seats until the plane comes to a full stop.
*Bleiben Sie sitzen, bis das Flugzeug zu einem völligen Stillstand gekommen ist.*

**remember, to** [riMEMbə*r*] *v.* • sich erinnern
I still remember my old phone number.
*Ich erinnere mich noch an meine alte Telefonnummer.*

**remind, to** [riMEIND] *v.* • erinnern
Please remind me to take my medicine.
*Erinnere mich bitte daran, meine Medizin zu nehmen.*

**remove, to** [riM*OOV*] *v.* • entfernen
We must remove the decorations tonight.
*Wir müssen heute abend den Schmuck entfernen.*

**rent, to** [RENT] *v.* • mieten
Do you rent this home or own it?
*Mieten Sie dieses Haus oder gehört es Ihnen?*

**repair, to** [riP*EJ*R] *v.* • reparieren
The mechanic repaired our car.
*Der Mechaniker hat unser Auto repariert.*

**repeat, to** [riPIET] *v.* • wiederholen
Please repeat what you said but more slowly.
*Wiederholen Sie bitte, was Sie gesagt haben, aber etwas langsamer.*

**replace, to** [riPL*EJ*S] *v.* • ersetzen
I replaced the broken windowpane.
*Ich habe die zerbrochene Fensterscheibe ersetzt.*

**reply, to** [riPLEI] *v.* • antworten
I always reply to his letters.
*Ich antworte immer auf seine Briefe.*

**rescue, to** [RESkj*oo*] *v.* • retten
The lifeguard rescued the swimmer.
*Der Bademeister rettete den Schwimmer.*

**respond, to (to answer)** [riSPAHND] *v.* • beantworten
**response** *n.* • Antwort, die
Can someone respond to the question?
*Kann jemand die Frage beantworten?*

**responsibility** [rispahnsəBILətie] *n.* • Verantwortung, die
By making this decision, we took on a big responsibility.
*Mit dieser Entscheidung haben wir eine schwere Verantwortung übernommen.*

**restaurant** [RESt*ər*ahnt] *n.* • Restaurant, das
We know a good restaurant that's not too expensive.
*Wir kennen ein gutes Restaurant, das nicht zu teuer ist.*

**rest, to** [REST] *v.* • ausruhen
The doctor told me to rest all day.
*Der Doktor verordnete mir, den ganzen Tag auszuruhen.*

**return, to (to come back; to go back)** [riTƏ*R*N] *v.* • zurückkommen
**return, to (to give back)** *v.* • zurückgeben
They are returning from their trip.
*Sie kommen von ihrer Reise zurück.*

**rhinoceros** [reiNAHSə*r*əs] *n.* • Nashorn, das
The rhinoceros has a horn on its head.
*Das Nashorn trägt ein Horn auf seiner Stirn.*

**ribbon** [RIBən] *n.* • Band, das
This little girl has ribbons in her hair.
*Das kleine Mädchen trägt Bänder im Haar.*

**rice** [REIS] *n.* • Reis, der
I like chicken with rice.
*Ich mag gern Huhn mit Reis.*

**rich** [RI*TSH*] *adj.* • reich
My rich uncle owns five cars.
*Mein reicher Onkel besitzt fünf Autos.*

**ride, to** [REID] *v.* • fahren
**to ride a bike** • Fahrrad fahren
**to ride a horse** • reiten
Let's ride the bus downtown.
*Laßt uns mit dem Bus in die Stadt fahren.*

**right** [REIT] *adj.* • recht
**right away** • sofort
**the right hand** • rechte Hand, die
**to be right** • recht haben
**to the right (of)** • rechts (von)
Most people write with their right hand.
*Die meisten Leute schreiben mit der rechten Hand.*

**ring** [RING] *n.* • Ring, der
She is wearing a wedding ring on her left hand.
*Sie trägt einen Ehering an der linken Hand.*

**ripe** [REIP] *adj.* • reif
Is this melon ripe yet?
*Ist diese Melone schon reif?*

**river** [RI*V*ər] *n.* • Fluß, der
The best farmland is near the river.
*Das beste Ackerland liegt in der Nähe des Flusses.*

**road** [ROHD] *n.* • Straße, die
Does this road go to Paris?
*Führt diese Straße nach Paris?*

**roast, to** [ROHST] *v.* • braten
**roast beef** • Rinderbraten, der
We are roasting a turkey for dinner.
*Wir braten einen Truthahn zum Abendessen.*

**rob, to** [RAHB] *v.* • ausrauben
**robber** *n.* • Räuber, der (-in, f.)
**robbery** *n.* • Raubüberfall, der
The police caught the man who had robbed the store.
*Die Polizei fing den Mann, der den Laden ausgeraubt hatte.*

**rock** [RAHK] *n.* • Fels, der
Let's climb this big rock.
*Laßt uns auf diesen großen Felsen klettern.*

**rocket** [RAHKet] *n.* • Rakete, die
The weather satellite was launched by a rocket.
*Der Wettersatellit wurde von einer Rakete abgeschossen.*

**role (theater)** [ROHL] *n.* • Rolle, die
**the lead rolc** • Hauptrolle, die
Which role do you have in the play?
*Welche Rolle spielst du in dem Stück?*

**roll** [ROHL] *n.* • Brötchen, das
I put butter on the roll.
*Ich habe Butter auf das Brötchen gestrichen.*

**roll, to** [ROHL] *v.* • rollen
**roller coaster** *n.* • Berg-und-Tal-Bahn, die
**roller skate** *n.* • Rollschuh, der
The ball rolled into the street.
*Der Ball rollte auf die Straße.*

**roof** [R*OO*F] *n.* • Dach, das
There is snow on the roof.
*Auf dem Dach liegt Schnee.*

**room** [R*OO*M] *n.* • Zimmer, das; Raum, der
**bathroom** *n.* • Badezimmer, das
**classroom** *n.* • Klassenzimmer, das
**dining room** *n.* • Eßzimmer, das
Our house has eight rooms.
*Unser Haus hat acht Zimmer.*

**rooster** [R*OO*Stə*r*] *n.* • Hahn, der
The rooster wakes us up in the morning.
*Der Hahn weckt uns morgens auf.*

**rope** [ROHP] *n.* • Seil, das
This rope is used to tie up boats.
*Dieses Seil wird benutzt, um Boote festzumachen.*

**rose** [ROHZ] *n.* • Rose, die
I love the smell of roses.
*Ich mag den Duft von Rosen.*

**round** [RAUND] *adj.* • rund
**round trip ticket** • Rückfahrkarte, die
Please hand me the round tray.
*Gib mir bitte das runde Tablett!*

**row** [ROH] *n.* • Reihe, die
There are thirty rows of seats in the theater.
*Im Theater sind dreißig Sitzreihen.*

**rubber** [RəBə*r*] *n.* • Gummi, das
**made of rubber** • aus Gummi
Rubber is an important export for Brazil.
*Gummi ist ein wichtiges Exportprodukt für Brasilien.*

These tires are made of rubber.
*Diese Reifen sind aus Gummi.*

**rug** [RƏG] *n.* • Teppich, der
There is a thick rug on the floor.
*Auf den Boden liegt ein dicker Teppich.*

**rule** [R*OO*L] *n.* • Regel, die
Have your learned the rules of the game?
*Hast du die Spielregeln gelernt?*

**ruler (for measuring)** [R*OO*Lə*r*] *n.* • Lineal, das
**ruler (sovereign)** *n.* • Herrscher, der (-in, f.)
I measure the paper with a ruler.
*Ich messe das Papier mit einem Lineal.*

**run, to** [RƏN] *v.* • laufen
**to run (of a car)** *v.* • fahren
**to run (to operate)** *v.* • bedienen
**to run away** • fortlaufen
Run or you'll miss the bus!
*Lauf oder du verpaßt den Bus!*

The car runs on gasoline.
*Das Auto fährt mit Benzin.*

I don't know how to run the machine.
*Ich weiß nicht, wie man die Maschine bedient.*

When the dog comes in, the cat runs away.
*Wenn der Hund hereinkommt, läuft die Katze fort.*

**Russia** [RƏSHə] *n.* • Rußland
**Russian (person)** *n.* • Russe, der (-in, f.)
**Russian** *adj.* • russisch
Russia is a huge country.
*Rußland ist ein riesiges Land.*

The Russian ballet is in New York for a week.
*Das russische Ballett ist eine Woche lang in New York.*

# S

**sad** [S*A*D] *adj.* • traurig
She is very sad about the loss of her cat.
*Sie ist sehr traurig über den Verlust ihrer Katze.*

**safety** [S*EJ*Ftie] *n.* • Sicherheit, die
**safety-belt (seat belt)** *n.* • Sicherheitsgurt, der
The lifeguard is responsible for the safety of the swimmers.
*Der Bademeister ist für die Sicherheit der Schwimmer verantwortlich.*

**sailboat** [S*EJ*Lboht] *n.* • Segelboot, das
See the sailboats on the lake!
*Schau dir nur die Segelboote auf dem See an!*

**sailor** [S*EJ*lər] *n.* • Seeman, der
The sailor works on the ship.
*Der Seeman arbeitet auf dem Schiff.*

**salad** [S*A*Ləd] *n.* • Salat, der
Julia has a salad for lunch.
*Julia ißt einen Salat zu Mittag.*

**sale** [S*EJ*L] *n.* • Schlußverkauf, der
**for sale** • zum Verkauf
**on sale** • im Schlußverkauf sein
**salesman; saleswoman** *n.* • Verkäufer, der (-in, f.)
This store is having a sale on summer clothes.
*In diesem Laden gibt es einen Schlußverkauf von Sommerkleidung.*

There's a house for sale on our street.
*In unserer Straße steht ein Haus zum Verkauf.*

I only buy shoes when they're on sale.
*Ich kaufe nur Schuhe, wenn sie im Schlußverkauf sind.*

My cousin is a salesman in this store.
*Mein Cousin (Vetter) ist Verkäufer in diesem Geschäft.*

**salt** [S*A*WLT] *n.* • Salz, das
The soup needs a little more salt.
*Die Suppe braucht etwas mehr Salz.*

**same** [S*EJ*M] *adj.* • derselbe; dieselbe; dasselbe
You have the same jacket as your brother.
*Du hast dieselbe Jacke wie dein Bruder.*

It's all the same to me.
*Für mich ist es alles dasselbe.*

**sand** [SAND] *n.* • Sand, der
We are building a sand castle on the beach.
*Wir bauen eine Sandburg am Strand.*

**sandwich** [SAN(D)*witsh*] *n.* • (Butter) brot, das; Sandwich, das
I would like a ham sandwich for lunch.
*Ich möchte ein Schinkenbrot zu Mittag.*

**Saturday** [SATərd*ej*] *n.* • Samstag, der
We are going to the theater on Saturday.
*Wir gehen am Samstag ins Theater.*

**sauce** [S*A*WS] *n.* • Soße, die
Pour some sauce over my spaghetti, please.
*Gieß bitte etwas Soße auf meine Spaghetti.*

**saucer** [S*A*WSə*r*] *n.* • Untertasse, die
Put the cups on the saucers.
*Stell die Tassen auf die Untertassen.*

**sauerkraut** [SAUərkraut] *n.* • Sauerkraut, das
Sauerkraut is made with cabbage.
*Sauerkraut wird aus Kohl hergestellt.*

**sausage** [S*AW*si*dzh*] *n.* • Wurst, die
We buy sausages at the delicatessen.
*Wir kaufen Wurst im Feinkostgeschäft.*

**save, to** [S*EJV*] *v.* • retten
**to save money** • Geld sparen
The fire fighter saved the child's life.
*Der Feuerwehrmann rettete das Leben des Kindes.*

**saxophone** [S*A*Ksəfohn] *n.* • Saxophon, das
My brother plays the saxophone.
*Mein Bruder spielt Saxophon.*

**say, to** [S*EJ*] *v.* • sagen
**Say!** *interj.* • Hör mal!
**that is to say** • das bedeutet
Can you say "Hello" in German?
*Kannst du "Hallo" auf Deutsch sagen?*

**scare, to** [SK*EJ*R] *v.* • erschrecken
The barking dog scared the baby.
*Der bellende Hund erschreckte das Baby.*

**scarf** [SK*AH*RF] *n.* • Schal, der
I wear a scarf in the winter.
*Ich trage im Winter einen Schal.*

**schedule** [SKE*DZH*ul] *n.* • Plan, der
What is your schedule for this week?
*Wie sieht dein Plan für diese Woche aus?*

**school** [SK*OO*L] *n.* • Schule, die
**high school** *n.* • Gymnasium, das
What's the name of your school?
*Wie heißt deine Schule?*

**science (natural)** [SEIəns] *n.* • Naturwissenschaft, die
**scientific** *adj.* • wissenschaftlich
**scientist** *n.* • Wissenschaftler, der (-in, f.)
We learned about magnetism in science class.
*Wir haben den Magnetismus im Naturwissenschaftsunterricht besprochen.*

**scissors** [SIZərz] *n.* • Schere, die
You need sharp scissors to cut through cloth.
*Man braucht eine scharfe Schere, um Stoff durchzuschneiden.*

**scold, to** [SKOHLD] *v.* • ausschimpfen
Dad scolds us when we are naughty.
*Vati schimpft uns aus, wenn wir unartig sind.*

**Scotland** [SKAHTlənd] *n.* • Schottland
**Scot** *n.* • Schotte, der (-in, f.)
**Scottish** *adj.* • schottisch
Scotland is north of England.
*Schottland liegt nördlich von England.*

**scout** [SKAUT] *n.* • Pfadfinder, der
My brothers are Boy Scouts.
*Meine Brüder gehören zu den Pfadfindern.*

**scream, to** [SKRIEM] *v.* • schreien
I screamed in pain when I broke my arm.
*Ich schrie vor Schmerzen, als ich mir den Arm brach.*

**sculptor** [SKƏLPtər] *n.* • Bildhauer, der
The sculptor was carving a statue from wood.
*Der Bildhauer schnitzte eine Figur aus Holz.*

**sea** [SIE] *n.* • See, die; Meer, das
**seashore** *n.* • Meeresküste, die
We like to swim in the sea.
*Wir schwimmen gern im Meer.*

**search, to** [SƏ*RTSH*] *v.* • suchen
We are searching for our lost dog.
*Wir suchen nach unserem entlaufenen Hund.*

**season** [SIE*z*ən] *n.* • Jahreszeit, die
Is autumn your favorite season?
*Ist der Herbst deine Lieblingsjahreszeit?*

**seat** [SIET] *n.* • Platz, der
**to remain seated** • sitzen bleiben
Is the seat next to you taken?
*Ist der Platz neben Ihnen besetzt?*

**second** [SEKənd] *adj.* • zweite
This is her second trip to France.
*Dieses ist ihre zweite Reise nach Frankreich.*

**secret** [SIEKrət] *n.* • Geheimnis, das
Do you know how to keep a secret?
*Kannst du ein Geheimnis behalten?*

**secretary** [SEKrəterie] *n.* • Sekretär, der (-in, f.)
My secretary answers the phone.
*Meine Sekretärin beantwortet das Telefon.*

**see, to** [SIE] *v.* • sehen
**See you soon!** • Bis bald!
**to see again** • wiedersehen
I see better with my new glasses.
*Ich sehe besser mit meiner neuen Brille.*

**seed** [SIED] *n.* • Samen, der
We plant flower seeds in our garden.
*Wir säen Blumensamen in unserem Garten.*

**seem, to** [SIEM] *v.* • scheinen
You seem to be in a bad mood.
*Du scheinst in einer schlechten Laune zu sein.*

**seesaw** [SIEs*aw*] *n.* • Wippe, die
There is a seesaw in the park.
*Im Park ist eine Wippe.*

**sell, to** [SEL] *v.* • verkaufen
My brother sells cars.
*Mein Bruder verkauft Autos.*

**send, to** [SEND] *v.* • verschicken
We send many packages at Christmas.
*Wir verschicken zu Weihnachten viele Pakete.*

**sense** [SENS] *n.* • Sinn, der
**common sense** • gesunde Menschenverstand, der
**good sense** • gesunde Menschenverstand, der
**sensible** *adj.* • vernünftig
**sensitive** *adj.* • sensibel
This assignment makes no sense at all.
*Diese Aufgabe macht überhaupt keinen Sinn.*

**sentence** [SENtənts] *n.* • Satz, der
Write five sentences in German!
*Schreibt fünf Sätze auf deutsch!*

**September** [sepTEMbə*r*] *n.* • September, der
We go back to school again in September.
*Im September gehen wir wieder zurück zur Schule.*

**serious** [SIERie-əs] *adj.* • ernst(haft)
Stop giggling and be serious!
*Hört auf zu kichern und seid ein bißchen ernst!*

**serve, to** [Sə*RV*] *v.* • bedienen
**at your service** • zu Ihren Diensten
**service** *n.* • Service, der
**to serve as** • dienen als
First, we serve our guests.
*Zuerst bedienen wir unsere Gäste.*

**set, to** [SET] *v.* • stellen
**to set the table** • den Tisch decken
Set the box down on the table.
*Stell die Kiste auf den Tisch!*

**seven** [SE*V*ən] *n.; adj.* • sieben
There are seven days in the week.
*Die Woche hat sieben Tage.*

**seventeen** [se*v*ənTIEN] *n.; adj.* • siebzehn
I was only seventeen when I started college.
*Ich war erst siebzehn, als ich anfing zu studieren.*

**seventy** [SE*V*əntie] *n.; adj.* • siebzig
My grandfather is seventy years old.
*Mein Großvater ist siebzig Jahre alt.*

**several** [SE*V*rəl] *adj.* • einige
Let's wait for him several more minutes.
*Laßt uns noch einige Minuten auf ihn warten.*

**sew, to** [SOH] *v.* • nähen
**sewing machine** • Nähmaschine, die
Can you sew a new button on for me?
*Kannst du mir einen neuen Knopf annähen?*

**shade** [SH*EJ*D] *n.* • Schatten, der
Let's sit in the shade of this tree.
*Laßt uns im Schatten dieses Baumes sitzen.*

**shadow** [SH*A*Doh] *n.* • Schatten, der
Shadows are shortest at noon.
*Der Schatten ist über Mittag am kürzesten.*

**shake, to** [SH*EJ*K] *v.* • zittern
**to shake hands** • Hände schütteln
I'm so scared I'm shaking all over.
*Ich habe solche Angst, daß ich am ganzen Körper zittere.*

**shampoo** [sh*a*mP*OO*] *n.* • Shampoo, das
**to shampoo (to wash one's hair)** *v.* • die Haare waschen
The shampoo makes my hair smell clean.
*Das Shampoo läßt mein Haar frisch duften.*

**shape** [SH*EJ*P] *n.* • Form, die
Look at the shape of that cloud.
*Schau dir die Form dieser Wolke an!*

**share, to** [SH*EJ*R] *v.* • sich teilen
We can share this serving of cake.
*Wir können uns dieses Stück Kuchen teilen.*

**shave, to** [SH*EJ*V] *v.* • rasieren, sich
Father shaves in the morning.
*Vater rasiert sich am Morgen.*

**she** [SHIE] *pron.* • sie
She is my mother's sister.
*Sie ist die Schwester meiner Mutter.*

**sheep** [SHIEP] *n.* • Schafe, die (pl.)
The sheep are following the shepherd.
*Die Schafe folgen dem Hirten.*

**sheet** [SHIET] *n.* • Bettuch, das
**sheet of paper** *n.* • Blatt Papier, das
The maid changed the sheets on the bed.
*Das Zimmermädchen wechselte die Bettücher.*

**shelf** [SHELF] *n.* • Regal, das
The cups are on the bottom shelf.
*Die Tassen stehen auf dem untersten Regal.*

**shell** [SHEL] *n.* • Muschel, die
I look for shells on the beach.
*Ich suche Muscheln am Strand.*

**shepherd** [SHEPərd] *n.* • Hirte, der
**German shepherd (dog)** *n.* • Deutsche Schäferhund, der
**shepherdess** *n.* • Hirtin, die
The shepherd watches the sheep.
*Der Hirte hütet die Schafe.*

**shine, to** [SHEIN] *v.* • scheinen
The stars shine at night.
*Die Sterne scheinen bei Nacht.*

**ship** [SHIP] *n.* • Schiff, das
The ship crosses the ocean.
*Das Schiff überquert den Ozean.*

**shirt** [SHə*R*T] *n.* • Hemd, das
He wears a shirt and tie to work.
*Er trägt ein Hemd und eine Krawatte bei der Arbeit.*

**shoe** [SH*OO*] *n.* • Schuh, der
I bought a new pair of shoes.
*Ich habe ein neues Paar Schuhe gekauft.*

**shoot, to** [SH*OO*T] *v.* • schießen
The hunter shoots his gun.
*Der Jäger schießt mit seinem Gewehr.*

**shop** [SHAHP] *n.* • Laden, der
**to go shopping** • einkaufen gehen
What do they sell in this shop?
*Was verkaufen sie in diesem Laden?*

**shore** [SHOHR] *n.* • Küste, die
They live near the shore.
*Sie leben (wohnen) in der Nähe der Küste.*

**short** [SH*A*WRT] *adj.* • klein; kurz
The little girl is too short to reach the top shelf.
*Das kleine Mädchen ist zu klein, um das oberste Regal zu erreichen.*

**shorts** [SHA*W*RTS] *n.* • Shorts, die
We wear shorts when it's hot.
*Wir tragen Shorts, wenn es heiß ist.*

**shot** [SHAHT] *n.* • Spritze, die
I do not like it when the doctor gives me a shot.
*Ich mag es nicht, wenn der Arzt mir eine Spritze gibt.*

**shoulder** [SHOHLdə*r*] *n.* • Schulter, die
Martine has a sore shoulder.
*Martine hat eine steife Schulter.*

**shout, to** [SHAUT] *v.* • schreien
The children shout when they play baseball.
*Die Kinder schreien, wenn sie Baseball spielen.*

**shovel** [SHƏ*V*əl] *n.* • Schaufel, die
The little boy plays in the sand with a shovel.
*Der kleine Junge spielt mit einer Schaufel im Sand.*

**shower** [SHAUə*r*] *n.* • Dusche, die
Do you prefer a shower or a bath?
*Ziehen Sie eine Dusche oder ein Bad vor?*

**show, to** [SHOH] *v.* • zeigen
**show** *n.* • Show, die
Show me your new book.
*Zeig mir dein neues Buch.*

**shrimp** [SHRIMP] *n.* • Garnelen, die (pl.)
When we go to this restaurant, I usually order shrimp.
*Wenn wir in dieses Restaurant gehen, bestelle ich gewöhnlich Garnelen.*

**shut, to** [SHƏT] *v.* • schließen
**to shut up (be quiet)** • den Mund halten
Please shut the window! It's cold!
*Schließen Sie bitte das Fenster! Es ist kalt!*

**shy** [SHEI] *adj.* • schüchtern
Nicole is shy around strange people.
*Nicole ist schüchtern bei fremden Leuten.*

**sick** [SIK] *adj.* • krank
**sickness** *n.* • Krankheit, die
I stay in bed when I am sick.
*Ich bleibe im Bett, wenn ich krank bin.*

**side** [SEID] *n.* • Seite, die
He lives on the other side of the street.
*Er wohnt auf der anderen Seite der Straße.*

**sidewalk** [SEID*wawk*] *n.* • Bürgersteig, der
**sidewalk café** • Straßencafé, das
The dog walks on the sidewalk.
*Der Hund läuft auf dem Bürgersteig.*

**silence** [SEIləns] *n.* • Ruhe, die
**silent** *adj.* • ruhig
The teacher asked the class for silence.
*Der Lehrer bat die Klasse um Ruhe.*

**silly** [SILie] *adj.* • dumm
That's a silly joke.
*Das ist ein dummer Witz.*

**silver** [SIL*v*ər] *n.* • Silber, das
**made of silver** • aus Silber gemacht
My mother has a silver ring.
*Meine Mutter hat einen Ring aus Silber.*

**similar** [SIMilər] *adj.* • ähnlich
The brothers are similar in appearance.
*Die Brüder sehen sich ähnlich.*

**since** [SINS] *conj.* • da
**since when?** • seit wann?
Since you are here, stay for lunch!
*Da du schon hier bist, bleib doch zum Mittagessen!*

**sincere** [sinSIER] *adj.* • ernst
She is sincere about her love for animals.
*Sie nimmt die Tierliebe ernst.*

**sing, to** [SING] *v.* • singen
**singer** *n.* • Sänger, der (-in, f.)
The class sang a song to end the show.
*Die Klasse sang ein Lied, um die Show zu beenden.*

**sink** [SINGK] *n.* • Spülbecken, das
We wash the dishes in the sink.
*Wir spülen das Geschirr im Spülbecken.*

**sir** [Sə*R*] *n.* • Herr (der, mein, gnädige[r])
May I take your hat, sir?
*Darf ich Ihren Hut nehmen, mein Herr?*

**sister** [SIStə*r*] *n.* • Schwester, die
Your sister seems like a nice girl.
*Deine Schwester scheint ein nettes Mädchen zu sein.*

**sit, to** [SIT] *v.* • sitzen
He always sits in this chair.
*Er sitzt immer auf diesem Stuhl.*

**six** [SIKS] *n.; adj.* • sechs
I was six years old in first grade.
*Ich war im ersten Schuljahr sechs Jahre alt.*

**sixteen** [siksTIEN] *n.; adj.* • sechzehn
Many people learn to drive at sixteen.
*Viele Leute lernen mit sechzehn, Auto zu fahren.*

**sixty** [SIKStie] *n.; adj.* • sechzig
There are sixty minutes in an hour.
*Eine Stunde hat sechzig Minuten.*

**size** [SEIZ] *n.* • Größe, die
Is this the right size?
*Ist dies die richtige Größe?*

**skate, to** [SK*EJ*T] *v.* • Eis laufen; eislaufen
**skater** *n.* • Eisläufer, der (-in, f.)
Do you know how to skate?
*Kannst du Eis laufen?*

**skeleton** [SKELətən] *n.* • Skelett, das
How many bones are in a skeleton?
*Wie viele Knochen hat ein Skelett?*

**ski** [SKIE] *n.* • Ski, der
**skiing** *n.* • Skilaufen, das
**to ski** *v.* • Ski laufen
**to water ski** *v.* • Wasserski laufen
Have you seen my other ski?
*Hast du meinen anderen Ski gesehen?*

**skin** [SKIN] *n.* • Haut, die
The baby has soft skin.
*Das Baby hat eine weiche Haut.*

**skinny** [SKINie] *adj.* • mager; dünn
You look skinny. You should eat more.
*Du siehst mager aus. Du solltest mehr essen.*

**skirt** [SKə*R*T] *n.* • Rock, der
She is wearing a new skirt to the party.
*Sie trägt einen neuen Rock für die Party.*

**sky** [SKEI] *n.* • Himmel, der
**skyscraper** *n.* • Wolkenkratzer, der
The sun shines; the sky is blue; the weather is great!
*Die Sonne scheint; der Himmel ist blau; das Wetter ist toll!*

**slang** [SL*A*NG] *n.* • Jargon, der
Student slang is very funny.
*Der Studentenjargon ist sehr lustig.*

**sled** [SLED] *n.* • Schlitten, der
My sled goes down the hill fast.
*Mein Schlitten fährt schnell den Hügel hinunter.*

**sleep, to** [SLIEP] *v.* • schlafen
**sleeping bag** ] *n.* • Schlafsack, der
**to be very sleepy** • sehr schläfrig sein
**to go to sleep; to fall asleep** • einschlafen
**to sleep late** • lange schlafen
The cat is sleeping on the couch.
*Die Katze schläft auf dem Sofa.*

Did you sleep well last night?
*Hast du letzte Nacht gut geschlafen?*

**sleeve** [SLIE*V*] *n.* • Ärmel, der
The sleeves are too short!
*Die Ärmel sind zu kurz!*

**slice** [SLEIS] *n.* • Scheibe, die
Would you like a slice of ham?
*Möchtest du eine Scheibe Schinken?*

**slide, to** [SLEID] *v.* • gleiten
The skaters slide across the ice.
*Die Eisläufer gleiten über das Eis.*

**slim** [SLIM] *adj.* • schlank
You're looking very slim after your diet.
*Du siehst nach deiner Diät sehr schlank aus.*

**slip, to** [SLIP] *v.* • ausrutschen
Be careful! Don't slip on the ice!
*Sei vorsichtig! Rutsch nicht auf dem Eis aus!*

**slipper** [SLIPə*r*] *n.* • Hausschuh, der
Grandmother wears her slippers at home.
*Großmutter trägt zu Hause ihre Hausschuhe.*

**slow** [SLOH] *adj.* • langsam
**to slow down** • verlangsamen
**slowly** *adv.* • langsam
This slow train will make us late.
*Dieser langsame Zug wird uns verspätet ankommen lassen.*

They had to slow the car down.
*Sie mußten die Geschwindigkeit des Autos verlangsamen.*

**small** [SM*A*WL] *adj.* • klein
These shoes are too small!
*Diese Schuhe sind zu klein!*

**smart** [SMAHRT] *adj.* • klug
All these students are smart.
*Alle diese Studenten sind klug.*

**smash, to** [SM*A*SH] *v.* • zerschlagen
He smashed the glass with a hammer.
*Er zerschlug das Glas mit einem Hammer.*

**smell, to** [SMEL] *v.* • riechen (an)
The lady is smelling the flowers.
*Die Dame riecht an den Blumen.*

**smile, to** [SMEIL] *v.* • lächeln
We ought to smile for the picture.
*Wir sollten für das Bild lächeln.*

**smoke** [SMOHK] *n.* • Rauch, der
**No smoking!** • Rauchen verboten!
**to smoke** *v.* • rauchen
There's a lot of smoke in the air today.
*Heute gibt es viel Rauch am Himmel.*

**snack** [SN*A*K] *n.* • Zwischenmahlzeit, die
We have a snack when we get home from school.
*Wir haben eine Zwischenmahlzeit, wenn wir nach Hause kommen.*

**snail** [SN*EJ*L] *n.* • Schnecke, die
You can order snails in this restaurant.
*Man kann in diesem Restaurant Schnecken bestellen.*

**snake** [SN*EJ*K] *n.* • Schlange, die
A cobra is a dangerous snake.
*Eine Kobra ist eine gefährliche Schlange.*

**snow** [SNOH] *n.* • Schnee, der
**snowman** *n.* • Schneemann, der
**to snow** *v.* • schneien
It's snowing.
*Es schneit.*

Let's go play in the snow!
*Laß uns im Schnee spielen!*

**so** [SOH] *adv.* • so
**and so on** • und so weiter
**so much (many)** • so viel (viele)
**so-so** • so-so
This suitcase is so light.
*Dieser Koffer ist so leicht.*

**soap** [SOHP] *n.* • Seife, die
I wash my hands with soap before every meal.
*Ich wasche mir die Hände vor jedem Essen mit Seife.*

**soccer** [SAHKə*r*] *n.* • Fußball(spiel), das
**to play soccer** • Fußball spielen
Soccer is becoming popular in the U.S.
*Fußball wird in den U.S.A. beliebt.*

**social studies** [SOHSHəl STədie*z*] *n.* • Sozialkunde, die
Who is your social studies teacher?
*Wer ist dein Lehrer in Sozialkunde?*

**sock** [SAHK] *n.* • Socke, die
Do these two socks go together?
*Passen diese beiden Socken zusammen?*

**sofa** [SOHfə] *n.* • Sofa, das
The cat is sleeping on the sofa.
*Die Katze schläft auf dem Sofa.*

**soft** [SAWFT] *adj.* • weich
This blanket is soft.
*Diese Decke ist weich.*

**soil, to** [SEUL] *v.* • beschmutzen
Don't soil the rug with your dirty shoes!
*Beschmutze nicht den Teppich mit deinen schmutzigen Schuhen!*

**soldier** [SOHL*dzh*ər] *n.* • Soldat, der
The soldiers are waiting for their orders.
*Die Soldaten warten auf ihre Befehle.*

**solid** [SAHLid] *adj.* • fest
The ice on the lake is solid.
*Das Eis auf dem See ist fest.*

**some** [SƏM] *adj.* • etwas
**somebody** *pron.* • jemand
**something** *pron.* • etwas
**sometimes** *adv.* • manchmal
**somewhere** *adv.* • irgendwo
**to have something to eat** • etwas zu essen haben
Do you want some cake?
*Möchtest du etwas Kuchen?*

**son** [SƏN] *n.* • Sohn, der
Grandfather and grandmother have six sons.
*Großvater und Großmutter haben sechs Söhne.*

**song** [SAWNG] *n.* • Lied, das
The music teacher taught us a new song.
*Der Musiklehrer hat uns ein neues Lied beigebracht.*

**soon** [S*OO*N] *adv.* • bald
**as soon as** • sobald wie
**See you soon!** • Bis bald!
The plane will arrive soon.
*Das Flugzeug wird bald ankommen.*

**sorry, to be** [SAHRie] *v.* • leid tun
**I am sorry** • Es tut mir leid
I am sorry I am late.
*Es tut mir leid, daß ich so spät komme.*

**sort (kind)** [S*A*W*R*T] *n.* • Sorte, die
What sort of cake is this?
*Was für eine Sorte Kuchen ist das?*

**sound** [SAUND] *n.* • Klang, der
This instrument has a good sound.
*Dieses Instrument hat einen guten Klang.*

**soup** [S*OO*P] *n.* • Suppe, die
Hot soup is good in the winter.
*Heiße Suppe ist etwas Gutes im Winter.*

**sour** [SAUə*r*] *adj.* • sauer
Lemon juice is sour.
*Zitronensaft ist sauer.*

**south** [SAU*TH*] *n.; adj.* • Süden, der
**South America** *n.* • Südamerika
We traveled into the south of Mexico.
*Wir sind in den Süden Mexikos gereist.*

**space** [SP*EJ*S] *n.* • Weltraum, der
**space ship** *n.* • Raumschiff, das
Do you want to go into space one day?
*Möchtest du eines Tages in den Weltraum fliegen?*

**Spain** [SP*EJ*N] *n.* • Spanien
**Spaniard** *n.* • Spanier, der (-in, f.)
**Spanish** *adj.* • spanisch

My friends spent their vacation in Spain.
*Meine Freunde haben ihre Ferien in Spanien verbracht.*

**speak, to** [SPIEK] *v.* • sprechen
I will speak with the teacher after class.
*Ich werde nach dem Unterricht mit dem Lehrer sprechen.*

**special** [SPESHəl] *adj.* • besonders
**specially** *adv.* • besonders
There is a special show on T.V. tonight.
*Heute abend kommt eine besondere Show im Fernsehen.*

**speech** [SPIE*TSH*] *n.* • Rede, die
**to give a speech** • eine Rede halten
Your speech is very clear and distinct.
*Deine Rede ist sehr klar und deutlich.*

**spend, to (time)** [SPEND] *v.* • verbringen (Zeit)
**to spend (money)** *v.* • (Geld) ausgeben
Paul spends a month at summer camp.
*Paul verbringt einen Monat im Sommerlager.*

**spider** [SPEIdər] *n.* • Spinne, die
Are you afraid of spiders?
*Hast du Angst vor Spinnen?*

**spill, to** [SPIL] *v.* • verschütten
The child spilled her milk.
*Das Kind hat die Milch verschüttet.*

**spinach** [SPINi*tsh*] *n.* • Spinat, der
The salad is made with spinach.
*Der Salat ist mit Spinat gemacht.*

**splendid** [SPLENdid] *adj.* • grandios
The fireworks are splendid!
*Das Feuerwerk ist grandios!*

**sponge** [SPƏN*DZH*] *n.* • Schwamm, der
You clean the bathtub with a sponge.
*Man reinigt die Badewanne mit einem Schwamm.*

**spoon** [SP*OO*N] *n.* • Löffel, der
How many spoons are there on the table?
*Wie viele Löffel sind auf dem Tisch?*

**sport** [SP*AW*RT] *n.* • Sport, der
Did you play sports in college?
*Hast du an der Universität Sport getrieben?*

**spot** [SPAHT] *n.* • Fleck, der
**spotted** *adj.* • befleckt
He has a spot on his shirt.
*Er hat einen Fleck auf seinem Hemd.*

**spring** [SPRING] *n.* • Frühling, der
It rains a lot in the spring.
*Im Frühling regnet es viel.*

**square** [SK*WEJ*R] *adj.* • quadratisch
The napkin is square.
*Die Serviette ist quadratisch.*

**squirrel** [SK*W*Ə*R*l] *n.* • Eichhörnchen, das
There is a grey squirrel in the tree.
*Auf dem Baum sitzt ein graues Eichhörnchen.*

**stadium** [ST*EJ*die-əm] *n.* • Stadion, das
We are going to a game at the stadium.
*Wir gehen zu einem Spiel im Stadion.*

**stain** [ST*EJ*N] *n.* • Fleck, der
Nancy is trying to get the stain out of her blouse.
*Nancy versucht, den Fleck aus ihrer Bluse herauszubekommen.*

**stair(s)** [ST*EJ*R(Z)] *n.* • Treppe(n), die
We climb the stairs.
*Wir steigen die Treppen hinauf.*

**stamp (postage)** [ST*A*MP] *n.* • Briefmarke, die
My sister collects stamps.
*Meine Schwester sammelt Briefmarken.*

**stand, to** [ST*A*ND] *v.* • stehen
**standing** *adj.* • stehend
**to stand up** • aufstehen
The saleswoman stands all day.
*Die Verkäuferin steht den ganzen Tag.*

**star** [STAHR] *n.* • Stern, der
**movie star** *n.* • Filmstar, der
There are many stars in the sky tonight.
*Heute abend sind viele Sterne am Himmel.*

**start, to (to begin)** [STAHRT] *v.* • beginnen
**to start (to take off; to run)** *n.* • starten
The movie starts at 7:30 p.m.
*Der Film beginnt um 19.30 Uhr.*

**state** [ST*EJ*T] *n.* • Staat, der
There are fifty states in the United States.
*Die U.S.A. bestehen aus fünfzig Staaten.*

**station** [ST*EJ*shən] *n.* • Station, die
**police station** *n.* • Polizeistation, die
The bus finally reached the station.
*Der Bus erreichte endlich die Station.*

**statue** [ST*A*tshoo] *n.* • Statue, die
The "Venus de Milo" is a famous statue.
*Die "Venus von Milo" ist eine berühmte Statue.*

**stay, to** [ST*EJ*] *v.* • bleiben
I am staying at my friend's house tonight.
*Ich bleibe heute abend bei meinem Freund.*

**steak** [ST*EJ*K] *n.* • Steak, das
I would like my steak well done.
*Ich möchte mein Steak gut durchgebraten.*

**steal, to** [STIEL] *v.* • stehlen
The fox is stealing a chicken.
*Der Fuchs stiehlt ein Huhn.*

**steamship** [STIEMship] *n.* • Dampfer, der
The steamship arrived in New York.
*Der Dampfer kam in N.Y. an.*

**step** [STEP] *n.* • Schritt, der
**step (stairs)** *n.* • Stufe, die
How many steps are there in the directions?
*Wie viele Schritte enthalten die Anweisungen?*

**stepmother** [STEPmə*dh*ə*r*] *n.* • Stiefmutter, die
**stepdaughter** *n.* • Stieftochter, die
**stepfather** *n.* • Stiefvater, der
**stepson** *n.* • Stiefsohn, der
May I introduce my stepmother to you?
*Darf ich Ihnen meine Stiefmutter vorstellen?*

**steward (flight attendant)** [ST*OO*ərd] *n.* • Steward, der; Flugbegleiter, der
**stewardess** *n.* • Stewardess, die
The steward brings our drinks.
*Der Steward bringt unsere Getränke.*

**still** [STIL] *adv.* • noch
He still remembered my name after many years.
*Er erinnerte sich nach vielen Jahren noch an meinen Namen.*

**sting, to** [STING] *v.* • stechen
These bugs sting!
*Diese Käfer stechen!*

**stingy** [STIN*dzh*ie] *adj.* • geizig
He is too stingy to share his food.
*Er ist zu geizig, um sein Essen zu teilen.*

**stir, to** [STə*R*] *v.* • umrühren
Father is stirring the soup.
*Vater rührt die Suppe um.*

**stocking** [STAHKing] *n.* • Strumpf, der
Are these stockings dry?
*Sind diese Strümpfe trocken?*

**stomach** [STəMək] *n.* • Magen, der
**tomach ache** *n.* • Magenschmerzen, die
My stomach is still full from dinner.
*Mein Magen ist noch immer vom Abendessen voll.*

**stone** [STOHN] *n.* • Stein, der
Let's throw stones in the lake.
*Laßt uns Steine in den See werfen.*

**stop, to** [STAHP] *v.* • anhalten
**to stop (oneself)** *v.* • aufhören
Let's stop at the gas station.
*Laßt uns an der Tankstelle anhalten.*

**store** [ST*AW*R] *n.* • Laden, der
**book store** • Buchladen, der
**department store** • Kaufhaus, das
**store window** • Schaufenster, das
Did you shop at the new store?
*Hast du in dem neuen Laden eingekauft?*

**storm** [ST*AW*RM] *n.* • Sturm, der
The storm blew the tree down.
*Der Sturm hat den Baum entwurzelt.*

**story** [STOHRie] *n.* • Geschichte, die
Tell me the story of how you met her.
*Erzähl mir die Geschichte, wie du sie kennengelernt hast.*

**stove** [STOH*V*] *n.* • Herd, der
The sauce is cooking on the stove.
*Die Soße kocht auf dem Herd.*

**strange** [STR*EJ*N*DZH*] *adj.* • seltsam
**stranger** *n.* • Fremde, der
Your voice sounds strange. Are you well?
*Deine Stimme klingt seltsam. Geht es dir gut?*

**straw** [STR*AW*] *n.* • Stroh, das
The animals sleep on the straw.
*Die Tiere schlafen im Stroh.*

**strawberry** [STR*AW*berie] *n.* • Erdbeere, die
Here is some strawberry jam for your bread.
*Hier ist etwas Erdbeermarmelade für dein Brot.*

**stream** [STRIEM] *n.* • Bach, der
Little streams become great rivers.
*Kleine Bäche werden große Flüsse.*

**street** [STRIET] *n.* • Straße, die
**street cleaner** • Straßenkehrer, der
What is the name of this street?
*Wie heißt diese Straße?*

**strict** [STRIKT] *adj.* • streng
These rules are very strict.
*Diese Regeln sind sehr streng.*

**string** [STRING] *n.* • Schnur, die
**string beans** *n. pl.* • Gartenbohnen, die
I need some string for my kite.
*Ich brauche eine Schnur für meinen Drachen.*

**strong** [STR*AW*NG] *adj.* • stark
This athlete is very strong.
*Dieser Athlet ist sehr stark.*

**stubborn** [STƏBə*r*n] *adj.* • stur
They say that goats are stubborn.
*Man sagt, daß Ziegen stur sind.*

**student** [ST*OO*dənt] *n.* • Student, der (-in, f.)
These students go to the university.
*Diese Studenten gehen zur Universität.*

**study, to** [STƏDie] *v.* • studieren
We are studying German.
*Wir studieren Deutsch.*

**stupid** [ST*OO*Pid] *adj.* • dumm
He made a stupid mistake.
*Er hat einen dummen Fehler gemacht.*

**subject** [SƏB*dzh*ekt] *n.* • Gegenstand, der
What is the subject of this discussion?
*Was ist der Gegenstand dieser Diskussion?*

**suburb** [SƏBə*r*b] *n.* • Vorort, der
My friend lives in a suburb of Paris.
*Mein Freund lebt in einem Vorort von Paris.*

**subway** [SƏB*wej*] *n.* • Untergrundbahn, die (U-Bahn)
Do you want to ride the subway?
*Willst du mit der U-Bahn fahren?*

**succeed, to** [səkSIED] *v.* • Erfolg haben
**success** *n.* • Erfolg, der
She succeeds at her work.
*Sie hat Erfolg bei ihrer Arbeit.*

**suddenly** [SƏDnlie] *adv.* • plötzlich
Suddenly he jumped up from his seat.
*Plötzlich sprang er von seinem Sitz auf.*

**sugar** [SHUGə*r*] *n.* • Zucker, der
Do you take sugar in your coffee?
*Nimmst du Zucker in deinen Kaffee?*

**suit** [S*OO*T] *n.* • Anzug, der
Father is wearing his blue suit today.
*Vater trägt heute seinen blauen Anzug.*

**suitcase** [S*OO*Tk*ej*s] *n.* • Koffer, der
**to pack one's suitcase** • seinen Koffer packen
How many suitcases are they bringing?
*Wie viele Koffer bringen sie mit?*

**summer** [SƏMə*r*] *n.* • Sommer, der
This summer we're spending our vacation in Canada.
*Diesen Sommer verbringen wir unsere Ferien in Kanada.*

**sun** [SƏN] *n.* • Sonne, die
The cat is sleeping in the sun.
*Die Katze schläft in der Sonne.*

**Sunday** [SƏNd*ej*] *n.* • Sonntag, der
We are going to Grandmother's on Sunday.
*Wir gehen am Sonntag zu Großmutter.*

**supermarket** [S*OO*Pə*r*mahrkət] *n.* • Supermarkt, der
This supermarket has its own bakery.
*Dieser Supermarkt hat eine eigene Bäckerei.*

**sure** [SHUR] *adj.* • sicher
Are you sure you can go?
*Bist du sicher, daß du gehen kannst?*

**surgeon** [SƏ*Rdzh*ən] *n.* • Chirurg, der (-in, f.)
**surgery** *n.* • chirurgische Eingriff, der; Operation, die
The surgeon works at the hospital.
*Der Chirurg arbeitet im Krankenhaus.*

**surprise** [səPREIZ] *n.* • Überraschung, die
**surprising** *adj.* • überraschend
Don't tell anyone because it's a surprise!
*Erzähl es niemandem, denn es ist eine Überraschung!*

**sweater** [SWETə*r*] *n.* • Pullover, der
I'm cold! Where is my sweater?
*Ich friere! Wo ist mein Pullover?*

**Sweden** [SWIEDn] *n.* • Schweden
**Swede** *n.* • Schwede, der (Schwedin, die)
**Swedish** *adj.* • schwedisch
We're going to Sweden this Summer.
*Wir fahren in diesem Sommer nach Schweden.*

**sweep, to** [SWIEP] *v.* • fegen
My sister is sweeping the floor.
*Meine Schwester fegt den Boden.*

**sweet** [SWIET] *adj.* • süß
This dessert is too sweet.
*Dieser Nachtisch ist zu süß.*

**swim, to** [SWIM] *v.* • schwimmen
**swimming pool** *n.* • Schwimmbecken, das; Swimmingpool, der
**swimsuit** *n.* • Badeanzug, der
I learned to swim at summer camp.
*Ich habe im Sommerlager schwimmen gelernt.*

**swing** [SWING] *n.* • Schaukel, die
There are swings for the children in the park.
*Im Park sind Schaukeln für die Kinder.*

**Switzerland** [SWITsərlənd] *n.* • Schweiz, die
**Swiss (person)** *n.* • Schweizer, der (-in, f.)
**Swiss** *adj.* • schweizerisch
Bern is the capital of Switzerland.
*Bern ist die Hauptstadt der Schweiz.*

# T

**table** [T*EJ*Bl] *n.* • Tisch, der
**tablecloth** *n.* • Tischdecke, die
**to set the table** • den Tisch decken
The table is in the dining room.
*Der Tisch ist im Eßzimmer.*

**tail** [T*EJ*l] *n.* • Schwanz, der
The dog wags his tail when he is happy.
*Der Hund wedelt mit dem Schwanz, wenn er froh ist.*

**tailor** [T*EJ*lər] *n.* • Schneider, der (-in, f.)
The tailor is making a suit.
*Der Schneider macht einen Anzug.*

**take, to** [T*EJ*K] *v.* • nehmen
**to take a bath** • ein Bad nehmen
**to take a test** • eine Prüfung ablegen
**to take a trip** • eine Reise machen
**to take a walk** • einen Spaziergang machen
**to take off (airplane)** • abfliegen
**to take off; to remove** *v.* • absetzen
We took the train at noon.
*Wir nahmen den Mittagszug.*

I took off my hat.
*Ich habe meinen Hut abgesetzt.*

The plane took off at 8 o'clock for Munich.
*Das Flugzeug flog um 8 Uhr nach München ab.*

**tale** [T*EJ*l] *n.* • Geschichte, die
**fairy tale** *n.* • Märchen, das
Grandmother entertained the children with her tales of long ago.
*Großmutter unterhielt die Kinder mit ihren Geschichten von anno dazumal.*

**talk, to** [T*A*WK] *v.* • reden
**talk** *n.* • Gespräch, das
**talkative** *adj.* • gesprächig
The boy talks too much.
*Der Junge redet zuviel.*

**tall** [T*A*WL] *adj.* • groß
He must be tall if he can reach the ceiling.
*Er muß schon groß sein, wenn er die Decke berühren kann.*

**tape (cassette)** [T*EJ*P] *n.* • Cassette, die
**tape (adhesive)** *n.* • Band, das; Klebeband, das
**tape recorder** *n.* • Cassettenrekorder, der
He is listening to a tape of his favorite song.
*Er hört sich eine Cassette mit seinem Lieblingslied an.*

**taste, to** [T*EJ*ST] *v.* • probieren
Taste this cheese! It's really good!
*Probiere diesen Käse! Er ist wirklich gut!*

**taxi** [T*A*Ksie] *n.* • Taxi, das
**taxi stand** • Taxistand, der
We'll take a taxi to the hotel.
*Wir nehmen ein Taxi zum Hotel.*

**tea** [TIE] *n.* • Tee, der
I would like some milk in my tea, please.
*Ich hätte gern etwas Milch in meinen Tee.*

**teach, to** [TIE*TSH*] *v.* • lehren
**teacher** *n.* • Lehrer, der (-in, f.)

My mother teaches high school.
*Meine Mutter lehrt an einem Gymnasium.*

**team** [TIEM] *n.* • Mannschaft, die
Our basketball team has twelve players.
*Unsere Korbballmannschaft hat zwölf Spieler.*

**tear** [TIER] *n.* • Träne, die
She has tears in her eyes.
*Sie hat Tränen in ihren Augen.*

**tear, to** [T*EJ*R] *v.* • zerreißen
Don't tear the paper.
*Zerreiß das Papier nicht!*

**tease, to** [TIEZ] *v.* • necken
Don't tease your sister!
*Necke deine Schwester nicht!*

**teenager** [TIEN*ejdzhər*] *n.* • Teenager, der
His son is a teenager in high school.
*Sein Sohn ist ein Teenager, der zum Gymnasium geht.*

**teeth** [TIE*TH*] *n.* • Zähne, die
The dentist looks at my teeth.
*Der Zahnarzt untersucht meine Zähne.*

**telephone** [TELəfohn] *n.* • Telefon, das
**telephone booth** • Telefonzelle, die
**telephone number** • Telefonnummer, die
The telephone rang five times.
*Das Telefon klingelte fünf Mal.*

**television** [TELə*vizh*ən] *n.* • Fernsehen, das
**television set** • Fernsehgerät, das
**T.V.** *n.* • Fernsehen, das
Do you watch much television at night.
*Siehst du viel Fernsehen am Abend?*

**tell, to** [TEL] *v.* • erzählen
Grandfather tells us a story every night.
*Großvater erzählt uns jeden Abend eine Geschichte.*

**ten** [TEN] *n.; adj.* • zehn
I've lived in this house for ten years.
*Ich wohne seit zehn Jahren in diesem Haus.*

**tennis** [TENəs] *n.* • Tennisspielen, das
**to play tennis** • Tennis spielen
He plays tennis very well.
*Er spielt sehr gut Tennis.*

**tent** [TENT] *n.* • Zelt, das
I like to sleep in a tent.
*Ich schlafe gern in einem Zelt.*

**terrible** [TERibəl] *adj.* • schrecklich
The tornado caused terrible destruction.
*Der Tornado verursachte schreckliche Verwüstungen.*

**test** [TEST] *n.* • Prüfung, die
**to fail a test** • durch eine Prüfung fallen
**to pass a test** • eine Prüfung bestehen
**to take a test** • eine Prüfung ablegen
We have three tests tomorrow!
*Wir haben morgen drei Prüfungen!*

**thank, to** [*TH*ANGK] *v.* • danken
**thank you** • Vielen Dank!
They thank the hostess before leaving.
*Sie danken der Gastgeberin, bevor sie gehen.*

**that** [*DH*AT] *adj.* • jener, -e, -es
**that is** • das ist
**that's all** • das ist alles
**that's too bad!** • das ist schade!
Please pass me that book over there.
*Geben Sie mir bitte jenes Buch dort drüben.*

**the** [*DH*ə] *def. art.* • der; die; das; die (pl.)
The books are on the table.
*Die Bücher sind auf dem Tisch.*

**theater** [*TH*IEətər] *n.* • Theater, das
**movie theater** • Kino, das
We see a play at the theater.
*Wir sehen uns ein Schauspiel im Theater an.*

**their** [*DH*E*J*R] *pron.* • ihr, ihre
Is this their own house or do they rent it?
*Ist dies ihr eigenes Haus oder mieten sie es?*

**them** [*DH*EM] *pron.* • ihnen
**to them** • ihnen
I told them all to be quiet.
*Ich habe ihnen allen gesagt, ruhig zu sein.*

**then** [*DH*EN] *adv.* • dann
We'll get home; then we'll make dinner.
*Wir fahren nach Hause; dann machen wir Abendbrot.*

**there** [*DH*E*J*R] *adv.* • da
**down there** • da unten
**over there** • da drüben
**there is; there are** • es gibt
**up there** • da oben
Hello, is your father there?
*Hallo, ist dein Vater da?*

**these** [*DH*IE*Z*] *adj.* • diese
I recognize these children.
*Ich erkenne diese Kinder.*

**they** [*DH*E*J*] *pron.* • sie
Where are they?
*Wo sind sie?*

**thick** [*TH*IK] *adj.* • dick
This is a thick blanket.
*Dies ist eine dicke Decke.*

**thief** [*TH*IEF] *n.* • Dieb, der
The thief escaped through the window.
*Der Dieb entkam durch das Fenster.*

**thin** [*TH*IN] *adj.* • dünn
The giraffe has thin legs.
*Die Giraffe hat dünne Beine.*

**thing** [*TH*ING] *n.* • Ding, das
**How are things?** • Wie geht's?
**something** *pron.* • etwas
I have too many things to do.
*Ich muß zu viele Dinge erledigen.*

**think** [*TH*INGK] *v.* • denken
**to think about** • nachdenken über
**to think of** • denken an
I think we are late!
*Ich denke, wir kommen zu spät!*

**thirst** [*TH*ə*R*ST] *n.* • Durst, der
**to be thirsty** • durstig sein; durst haben
May I have some water? I am thirsty.
*Kann ich etwas Wasser haben? Ich bin durstig.*

**thirteen** [*th*ə*r*t-TIEN] *n.; adj.* • dreizehn
There are thirteen candles on the cake.
*Auf dem Kuchen sind dreizehn Kerzen.*

**thirty** [*TH*ə*R*die] *n.; adj.* • dreißig
There are thirty days in September.
*Der September hat dreißig Tage.*

**this** [*DH*IS] *adj.* • dieser
**this is** • dieses ist
This man is my father.
*Dieser Mann ist mein Vater.*

**those** [*DH*OHZ] *adj.* • jene, -r, -s
**those are** • das sind

I want those earrings.
*Ich will jene Ohrringe.*

**thousand** [*TH*AUzənd] *n.; adj.* • tausend
My brother has a thousand dollars cash!
*Mein Bruder hat tausend Dollar in bar.*

**thread** [*TH*RED] *n.* • Faden, der
You need thread to sew.
*Man braucht einen Faden, um zu nähen.*

**three** [*TH*RIE] *n.; adj.* • drei
The young child is three years old.
*Das kleine Kind ist drei Jahre alt.*

**throat** [*TH*ROHT] *n.* • Hals, der
Richard has a sore throat.
*Richard hat eine Halsentzündung.*

**throw, to** [*TH*ROH] *v.* • werfen
Throw the ball against the wall!
*Werf den Ball an die Wand.*

**thunder** [*TH*əNdər] *n.* • Donner, der
My little sister is afraid of thunder.
*Meine kleine Schwester hat Angst vor Donner.*

**Thursday** [*TH*ə*RZ*de*j*] *n.* • Donnerstag, der
The class meets on Tuesday and Thursday.
*Die Klasse trifft sich am Dienstag und am Donnerstag.*

**ticket** [TIKit] *n.* • Eintrittskarte, die
**ticket office** • Kartenschalter, der
Do you have the tickets for the zoo?
*Hast du die Entrittskarten für den Zoo?*

**tie** [TEI] *n.* • Krawatte, die
Do you like to wear a tie?
*Trägst du gern eine Krawatte?*

**tiger** [TEIgər] *n.* • Tiger, der
There are some tigers at the zoo.
*Im Zoo sind Tiger.*

**tight** [TEIT] *adj.* • eng
These shoes are too tight.
*Diese Schuhe sind zu eng.*

**time** [TEIM] *n.* • Zeit, die
**a long time** • eine lange Zeit
**next time** • nächstes Mal
**on time** • pünktlich
**two at a time** • zwei auf einmal
**What time is it?** • Wie spät ist es?
How much time do we have?
*Wieviel Zeit haben wir?*

**tip** [TIP] *n.* • Trinkgeld, das
We leave a tip for the waitress.
*Wir lassen der Kellnerin ein Trinkgeld.*

**tire** [TEIR] *n.* • Reifen, der
The car has a flat tire.
*Das Auto hat einen platten Reifen.*

**tired** [TEIRD] *adj.* • müde
I am tired after the game.
*Ich bin müde nach dem Spiel.*

**to** [T*OO*] *prep.* • zu
I am going to my sister's today.
*Ich gehe heute zu meiner Schwester.*

**toast** [TOHST] *n.* • Toastbrot, das
Helen puts butter on her toast.
*Helen streicht Butter auf ihr Toastbrot.*

**today** [tuD*EJ*] *adv., n.* • heute
Today is my birthday.
*Heute ist mein Geburtstag.*

**toe** [TOH] *n.* • Zeh, der
My toe hurts from the tight shoes.
*Mein Zeh schmerzt von den engen Schuhen.*

**together** [tuGE*DH*ər] *adv.* • zusammen
The two friends sit together.
*Die zwei Freunde sitzen zusammen.*

**toilet** [TEUlət] *n.* • Toilette
The toilet is at the end of the hallway.
*Die Toilette ist am Ende des Ganges.*

**tomato** [tuM*EJ*toh] *n.* • Tomate, die
Tomatoes taste good with basil.
*Tomaten schmecken gut mit Basilikum.*

**tomorrow** [tuMAHRoh] *adv.* • morgen
**day after tomorrow** • übermorgen
Where are we going tomorrow?
*Wohin gehen wir morgen?*

**tongue** [TəNG] *n.* • Zunge, die
The dog's tongue is pink.
*Die Zunge des Hundes ist rosa.*

**too** [T*OO*] *adv.* • auch
Monique wants to come, too.
*Monika möchte auch kommen.*

**tooth** [T*OOTH*] *n.* • Zahn, der
**to have a toothache** • Zahnschmerzen haben
**toothbrush** *n.* • Zahnbürste, die
**toothpaste** *n.* • Zahnpasta, die
The dentist fixed my sore tooth.
*Der Zahnarzt heilte meinen entzündeten Zahn.*

**tornado** [t*aw*rN*EJ*doh] *n.* • Tornado, der
There are often tornadoes in the summer.
*Im Sommer gibt es oft Tornados.*

**touch, to** [TəTSH] *v.* • anfassen
Don't touch the dog! He bites!
*Faß den Hund nicht an! Er beißt!*

**tour** [TOOR] *n.* • Ausflug, der
**tourism** *n.* • Tourismus, der
**tourist** *n.* • Tourist, der (-in, f.)
We are taking a tour of Berlin.
*Wir machen einen Ausflug durch Berlin.*

**toward** [TWAWRD] *prep.* • entgegen
The dog is coming toward me.
*Der Hund kommt mir entgegen.*

**towel** [TAUəl] *n.* • Handtuch, das
**bath towel** • Badetuch, das
I need a dry towel.
*Ich brauche ein trockenes Handtuch.*

**tower** [TAUər] *n.* • Turm, der
The Eiffel Tower is very famous.
*Der Eiffelturm ist sehr berühmt.*

**town** [TAUN] *n.* • Stadt, die
**in town** • in der Stadt
**town hall** • Stadthalle, die
This town has only one store.
*Diese Stadt hat nur einen Laden.*

**toy** [TEU] *n.* • Spielzeug, das
The child wants toys for his birthday.
*Das Kind möchte Spielzeug zu seinem Geburtstag.*

**traffic** [TRAFik] *n.* • Verkehr, der
Watch out for the traffic when you cross the street!
*Achte auf den Verkehr, wenn du die Straße überquerst!*

**train** [TREJN] *n.* • Zug, der
**train station** • Bahnhof, der

What time does the train arrive?
*Um wieviel Uhr kommt der Zug an?*

**translate, to** [TRANZl*ej*t] *v.* • übersetzen
He translated an English text into German.
*Er übersetzte einen englischen Text ins Deutsche.*

**travel, to** [TR*AV*əl] *v.* • reisen
**traveler** *n.* • Reisende, der (die, f.)
I travel with my family every summer.
*Ich reise jeden Sommer mit meiner Familie.*

**tree** [TRIE] *n.* • Baum, der
Let's go under the shade of this tree.
*Laßt uns in den Schatten dieses Baumes gehen.*

**trial** [TREIəl] *n.* • Verhandlung, die
The judge set the trial for November 8.
*Der Richter legte die Verhandlung für den 8. November fest.*

**trip** [TRIP] *n.* • Reise, die
**on a trip** • auf einer Reise
**to take a trip** • eine Reise machen
We are leaving on a trip.
*Wir brechen zu einer Reise auf.*

**trouble** [TRƏBl] *n.* • Ärger, der
He is having trouble with his car.
*Er hat Ärger mit seinem Auto.*

**trousers** [TRAUzə*rz*] *n.* • Hose, die
Are these trousers too long?
*Ist diese Hose zu lang?*

**truck** [TRƏK] *n.* • Lastwagen, der
My uncle drives a truck.
*Mein Onkel fährt einen Lastwagen.*

**true** [TR*OO*] *adj.* • wahr
**truly** *adv.* • wahrhaft
Is this story true or false?
*Ist diese Geschichte wahr oder falsch?*

**trumpet** [TRəMpət] *n.* • Trompete, die
My friend plays the trumpet.
*Mein Freund spielt Trompete.*

**trunk** [TRəNGK] *n.* • Truhe, die
Let's open Grandmother's old trunk!
*Laßt uns Großmutters alte Truhe öffnen!*

**truth** [TR*OOTH*] *n.* • Wahrheit, die
Is she telling the truth?
*Erzählt sie die Wahrheit?*

**try, to** [TREI] *v.* • versuchen
I am trying to write a letter in German.
*Ich versuche, einen Brief auf deutsch zu schreiben.*

**Tuesday** [T*OOZ*d*e*j] *n.* • Dienstag, der
Tickets are half price on Tuesday.
*Die Karten sind am Dienstag für den halben Preis zu haben.*

**tuna** [T*OO*nə] *n.* • Thunfisch, der
Buy a can of tuna to make sandwiches.
*Kaufe eine Dose Thunfisch, damit wir belegte Brote machen können.*

**turkey** [Tə*R*kie] *n.* • Truthahn, der
We eat turkey on holidays.
*Wir essen an Feiertagen Truthahn.*

**turn, to** [Tə*R*N] *v.* • drehen
**to turn off** • abdrehen
**to turn on** • andrehen
**turn** *n.* • Biegung, die

Turn the meat over and cook the other side.
*Drehe das Fleisch um und brate es auf der anderen Seit.*

**turtle** [TƏ*R*Tl] *n.* • Schilkröte, die
We saw a giant turtle at the zoo.
*Wir sahen eine riesige Schildkröte im Zoo.*

**T.V.** [TIE *V*IE] *n.* • Fernsehen, das
  **T.V. channel** • Fernsehkanal, der
  **T.V. news** • Fernsehnachrichten, die
At what time do you watch T.V.?
*Wann um wieviel Uhr siehst du Fernsehen?*

**twelve** [T*W*ELV] *n.; adj.* • zwölf
My friend is twelve years old.
*Mein Freund ist zwölf Jahre alt.*

**twenty** [T*W*ENtie] *n.; adj.* • zwanzig
It takes twenty minutes to go downtown.
*Es dauert zwanzig Minuten, um in die Stadt zu gehen.*

**twice** [T*W*EIS] *adv.* • zweimal
He eats only twice a day.
*Er ißt nur zweimal am Tag.*

**twin** [T*W*IN] *n.* • Zwilling, der (die, f.)
My sister has twins.
*Meine Schwester hat Zwillinge.*

**two** [T*OO*] *n.; adj.* • zwei
Our family owns two cars.
*Unsere Familie besitzt zwei Autos.*

**type, to** [TEIP] *v.* • tippen
  **typewriter** *n.* • Schreibmaschine, die
  **typist** *n.* • Typist, der (-in, f.)
I learned to type when I was 16 years old.
*Ich habe tippen gelernt, als ich 16 Jahre alt war.*

**typical** [TIPikəl] *adj.* • typisch
**typically** *adv.* • typisch
Cold weather is not typical of summer.
*Kaltes Wetter ist nicht typisch für den Sommer.*

# U

**ugly** [əGlie] *adj.* • häßlich
Purple is an ugly color for a house.
*Purpur ist eine häßliche Farbe für ein Haus.*

**umbrella** [əmBRELə] *n.* • Regenschirm, der
It's raining! Where is the umbrella?
*Es regnet! Wo ist der Regenschirm?*

**unbelievable** [ənbiLIEVəbəl] *adj.* • unglaublich
That's an unbelievable story.
*Das ist eine unglaubliche Geschichte.*

**uncle** [əNGkəl] *n.* • Onkel, der
Where do your aunt and uncle live?
*Wo wohnen deine Tante und dein Onkel?*

**uncomfortable** [ənKəMfə*r*təbəl] *adj.* • unbequem
This chair is uncomfortable.
*Dieser Stuhl ist unbequem.*

**under** [əNdə*r*] *prep.* • unter
The dog is under the table.
*Der Hund ist unter dem Tisch.*

**understand, to** [əndə*r*STAND] *v.* • verstehen
I understand German, but I can't write it.
*Ich verstehe Deutsch, aber ich kann es nicht schreiben.*

**unexpected** [ənekSPEKtəd] *adj.* • unerwartet
This invitation is unexpected.
*Diese Einladung kommt unerwartet.*

**unfortunately** [ənFAWRtshənətlie] *adv.* • leider
Unfortunately, we have no car.
*Leider haben wir kein Auto.*

**unhappy** [ənHAPie] *adj.* • unglücklich
She is unhappy when she is alone.
*Sie ist unglücklich, wenn sie allein ist.*

**united** [jooNEItəd] *adj.* • vereint
**to unite** *v.* • vereinigen, vereinen
**United Nations** *n.* • Vereinten Nationen, die
**United States** *n.* • Vereinigten Staaten, die
We are united in our desire for peace.
*Wir sind vereint in unserem Wunsch nach Frieden.*

**university** [jooniVƏRsətie] *n.* • Universität, die
There is a university in my home town.
*In meiner Heimatstadt gibt es eine Universität.*

**unknown** [ənNOHN] *adj.* • unbekannt
The thief's identity was unknown.
*Die Identität des Diebes war unbekannt.*

**until** [ənTIL] *prep.* • bis
I study until four o'clock.
*Ich lerne bis vier Uhr.*

**unusual** [ənJOOzhooəl] *adj.* • ungewöhnlich
Garlic is an unusual flavor for ice cream.
*Knoblauch ist eine ungewöhnliche Geschmackssorte für Eis.*

**up** [əP] *adv.* • hinauf
**to go up** • hinaufgehen
**upstairs** *adv.* • oben
The cat climbed up the tree and got stuck.
*Die Katze kletterte auf den Baum hinauf und blieb stecken.*

Our bedrooms are upstairs.
*Unsere Schlafzimmer sind oben.*

**us** [əS] *pron.* • uns
This present is for both of us.
*Dieses Geschenk ist für uns beide.*

**use, to** [J*OOZ*] *v.* • benutzen
**used car** • Gebrauchtwagen, der
**useful** *adj.* • nützlich
**useless** *adj.* • nutzlos
I used the dictionary to look up words.
*Ich benutzte das Lexikon, um Wörter nachzuschlagen.*

**usual** [J*OOzhoo*əl] *adj.* • gewöhnlich
This isn't my usual seat.
*Dieses ist nicht mein gewöhnlicher Platz.*

# V

**vacation** [*vej*K*EJ*SHən] *n.* • Ferien, die
**on vacation** • in Ferien
**to take a vacation** • Ferien machen
We take a vacation every summer.
*Wir machen jeden Sommer Ferien.*

**vacuum cleaner** [*VA*Kj*oo*m KLIEn*ər*] *n.* • Staubsauger, der
**to vacuum** *v.* • staubsaugen
The vacuum cleaner gets the dirt out of the rugs.
*Der Staubsauger bekommt den Schmutz aus den Teppichen.*

Who vacuums at your house?
*Wer saugt bei euch Staub?*

**valley** [*VA*Lie] *n.* • Tal, das
There is a pretty valley between the mountains.
*Es gibt ein hübsches Tal in den Bergen.*

**van** [*VAN*] *n.* • Transporter, der
We take our own van to deliver the merchandise.
*Wir benutzen unseren eigenen Transporter, um die Ware auszuliefern.*

**vanilla** [*v*əNILə] *n.* • Vanille, die
Grandmother wants some vanilla ice cream.
*Großmutter möchte etwas Vanilleeis.*

**vase** [*VEJ*S] *n.* • Vase, die
Put the flowers in this vase.
*Stell die Blumen in die Vase.*

**vegetable** [*V*E*DZH*təbəl] *n.* • Gemüse, das
Which vegetables do you like best?
*Welches Gemüse ißt du am liebsten?*

**very** [*V*ERie] *adv.* • sehr
**very much** • sehr viel
This soup is very good!
*Diese Suppe ist sehr gut!*

**veterinarian** [*v*etə*r*əNERie-ən] *n.* • Tierarzt, der (-in, f.)
Veterinarians take care of animals.
*Tierärzte kümmern sich um Tiere.*

**video cassette recorder (VCR)** [*V*IDieoh kəSET riK*AW*RDə*r*] *n.* • Videorekorder, der
**video cassette** *n.* • Videocassette, die
We watched the movie on the VCR.
*Wir haben uns den Film auf dem Videorekorder angesehen.*

**view** [*V*JOO] *n.* • Blick, der
There is a fine view from the mountain top.
*Man hat einen guten Blick vom Berggipfel.*

**village** [*V*ILi*dzh*] *n.* • Dorf, das
The church is in the center of the village.
*Die Kirche ist in der Dorfmitte.*

**violet** [*V*EIələt] *n.* • Veilchen, das
The little girl is picking some violets.
*Das kleine Mädchen pflückt ein paar Veilchen.*

**violin** [*v*eiəLIN] *n.* • Geige, die
Do you like violin music?
*Magst du Geigenmusik?*

**visit, to** [*V*IZit] *v.* • besichtigen
**to visit a person** • besuchen
**visit** *n.* • Besuch, der
**visitor** *n.* • Besucher, der (-in, f.)
We are visiting a castle on the Rhine.
*Wir besichtigen ein Schloß am Rhein.*

**voice** [*V*EUS] *n.* • Stimme, die
The singer has a beautiful voice.
*Der Sänger hat eine schöne Stimme.*

**volcano** [*vaw*lK*EJ*noh] *n.* • Vulkan, der
There are volcanoes on this island.
*Auf dieser Insel gibt es Vulkane.*

**volleyball** [*V*AHLieb*aw*l] *n.* • Volleyballspiel, das
**to play volleyball** • Volleyball spielen
We played volleyball on the beach.
*Wir spielten am Strand Volleyball.*

**vote, to** [*V*OHT] *v.* • wählen
Did you vote in the last election?
*Hast du bei der letzten Wahl gewählt?*

# W

**waist** [*WEJ*ST] *n.* • Taille, die
She wears belts to show off her small waist.
*Sie trägt Gürtel, um ihre enge Taille zu zeigen.*

**wait, to** [*WEJ*T] *v.* • warten
**waiting room** • Wartezimmer, das
I'm going to wait in the anteroom.
*Ich warte im Vorzimmer.*

**waiter; waitress (f.)** [*WEJ*tər; *WEJ*trəs] *n.* • Kellner, der; Kellnerin, die
We gave a tip to the waiter.
*Wir haben dem Kellner ein Trinkgeld gegeben.*

**wake (up), to** [*WEJ*K] *v.* • aufwachen
Patrick wakes up at 7:00 a.m.
*Patrick wacht um 7 Uhr auf.*

**walk** [*WAW*K] *n.* • Spaziergang, der
**take a walk** • spazierengehen
**to walk** *v.* • gehen (spazieren)
We wanted to take a walk.
*Wir wollten einen Spaziergang machen.*

**wall** [*WAW*L] *n.* • Wand, die
There is a mirror hanging on the wall.
*An der Wand hängt ein Spiegel.*

**wallet** [*WAH*Lət] *n.* • Brieftasche, die
He puts money in his wallet.
*Er steckt Geld in seine Brieftasche.*

**want, to** [*W*AHNT] *v.* • wollen
We want to come with you.
*Wir wollen mit dir kommen.*

**war** [*WAW*R] *n.* • Krieg, der
These people are demonstrating against war.
*Diese Leute demonstrieren gegen den Krieg.*

**warm** [*WAW*RM] *adj.* • warm
**it is warm** • es ist warm
**to be warm (person)** • warmherzig sein
It was a nice, warm Summer day.
*Es war ein schöner, warmer Sommertag.*

**wash, to** [*WAW*SH] *v.* • waschen
**to wash oneself** • sich waschen
**washing machine** • Waschmaschine, die
We must wash the dirty car.
*Wir müssen das schmutzige Auto waschen.*

**watch, to** [*W*AH*TSH*] *v.* • ansehen
**to watch over** • aufpassen
**watch** *n.* • Uhr, die
We are watching a new show on T.V.
*Wir sehen uns eine neue Show im Fernsehen an.*

Do you wear your watch on your left wrist?
*Trägst du deine Uhr auf dem linken Arm?*

**water** [*WAW*Tə*r*] *n.* • Wasser, das
**mineral water** • Mineralwasser, das
I'm thirsty. May I have a glass of water?
*Ich bin durstig. Darf ich ein Glas Wasser haben?*

**wave** [*WEJV*] *n.* • Welle, die
Huge waves came ashore in the storm.
*Riesige Wellen schlugen im Sturm an Land.*

**way** [*WEJ*] *n.* • Weg, der
**in this way** • auf diese Weise

We are going the same way.
*Wir haben denselben Weg.*

**weak** [*W*IEK] *adj.* • schwach
The baby birds are weak.
*Die jungen Vögel sind schwach.*

**wealthy** [*W*EL*th*ie] *adj.* • wohlhabend
This wealthy family is very generous.
*Diese wohlhabende Familie ist sehr großzügig.*

**wear, to** [*WEJ*R] *v.* • tragen
He is wearing his blue sweater.
*Er trägt seinen blauen Pullover.*

**weather** [*W*E*DH*ər] *n.* • Wetter, das
What is the weather like today?
*Wie ist das Wetter heute?*

**wedding** [*W*EDing] *n.* • Hochzeit, die
There is a wedding at the church today.
*In der Kirche findet heute eine Hochzeit statt.*

**Wednesday** [*W*ENZd*ej*] *n.* • Mittwoch, der
Wednesday is the third day of the work week.
*Mittwoch ist der dritte Tag der Arbeitswoche.*

**week** [*W*IEK] *n.* • Woche, die
**weekend** *n.* • Wochenende, das
What are the days of the week in German?
*Wie heißen die Wochentage auf Deutsch?*

**weigh, to** [*WEJ*] *v.* • wiegen
**to gain weight** • zunehmen
**to lose weight** • abnehmen
**weight** *n.* • Gewicht, das
The grocer weighs the fruit.
*Der Lebensmittelhändler wiegt das Obst.*

**welcome** [*W*ELkəm] *n.* • Willkommen, das
**you're welcome** • du bist willkommen; bitte (schön)!
Welcome to our home!
*Willkommen bei uns zu Hause!*

**well** [*W*EL] *adv.* • gut
**as well as** • so gut wie
**I am well.** • Es geht mir gut.
**well-behaved** *adj.* • gut erzogen
Doreen plays the piano very well.
*Doreen spielt sehr gut Klavier.*

**west** [*W*EST] *n.* • Westen, der
California is in the west of the U.S.
*Kalifornien liegt im Westen der U.S.A.*

**wet** [*W*ET] *adj.* • naß
My hair is still wet from the shower.
*Meine Haare sind noch naß von der Dusche.*

**what** [*W*əT] *pron.* • welche, -r, -s
**What (did you say)?** • Was (hast du gesagt)?
What street are we supposed to take?
*Welche Straße sollen wir nehmen?*

**wheat** [*W*IET] *n.* • Weizen, der
The bread is made with wheat flour.
*Das Brot ist aus Weizenmehl gemacht.*

**wheel** [*W*IEL] *n.* • Rad, das
**steering wheel** • Steuerrad, das
**wheelbarrow** *n.* • Schubkarre, die
**wheel chair** *n.* • Rollstuhl, der
A bicycle has two wheels.
*Ein Fahrrad hat zwei Räder.*

**when** [*W*EN] *adv.; conj.* • wann
Tell me when you want to leave.
*Sag mir, wann du gehen willst.*

**where** [*WEJ*R] *adv.* • wo
**anywhere; wherever** *adv.* • irgendwo; wo (hin) immer
**where . . . from (how)** • woher
Where are my shoes?
*Wo sind meine Schuhe?*

How do you know that?
*Woher weißt du das?*

**whether** [*W*E*DH*ər] *conj.* • ob
John doesn't know whether he can go or not.
*Johann weiß nicht, ob er gehen kann oder nicht.*

**which** [*W*I*TSH*] *adj.* • welche, -r, -s
Which book do you want?
*Welches Buch willst du?*

**while** [*W*EIL] *conj.* • während
She plays while I work.
*Sie spielt, während ich arbeite.*

**whistle, to** [*W*ISəl] *v.* • pfeifen
I am teaching my brother to whistle.
*Ich bringe meinem Bruder bei zu pfeifen.*

**white** [*W*EIT] *adj.* • weiß
The paper is white.
*Das Papier ist weiß.*

**who** [H*OO*] *pron.* • wer
Who wants to play soccer?
*Wer will Fußball spielen?*

**whole** [HOHL] *adj.* • ganze, -r, -s
He is going to stay with us a whole month.
*Er wird einen ganzen Monat bei uns bleiben.*

**whom** [H*OO*M] *pron.* • den; die; das
The man whom we saw at the station teaches in my school.
*Der Mann, den wir am Bahnhof sahen, unterrichtet an meiner Schule.*

**why** [*W*EI] *adv.* • warum
Why are you so sad?
*Warum bist du so traurig?*

**wide** [*W*EID] *adj.* • breit
The Grand Canyon is very wide.
*Der Grand Canyon ist sehr breit.*

**wife** [*W*EIF] *n.* • (Ehe)frau, die
His wife's name is Madeleine.
*Seine (Ehe)frau heißt Madeleine.*

**wild** [*W*EILD] *adj.* • wild
There are many wild animals in the jungle.
*Es gibt viele wilde Tiere im Dschungel.*

**win, to** [*W*IN] *v.* • gewinnen
You will win often if your team plays well together.
*Ihr werdet oft gewinnen, wenn eure Mannschaft gut zusammenspielt.*

**wind** [*W*IND] *n.* • Wind, der
**windmill** *n.* • Windmühle, die
The wind is blowing from the north.
*Der Wind weht von Norden her.*

**window** [*W*INdoh] *n.* • Fenster, das
**store window** • Schaufenster, das
**window display** • Fensterauslage, die
**window pane** • Fensterscheibe, die
Look out the window and see if he's here.
*Schau aus dem Fenster und sieh, ob er da ist.*

**wine** [*W*EIN] *n.* • Wein, der
This red wine comes from France.
*Dieser rote Wein kommt aus Frankreich.*

**wing** [*W*ING] *n.* • Flügel, der
The bird flies with its wings.
*Der Vogel fliegt mit seinen Flügeln.*

**winter** [*W*INtər] *n.* • Winter, der
In winter we go skiing.
*Im Winter gehen wir Ski laufen.*

**wise** [*W*EIZ] *adj.* • weise
We asked advice of the wise old man.
*Wir fragten den weisen, alten Mann um Rat.*

**wish, to** [*W*ISH] *v.* • wünschen
**best wishes** • gute Wünsche
**wish** *n.* • Wunsch, der
What do you wish for Christmas?
*Was wünschst du dir zu Weihnachten?*

**with** [*WITH*] *prep.* • mit
**to go with** • mitgehen
**with care** • sorgfältig
**without** *prep.* • ohne
Joelle is going dancing with her friends.
*Joelle geht mit ihren Freunden tanzen.*

**wolf** [*W*ULF] *n.* • Wolf, der
Are you afraid of wolves?
*Hast du Angst vor Wölfen?*

**woman** [*W*UMən] *n.* • Frau, die
This woman is my teacher.
*Diese Frau ist meine Lehrerin.*

**wonderful** [*W*əNdərful] *adj.* • wunderbar
My mother is a wonderful cook.
*Meine Mutter ist eine wunderbare Köchin.*

**wood** [*W*UD] *n.* • Holz, das
**wooden** *adj.* • aus Holz; hölzern
**woods** *n. pl.* • Wald, der
The furniture is made of wood.
*Die Möbel sind aus Holz gemacht.*

**wool** [*W*UL] *n.* • Wolle, die
**woolen** *adj.* • aus Wolle; wollen
My aunt knitted me a sweater of pure wool.
*Meine Tante hat mir einen Pullover aus reiner Wolle gestrickt.*

**word** [*W*Ə*R*D] *n.* • Wort, das
I looked up the word in the dictionary.
*Ich habe das Wort im Lexikon nachgeschlagen.*

**work** [*W*Ə*R*K] *n.* • Arbeit, die
**to work** *v.* • arbeiten
**to work (on something); to process** *v.* • bearbeiten
The scientists do important work.
*Die Wissenschaftler leisten wichtige Arbeit.*

**world** [*W*Ə*R*LD] *n.* • Welt, die
Someday I want to travel around the world.
*Eines Tages möchte ich um die Welt reisen.*

**worm** [*W*Ə*R*M] *n.* • Wurm, der
**earthworm** *n.* • Regenwurm, der
We use the worms for bait.
*Wir benutzen die Würmer als Köder.*

**worried** [*W*Ə*R*ied] *adj.* • besorgt
Paul is worried about his grades.
*Paul ist um seine Noten besorgt.*

**write, to** [REIT] *v.* • schreiben
Janine is writing a letter to her pen pal.
*Janine schreibt einen Brief an ihre Brieffreundin.*

**wrong** [RAWNG] *adj.* • falsch
**to be wrong** • sich irren
**What's wrong?** • Was ist los?
Your addition here is wrong.
*Deine Addition hier ist falsch.*

# X

**xylophone** [ZEIləfohn] *n.* • Xylophon, das
A xylophone is played with a wooden mallet.
*Das Xylophon wird mit einem Holzklöppel gespielt.*

# Y

**year** [JIER] *n.* • Jahr, das
**New Year's Day** • Neujahrstag, der
I am in my first year of German.
*Ich lerne im ersten Jahr Deutsch.*

**yellow** [JELoh] *adj.* • gelb
The school bus is yellow.
*Der Schulbus ist gelb.*

**yes** [JES] *adv.* • ja
Yes, I would like some dessert!
*Ja, ich möchte gern etwas Nachtisch!*

**yet** [JET] *adv.* • noch nicht
Aren't they here yet?
*Sind sie noch nicht hier?*

**you** [JOO] *pron.* • dich, Sie, euch, du
**you never know** • Man weiß nie
This present is for you.
*Dieses Geschenk ist für dich (Sie, euch).*

You can't do that!
*Du kannst nicht tun!*

**young** [JəNG] *adj.* • jung
**young man; youth** *n.* • Jugendliche, der (die); Jugend, die
He is too young to drive.
*Er ist zu jung, um Auto zu fahren.*

**your** [JUR] *adj.* • dein, Ihr, euer
Where is your notebook?
*Wo ist dein (Ihr, euer) Heft?*

# Z

**zebra** [ZIEBrə] *n.* • Zebra, das
Zebras have black and white stripes.
*Zebras haben schwarze und weiße Streifen.*

**zero** [ZIERoh] *n.* • null
Two minus two is zero.
*Zwei minus zwei ist null.*

**zoo** [ZOO] *n.* • Zoo, der
You see all sorts of animals at the zoo.
*Man kann alle möglichen Arten von Tieren im Zoo sehen.*

# Appendices/*die Anhänge*

## German Names—*die Vornamen*

### Masculine Names

|  |  |
|---|---|
| Andrew | *Andreas* |
| Anthony | *Anton* |
| Arthur | *Artur* |
| Bernard | *Bernhard* |
| Charles | *Karl* |
| Clement | *Klemens* |
| Conrad | *Konrad* |
| Cyril | *Zyrillus* |
| Derrick | *Dietrich* |
| Edward | *Eduard* |
| Eric | *Erich* |
| Ernest | *Ernst* |
| Eugene | *Eugen* |
| Francis, Frank | *Franz* |
| Frederick | *Friedrich* |
| Geoffrey | *Gottfried* |
| Gerald | *Gerhard* |
| Gregory | *Gregor* |
| Gus, Gustavus | *Gustel, Gustav* |
| Guy | *Guido* |
| Harry | *Heinz* |
| Henry | *Heinrich* |
| Hugh | *Hugo* |
| Jack | *Hans* |
| Jacob | *Jakob* |
| Jasper | *Kasper* |
| Jerome | *Hieronymus* |
| John | *Johann* |
| Johnny | *Hänsel* |
| Lawrence | *Lorenz* |
| Leonard | *Leonhard* |
| Lewis, Louis | *Ludwig* |
| Lucas | *Lukas* |
| Mark | *Markus* |
| Matthew | *Mathäus, Mathias* |
| Maurice | *Moritz* |
| Nick | *Klaus* |
| Percival | *Parzival* |
| Puck | *Kobold* |
| Ralph | *Rudolf* |
| Reginald | *Reinhold* |
| Reynard | *Reinhard* |
| Robin | *Robert* |
| Rodney | *Roderich* |
| Roger | *Rüdiger* |
| Rupert | *Ruprecht* |
| Samson | *Simson* |
| Timothy | *Timotheus* |
| Vincent | *Vinzenz* |
| William | *Wilhelm* |

### Feminine Names

|  |  |
|---|---|
| Amelia | *Amalia* |
| Anne | *Anna* |
| Belle | *Anabel* |
| Bessie | *Betti* |
| Bridget | *Brigitte* |
| Carrie | *Lina* |
| Catherine | *Katharine* |
| Cecilia | *Cäcilie* |
| Connie | *Stanze* |
| Constance | *Konstanze* |
| Daisy | *Grete* |
| Dolly | *Dörthe* |
| Eleanor, Leonora | *Lenore* |
| Emily | *Emilia* |
| Gertie | *Trude* |
| Gillian | *Juliane* |
| Harriet | *Jettchen* |
| Helen | *Helena* |
| Isabel | *Isabella* |
| Jane, Joan | *Johanna* |

**Feminine Names (continued)**

| | | | |
|---|---|---|---|
| Janet | *Hannchen* | Maud | *Tilde* |
| Jenny | *Hannele* | Millicent | *Melisande* |
| Jessica | *Jetta* | Molly | *Mariechen* |
| Kate | *Kättchen* | Peggy | *Grete* |
| Kitty | *Katti* | Phoebe | *Luna* |
| Laura | *Lore* | Rachel | *Rahel* |
| Lilian | *Lilli* | Rose | *Rosa* |
| Lizzie | *Liesel* | Rosemary | *Rosemarie* |
| Lottie | *Lotte* | Sheba | *Saba* |
| Louisa, Louise | *Luise* | Sibyl | *Sibylle* |
| | | Sophia | *Sophi* |
| Lucy | *Luzie* | Susan, Suzanne | *Susanne* |
| Madeline | *Magdalene* | | |
| Madge | *Magda* | Theresa | *Therese* |
| Maggie | *Gretchen* | Tilly | *Thilde* |
| Maryann | *Marianne* | Trixy | *Beate* |

## Family Members—*die Familienmitglieder*

| | |
|---|---|
| parents | *die Eltern* |
| mother, mom | *die Mutter, Mutti* |
| father, dad | *der Vater, Vati* |
| son; daughter | *der Sohn; die Tochter* |
| brother; sister | *der Bruder; die Schwester* |
| grandmother; grandfather | *die Großmutter; der Großvater* |
| grandson; granddaughter | *der Enkel; die Enkelin* |
| uncle; aunt | *der Onkel; die Tante* |
| nephew; niece | *der Neffe; die Nichte* |
| cousin | *der Vetter (Cousin); die Cousine* |
| father-in-law; stepfather | *der Schwiegervater; der Stiefvater* |
| mother-in-law; stepmother | *die Schwiegermutter; die Stiefmutter* |
| brother-in-law; stepbrother | *der Schwager; der Stiefbruder* |
| sister-in-law; stepsister | *die Schwägerin; die Stiefschwester* |
| son-in-law; stepson | *der Schwiegersohn; der Stiefsohn* |
| daughter-in-law; stepdaughter | *die Schwiegertochter; die Stieftochter* |

## The Body—*der Körper*

| | | | |
|---|---|---|---|
| ankle | *der Fußknöchel* | hand | *die Hand* |
| arm | *der Arm* | head | *der Kopf* |
| back | *der Rücken* | heart | *das Herz* |
| beard | *der Bart* | hips | *die Hüften* |
| blood | *das Blut* | knee | *das Knie* |
| bone | *der Knochen* | leg | *das Bein* |
| buttocks | *die Hinterbacke* | lips | *die Lippen* |
| cheek | *die Backe* | mouth | *der Mund* |
| chest | *die Brust* | muscle | *die Muskel* |
| chin | *das Kin* | mustache | *der Schnurrbart* |
| ear | *das Ohr* | neck | *der Hals* |
| elbow | *der Ellbogen* | nose | *die Nase* |
| eye | *das Auge* | shoulder | *die Schulter* |
| face | *das Gesicht* | skin | *die Haut* |
| finger | *der Finger* | stomach | *der Magen* |
| fingernail | *der Fingernagel* | toe | *die Zähe* |
| fist | *die Faust* | tongue | *die Zunge* |
| foot | *der Fuß* | tooth | *der Zahn* |
| forehead | *die Stirn* | waist | *die Taille* |
| hair | *das Haar* | wrist | *das Handgelenk* |

## Countries—*die Länder*

| | | | |
|---|---|---|---|
| Australia | *Australien* | Holland | *Holland* |
| Austria | *Österreich* | Iceland | *Island* |
| Belgium | *Belgien* | Ireland | *Irland* |
| Bolivia | *Bolivien* | Italy | *Italien* |
| Brazil | *Brasilien* | Japan | *Japan* |
| Canada | *Kanada* | Korea | *Korea* |
| China | *China* | Mexico | *Mexiko* |
| Denmark | *Dänemark* | Morocco | *Marokko* |
| Egypt | *Ägypten* | Norway | *Norwegen* |
| England | *England* | Portugal | *Portugal* |
| Finland | *Finnland* | Russia | *Rußland* |
| France | *Frankreich* | Scotland | *Schottland* |
| Germany | *Deutschland* | Spain | *Spanien* |
| Great Britain | *Groß Britanien* | Sweden | *Schweden* |
| Greece | *Griechenland* | Switzerland | *die Schweiz* |
| Haiti | *Haiti* | U.S.A. | *die Vereinigten Staaten, U.S.A.* |

## Nationalities (Nationalitäten) -*die Staatsangehörigkeiten*

| | | |
|---|---|---|
| American | *der Amerikaner, (-in)* | *amerikanisch* |
| Australian | *der Australier, (-in)* | *australisch* |
| Austrian | *der Österreicher, (-in)* | *österreichisch* |
| Belgian | *der Belgier, (-in)* | *belgisch* |
| Bolivian | *der Bolivianer, (-in)* | *bolivianisch* |
| Brazilian | *der Brasilianer, (-in)* | *brasilianisch* |
| Canadian | *der Kanadier, (-in)* | *kanadisch* |
| Chinese | *der Chinese, (-in)* | *chinesisch* |
| Danish | *der Däne, (-in)* | *dänisch* |
| Egyptian | *der Ägypter, (-in)* | *ägyptisch* |
| English | *der Engländer, (-in)* | *englisch* |
| Finlander | *der Finländer, (-in)* | *finnisch* |
| French | *der Franzose, (-in)* | *französisch* |
| German | *der Deutsche(r), (m. & f.)* | *deutsch* |
| British (pl.) | *die Briten (pl.)* | *britisch* |
| Briton (s.) | *der Brite, (-in)* | *britisch* |
| Greek | *der Grieche, (-in)* | *griechisch* |
| Haitian | *der Haitianer, (-in)* | *haitisch* |
| Dutch | *der Holländer, (-in)* | *holländisch* |
| Icelander | *der Isländer, (-in)* | *isländisch* |
| Irish | *der Irländer, (-in)* | *irländisch* |
| Italian | *der Italiener, (-in)* | *italienisch* |
| Japanese | *der Japaner, (-in)* | *japanisch* |
| Korean | *der Koreaner, (-in)* | *koreanisch* |
| Mexican | *der Mexikaner, (-in)* | *mexikanisch* |
| Moroccan | *der Marokkaner, (-in)* | *marokkanisch* |
| Norwegian | *der Norweger, (-in)* | *norwegisch* |
| Portuguese | *der Portugiese, (-in)* | *portugiesisch* |
| Scottish | *der Schotte, (-in)* | *schottisch* |
| Russian | *der Russe, (-in)* | *russisch* |
| Spanish | *der Spanier, (-in)* | *spanisch* |
| Swedish | *der Schwede, (-in)* | *schwedisch* |
| Swiss | *der Schweizer, (-in)* | *schweizerisch* |

## Food—*das Lebensmittel, Essen, Nahrungsmittel*

| | | | |
|---|---|---|---|
| broccoli | *der Spargelkohl* | hamburger | *der Hamburger* |
| cake | *der Kuchen* | ice cream | *das Eis* |
| celery | *der Sellerie* | jam | *die Marmelade* |
| chicken | *das Huhn* | ketchup | *der Ketchup* |
| coffee | *der Kaffee* | mushroom | *der Champignon, eßbarer Pilz* |
| cream | *die Sahne* | | |
| eggs | *die Eier* | mustard | *der Senf* |
| fish | *der Fisch* | noodles | *die Nudeln* |
| ham | *der Schinken* | omelet | *das Omelett* |

## Food—*das Lebensmittel, Essen, Nahrungsmittel* (continued)

| | | | |
|---|---|---|---|
| pepper | *der Pfeffer* | soft drink | *das alkohofreie Getränk, Sprudelwasser* |
| rice | *der Reis* | soup | *die Suppe* |
| salad | *der Salat* | steak | *das Steak* |
| salt | *das Salz* | sugar | *der Zucker* |
| sandwich | *das belegte Brot, Sandwich* | tea | *der Tee* |
| sausages | *die Wurst* | toast | *der Toast* |

## Sports—*der Sport*

| | |
|---|---|
| boxing | *der Boxsport* |
| car racing | *das Autorennen* |
| cross-country skiing | *das Geländeskilaufen* |
| cycling | *das Radfahren* |
| downhill skiing | *das Skilaufen* |
| fencing | *das Fechten* |
| gymnastics | *das Turnen* |
| hockey | *das Hockey* |
| horseback riding | *das Pferdereiten* |
| jogging | *das Trotten* |
| sailing | *das Segeln* |
| skating | *das Schlittschuhlaufen* |
| soccer | *das Fußballspielen* |
| swimming | *das Schwimmen* |
| tennis | *das Tennis* |
| volleyball | *das Volleyball* |
| weight lifting | *das Gewichtheben* |
| wrestling | *das Ringen* |

## At the Zoo—*Im Tiergarten*

| | | | |
|---|---|---|---|
| alligator | *der Alligator* | lizard | *die Eidechse* |
| bear | *der Bär* | ostrich | *der Strauß* |
| camel | *das Kamel* | panda | *der Katzenbär* |
| deer | *das Wild* | parrot | *der Papagei* |
| eagle | *der Adler* | peacock | *der Pfau* |
| elephant | *der Elefant* | penguin | *der Pinguin* |
| flamingo | *der Flamingo* | polar bear | *der Eisbär* |
| fox | *der Fuchs* | rhinoceros | *der Nashorn* |
| giraffe | *die Giraffe* | seal | *der Seehund* |
| gorilla | *der Gorilla* | tiger | *der Tiger* |
| hippopotamus | *das Nilpferd* | turtle | *die Schildkröte* |
| jaguar | *der Jaguar* | walrus | *das Walroß* |
| leopard | *der Leopard* | wolf | *der Wolf* |

## Months of the Year—*die Monaten*

| | | | |
|---|---|---|---|
| January | *der Januar* | July | der Juli |
| February | *der Februar* | August | der August |
| March | *der März* | September | der September |
| April | *der April* | October | der Oktober |
| May | *der Mai* | November | der November |
| June | *der Juni* | December | der Dezember |

## Days of the Week—*die Wochentage*

| | | | |
|---|---|---|---|
| Monday | *der Montag* | Friday | *der Freitag* |
| Tuesday | *der Dienstag* | Saturday | *der Samstag, Sonnabend* |
| Wednesday | *der Mittwoch* | | |
| Thursday | *der Donnerstag* | Sunday | *der Sonntag* |

## Numbers—*die Zahlen*

| | | | | | |
|---|---|---|---|---|---|
| 0 | zero | *null* | 15 | fifteen | *fünfzehn* |
| 1 | one | *eins* | 16 | sixteen | *sechzehn* |
| 2 | two | *zwei* | 17 | seventeen | *siebzehn* |
| 3 | three | *drei* | 18 | eighteen | *achtzehn* |
| 4 | four | *vier* | 19 | nineteen | *neunzehn* |
| 5 | five | *fünf* | 20 | twenty | *zwanzig* |
| 6 | six | *sechs* | 30 | thirty | *dreißig* |
| 7 | seven | *sieben* | 40 | forty | *vierzig* |
| 8 | eight | *acht* | 50 | fifty | *fünfzig* |
| 9 | nine | *neun* | 100 | one hundred | *einhundert* |
| 10 | ten | *zehn* | 200 | two hundred | *zweihundert* |
| 11 | eleven | *elf* | 1,000 | one thousand | *eintausend* |
| 12 | twelve | *zwölf* | 2,000 | two thousand | *zweitausend* |
| 13 | thirteen | *dreizehn* | 10,000 | ten thousand | *zehntausend* |
| 14 | fourteen | *vierzehn* | | | |

## Temperature—*die Temperatur*

| | *Fahrenheit* | *Centigrade/Celsius* | |
|---|---|---|---|
| Water freezes at<br>*das Wasser friert bei* | 32° | 0° | degrees<br>*Grad* |
| Water boils at<br>*das Wasser kocht bei* | 212° | 100° | degrees<br>*Grad* |

To convert Centigrade into Fahrenheit:
*Um Celsius auf Fahrenheit zu konvertieren:*
(C° × 9) / 5 + 32 = F°

To convert Fahrenheit into Centigrade:
*Um Fahrenheit auf Celsius zu konvertieren:*
(F° – 32) × 5/9 = C°

## Weights and Measures—*die Gewichte und Messungen*

Acre = *40 Are (4,000 Quadratmeter)*
Bushel = 36 Liter
Cubic Inch = *17 Kubikzentimeter*
Foot = *0.3 Meter*
Hundredweight = *50 Kilogramm*
Inch = *2.5 Zentimeter*
Mile = *1,600 Meter*
Ounce = *28 Gramm*
Pint = *0.6 Liter*
Pound = *0.45 Kilogramm*
Quart = *1.2 Liter*
Square Mile = *2.6 Quadratkilometer (260 Hektar)*
Ton = a fraction over *1,000 Kilogramm*
Yard = *0.9 Meter*

*das Ar* = 120sq. yds., or 0.025 acre
*das Gramm* = 15 grains troy, or 0.03 ounce avoir du pois
*der Hektar* = 2.5 acres
*das Kilogramm* = 2.2 lb.
*das Kilometer* = 0.6 mile
*das Kubikzentimeter* = 0.06 cu. in.
*der Liter* = 60 cu. in., or 2.1 U.S. pints
*der Meter* = 39.5 in.
*der Millimeter* = 0.04 in.
*der Quintal* = 220 lb. (a fraction less than 2 cwt.)
*die Tonne* = 2,200 lb. (40 lb. less than 1 ton)
*der Zentimeter* = 0.4 in.

SWEDEN
DENMARK
NETHERLANDS
Hamburg
Bremen
POLAND
Berlin
Hanover
Potsdam
Essen
Düsseldorf
Leipzig
Cologne
BELGIUM
GERMANY
Dresden
Bonn
Frankfurt
CZECH
REPUBLIC
LUXEMBURG
Mannheim
Nuremburg
FRANCE
Stuttgart
Ulm
Munich
AUSTRIA
SWITZERLAND
ITALY

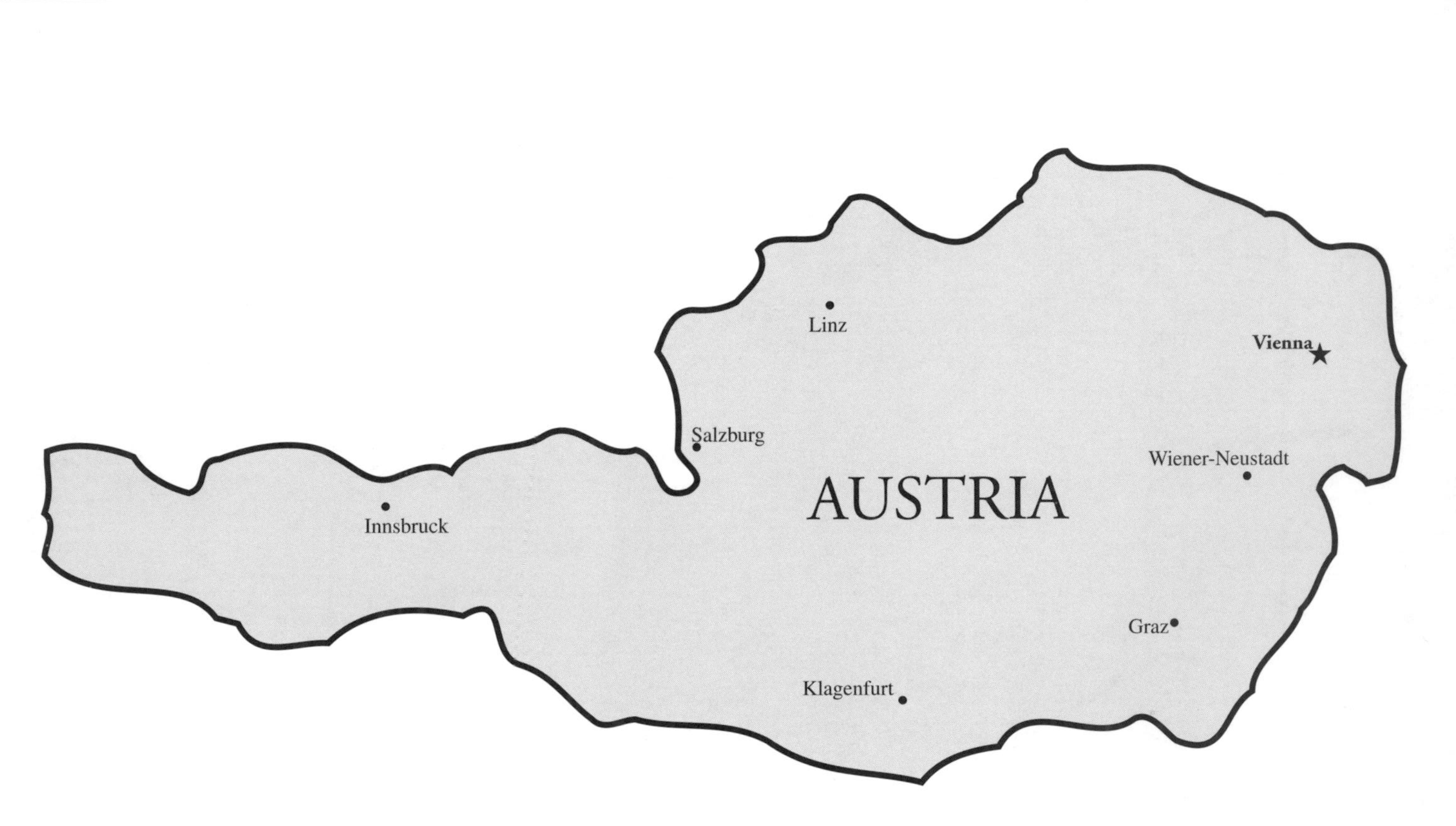
Linz
Vienna
Salzburg
Wiener-Neustadt
AUSTRIA
Innsbruck
Graz
Klagenfurt

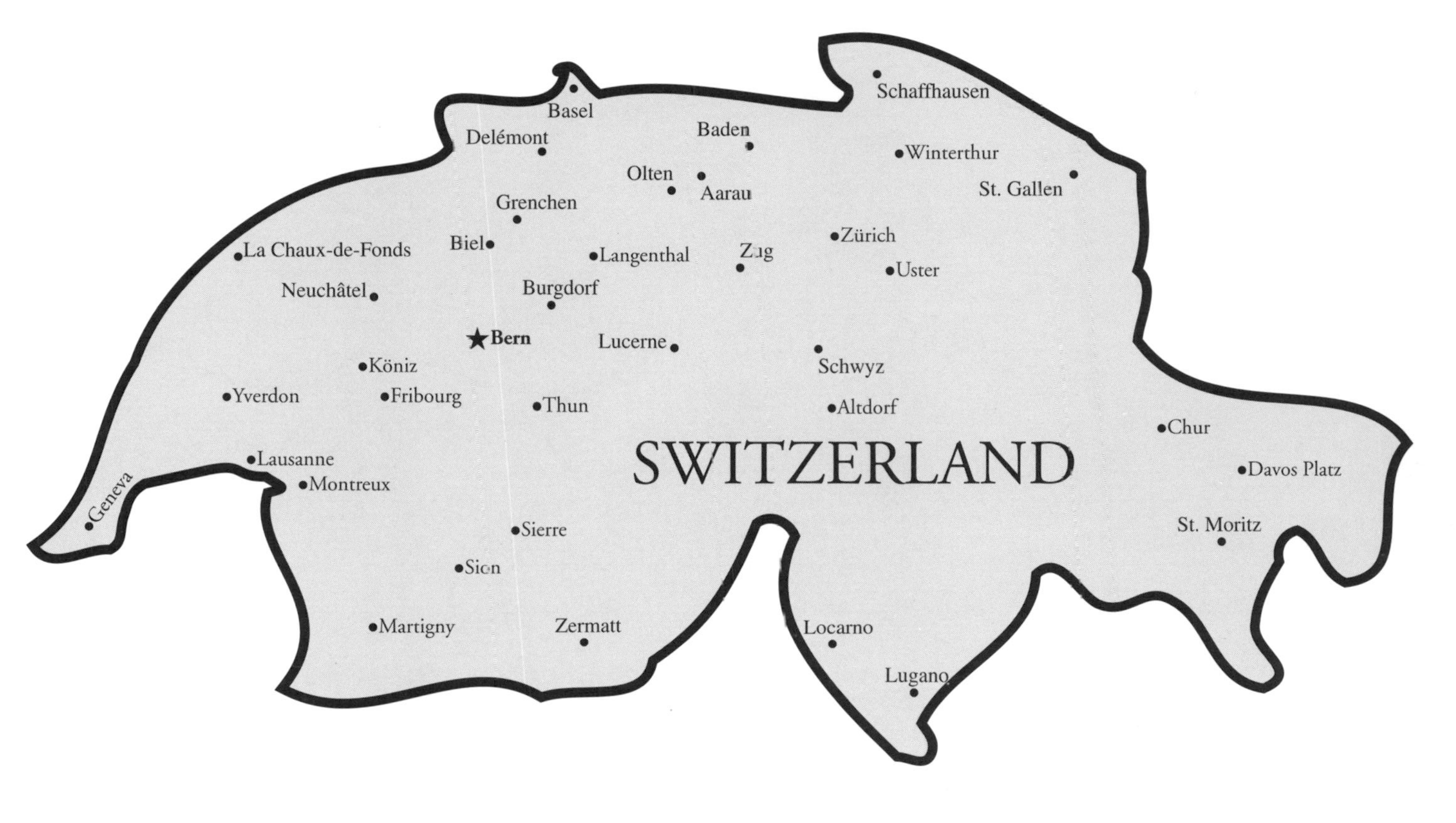
SWITZERLAND
Basel
Schaffhausen
Delémont
Baden
Winterthur
Olten
Aarau
St. Gallen
Grenchen
La Chaux-de-Fonds
Biel
Langenthal
Zug
Zürich
Uster
Neuchâtel
Burgdorf
Bern
Lucerne
Schwyz
Köniz
Yverdon
Fribourg
Thun
Altdorf
Chur
Lausanne
Montreux
Davos Platz
Geneva
St. Moritz
Sierre
Sion
Martigny
Zermatt
Locarno
Lugano

# NTC GERMAN LANGUAGE TEXTS AND MATERIALS

**Computer Software**
German Basic Vocabulary Builder on Computer

**Language Learning Materials**
NTC Language Learning Flash Cards
NTC Language Posters
NTC Language Puppets
Language Visuals

**Exploratory Language Books**
Let's Learn German Coloring Book
German for Beginners
Getting Started in German
Just Enough German
Multilingual Phrase Book

**Graded Workbooks**
Aufsätze mit Bildern
German Verb Drills
Jetzt schreiben wir
Wir können doch schreiben

**Text and Audiocassette Packages**
Just Listen 'n Learn German
Just Listen 'n Learn German Plus
Conversational German in 7 Days
Practice & Improve Your German
Practice & Improve Your German Plus
Auf Deutsch, bitte
How to Pronounce German Correctly

**Wir Sprechen Deutsch Series**
Ich bin Berliner
Ich bin Hamburger
München—Heimliche Hauptstadt

**Black-Line and Duplicating Masters**
German Verbs and Vocabulary Bingo Games
German Crossword Puzzles
German Word Games for Beginners
The Magazine
Basic Vocabulary Builder
Practical Vocabulary Builder

**Puzzle and Word Game Books**
Easy German Crossword Puzzles
Easy German Word Games and Puzzles

**Teaching Guide**
Teaching German: A Practical Guide

**Grammar References**
Guide to German Idioms
German Verbs and Essentials of Grammar
Nice 'n Easy German Grammar

**Bilingual Dictionaries**
Klett's Modern German/English Dictionary
Klett's Super-Mini German/English Dictionar
Schöffler-Weis German/English Dictionary
Let's Learn German Picture Dictionary
German Picture Dictionary

**Cross-Cultural Awareness**
Let's Play Games in German
Songs for the German Class

For further information or a current catalog, write:
National Textbook Company
a division of *NTC Publishing Group*
4255 West Touhy Avenue
Lincolnwood, Illinois 60646-1975 U.S.A.